To Ron Lee
with my best wishes
& thanks
Charles Willard

LIBERALISM AND THE PROBLEM OF KNOWLEDGE

New Practices of Inquiry

A series edited by D. N. McCloskey & John S. Nelson

LIBERALISM AND THE PROBLEM OF KNOWLEDGE

A New Rhetoric for Modern Democracy

Charles Arthur Willard

THE UNIVERSITY OF CHICAGO PRESS • *Chicago & London*

Charles Willard is professor and chair of the Department of Communication at the University of Louisville.

The University of Chicago Press, Chicago 60637
The University of Chicago Press, Ltd., London

Printed in the United States of America

05 04 03 02 01 00 99 98 97 96 1 2 3 4 5
ISBN:0-226-89845-8 (cloth)
0-226-89846-6 (paper)

Library of Congress Cataloging-in-Publication Data

Willard, Charles Arthur.
Liberalism and the problem of knowledge : a new rhetoric for modern democracy / Charles Arthur Willard.
p. cm. — (New practices of inquiry)
Includes bibliographical references and index.
1. Liberalism. 2. Democracy. 3. Epistemics. I. Title.
II. Series.
JC574.W55 1996 95-51761
320.5—dc20 CIP

∞ The paper used in this publication meets the minimum requirements of the American National Standard for Information Sciences—Permanence of Paper for Printed Library Materials, ANSI Z39.48-1984.

To the signers of the Treaty of Maastricht—
who found that the fiscal side of a common currency
is easier to negotiate than the allegorical

Contents

Acknowledgments ix

Introduction: The Yankee Way to Knowledge 1

PART I: **The Public and Its Problems: One More Time** 11

1 Authenticity and the Rhetoric of Trauma 25

2 Romancing the *Gesellschaft:* Community and the Fallacy of Common Ground 40

3 Commensuration and Unificationism 68

4 Foucault's Trap 87

5 Pluralism, the Public, and the Problem of Knowledge 119

6 Democracy in America: A Thought Experiment 150

PART II: **Discourse across Differences** 181

7 Epistemics 189

8 The Uses of Argument Fields 217

9 Fields as Organizations 245

10 A Theory of Presumption 277

11 Desperately Seeking Dewey 293

12 Epilogue: A Rhetoric for Modern Democracy 312

Bibliography 333

Index 373

Acknowledgments

I am grateful to the Royal Netherlands Academy of Arts and Sciences. My Fellowship at the Netherlands Institute for Advanced Study made this book possible—and put me in a position to observe the startling events of 1989. I expected to study the evolution of Federated Europe to illustrate some ideas in this book. Instead I found myself watching the embryonic federation grapple with events that would threaten even a mature organization—the dominolike disintegration of the Eastern European police states.

I have profited as well from opportunities to present aspects of this book in lectures and at conferences. These occasions have been valuable sources of feedback. I thank G. Thomas Goodnight (Northwestern University), Joseph W. Wenzel (University of Illinois), Ralph Johnson and J. Anthony Blair (University of Windsor), Dirk J. van de Kaa (Netherlands Institute for Advanced Study), Frans van Eemeren and Rob Grootendorst (University of Amsterdam), Robert Maier (University of Utrecht), Michael Gilbert (York University), Michael D. Hazen and David Williams (who directed four Wake Forest University conferences), Kuno Lorenz and Norbert Gutenberg (Universität des Saarlands), Michel Meyer (Free University of Brussels), Christian Plantin (University of Lyon), and the Centre Culturel International de Cerisy-La-Salle (Cerisy-La-Salle, France). Special thanks in this regard are due to Malcolm O. Sillars, University of Utah, who has been the driving force behind the conferences on argumentation at Alta, Utah.

I am especially grateful to friends and colleagues who helped me improve this book: Daniel J. O'Keefe, John Nelson, and Steve Fuller provided extensive critiques. And I have profited from advice and criticism from Eric Doxtader, Thomas Goodnight, Bill Lynch, Barbara J. O'Keefe, Sujatha Raman, Joseph W. Wenzel—and from my corridor colleagues Thomas J. Hynes, Shirley Willihnganz, John Ferre, William Keith, and Mark E. Blum.

My sketch of Epistemics is based on an earlier piece, "L'Argumentation et les Fondements Sociaux de la Connaisance" in Alain Lempereur, ed., *L'Argumentation: Colloque de Cerisy* (Leige: Mardaga, 1987). In addition, some of my arguments are expansions upon themes found in my essay "The Problem of the Public Sphere: Three Diagnoses," in David C. Williams and Michael D. Hazen, eds., *Argumentation and the Rhetoric of Assent* (Tuscaloosa: University of Alabama Press, 1989). The reader may notice that some of my conclusions have since changed. Finally, some of my arguments about authority-dependence are taken from my essay "Authority" in *Informal Logic* (1990) 12:11–22. Permission from the publisher is gratefully acknowledged.

INTRODUCTION

The Yankee Way to Knowledge

Pragmatists often say that progress toward greater human solidarity will come not from discovering timeless truths but from creating new ones—new ways of talking about difference that make differences manageable. Solidarity lies not in merging diverse cultures and beliefs into a single commensurating system or in reaching complete agreement about the facts of the world. It arises in cooperative projects—ventures people undertake because, in an interdependent world, they find it "increasingly difficult to get out of each other's way" (Geertz 1988, 147). The challenge is to "enlarge the possibility of intelligible discourse" by lowering the price of collaboration—by surrendering what John Dewey disparaged as the quest for certainty. "We should," Richard Rorty says, "try *not* to want something which stands beyond history and institutions" (1989, 189), a universal arbiter of knowledge claims, a mirror of nature. We should, as Nancy Reagan might say, "just say 'no'" to realism.

The paradigm case of such creativity is found in every American's purse or pocket—just above the eagle on a quarter. E pluribus unum is a genuinely revolutionary idea—as much an innovation as designer genes. For like recombinant DNA, it is human handiwork, not a natural category. Thomas Jefferson saw it as a creative act—a rhetorical experiment. "We hold these truths to be self-evident," he wrote, knowing full well they were not. No Hapsburg would have agreed that "all men are created equal." No shogun would have thought his slaves "endowed by their creator with certain inalienable rights." The Founders themselves disagreed about what those rights were. They knew that any claim to truth might be contested. "Liberty is to faction as air is to fire," Madison would later write in *Federalist* 10, and from factions the Founders expected only factiousness.

So Jefferson's key idea is expressed by the words "we hold." The Founders were taking a stand, declaring a creed—and inventing, in the bargain, a new race. It was a race one "joined" much as one joins AA by taking the pledge or enlists in the army by pledging allegiance. Becoming an American was a decision one made, and, being a rational man, Jefferson thought it was a rational decision. One came to a conclusion. If one was an immigrant, one changed one's mind. Cognitive dissonance theory hadn't been invented, but Jefferson had the rough idea: Serb and Croat might have their blood feuds in Europe, but they would be neighborly in America. Having made the decision to be Americans, they would be free to jettison their rancor.

It was a better mousetrap. By Teddy Roosevelt's day, America had become "a nation of immigrants," Emma Lazarus was chiseled onto the Statue of Liberty, and Jefferson's rational change of mind had acquired a warm, romantic glow. *The Melting Pot* was the title of a popular play. Imagine *Romeo and Juliet* with a happy ending and you have the plot: Jew and Gentile fall in love, subdue ancient hatreds, and live happily ever after. Ellis Island, it seemed, was a place of magic transformations, where Goffmanesque face shifts radiated inward to the soul. One was suddenly not-Italian (or whatever), or at least burning with resolve to become not-Italian as quickly as possible.

What one then became was vague. When manifest destiny was in flower, Roosevelt and others pedaled something called the "English-speaking Teutonic people." But with the rise of mass media, English-speaking consumers would do, and assimilation into the mongrel mass culture was, by all accounts, merely a matter of buying into it. That such transformations were possible—and successful on a mass scale—is suggested by two sizable literatures. To hear Marxists tell it, authentic identity is a scarce commodity, and to hear communitarians tell it, genuine community is a thing of the past. Both camps see American culture as an "empty sameness," an homogenized, shallow void glittering with fast food ideas and drive-in funerals. The melting pot culture absorbs everything, like the howling Nothing in *The Neverending Story.*

I hope the melting pot is that powerful. The world might be a better place if identities like Serb, Kurd, and Hutu acquired the same depth and emotional power as Pepsi Generation or Hoosier. The latter identities are creatures of mass culture, and intellectuals, as a rule, detest their triviality and ephemerality. Persuasion researchers call them *granfalloons*—"proud and meaningless associations" (Pratkanis and Aronson 1992, 168)—just the opposite of the authenticity Marxists want and the enduring meanings communitarians want. But Trekkers and Trekkies, I submit, have lower body counts than Tatars and Tajiks. Those who most loath the melting pot culture—who want to enrich it, or replace it with deeper, more authentic and intensely felt public meanings—should consider, perhaps more deeply than they have, the social engineering their calls for unity would require. For we have a fact before us: In the wreckage of the Stalinist police states, and in the power vacuum left by the end of the Cold War, from Bosnia and Tatarstan to Myanmar and East Timor, a chain of race wars virtually encircles the globe. Historic peoples are recovering their rich cultural heritages by slaughtering their neighbors—in Azerbaijan, Slovenia, Croatia, Moldova, South Ossetia, Nagorno-Karabakh, and further afield, in Angola, Burundi, Rwanda, Zaire, Turkey, the Sudan, Bhutan, Sri Lanka, and Papua New Guinea. Identity, apparently, abhors a vacuum,and when people set out to fill this void, they often fill it with corpses.

It is an open question whether the melting pot will be strong enough to keep the aboriginal demons at bay. From Tocqueville on, every visitor who has marveled in print at the power of the polyglot culture has also paused to fret that the pull of history might prove too strong. Some say the pot never melted (Moynihan 1993). Others doubt that the pot's most recent and most cosmopolitan incarnation—Euroculture—can dilute ancient sovereignties and animosities. And for similar reasons, to return to the pragmatists' point, it is an open question whether the partisans of competing theories can be persuaded that by compromising some of their sovereignty they might profit from common projects. Sovereignty, political and intellectual, seems to be the sticking point—so much so, indeed, that one wonders whether any flowers, let alone a thousand, can bloom in the no-man's land between warring peoples and paradigms.

I propose to open this question by defending a rhetorical turn—a move away from one discourse, liberalism, to a different discourse, which I will call "epistemics." Liberalism, I will argue, is a family of rhetorics whose themes and battlelines obscure what might be called the problem of competence. A fixation on unity diverts attention from the knowledge problems of democracy. A fixation on the status of intellectuals in modernity makes it difficult to understand the creation, negotiation, and uses of public knowledge and diverts attention from the behavior of experts and expert fields in public life. What is needed is a different agenda of topics—one that salvages liberalism's most important intuitions while bypassing its most intransigent disputes. The goal, in other words, is to create a rhetorical ground on which theorists who largely ignore one another might find common interests.

The problem is to convince various partisans that the new ground is worth traversing and that the price of passage is a surrender only of some public postures, not their deepest convictions. The move from liberalism to epistemics will be not unlike moving from an historically occurring culture to a contrived one, from a natural language to Esperanto. So the point in critiquing liberalism's themes—authenticity, community, commensuration—isn't to celebrate inauthenticity, disunity, and relativity. The point, rather, is to show that liberalism's rhetorical methods are constricting the pragmatic value of its claims.

Take one example: Because they have an oversimple view of communication—of what it is, how it works, and what it can accomplish—some authors presume that the opposite of authentic communication is false or dishonest, as opposed to conventional or rhetorical. Because they bring this view of communication to their thinking about unity, they are inevitably disappointed by the sorts of unity heterogeneous societies in fact achieve. This disappointment has become a ritual: One holds modernity up to inflated ideals, convicts it of not meeting them, and then announces that there is a crisis of liberal democracy (Frankel 1962). This "crisis" has been a staple of American intellectual life for a century now, and it deserves a skeptical look, for calamity-howling diverts attention from other problems—and often has consequences that feed state power. Steve Fuller calls this my most dubious thesis—"an almost libertarian fear of states" (1987, private correspondence). Still, a libertarian fear of states has its uses, and the libertarian case is one communitarians need to hear. For now, I will quote a demagogue whose track record is part of my argument. "Everything," Danton said, "belongs to the fatherland when the fatherland is in danger." There are, I will argue, ways of talking about fatherlands that make them seem always to be in danger.

But the libertarian fear of states must be tempered if one believes that the purpose of states is to offset the side effects of capitalism. States have gotten better at this over the centuries as intellectual movements have forced governments to institutionalize reforms. But this evolutionary process is unquestionably incomplete: Structural and cyclical unemployment are as obdurate in the 1990s as they were in the 1890s. So liberalism's indispensable function—pressing the case for distributive justice—will not be at issue here. The modern welfare state, warts and all, is what we have. The point is not to line the libertarians up against the communitarians and then leave them locked in trench warfare. The point is to lure them into a common project and thereby make their differences less intransigent. One question that taps both communitarian and libertarian interests is why the modern state does no better than it does. Communitarians and libertarians alike can stare with fascination at states that are as inept at being lackeys of capitalism as they are at restraining it and cushioning its side effects. And neither wants a modern state that is ruled more by momentum than deliberation—preserved more by luck than by design.

Of course the frailties of the modern welfare state pose enormously complex questions. Their complexity, indeed, is an important part of my argument, for when questions cross many disciplinary lines and force policy-makers to adjudicate among competing expert claims, they are best seen as corporate challenges. No single intelligence can grasp them; no panoptic, overarching point of view is available to tie all the loose ends together. This is one facet of what I will call "the problem of knowledge," and while I will make no pretense of solving it—and certainly no pretense of fully addressing the problems of the modern welfare state—I will venture some arguments about why states blunder rather more than they should and why their decisions are often less rational than we would like. Mine will not be the usual explanation—that once politics meddles with expertise, the result is a grotesque tangle of, say, half-baked economics and self-serving bravado. I don't doubt that this is so, but I want to call attention to the other side of this coin—the behavior of experts and the postures of expert fields. Those who presume to instruct government, I will argue, are obliged to enlighten it, and however modest this standard may seem, it is not by any stretch one that the expert fields have met.

So in describing epistemics, I will have some suggestions for how intellectuals might better confront epistemic problems. By "epistemic problems" I mean the predicaments of modern decision-makers—their dependence on authority, their inability to assess the states of consensus in disciplines, their incompetence in the face of burgeoning literatures, and their pronenesses to mistaken agreements. By "decision-maker" I mean anyone who deals with public problems: the senator or agency administrator who must assess expert testimony, the academic who tries to fathom the implications of ideas in other fields, and the teacher who attempts to package a vision of modern intellectual life for novices. All such people grapple with the reliability of knowledge claims and the credibility of advocates. Epistemics will thus focus on the ways people communicate across differences, the flow and transformation of ideas across field borders, and the ways in which differences become disputes.

More about the problem of competence later, and more too about the spirit this example has been meant to illustrate. For now, suffice it to say that at the end of this book I hope the reader will see a clearcut choice between two topic agendas. The question will be: What are modern states best asked to do? Do we want them worrying about identity and unity, or about their own epistemic incompetence?

If enough has been said to introduce the problem of knowledge and the pragmatic spirit with which I hope to confront it, not enough has been said about two other key terms in my title. "Liberalism" isn't the clearest word in the world, and "rhetoric" is hardly the least controversial, so I will offer a brief definition of the former to get my cast of characters straight, and a definition of the latter to get my attitude toward realism straight.

The label "liberalism" is purely a convenience—shorthand, if you prefer, for the liberal democratic tradition or the discourse of liberal democracy. I will describe liberalism by grouping its chief "ists" and "isms" along some definitive argument fissures. The "ists" I will call "pluralists," "modernists," and "postmodernists," and their "isms" I will describe as "rhetorics"—three distinct ways of talking about democracy that prefigure the positions their advocates take. I propose, indeed, to treat liberalism as an argument field—a group defined and held together by disputes as well as agreements, a discourse made up of divergent rhetorics and hostile positions. Pluralism, modernism, and postmodernism, in other words, will figure here as competing positions in a debate.

Pluralists, as I depict them, are too complacent about the "intelligence of democracy." They think the marketplace of ideas is a level playing field: The voices worth hearing get a fair hearing. And they believe in meritocracy: The rule-by-experts is inevitable, preferable to populism, and on the whole the best of all possible arrangements. Modernists, on the other hand, see pluralism as an unrealized ideal. They hope to critique and reconstruct modernity from within. And postmodernists see pluralism as an illusion. They see themselves as outsiders, free of the system, whose epistemic imperialism they liken to a selfish gene. The modernists, I argue, are too hopeful about what individuals can accomplish in complex societies. They put the onus for an idealized rational mastery on individuals —and demand that we acquiesce only to epistemic fields whose operations are transparent. This ignores organizational scale and authority-dependence. It demands a scope of vision individuals rarely have. And the postmodernists, I argue, are too pessimistic about the prospects for critique. They so inflate system determinism that foreigner status is the only tenable critical ground. This poses a Hobson's choice I will call "Foucault's Trap": If discourses are hermetically sealed and all-determining, then internal critique is self-confirming and outside critique is irrelevant. One is either a compromised native or an inept foreigner.

Incidentally, there are no shenanigans afoot with these labels. Modernity and postmodernity have a notoriously wide range of meanings, but my reasons for using these terms as I do will be clear as things proceed. And for the reader who has noticed that certain Marxists will be postmodernists in my usage, by virtue of their claim to outsider status, rest assured that I realize that Marxists have their own vision of postmodernity and do not much like it. And perhaps it needs to be said: In discussing Marxists within the liberalism rubric, I do not mean to tar them as political liberals. I mean only to include them within the discourse of liberal democracy.

Though the book is divided into two halves—part 1 about liberalism, part 2 about epistemics—you will meet epistemics much earlier. In fact you already have. In asking whether the trivialities of popular culture might be preferable modes of identity to more "authentic" ones, I have given you a glimpse of epistemics' political message: What liberals fail to see, I will argue, is that what unifies people the most is also what is most superficial about them. And this political point suggests, in turn, how epistemics critiques two premier intellectual virtues—depth and systematicity of thought. Both are unquestionably virtues *inside* discourses, but they make for neurotic behavior *across* discourses. Sometimes, at least, when complex questions make us track multiple discourses, when political diversity makes us accommodate competing interests, compromise is a cardinal virtue. These conditions are the rule in public discourse—which means that the problem of adjusting specialized expert discourses to public needs is often a difficult one. It has been exacerbated, I will argue, by the behavior of experts; and it may be corrected if the academic specialties rethink their views of how their knowledge should function in public life.

When accommodation and compromise figure as virtues, and the quest for certainty is left to true believers, the conversation has plainly taken a rhetorical turn. Whether this is a turn for the worse depends on the sort of rhetoric one has in mind. Rhetoric, after all, has few good connotations in popular parlance. For American journalists, it is the antonym of truth and reality. At best it means oratory—an art more often maligned than prized. And at worst it means grandiloquence and verbosity. So *A New Rhetoric for Modern Democracy* may seem more a threat than a promise. Democracy, one may think, has quite enough rhetoric. What it needs is more "plain speaking," as Harry Truman used to say—or as Ross Perot says, "less rhetoric, more reality."

Rational argument is no doubt scarcer—and Beltway bombast more abundant—than either ought to be. But the demand for plain speaking supposes that truth is simple, self-evident, and intelligible—obscured only by political prattle or the obfuscations of experts. This article of faith has the virtue of sparking a skepticism toward credibility. Journalists are adept at exposing demagoguery—and sometimes effective in debunking the deliberately arcane. But complexity and specialism are not always fraudulent, and the degree to which jargon (the journalists' ultimate devil term) can in fact be translated into language that may be understood by everyone is, or ought to be, an open question. It takes, I will argue, a leap of faith to insist that the issues surrounding, for example, the capital gains tax or NAFTA or the supercollider be translatable into a widely accessible language. And it takes a certain insouciance about one's rhetorical bedfellows: For in the rogues' gallery of demagogues usually studied in university persuasion courses—from Pitchfork Ben Tillman to Joe McCarthy to (I am sorry to say) Ross Perot—the common theme among them is that truth is simple. "Simplify," indeed, is the cardinal rule in what is perhaps the only extant handbook for demagogues, *Mein Kampf*.

As the persuasion theorist sees it, demagoguery is democracy's closest analogue to cancer, and simplification is the demagogue's method of choice. This is rhetoric's dark side, and it will figure in this book as a variation on the irony of democracy—a famous idea with famously disparate meanings. To the left, it means that the people have no genuine voice. To the right, it suggests the fear that the people, given full voice in a democracy, might be undemocratic, intolerant, and authoritarian. This fear, in my opinion, is almost always misstated, for it is less a matter of human nature than a quirk of mass discourse that unity on a mass scale is most easily ignited by demagoguery. When Alexander Hamilton said "your people, sir, is a great beast," he might better have said "your discourse, sir, has limits," for there are only so many ways of unifying diverse masses. Race, ethnicity, and religion are the simplest, most easily deployed. They are especially ugly mingled with nationalism. And mingling they are: The themes perfected in the 1930s by Hitler and Goebbels—a romanticized purity interspersed with xenophobia—have returned not much changed in our own time. So the German Question, I will argue, is everyone's question.

But it is one thing to share the pluralists' distrust of mass discourse and quite another to trust the rule of experts. The problem of knowledge, I will argue, has little to do with the virtues and vices traditionally imputed to the public. It centers on the limits of expertise—and on the need to debunk the pluralists' epistemic hubris. This arrogance goes back to Plato, who impugned rhetoric as a "knack akin to cookery," yet feared it so much he restricted its use to philosopher kings, who were to determine the Truth and then use rhetoric to dupe the public into behaving well. This may be the oldest extant defense of false consciousness as an instrument of social control. Adams and Jefferson—still a century before Marx—joined their classical educations to their appreciation of Realpolitik to read Plato as condoning republican social control. Like Adam Smith (1776), they feared that workers might be alienated by dull, repetitive labor. They read Rousseau as wanting a hidden hand to create illusions of self-government to socialize individuals into the collective will. And so, "If the people think they govern," William Penn intoned, "they will be governed." By the 1930s, Walter Lippmann was calling for an "engineering of consent." And today, as we shall see, pluralists unblushingly duplicate Plato's arguments for the vile necessity of rhetoric. Thus, in the Platonic vision, rhetoric is either terrible or trifling—truth's enemy or its simpleton servant. Persuasion researchers are at worst the servants of power, or at best the dung beetles of the social sciences.

I ask readers who have these qualms to stay with me. Here the word *rhetoric* means the theory, practice, and criticism of persuasion, the study of the constitution of discourses—of how people collectively form, enact, and represent their activities. A rhetoric for modern democracy thus refers to democracy's inner workings, its methods of influence and decision-making. It refers to the ways people represent democracy (and their roles in it) to themselves and others. These innards include the worst shenanigans of rhetoric's dark side, but they also include argument and negotiation—activities open to critique and reconstruction. And the study of argumentation and negotiation brings into the open an important problem of democracy—knowledge claims that conceal the grounds of their own creation.

To appreciate this last idea, it needs to be recognized that the positivists are winning. Not perhaps in the higher reaches of academe, where *Weltanschauungen* flourish and rhetorics of this and that abound. But if logical positivism has lost ground as an academic venture, one wouldn't know it in the outside world. For the language of positivism is alive and well in the public sphere—the rhetoric of choice in grant proposals, expert testimony, legal proceedings, and public decision-making. As we shall see, two offshoots of positivism (policy science and cost-benefit analysis) are often said to be the diseases of public discourse. And the doctrine of operationism has been kept alive, mostly by professional educators. Now called outcomes assessment, it lends the aura of science to budgetary knives and ensures in the bargain that the language of positivism will eventually revisit the higher reaches of academe.

As might be guessed, much of what I have to say comes down to a case against ontological style talk. For readers who find this expression puzzling, or who want to maintain a strict dichotomy between rhetoric and reality, we should muse a moment about the word *realism,* whose political and philosophical meanings have interesting intersections. In politics, realists are the smug folk who dismiss their opponents as idealists—Realpolitik being what sets in after idealism is disillusioned. One claims to know how things really are, to see through appearances to the essence of things. One is thus a realist, a pragmatist, a cynic. In this same world, realism is also a claim to truth—scientific and otherwise: The policy scientist claims to have pristine, self-evident facts, the cost-benefit analyst claims to have advice untainted by human frailty, and the charismatic leader claims to see realities invisible to others. These are rhetorics of settled realities and narrowed possibilities; they aim to judge and adjudicate, to terminate debate—the opposite of what Rorty calls "keeping the conversation going."

If democracy is a continuing discourse, as Dewey said, then one problem of modernity is to thwart attempts to bring the process to a halt. In that spirit, even the reader who is ill-disposed to rhetorics of science can entertain a rhetoric for modern democracy. And those who want to maintain some version of realism against the various rhetorics of science can nonetheless entertain the claim that the rhetoric-versus-reality trope nourishes despotic discourses. Surely Mr. Goebbels has proved that rhetoric is as real as anything else. Despotism and fanaticism always come wrapped as Truth, and they are most insidious when they ignore, conceal, or deny their own rhetorical character.

Indeed, readers with Platonic intuitions may be reassured by something that others will find more disturbing. The move to epistemics replaces a rich, poignant, aesthetically-pleasing discourse with a dull, technical, and functional agenda—on a rationale that roughly resembles the case for dietary fiber. It sees democracy as a family of knowledge problems—and the veneration of culture, authenticity, community, and commensuration as impediments to discourse across differences. It is meant to be a bland diet for an interdependent world, a healthier alternative, as it were, to rhetorics that have gotten a bit overweight. And the question, when all is said and done, will be whether it is too lean.

Part I

The Public and Its Problems—One More Time

"What if there is no crisis of liberal democracy?"

—Salkever 1987, 246

For many people, "the public" is the archetypal democratic institution—along with freedom, democracy's most indispensable idea. Articulated by Jefferson, mythologized by Tocqueville, and placed at the center of political philosophy by Dewey, "the public" is largely an idea about American democracy. It is an entry point to a way of speaking about democratic life. It gives meaning and value to institutions such as the press and jurisprudence. It is the commonweal made flesh—a vehicle for idealizing democratic discourse, for describing a discourse space distinct from market and state and from private and technical discourses.

In these guises, "the public" has been a tragic figure. Habermas's (1989a) public sphere is a victim, smothered between the state and the market. Goodnight (1982) laments a lost art—deliberative rhetoric—that has sunk Atlantis-like beneath the forces of privatism and the more articulate technical discourses. Both see the tragedy of modernity as a failure to realize Dewey's civic-minded, articulate public and a co-optation of public discourse by advertising and public relations. The marketplace of ideas has become a convenience store—crammed with glittery but shoddy merchandise.

Indeed the crisis of liberal democracy (Deutsch and Soffer 1987) has many faces. For some it is a fall from grace—a loss of community and civic virtue (Etzioni 1993). Others denounce elite oligarchy (Parenti 1983, Reiter 1987). And others mourn a lost opportunity: Television might have been an electronic agora, Norman Rockwell's idealized town meeting writ large; instead it has "cretinized" the public (Birnbaum 1988), trivialized discourse (Postman 1985), reduced public time to post facto sound-bites (Rosen 1991), sparked a retreat to privacy (Elliott 1974), masked reality with pseudo-events (Boorstin 1961) and peddled consumerism at the expense of a public patriae (Ewen 1976).

The public, it seems, is "the deepest and most fundamental concept" in the liberal tradition (Carey 1992, 9); it is emblematic of democratic values, synonymous with the very idea of democracy. And it is in a sorry way—disenfranchised by technocracy, lobotomized by television, and compromised by consumerism. It lacks community, civic virtue, and public space. So the choices, apparently, are among calamities: Democracy in America is either dead, dying, a caricature, or a hoax.

Of course people have been squinting suspiciously at liberal institutions since the Enlightenment. The recurring theme has been the internal contradiction. Tocqueville said that good regimes promote safety and affluence; these comforts promote individualism; so individuals withdraw into privacy, leaving the public sphere to stagnate. Others argue that democratic institutions are based on self-negating logic (Blumenberg 1983, Connerton 1980, Galgan 1982), or that freedom is menaced by the organization and rationalization that make it possible (Weber 1905, 1946, 1947). If you read a description of the aerodynamics of helicopters (the physical principles that let them fly also give them an urge to flip upside down), you have the drift of political philosophy since Hobbes.

For some, this precariousness evokes a mood of futility. One feels that it doesn't matter what intellectuals say. Democracy goes its merry way, governed only by bureaucratic stubbornness and policy momentum—which puts political philosophy on a par with grousing about the weather. For others, the mood is a queasy foreboding, the herd jitters Yeats sensed: Things are about to fall apart; the center isn't holding. Like the atmosphere in a Kubrick film, dread sets the stage; nothing seems innocent. Auden called the 1930s the "Age of Anxiety," but he in fact named the common cold of democracies—liberal angst.

Others fear that the center is holding, that modernity is an all-encompassing, inexorable system whose logic is so self-confirming that the only haven is outside. The result is two orders of disease. *Ideology and Utopia* (Mannheim 1936) isolated an anxiety—call it "Mannheimia," a claustrophobic need to flee one's society. Left untreated for 40 years, the syndrome became a chronic estrangement—"severe Lyotardation"—a confusion of critique with guerrilla warfare, sabotage, vandalism, or graffiti (Lyotard 1984).

I think there is something fishy about this. There are too many cliffhangers; the angst and alienation are too operatic; the narratives of loss and redemption are too biblical—or too disgruntled, like grousing about the good old days or a nostalgia for somebody else's past. And there is something not quite kosher about a crisis due for a Diamond Jubilee: Ms. Clinton's "crisis of meaning," the belief that Americans are "yearning" for coherence and "the meaning of life" (Bellah et al. 1985, 295), goes back to the "crisis of the spirit" of the Progressive Era (Wyle 1912). And it is at least suspect that the expatriate's manifesto—a genre perfected by Rousseau—is still au courant. Is it a literary formula? Is modernity being held up to ideals so extravagant and romantic that the only possible denouement is an emergency? Is the crisis of liberal democracy an artifact of how democracy's critics make their cases?

I propose to nurse these suspicions. I want to play the hunch that there is something wrong with the conventions and dynamics of this genre, with how its scene-setting trades upon and feeds its narratives. And I have a parallel in mind.

Agatha Christie didn't invent narrative-as-concealment, but she raised camouflage to a new height by violating a literary convention. *The Murder of Roger Ackroyd* is baffling: Everything is a red herring; nothing makes sense—until you tumble to the trick. The trick was invisible because it was unknown in the genre until Christie did it. Once you glimpse the possibility of the trick, everything falls into place; the solution is obvious. The narrator is the murderer. I want to tell a similar story here. The puzzle is the crisis of liberal democracy; the victim is the public, a.k.a. "the public sphere"; and the name of the narrator is . . .

THE CRITICS OF LIBERAL DEMOCRACY

I will lump democracy's critics into two camps—modernist and postmodernist. Modernists (Dewey and Habermas) hope to complete the enlightenment project of rationalizing and humanizing modernity. Whereas the case for political freedom in Spinoza, Mill, and Locke is articulated in the language of religious freedom, modernists make the case in the language of the Frankfurt school limned with a vocabulary of intellectual mastery. Their public is a prisoner of systematically distorted communication to be emancipated by the critique and reconstruction of discourses (Bernstein 1968, 1983).

Postmodernists (Lyotard and Foucault) hope to subvert the grand narratives on which modern institutions are based. They are, as a rule, preoccupied with their prerogatives—their positions in society, their limits, abilities, and ideals. This narcissism grew from Marx and Nietzsche, but it is chiefly an expatriate's story told by Adorno and Horkheimer (1972) and by Mannheim (1936), who brought to America a way of portraying the promises of modernity and the prospects of intellectuals as if they were synonymous. *Ideology and Utopia* defined the role of intellectuals in modernity: It was a rationale for estrangement, a philosophical battle plan that exempted prodigal critics from the existential determination of thought.

Mannheim's free-floating intellectual is an outsider—homeless, groupless, free of the Newtonian determinisms of culture, class, and race—whose marginality is a platform of epistemic privilege that enables criticism and reflective thinking.

The two sides are united by many values—critique, emancipation, reconstruction—but divided by their beliefs about the ground criticism occupies. Their breach can be described as liberal versus radical, native versus foreigner—all variations on inside versus outside, internal versus external.

This argumentative fissure doesn't spawn a satisfactory debate. As the issues become sharpest, the debate is less like a field-defining dispute—a central tension that defines a discourse—than an accident of focus or even a border between two sovereign fields. The competitors are in *Zugzwang*, a chess standoff: Neither side can change its position without disaster. Neither can concede the other's view of critical ground, yet each draws blood from the other on the issue of efficaciousness: Modernists risk being compromised by their institutions; postmodernists risk being neoconservative —as Habermas (1985b) dubs Foucault—by virtue of being ineffectual. The result is an intransigent tension within which the prudent stance is timidity. One enjoys the fruits of modernity tinged with postmodern anxiety. One proceeds as if critique can expose systematically distorted communication, but ever so cautiously, as if one is using a tool that can at any moment break. Postmodernists have cozied up to this trepidation playfully and seriously. Critique is high jinx, vandalism, graffiti, or guerrilla war. And the modernists have become more earnest: If the business of America is business, then critique must be its conscience.

Admittedly the labels "modern" and "postmodern" are a bit like Rorschach inkblots. Both are chameleons put to different uses by theologians, political scientists, architects, aestheticians, critical theorists, sociologists, anthropologists, urban planners, political philosophers, journalists, and historians. Across this territory, there is no agreement on whether postmodernity is the status quo or a future possibility, holistic or partial, good or bad, delightful or loathsome, a new or a false consciousness. Perhaps their only common function is as arguments in the realist style. Marxists call it "periodizing" (Jameson 1988), by which they mean—with some claim to objective truth—the origins of current conditions and transitions to new ones. The times are changing, usually for the worse: This is being supplanted by that. Modernity is "everything after" or "post-," and then, from writer to writer, pick the noun: -feudalism, -industrial revolution, -Hobbes, -Hegel, -Descartes and Kant, -Bacon and

Hume. So, for instance, modernity was born just after the economic crisis of 1850 with the creation of new systems of credit, corporate organization, and the expansion of foreign trade and infrastructure (Harvey 1989); the passing of modernity has been sparked by new communication technologies (Mowlana and Wilson 1990); and postmodernity, then, is post-whatever. Depending on who you read, it is what you will have or now have; it is good or bad; and it does or doesn't affect everything.

So different claims are being made, for different purposes, at different points in time; their commonality is that they are arguments that use comparisons with the past as leverage for making claims about the present or future. Both terms, in other words, can be seen not as any particular condition but as strategies the denizens of any epoch might use to define and evaluate their times. "Modernity" (whose meaning will differ for our progeny in ways we can't envision) is how someone describes everything going on right now: modern times, the status quo—the ideas, institutions, arts, and organizations that affect our lives and our search for reflective mastery over them. Modernism attempts to critique and reconstruct modernity. For their times, Descartes, Hegel, and Habermas are modernists—modernity's therapists, so to speak. So are the pedagogies that claim to provide general intellectual skills. "Postmodernism," in this view, is a current name for a current opposition to a current condition: perhaps modernity's next step (Mandel 1975), or feelings of powerlessness (Eisenstadt 1973), or a competing narrative—criticism from the margins (Conner 1989). Aghast at everything going on right now, one makes a counterproposal or envisions a sequel.

Like all lines of argument, periodizing covaries with the theories and grievances of the periodizers. Some periodizations can be grouped under the rubric "epistemological postmodernism," an antifoundationalism devoted to debunking grand narratives (Featherstone 1988). In this view, modernity is totalitarian enlightenment embodied in modern institutions; postmodernism is the attempt to puncture or deface it. Other periodizations might be clustered under the rubric "renovationism." Renovationists hold that antifoundationalism, relativism, and depthlessness (what I just called epistemological postmodernism) are the crisis of modernity. Their ranks include antirelativists, nostalgic foundationalists, cultural defenders, and Marxists who see modernity (or postmodernity as status quo) as fragmented and relativized. In this view, a cancer in philosophy has metastasized into public life.

The sheer number of these grim diagnoses warrants a wary glance at the physicians. For if the crisis of liberal democracy is an iatrogenic disease

(Salkever 1987), the malpractice, if I may call it that, perhaps lies in a strategy I will call "arguing from hyperbolic standards." One condemns current practices for falling short of exaggerated standards. Rescher (1977b) sees this tactic in epistemological skepticism: A hyperbolic standard of knowledge—certainty—fuels a general skepticism where a more modest standard would not. This tactic, I submit, is operating in the themes of the first five chapters of this book: authenticity, community, commensuration, freedom, and critique.

Chapter 1 describes a primitive view of communication that, mingled with political philosophy, becomes a rationale for expressive politics. It begins with Rousseau's idealization of authenticity. If communication is genuine only insofar as it expresses one's beliefs, or realistically connects nouns with objects, then most communication is counterfeit, most leadership is deceitful (Bailey 1987), and mass media simulations will seem to have replaced the authentic links between language and reality (Baudrillard 1983a). Behind this thinking is a naive realism: Communication is a process of making known one's thoughts and feelings; its purpose is to convey one's thoughts and feelings to others; it either conveys one's internal reality or conceals it—it is either true or false. Honest communication is authentic, accurate, a mirror of inner reality. In a word, it is *expressive*.

One who sees communication this way will see conventional rules, etiquettes, and norms as inauthentic and rhetorical achievements—the creation of new situations and selves to get around conventional obstructions—as deceitful. This primitive view of communication is an interpersonal handicap, and it is angst-inspiring when it fosters the expectation that states and organizations be as authentic as people. The expectation that ITT or IBM be surrogate humans, embracing the individual in the warm arms of common ground is both a mistake and a predisposition to anomie. Mimicking kinship and friendship is not what the conventions of organizations and societies do best—so they inevitably seem counterfeit and inhuman. The result is a rhetoric of trauma—modernity is denounced for its suppression or distortion of some truth.

Chapter 2 argues that there are only so many "enduring truths" that can unite millions of people and that the track record of race, ethnicity, religion, and nationalism is ugly enough to warrant skepticism about calls for mass community—by which some writers mean religious unity, others mean a solution to relativity, and others mean reform-minded social engineering. These proposals are venturing, I submit, onto a slippery slope. Even locally, solidarity to some extent intensifies by exclusion; insiders stigmatize outsiders; and organizations obsessed with unity are distressed by dissent and skew their decision-making to achieve agreement at any cost. They dilute opposition—their best ally in achieving intellectual health. But with mass scale come greater risks: Unity does not come easily to heterogeneous societies, so mass persuasion often veers to the primitive as it seeks a basis for unity amid diversity. This primitive turn has ample precedent: In a world patterned by states, mass community has characteristically been consummated as nationalism and relativity "solved" by totalitarianism. But the telling evidence lies in the communitarian prose itself with its yearning for authentic, shared identity, in its search to find the meaning of life in a mode of government. Romanticism of this sort, I contend, finds its political voice most readily through expressive politics; so again, a disease is masquerading as a diagnosis.

Next comes social and political commensurability: One insists that people must hold the same beliefs, and, because they don't, one announces a crisis of fragmentation. Against this view, chapater 3 argues that relativity mustn't be an idée fixe that diverts attention from what is in fact a family of epistemic predicaments: literary proliferation, authority-dependence, political competition among authorities, and the closure and alienation caused by commensurating discourses. Relativity is an important member of this family, but it directs attention to unity as a solution, and thus largely misses the point, for unity may be the worst imaginable solution to problems whose synergism obstructs competence and coordination.

Chapters 4 and 5 explore the hiatus between postmodern outsiders and modernist insiders. Their common flaw is a hyperindividualism. One puts the onus for epistemic mastery on individuals, demanding that they acquiesce only to epistemic fields whose operations are transparent. Because omniscience is hard to come by in complex organizations, the postmodernist feels powerless; modernity seems out of control. Chapter 4 blames this feeling on an overblown determinism, a focus on lone individuals imprisoned in hermetically sealed discourses. This is an empirically tenuous view. Many fields have porous borders, peripheral subfields, border-spanning discourses, and common projects. But this is scarcely comforting to the modernists who (chapter 5 argues) exaggerate the prospects for individual epistemic mastery. They believe in general knowledge, and thus in the reflective critique and reconstruction of discourses. But they understate the degree to which critique is a group project and competence a group achievement, and they devalue the organizational virtues that make good decision-making possible. So a debate between (say) Foucault and Habermas is an "is-isn't" affair: Critique is (isn't) efficacious.

Chapter 5 also brings the pluralists into the fray, with a sympathy that betrays an author finally hoisting his colors. But rest assured, this book is the lunge of a desperate pluralist. Pluralists are most comfortable, I contend, as the winning side of the wrong debate. They take the technocratic side of the expertise-versus-democracy debate. They applaud the rule of experts, disparage the very idea of mass enfranchisement, and in general, I submit, get the better of it. Though populists will disagree, I think it is, or ought to be, an open question whether the prospects of democracy rest exclusively, or even mainly, with Dewey's public, or whether instead the intelligence of democracy lies with expertise and professionalism. I want liberals to shift their attention from the public to the behavior of experts and expert fields, not as a Platonic gesture to elite rule but as a way of interrogating the folkways and technical methods by which public knowledge is created and used.

The standoff between republicans and democrats, elitists versus populists, is democracy's oldest and most heated debate, and perhaps its most fundamental tension (Fischer 1990). But it is the wrong debate. The question has been, is elite oligarchy necessary? Can the public, through education and habituation to civil life, be the curator of democracy? And can a populace, 90 million of whom can barely read and write (*USA Today*, 9 September 1993, p. 1), serve as an effective check against technocracy? The question, in other words, has been about the public.

The question ought to be about elites. For no matter what one thinks about the mass public, there is little evidence that elite governance is any more competent. Indeed there are reasons to doubt that even the most splendidly-trained experts can achieve the kind of general knowledge pluralists take for granted. Pluralism seems plausible only when contrasted with populism. By itself it is a Potemkin village. As a source of confidence in elite governance, it can't point to anything more reassuring than good fortune to support its faith that modernity is muddling along.

What ought to be keeping pluralists up nights is the problem of knowledge, or more specifically, the problem of competence. By "competence" I mean (1) expertise and virtuosity as measured by professional or disciplinary standards; (2) an individual or group's grasp of the bases of knowledge claims, the evidence behind them, and the methods and techniques that produce them; and (3) the capacity of decision-makers to translate the claims of specialists into policy claims and to adjudicate among the competing claims of expert fields. According to this view, competent decision-making is more rational than accidental; the intelligence of democracy implies at least a little organizational sagacity—something better than policy momentum or luck. And the problem of competence, to be brief, begins with the limits of general knowledge.

General knowledge, I argue, is a dubious ideal even for specialists inside their own fields. As subject matters grow in complexity, their literatures grow unmanageable: too big and too interdependent with further literatures. Organizational complexity precludes breadth of vision. Complex fields aren't single conversations to which one can rationally acquiesce; their innards aren't fully transparent. Competence comes with focus. It waxes in microcosm and wanes in macrocosm. It multiplies specialties and narrows their focus. And general knowledge is doubly dubious seen as a field-spanning wisdom. It ignores the division of labor needed for decision-making in a complex society. There are too many knowledge claims in the world. No rational person would try to evaluate each one comprehensively. Public problems cross many field boundaries, but individual expertise can cross only a few, and so complex decision-making is surrounded by a penumbra of unintelligible communication.

Chapter 6 sets up a three-way debate—pluralism versus its modern and postmodern critics. Imagine a peace symbol from the 1960s, with pluralism in the bottom third, and you have the battlelines—and a clue to the spirit of the essay. It argues that pluralism's emphasis on competence needn't be dismissed as republican piety and that once the heat of the populism versus elitism schism cools, pluralism "cleans up" nicely and can be a presentable, even useful discourse. Once the pluralists and their critics agree that the knowledge problems of modernity start with a governing elite whose incompetence is exacerbated by the expert fields, a new agenda of debatable issues comes into play.

THREAT OR MENACE?

I am reluctant to think that the exposition to follow is antiliberal. But I will be disparaging the Quests (for community, etc.) and rubbing the renovationist's nose in precisely the features of modern life she most distrusts. I do not blame the impotence of critique on the hermeticism of fields. All fields are not equally hermetic, so the focus on local determinisms is misleading. I agree that localism delegitimates master narratives (Bové 1986), but not that all localities are prison-houses (Fish 1980). Interfield discourse is more common than many relativists realize. Nor do I see critique foreclosed by the invincibility of states that no longer need intellectuals to justify them.

The reader will also detect an antipathy for the postmodern attitude—the post-1960s abhorrence and cynicism (Ryan 1988) and cultural anomie felt by refugees from commodity capitalism (Kroker and Cook 1987). My complaint is partly a matter of degree. Berman (1982) makes a convincing case for despising Robert Moses, whose arrogant disregard for the consequences of demolishing neighborhoods to build the Cross-Bronx Expressway is as ignoble as his "ability to convince a mass public that he was the vehicle of impersonal world-historical forces, the moving spirit of modernity. For forty years he was able to preempt the vision of the modern" (294). Berman's case against *creative destruction* is persuasive because he sees in Faustian ideology a destruction of what is best in modernity itself.

But preempting the vision is also a common argument tactic among modernity's outside critics—a way of seeking the benefits of unequal status while seeming only to have the courage of one's convictions. The strategy is to devalue an opponent's claims by *diagnosing* the opponent's blindness. If I argue, for instance, that attempts to critique and reform modern institutions from within are doomed to perpetuate the system (using reason co-opts critique, for enlightened reason and organizational development have gone hand-in-hand), I have simultaneously devalued your arguments and deflected attention from the assumptions behind mine. Similarly, I might paint you as a victim of media-induced blindness. Reasoning that critique is duped by simulations and that opposition is co-opted by the media in the act of representing it, I thus play the role of a McLuhanite therapist: I see what you cannot. And again, if you deny the existence of the existential determination of thought, I can pathologize your denial, much as a psychiatrist might speak of a patient "in denial." Your arguments, I might say, "symptomize" false consciousness.

These are privileging tactics. Their effect is to create unequal status—priest and sinner, physician and patient. And their claim to epistemic privilege is disguised by a language of admonition and diagnosis. I am more-critical-than-thou, a seeing-eye free-floater, aloof, unsullied, locked in mortal struggle with Mammon, embarked on a higher road than the pawns of capitalism who would reform modernity from within. And if you disagree with me it proves my point; I have a diagnosis, you have a disease.

But surely the claim to outsider status merits skepticism. If the bibliography in this book is any indication of the paper tonnage devoted to cultural critique (it is in fact a tip of many icebergs), that critique is second only to acid rain as a threat to North America's trees. Manifestly, the all-encompassing spirit of capitalism has botched the job of silencing outsiders. The curiosity of a mainstream school of thought that claims to be disenfranchised is explained, I think, by the fact that leftist critics are making the case they claim can't be made, but they distrust representative democracy. They are representative advocates, but they often muddy the case for distributive justice with gestures toward the vox populi, an authentic pluralism. The disenfranchised must be allowed and enabled to speak for themselves. It isn't enough to make a case for someone else, and it is paternalistic to say that one makes the case better than others would. So the outsiders claim to be making the case the disenfranchised would make if emancipated and allowed authentic expression of their feelings. This stance trades upon selected disenfranchised groups (poor African Americans, not Ku Klux Klanners). And it dismisses the pluralists' fear that the disenfranchised, given full voice, will be undemocratic and intolerant.

This is an understandable mistake. The pluralists, we will see, positively wallow in the irony of democracy. H. L. Mencken made a career out of generalizing from the most benighted fundamentalists to the whole population; and his heirs similarly look at the Aryan Nation and see the face of America. This is empirically mistaken, but it lends legitimacy to a vision of the power elite that is, if anything, more smug and clubbish than C. Wright Mills feared. This vaguely social-Darwinist self-righteousness provokes leftists in a predictable way, for it is a near-Newtonian law of politics that for every caricature, there is an equal and opposite caricature. Populists have thus replied in kind with a Frank Capra idealization of the people that is, of course, a sitting duck for the ironist's artillery.

But as we back away from this cartoon clash, does there remain an irony of democracy that populists ought to consider? Is the vox populi more of a mixed bag than they might wish? Are there some voices that they might not want to hear? And if there are many such voices, are there thus rhetorical strategies that predictably veer to dangerously expressive politics? The tenor of the questions suggests my drift: The irony that I ask populists to consider is that the most readily-available vehicles of expressive politics are race, ethnicity, religion, and nationalism—four ideas that have rarely gone hand-in-hand with democracy.

If all this doesn't convict me of being a lackey of advanced capitalism, a final confession may clinch the case. Much of the rhetoric of trauma strikes me as little more than grousing about the good old days, disgruntled muttering masquerading as philosophy. The rhetorical theorists who want to recover the nobility and earnestness of Athenian discourse, or the great books champions who want to recover ancient wisdom are seeking a center that will hold. I think the unifying impulse is risky even on the small scale of expert fields. The canonical is as potentially authoritarian as any form of authority. A canon's raison d'être is exclusion, a kind of authority the human race has proved it can't wield with restraint. So I will endorse Foucault's point that we should be ambivalent about discipline. Disciplines are both beneficial and authoritarian. But the latter effect is heightened when thought systems become guiding intelligences for states, for it is all too easy to move from canon to cannon.

To argue that complexity and division of labor limit the prospects for intellectual mastery and that mass democracy can't be competent is to risk a slippery slope to apologetics, the sort of toadying Raymond Aaron used to be accused of, or the apologism Bernstein (1987) imputes to Rorty (1983). What I have to say is just the sort of thing critical theorists expect compromised intellectuals to say. The only question is whether I am a dupe or a scoundrel—modernity's patsy, ideologically hoodwinked, or a latter-day Justin the Martyr disguised as a critical theorist. A credo won't help. False consciousness is Descartes's demon in Bauhaus drag. Apologists take pains not to seem apologetic. So something better than George Bush's "I am an environmentalist" is needed. What follows is thus a protestation of intentions. These intentions can be weighed against subsequent developments, especially the critical program implied by field theory. They form a social contract: They are promises that will or won't be redeemed.

What follows is intended as an amicus curiae brief, for there is much in the liberal case that survives its presentation. Disregarding all talk of contradictions, one still hears the voices of Weber and Habermas. Modern organizations seem witless and venal. They are often as mysterious to us as nature was to primitive people. We doubt that we fully control or understand them. They are inscrutable giants, as likely to hurt as help us. We are as suspicious of their benevolence as primitives likely were of good weather. They are our version of the indifferent universe. And some organization theories don't seem much different from primitive religions. Modernity is a Chiller Theatre filled with things that go bump in the night—invisible hands, the spirit of capitalism, system entelechies, cultures, and historical forces. And we have our parallels to early science's attempts to replace religion: Taylorism's focus on profit and purpose, structuralism in many forms, but especially systems theory are all analogous to explanations of natural forces. They are ontologies of human handiwork colored by the feeling that things have gotten out of hand. Their vast Newtonian superstructures contain and affect quantum realities—expressed by a Jaguar worker, reacting to the news that Ford had purchased his company: "We're just little pawns caught up in the middle of giant corporations. All we can do is hope it all turns out alright" (BBC 1, 2 November 1989). And the giant corporations are not merely distant olympian abstractions: they are enmeshed in a multinational web that seems like a system whose complexity makes it invisible. When complexity seems invincible and unmanageable, emotivism becomes true by accident (MacIntyre 1981). The citizens of Bopahl can be pardoned if they still believe in dragons.

Liberalism may be overwrought, but it has been provoked. Beggaring the future is a way of reaping only the best of what you sow, so it isn't surprising that the intellectuals of the late twentieth century feel overmortgaged or victimized by a genetically transmitted disease. Any age that bequeaths its children a nuclear arsenal and ancient cliches to administer it deserves the rebellion it gets.

Moreover a flourishing opposition is integral to organizational health (Willard 1987c, Willard and Hynes 1991). The preference for agreement does to organizations what cancer does to living organisms, and a modernity unchecked by postmodern discourses may become just the lumbering monolith the critics fear. Advances beset by critics are likely to be the better for it. Nuclear plants are safer than they might have been thanks to their environmentalist foes. Sans opposition, they might have been deployed more widely or sited less cautiously. The environmental movements thus illustrate the possibilities of postmodernism. These movements (despite their Luddites) aim to preserve, critique, and check—three worthy tests of any advance.

Admittedly, a defense of competition has a social Darwinist tinge that bears watching. Social Darwinism has proved harder to eradicate than smallpox (Hofstadter 1944, 1963, 1967), and it is enough to spook any modernist when authors seem to have conservative programs—perhaps Whately's presumption or Bradley's ethics—waiting in the wings. A position of the sort I am taking can degenerate into public relations for current interests, so some readers may fear that I hope someday to say that modernity has passed history's tests. But the arguments to follow don't suppose that modern democracies have achieved distributive justice, escaped ideology, and conquered organizational stupidity. They assume the validity of Weber's qualms about rationalization and Lowi's (1969) "iron law of decadence" (organizations conserve themselves at the expense of innovation) and thus lend an urgency to the problem of competence. And nothing in the arguments to follow demands status quo veneration. The claim that nuclear plants are safer than they might have been scarcely means they are as safe as they might be.

My aim is to develop a focus on knowledge problems that may salvage some of liberalism's intuitions while bypassing its perpetual crises. Call it another tack postmodernism might take: The flaw in postmodern precariousness is not that we live in a consistent, safe, or happy world but that anxiety is impossible to act upon. This is an old complaint. We sympathize with Oedipus, but the view of fate fueling the plot makes us helpless. I want to play the hunch that this bum telos is what Berman would call a "world-historical alibi."

ONE

Authenticity and the Rhetoric of Trauma

Man is not borne free,
But everywhere he is in planes.

Imagine for a moment that you are embarked on one of modernity's definitive acts saddled with its definitive affliction. You are on a nonstop from Geneva to New York. Instead of an engaging seat mate, fate has dealt you a grumpy man on a grim expedition. His name, you gather, is Rousseau. His grievance, you gather, is with cities, and his immediate complaint is about leaving a pastoral, orderly community for a bustling "city of strangers" (Sennett 1974), a hodge-podge melting pot whose public spaces ring with the pluralistic jangle of mixed languages and motives. A flight from Geneva to New York, you gather, is a bleak descent—from honesty to deceit, good to evil. It prompts a stream of invective, and your companion is warming to the task.

These flights often pass over Paris. If the weather is clear, her vast public spaces are visible—the Place de la Concorde, the Champ de Mars, Baron Haussmann's grand boulevards—all set in relief by densely bunched buildings. The perspective of altitude yields a gestalt-shift figure like Wittgenstein's duck-rabbit: Look once and the open spaces define the private ones; look again and the private spaces leap to the foreground. The effect is startling. Once the gestalt shift is noticed, it is hard to recover the whole. The choice between public and private has become either-or. Paris thus epitomizes modernity's flaw—the incommensurability between public and private.

Rousseau has nothing good to say about either gestalt. The public expanses are diluted by their scale. They are places for enigmatic mannequins and inexplicable theatrics. Nothing authentic happens in them. People do not say what they mean. They go through motions. They hide their inner selves behind rituals. They are slaves to convention because they distrust intention. They wear their social roles and ranks like theatrical costumes and thus cannot communicate the values that might unite them in guileless community. And their private spaces are anomic hiding places—refuges from the theater of public life—that are ultimately untenable. Emile can't hide forever; the best he can do is keep moving.

But our seat mate is bracing for something uglier than Paris. New York looks nothing like Paris from the air—its private spaces seem to have metastasized and overgrown the public. But mass communications are but another sort of architecture, he thinks, modernity's latest perversion of public space (e.g., Meyrowitz 1985). New York is Paris writ large and modern, in neon and line signals, and our seat mate cannot conjure a more distressing image. It would be fitting if early Paul Simon songs are playing on the headphones—with New Yorkers lost in dangling conversations, shadows touching shadows. These toe-tappers for dour Genevans are the postmodern counterpoint to Rousseau's own opera, *Le Devin du Village,* a romantic celebration of bucolic life that now, in the belly of modernity, can find voice only in a pensive key.

It would be a nice coincidence if Richard Sennett is on our flight. His *Fall of Public Man* (1974) captures Rousseau's equation of communication with the expression of internal states. Judged by expressive standards, conventional communication is counterfeit. And rhetorical communication is theatrical"—a term so invidious that it is redundant to add "merely." As we fly over Paris, Sennett will see the incommensurability between public and private places as an artifact of perspective. At our altitude we cannot see the people, and someone looking up at us from the Champs du Mars can see only our contrails. She might wonder whether our view is a good one, but only from idle curiosity. Caught in the grounded milieu, she might doubt that our perspective affects her much. She might be right.

O'Keefe's Message Design Logics

It would be a splendid coincidence if Barbara O'Keefe is on our flight. Her (1988) typology of "message design logics" (MDLs) is a point of leverage for exposing the flaw in authenticity—as well as community and commensurability in the next two chapters. I have elsewhere (1989a) applied her MDLs to a theory of argument, so I will but briefly sketch her views here. Readers interested in the empirical grounding of her claims should consult her work directly (O'Keefe 1989a, 1990, 1992, O'Keefe and McCornack 1987).

Communication, O'Keefe argues, doesn't work the same way for everyone. There is no "universal sense of relevance or rationality that organizes all communication processes" (1989b, 4). People differ in their knowledge of what communication is, how it works, and what it can accomplish, and thus differ in their methods for creating messages relevant to contexts. The expressive MDL is, developmentally, the simplest. It involves a failure to distinguish between thought and expression. As an expressive, I think that the sole function of communication is to express my internal states. Stimulated by events, I dump my current mental states and assume that others do so as well. I see etiquette and conventional politesse as fraudulent and rhetorical creativity as deceptive. Any mask hides a reality. My crucial question is honesty. In dealing with others—say I want to criticize but not offend them—my alternatives are either to fully express my feelings or to tactfully conceal them. Communication that does not accurately express my inner state is inauthentic.

Communication may also be a conventional activity, a rule-governed enactment of public procedures exploiting working agreements and institutionalized methods for cooperative activity. Such communication doesn't require that speakers represent their private intentions, but instead of seeing it as dishonest, conventionals assume that communication may be guided by more complex motives—based on developmentally more complex knowledge and competencies—than the expression of internal states.

Communication can be a rhetorical activity, a reconstruction of situations and selves that makes coordinated action possible. The rhetorical MDL capitalizes on one's ability to create and refine rules, roles, and relations—to orchestrate faces and scenes so as to maximize the possibilities for cooperation (Goffman 1959, 1961a, 1961b, 1963, 1964, 1967, 1969, 1971, 1974). Diplomacy, for instance, requires a working consensus (Cicourel 1974), not common ground. Negotiators needn't hold the same opinions; they need only create agreements strong enough to ground future actions. They may want to smother differences beneath protocols, or transcend them by reconstructing situations and roles.

O'Keefe and Sennett use the word "expressive" differently, though their intentions are commensurate. O'Keefe sees expression as signaling internal states. An expressive is one who sees communication exclusively as making one's feelings and intentions known to others. When Sennett calls eighteenth-century public life "expressive," he captures what O'Keefe means by "rhetorical." Rhetorical gestures are distinctively public commodities; they involve sentiments not thought to be representative of anyone's private states. I will use quotation marks to denote this public/rhetorical sense of the "expressive." Think of the quotation marks as face paint, wig, and costume. Think of Rousseau as wanting to keep expression free of quotation marks—as seeing the difference between expressive and conventional MDLs as a titanic struggle between good and evil.

Rousseau's contempt for convention is widely shared. Buber, Heidegger, and Jaspers equate inauthenticity (and thus alienation) with convention. Mead's "I" is genuine; the "me" is fraudulent. Authenticity is linked to a sense of self that "stems from the experience of myself as the subject of my experiences, my thought, my feeling, my decision, my judgment, my action" (Fromm 1955, 130). As Miss Piggy says, "How does this affect *Moi*?" The answer, for critical theorists is "a deepening social crisis" in which a false economy of mass imagery keeps "individuals out of touch with themselves" (Hardt 1993, 54–55). Jameson's (1991) postmodernity is thus a miasma of fragmentation, ephemerality, playfulness, eclecticism, and aesthetization in which essential meanings are lost. The contrived depthlessness of architecture and culture, the commodification of history, the fragmentation of discourses, and the privatization and consumerism of late capitalism have turned urban denizens into the replicants of *Blade Runner* who can't "engage their own feelings." They are simulacra—imitations of the real thing, disempowered, dazed and distracted, wandering in an anarchic landscape, who can't find the basis for a coherent social order (Harvey 1989, 302). Just as image politics conceals its emptiness, the speculative logic of capital masks, fetishizes, and conceals its exploitation (Harvey 1989). It is a fraudulent discourse that forecloses the search for eternal human meaning.

The triumph of the "I" has animated research traditions concerning self-disclosure (Wheeless and Grotz 1976), information theory (Dretske 1982), therapy (Jourard 1974, Rogers 1970), and communication theory (Gibb 1961, Hart and Burkes 1972, Johannesen 1971). The idea is to keep Emile pure and honest, to find the Truth obscured by an alienating society.

And there is the Mother of All Dichotomies—Tönnies's (1957) *Gemeinschaft und Gesellschaft:* fellowship versus authority, kinship versus occupation, natural versus contrived relationships, family versus organization, premodernity versus modernity. Postmodernism is thus, in my view, devoted to finding a soul for the *Gesellschaft*—to make it more genuine, organic, and familial. A revival of authentic public spiritedness is seen as a remedy for narcissism and individualism (Jacoby 1975, Lasch 1979, 1984).

It is said that some savages, fearing loss of their souls, refuse to be photographed. A philosophical version of this belief is Baudrillard's (1983a, 1983b) theory of simulations. The evolution from authentic referential language to a perversion of reality through language to empty simulations of reality, is a process by which mass society is left only with a panic-stricken need to create facsimiles that seek to be more real—hyperreal—than reality itself (Conner 1989, 57). Mitroff and Bennis (1989, 21) indeed barely pause for breath before announcing that America "is on a collision course with reality. And reality may be losing, if it has not done so already." A calmer version of this point is Ginsberg's (1982, 1986) claim that public opinion is an artifact of polling, not a reflection of opinions people actually hold. Another is the idea that organizational actors create an illusion of rational control (and thus a fiction of rational decision-making) and then are duped by their own creation. But Baudrillard holds that opposition is only an appearance. The media can present only its simulation. This assumes, of course, a direct connection between words and things that the media are a priori guilty of concealing and reformulating. So the last vestige of honest communication is the political graffiti of the 1960s.

Graffiti suggests cities, and cities are postmodernism's bête noire. This animus goes back to Sodom and Gomorrah. Cities are wicked places where pastoral, agrarian (read genuine) values are smothered or corrupted. Romantic idealizations of peasants have always demonized cities (much as Hitler used the *Volk* tradition), but with the growth of the great European cities, romanticism found its idée fixe. Cities came to epitomize modernity-as-victimizer, and, by all appearances, they still do. Cities are seen as fallow places, nourishing only otherness, rootlessness, and fragmentation (Pfeil 1988).

Less romantic sensibilities have not been sanguine about cities. In the nineteenth century, they were the scenes in which industrialization, mechanization, technocratic control, and the industrial underclass were easiest to see, and today, it has to be admitted, they are stages for the startling contrast of the ragged homeless, wandering aimlessly, sitting dejectedly, passed-out in doorways, lost in the towering canyons of glitzy skyscrapers. Look at the buildings, then look at the human wrecks, and you think you see clearly the difference between rhetoric and reality. The discarded simulacra, made obsolescent by one of capitalism's paroxysms of creative destruction, are made invisible by the stage's scale.

REALISM AND THE RHETORIC OF TRAUMA

The flight from Sodom and Gomorrah may have been a postmodern act, but Rousseau can still be seen as the first postmodernist. He was the first to use the term *moderniste* as we now use it (Berman 1982, 17), and he pioneered the rhetoric of trauma. This rhetoric exploits a skepticism about modern times, a distrust of complexity, and a nostalgic utopianism, all fueled by the belief that the realities of family, crafts, and direct exchange have been lost beneath the theatricality of the city. Thus arises the most conspicuous face of postmodernisms: the traumatized refugee, a role Rousseau took literally. He fled the theatricality of Paris for an idyllic small town where individualism could flourish. Since individual uniqueness amounts to a daily inventory of one's sins (Sennett 1974), genuine community is possible only when small collectives are governed—tyrannically if need be—by a common religion. Bucolism backed by bayonets is what you want when modernity seems too big and bogus. Currier and Ives ideals ensure disappointment, which makes for reactionary politics. All current regimes are illegitimate, yet political activity is indispensable to moral development. The solution? Damn the problems of scale and economics! Revive the Greek polis (see Rapaczynski 1987, 257).

The rhetoric of trauma trades on an ethnographic assumption: The outsider's insights turn on the epistemic privilege of the foreigner buttressed by the ethnographic advantages of the expatriate. The prodigal critic sees what is invisible to the natives.

And it trades on an underlying realism. In social scientese, "realism" is the viewpoint of "naive social actors" who take it for granted that the world is as they see it, that their perceptions are unaffected by their ways of thinking, speaking, and listening. Such folk are susceptible to professional and charismatic authority—what I earlier called rhetorics in the ontological style. Using the realism strategy, one claims to know an underlying truth (or begs the question by assuming a truth) that is masked, distorted, or eclipsed by modernity's falseness. The mass media have been popular villains. Jensen (1990) sees this strategy in the work of Dwight McDonald (the dangers of Midcult), Daniel Boorstin (pseudo-events and the menace of unreality), Stuart Ewen (the media as ideological apparatuses), and Neil Postman (*Amusing Ourselves to Death*). And the variations on the internal contradiction are all mirrors of nature. The unsteadiness is in the institutions. There is not a whiff of metaphor anywhere in the vicinity of the belief that organizations are built on logic. If an organization could shimmy and shake through a deconstructive striptease, discarding not just its conventional clothing but its skin, the assumption is that we would see that its bones are logic, its heart a contradiction.

One objection to the realism strategy is that it debases the positions interlocutors might take. Argument requires give and take. It goes best when arguers put their views sincerely at risk, when they are willing to modify their claims, or compromise, based on what others have to say. It goes least well when it *doesn't matter* what one's interlocutor says. If one is going to say what one feels one simply must say *regardless* of what others say, if one claims to see realities invisible to others and to have a diagnosis of why others are blind, then there is no point in listening to others. One merely waits them out. And there are better words than "arguing" to describe the result, say, "preaching," "witnessing," or "kvetching."

By making argument irrelevant, the realism strategy has a peculiar potential for despotism: The scientism of policy science serves the same rhetorical functions as the privileged insight of the Marxist—both wrap feelings and intuitions in a cloak of authority. Values masquerade as facts. This epistemic privilege—in criticism and social engineering—authorizes a paternalistic cruelty, a singleminded service of the Truth, no matter the cost.

An alternative is to see realism as a rhetorical tactic, for once modernism and postmodernism are seen as rhetorical stances, the clarity of the insider versus outsider contrast dissolves and the Christie twist becomes plausible. If both narratives are open to suspicion, neither can stand unexamined as a diagnosis.

SENNETT'S PORTRAIT

Sennett's view is derived from an historical portrait whose richness can only be suggested here. It is worth sketching because it catches Rousseau's mistake in an especially clear way. Rousseau's claim that public life has been reduced to fraudulent rituals that lay no claim to an individual's loyalty is an argument from hyperbolic standards. Public life will always seem counterfeit if people expect it to express their beliefs and values. Sennett blames the decay of the public on this expectation. Narcissism feeds a tyranny of intimacy. One's self becomes one's principle burden (1974, 4). The Greek admonition "know thyself" becomes an end in itself.

The argument starts with an appreciation of how the eighteenth century raised inauthenticity to a high art. The eighteenth century had a "realm of objective discourse" that saw "the concept of a public rhetorical gesture as an expression at a distance from oneself" (ibid., 105). Public actors were performers whose scenes had historically secured, distinctively public meanings. The denizens of eighteenth-century Paris never saw their city from the air, but they appreciated the duck-rabbit incommensurability of the public and private domains. The privacy of family life was where one sought natural fulfillment; the public spaces were for one's creations. Neither domain was an expression of the other. Life was a question of balances. Do public things in public, private things in private. So Londoners and Parisians were comfortable with a division between their public codes and private lives. They did not see the former as expressions of the latter. Social meanings were sui generis.

Sennett is struck by the fact that eighteenth-century audiences were emotionally demonstrative, even though gussied up in wigs, face paint, elaborate costumes, and masks. How can folk who seem so counterfeit be so spontaneous and "expressive"?

> Their spontaneity rebukes the notion that you must lay yourself bare in order to be expressive. To conceive of the natural man as an expressive creature, and the social man as a being whose thoughts and feelings are weak, fractured, or ambivalent because they are not truly his own, became Romantic common sense after the Great Revolution, and then passed into both intellectual and popular culture. This point of view is pastoralism. Its latest expression was found in the 1960s among those small numbers of people who actually left (and large numbers who wanted to leave) the city and in the natural setting of the country tried to get "back in touch" with themselves. (ibid., 73)

There was nothing pastoral about the men and women who saw their bodies as children see dolls—mannequins to be dressed elaborately or express one's social station, occupation, or currently amusing theme:

> There were patches of red pigment smeared on nose or forehead or around the chin. Wigs were enormous and elaborate. So were the headdresses of women, containing in addition highly detailed model ships woven into the hair, or baskets of fruit, or even historical scenes represented by miniature figures. The skins of both men and women were painted either apoplexy-red or dull white. Masks would be worn, but only for the fun of frequently taking them off. The body seemed to have become an amusing toy to play with. (ibid., 65)

Costumes "express" public meanings that serve cosmopolitan functions. There were laws forbidding one from feigning higher class, but Sennett says that Londoners and Parisians observed the proprieties not because of the laws but because costuming was a way of managing discourse among strangers. The big cities forced diverse populations into contact. In simpler times, one might address another by citing the other's title along with a recitation of the other's achievements. Such niceties are impossible in a city of strangers, so clothing is "expressive." Later the Victorians came to fear that clothing is expressive.

The transition to the Victorian era can be appreciated by a literary comparison. On the one hand, Fielding and Balzac stress the theatricality of public life, the necessity of masks, and the control of appearances; Baudelaire's citified dandies invent, rather than discover themselves. On the other hand, Conan Doyle's novels are about concealment. Outer appearances may, if minutely observed and analyzed, yield clues about a person's inner character. Since the inner nature was assumed to be ugly, the idea was to conceal as much as possible. In a telling and typical passage ("Adventure of the Speckled Band"), Dr. Watson records a momentary lapse as a proper Victorian gentleman, in a fury, drops his mask: "Never has the stamp of evil been so plainly upon a face." Manners became shields rather than ends in themselves; clothing became expressive rather than "expressive"—kept drab, with subtle clues to status. Expression was for the home; convention was for public places; and the public discipline was concealment.

Sennett wants to show how much was lost in the transition from life-as-theatre to the concern for authenticity. He argues that the etiquette of the eighteenth century was transformed in the nineteenth into a cult of personality. Most people are too inhibited to display their inner selves, but some remarkable people are able to do so. Charisma thus arises from apparent revelations of private character, as in Nixon's Checkers speech. Jameson and Harvey think the same of Reagan's teflon presidency. An undistinguished actor becomes president—more a Frank Capra than an Albert Speer aestheticization of politics. But whereas Weber saw charismatic leadership as a near-magic union of leader and follower, and Jameson and Harvey see the teflon president as false, Sennett exposes a deeper trick. In a world that seems to be based on concealment, people who have the knack of convincing us that we see their inner selves become leaders.

Intimacy is the belief that the complexities of society can be measured by a common standard of truth—psychological truth. One's field of vision is localized: "the more this localizing rules, the more people seek out or put pressure on each other to strip away the barriers of custom, manners, and gesture which stand in the way of frankness and mutual openness" (ibid., 338). Authentic communication is supposed to yield openness and shared feeling, a congenial sociability and a merger of personalities. Common belief is common ground.

Of course expressive communication is relevant, even indispensable, to families and intimate relations. We nurture our children and love our mates by expressing ourselves. But there are limits to expression even in intimacy. Communication-by-blurting may tear families apart and sabotage intimacy. Successful families and relationships capitalize on conventions and, as family therapists know, often need rhetorical strategies. The limits of the expressive MDL become more pronounced as one moves from relatively private to relatively public affairs. Communication-by-blurting doesn't jibe with conventional activities. The expressive moves through organizational life either oblivious to or puzzled by his or her effects on others. "An honest person in a counterfeit world" will blunder through organizational space leaving a wake of fuming victims. No better chronicle is imaginable than Rousseau's Confessions. It is a catalog of former friends, fallings-out, paranoid escapes, and regrets—a sad ledger, its debits lying between the lines: A man who simply had to tell the truth was a better enemy than friend to many well-meaning people.

Beyond the confines of family and intimacy, as the scale of communication gets bigger, the expectation of intimacy becomes increasingly bizarre. ITT seems evil or unnatural because it can't be hugged. Mass communication, like Rousseau's big nation-states, seems fraudulent and grotesque, nothing at all like real community.

Expecting large-scale entities to mimic the social structure of small ones isn't idiosyncratic to Rousseau. A century later sociologists would be speaking of primary and secondary groups as if the latter is the former writ large. This is the social sciences' version of self-similarity—the physical doctrine that says that quantum particles share the formal structure of vast systems; you can see the universe in a grain of sand, and vice versa. The expressive thus expects large-scale abstractions—states, races, cultures, peoples—to yield the same rewards as intimate relations. Heidegger's solution to the blandness and alienation of mass culture, for instance, was a revival of the Volk. Conventionals and rhetoricals wouldn't expect large organizations to mimic families; the former will say that organizations serve different functions from families, and so have different rules, roles, and relations; the latter will say that public and family situations differ and so require different strategies.

But where intimate relations have outlets for expression, vast abstractions substitute institutionalized channels. Once abstractions are reified, we can express love and devotion to them only through their channels. Camaraderie can't be writ large without changing in kind. At best it becomes esprit de corps. At worst it becomes racial solidarity. Rousseau's mistake is seeing this as a kind of dishonesty—though he did see that only regimes and priesthoods benefit when states masquerade as neighborhoods and peoples masquerade as families.

So the rhetorical strategies of expressive politics pose a dilemma that has left American politics dominated by a cult of personality. One horn of the dilemma is hyper-individualism. As people became self-absorbed, obsessed with discovering their personalities, the eighteenth century's balance between public and private life eroded. "Men came to believe that they were the authors of their own characters, that every event in their lives must have a meaning . . . , but what this meaning was, the instabilities and contradictions of their lives made it difficult to say" (ibid., 339). "The society we inhabit today is burdened with the consequences of that history, the effacement of the res publica by the belief that social meanings are generated by the feelings of individual human beings" (ibid.). One effect of this history is that, while organizations expand, classes subdivide into new classes, and states become more interdependent. And as power is redistributed in an ever larger system, the denizens of the late twentieth century are increasingly obsessed with smallness. "Localism and local autonomy are becoming widespread political creeds, as though the experience of power relations will have more human meaning the more intimate the scale" (ibid.). Community is thus an antidote to bigness, for the crime of bigness is impersonality (Riesman et al. 1950, Whyte 1956).

The other horn of the dilemma is a loss of self (Hoffer 1951). One surrenders to the abstraction or becomes lost in institutionalized modes of expression. One is a good marine, a true believer, a Palestinian or Jew, and, with a little luck, gets the advantages of martyrdom without the side effects. This, it seems to me, is why states, peoples, and religions are petri dishes for fanatics. When abstractions become surrogates for family and friends, they inspire emotion that can be acted on only in institutionalized ways.

Certainly the whole world doesn't straddle this dilemma. The proponents of pastoralism and authenticity take pains to show that the "realities" they advocate are missing in modernity. And the eighteenth century's separation of public and private is arguably not as rare as Sennett thinks: Conventional and rhetorical discourses are thriving in the late twentieth century. An instructive example is the dress-for-success school, which never assumes that one's dress reflects one's internal states but that successful business dress reflects the mastery of a public code. This is *The Man in the Grey Flannel Suit* sans value judgments. Hypocrisy is no longer a crime and no longer equated with conformity. Also, though uniforms have always been ubiquitous, the denizens of the 1990s seem less prone than their 1960s predecessors to see the wearing of uniforms as expressive. As "expressions," however, modern life has a rich variety. We don't automatically take T-shirts that say boy toy, bare skin, or provocative dancing to be invitations to rape. We don't assume that tattoos mean just what they say. We take designer clothes, or shirts with messages, not as expressive but as "expressive" of an orientation, a membership in a culture—a function analogous to the eighteenth century's use of clothing to designate class. The leather-suited punk with orange, spiked hair and one eye painted presents an engaging picture side-by-side with an eighteenth-century Parisian woman whose elaborate wig is decked with a *pouf à sentiment,* face painted, and costume to match.

More important, expertise is impersonal. The language of experts—their claims, evidence, and methods of proof—are indexical not to the perspectives of particular speakers but to their fields. Technical discourses are local languages; they form a large part of public speech, for social and political issues pose technical challenges and presume factual states of affairs.

Also, American political life has always had close ties to the legal profession—which trains the majority of its politicians. A legal education is a mode of thinking and a distinctive attitude toward communication—arguably a paradigm case of conventional communication: It relies upon public positions that are seen as sui generis, not as evidence of private cognitive processes. This legal influence may be part of what Weber diagnoses as the rationalization of society. Rousseau would denounce it as evidence of the evils of scale. Bureaucracies, after all, are institutionalized discourses. So the familiar complaint that government is impersonal is perhaps an answer to Sennett: There are enough unhappy expressives to suggest that there are limits to Sennett's diagnosis.

One could infer from Sennett a kind of dualism—a mind-body problem for states. Governments are conventional; popular politics is expressive. The political disaffection he ascribes to pastoralism thus might be seen as an effect of expressive expectations butting up against the impersonality of government by convention. This dualism applies, perhaps, to some largely expressive movements. It might explain, for instance, some of the intransigence and animosity of the abortion dispute. But some publics—interest groups, unions, and political parties—are as institutionalized and conventional as any organization. They are not inauthentic simply because they are organized, nor do they necessarily foreclose rhetorical possibilities—the creation of new situations and selves, the social reconstruction of reality. Organizations undoubtedly circumscribe the options of their members (Clegg, 1979), but they are, as we shall see, quite imperfect at it (Bachrach and Lawler, 1980).

VIENNA CIRCLE JOURNALISM

Journalists often speak loosely of "information." They assail the "information society" and the gap between information-rich and information-poor citizens (Elliott 1982, D. Schiller 1986, H. I. Schiller 1981, 1986, Smith 1981); they stress the need to get reliable information to consumers (Bogart 1982) and the structural barriers to making information available (Abrams 1983, Bagdikian 1983, Demac 1984, May and Rowen 1982, McQuail 1984, 1986). Were it not for media conglomeration, corporate dominance, or governmental secrecy—if the citizens could just get the information—all might be well.

Information, in this literature, is often undefined, as if it is a transparent commodity that presents itself in a crude positivistic way; testimony is true or false, right or wrong; people express themselves badly or well. Information is a reality to be laid bare—and rarely, one gathers, is it ambiguous, arcane, or embedded in impenetrable contexts. The information-rich elites, one gathers, actually have what the public needs.

Using this vision of information, teachers of argument and informal logic see clarity as the precondition of successful discourse and misunderstanding as the main cause of conflicts. This is owed to Richards's (1965) definition of rhetoric as "the study of misunderstanding and its remedies," and to Bertrand Russell's view that philosophical problems arise from incorrect expressions. Once abstractions are reduced to concrete expressions, their flaws become apparent and remedies suggest themselves. Naess (1966) and Crawshay-Williams (1957) call this clarification *precization.*

But surely clarity has limits. In diplomacy, bargaining, and legislation, differences are sometimes best obscured. Labor negotiators do not seek compromise by rubbing everyone's nose in their differences. Clarifying the battlelines may heat up the hostilities; obscuring the differences can cool things down. Consider, for instance, the seven-year road to Palestine. It began in 1987, when Yasir Arafat seemed to say that Israel had a right to exist. The press, trained as it is to sniff out "real meanings," pressed for clarification. Did he in fact mean to signal a shift in PLO doctrine? Faced with these demands for explicitness, Arafat "backed down." But many deaths later, in 1989, he made more explicit concessions: The western powers wanted specific words—a rejection of terrorism and a recognition of Israel's right to exist; and by speaking the words—in a United Nations speech and in a position paper signed in France—Arafat gained diplomatic recognition from the United States and began to move in a language game made up of "expressive" social contracts. By 1993, those moves yielded a treaty, and by 1994 a new nation.

Perhaps the price of the seven years' delay was inescapable. Even in 1987, Arafat was straddling the worlds of conventional diplomacy and a miasma of expressive movements. Time brought the intifada, a succession of assassinations, and an explosion of violence as extremists on both sides tried to undo the Israeli-PLO treaty. Still, the possibility that a fixation on clarity may have killed a mockingbird deserves exploration. What if he hadn't been pressed so closely in 1987? Could his vagueness have solidified, increment by increment, into a policy commitment? It might not have mattered whether Arafat's statement was a mistake or a trial balloon. Subtle shifts can take on lives of their own in the public domain. Arafat wouldn't have been the first person to find himself saddled with a new position. And if the statement was a trial balloon—and Arafat's subsequent behavior suggests that it was—the outcome is all the more tragic. If people are divided by rigid doctrines, ageless hostilities, and intractable narrowness, trial balloons should be allowed to float. How else can people who take extreme public stands back down from them, modify them, or ease their more fanatical followers into accommodations?

This case is hardly conclusive, but it suggests a difference between asking what someone really means and asking what someone is trying to accomplish. The latter question is perhaps better suited to incremental negotiations, for the former question supposes that clarity is an ultimate value. Perhaps it isn't. Perhaps indeed, between Tatar and Russian, or Palestinian and Israeli, the better the understanding, the more intransigent the dispute.

The High and the Mighty—A Parting Glance

All in all, a bumpy flight. Our seat mate is thoroughly at home in the late twentieth century by virtue of despising every part of it. Such a thorough alienation requires a functional symbiosis with one's time, so Rousseau thrives in ours. He is a living contemporary; his ideas are at the center of things—kept alive by those who want the mass media to be an electronic agora or who hope to redeem the public sphere with a politics of authenticity. Depending on how we use the words, he is the archetypal postmodernist—the expatriate grousing at the margins—or the prototypical anti-postmodernist, for though he was no Marxist, Rousseau and Jameson alike are fixed on the concealments of modern times. Both want an expressive politics—a modernity in touch with its feelings. And both aspire to "theorizing totalities," an idea whose authoritarian potential will be a continuing theme here. So unlike most disagreeable traveling companions, Rousseau isn't going to rush out of our lives, grumbling his way down the concourse to catch the red-eye to Teheran. For all his theocratism, he belongs in New York. His view of the public sphere—that New York's electronic spaces are modern versions of Paris's public spaces—is entirely *au courant.*

Two

Romancing the *Gesellschaft:* Community and the Fallacy of Common Ground

Hillary Rodham Clinton may be remembered most for a speech, early on in the Clinton years, in which she called for a "politics of meaning." America, she said, is suffering "a sleeping sickness of the soul," a sense that prosperity and freedom are not enough, "that we lack at some core level meaning in our individual lives and meaning collectively." We are "crippled by alienation and despair and hopelessness." There is a "crisis of meaning." Society must be remolded "by redefining what it means to be a human being in the twentieth century, moving into a new millennium" (in Kelly 1993, D1).

This manner of speaking is something of a fixture in American life. One of the most quoted books of the 1980s saw Americans "yearning" for coherence and "the meaning of life" (Bellah et al. 1985, 295). Lyndon Johnson used the same language. And so did the progressives: "We are profoundly disenchanted," wrote Walter Wyle (1912, 1, 3), a "discontent is abroad in the land," a "deep and bitter disillusionment." "American democracy is in a process of decay."

The progressives had misgivings about the melting pot—about whether it was up to the job of absorbing "real" ethnicities. They pointed to the Know-Nothings as proof that the aboriginal demons are there, simmering beneath the surface. Woodrow Wilson had similar inklings as he lectured "hyphenated Americans" to mind their loyalties, as if the Italian side of an Italian-American was a genetic default setting. And in a book that sees the difference between primal demons and primitive rhetorics, Schlesinger (1991, 134) essays to "restore the balance between *unum* and *pluribus*" by quoting Herbert Croly's (1909) call for an "ultimate bond of union" based on a "democratic social ideal."

Americans—in 1909—were too dispersed to replicate the Greco-Roman audience—and seemed to bond together only in times of war. So the progressives wanted to exploit the social possibilities of war (Schambra 1990, xi), to turn war-scale solidarity to peaceful purposes. Democracy needs "cohesion within its ranks," Wyle wrote. "It must abate internal strife. It must gather an ever increasing number of recruits from the still unawakened but potentially democratic masses" (1912, 270). The wellspring of this unity was even then, Wyle thought, abroad in the land: "a new spirit, critical, concrete, insurgent" (1912, 4–5).

This spirit is often said to have died at Ypres. The optimism of the war to end all war soured with the spectacle of mechanized slaughter. So the progressives, it is said, lost their trust in modern institutions as instruments of reform (Hofstadter, Miller, and Aaron 1964, 305). But plainly the progressive spirit has survived—in reform-minded "wars" on poverty and crime, for example, and in the communitarian drift of Ms. Clinton's speech, though Wyle's martial imagery has given way to a New Age idealism owed to Michael Lerner: We want "a society based on love and connection, a society in which the bottom line would not be profit and power but ethical and spiritual sensitivity and a sense of community, mutual caring, and responsibility" (in Kelly 1993, D1).

Indeed, Ms. Clinton is speaking for a sizable literary tradition. Buber calls community "the primary aspiration of all history" (1958, 133). Kirkpatrick (1986) has a Christian vision of mutual fellowship and concern. MacIntyre (1981) wants a secular spiritual revival: to invigorate a public sphere with enough virtue and civility to transcend social divisions. Frankel (1962) links community to tolerance. Sullivan (1982) sees it as a stance citizens may learn to take where self-interest gives way to civic interests. And others hope that virtuous nations will create a virtuous world. Albert Schweitzer advocated a "higher patriotism which aims at ends worthy of the whole of mankind" (in Snyder 1976, 52); and the encyclical *Pacem in Terris* (11 April 1963), advocates a "universal moral order" backed by the vision of common good in the 1948 U.N. Declaration of Human Rights.

These are, to be sure, thoroughly humane proposals. As a lethal century draws to a close, one can scarcely defend unbridled self-interest as a governing mechanism—for individuals or states. And as an era of interdependence dawns, distributive justice is arguably a more distant goal than it was for Wyle and Croly. Disemployment is no longer a simple matter of buggy whips giving way to microchips. Jobs now move from Toledo to Taipei as profits disperse to scattered nodes in the developed world. The communitarians, it must be said, have never sent to know for whom these bells toll.

But conceding the decency of the communitarian drift, one notices withal a certain flimsiness in the communitarian argument. Ms. Clinton, for instance, simply announces the crisis of meaning—as if it is a perfectly ordinary thing to claim to know how 250 million Americans think and feel. And Jones (1994, 32) ventures, without a whiff of proof, that "people on the whole want to feel that they are part of a political community." One would have guessed otherwise from reading studies of citizen participation, especially voting (Neuman 1986); but the usual communitarian reply is that alienation causes low participation. This answer, mind you, rests on the same bedrock of evidence as the crisis of meaning. Indeed, it is fair to say, when communitarians attribute alienation and yearnings to the public, they characteristically proclaim it.

One would think that the communitarian literature would bristle with angst polls. Polling can almost always yield the results the pollster wants, so it must be tempting to raise one's diagnosis to the status of a scientific finding. But it is chiefly journalists who assign great credibility to polls and have turned loss-of-community polling into a ritual. Gannett's annual Mood of America poll, for instance, reports that Americans see their neighbors as less neighborly than they once were. Of course Gannett's respondents are answering the questions asked, whether or not their answers are opinions they in fact hold; they may be giving what they perceive to be the desired responses, and the fragrance of agenda-setting is especially pungent given journalism's professional stakes in rousing community involvement. Non-citizens are journalism's lost audience, so the finding that Americans yearn for community is arguably a bandwagon appeal with the aura of scientific truth.

In *Habits of the Heart* (Bellah et al. 1985) evidence is analogous to a runway from which one launches and then soars in free flight. It begins modestly: "We do not claim that we have talked to 'average' Americans or that we have a random sample" (ibid., x). This modesty, it turns out, is well warranted: With an *n* of 200+ white, middle-class Americans, the interviews are abstractly sketched; the questioning techniques are invisible. Still, the sketches are remarkable for the degree to which their recurring themes, even national-scale concerns, are personalized. *Habits*' respondents, like Gannett's, want local virtues—neighborliness, kindness from strangers, involvement in churches. But then with a breath-taking rush comes the conclusion (275–307), the material everyone quotes, where the prose slips the surly bonds of evidence. Suddenly we hear ancient voices (John Donne, "'tis all in peeces,"); we find ourselves searching for a core curriculum that will hold—and hearing claims that need more than wind beneath their wings: "There is a widespread feeling that the promise of the modern era is slipping away from us" (ibid., 277). We meet our old friend, melting-pot anxiety: The lifestyle enclaves of popular culture are "too evanescent," they inspire too little loyalty "to carry much public weight. Only at rare moments do such largely expressive solidarities create anything like a civic consciousness, as when a local . . . team wins a national championship and briefly gives rise to a euphoric sense of metropolitan belongingness" (ibid., 292). Can the social possibilities of football remedy the meaninglessness of work and alienation from public life? The answer is pure Rousseau: A national-scale camaraderie must be deeper, richer, more intrinsically rewarding than lifestyles and competition. It must be a form of "common worship," which reminds us that "we did not create ourselves" and puts us in touch with "the meaning of life" (ibid., 295).

Perhaps this way of arguing is simply a convention. Caught up in the rhythms and figural symmetries of a rhetorical tradition, one deploys the commonplaces—the images of crisis and decay—for expressing the intuition that all is not well. One then completes the ritual with a grand, synthetic finale cast in intense, evocative prose.

But notice the realism strategy: Communitarians are galvanized by the belief that genuine community is a scarce commodity. Some say it exists only in neighborhoods; some say it once existed in medieval villages and economies of direct exchange, or in religious communities and guilds. But the common diagnosis is that the virtues of the *Gemeinschaft* are missing in the *Gesellschaft.* Capitalism has replaced the authenticity of direct exchange with a false economy of goods and perceptions. The mass media have replaced the genuine, meaningful life of small towns with a hollow pseudo-culture, and authentic human voices have been drowned beneath a deafening wave of images and faux community.

These are expressive messages. They proclaim truths in a distinctively expressive way, as if the yearning for community is an obdurate reality, an "innate need of individuals for a sense of community" (Juergensmeyer 1993, 31). This realism is so pervasive that it infects, perhaps by osmosis, even anticommunitarians such as Robert Nisbet (1953), who describes a "yearning for community" that "cannot be denied." Like a Freudian drive, an instinct, or DNA instructions, it simply must find an outlet. Community thus arises as people bind together by expressing aspects of their inner being (Litt 1973, Pangle 1992). Public discourse is good when it authentically expresses everyone's inner feelings and thoughts. If people can cut through conventional pretensions and rhetorical deceits, and say what they really mean, an underlying unity will shine through. Community is thus absolute space for societies. It eliminates disturbances, so that everyone (like things in nature left undisturbed) returns to a preferred state.

Perhaps the yearning for community is a cultural truism—something so obvious to communitarians as to be taken for granted. But this possibility suggests another: "Cravings for 'historical identity'" Gunnar Myrdal said, have never come from the people; they are purely "upper class intellectual romanticism" (in Schlesinger 1992, 42). Historical romanticism, he might have said, for it is chiefly historians who crave historical identity. Consider Michael Stürmer's proposal that historians build positive images of the past so that nationalism will supply the meaning and order religion no longer provides: "Loss of orientation and the search for identity belong together. Whoever thinks that this has no consequences for politics and the future is unaware that in a country without history the future belongs to whoever fills memory, shapes the concepts and interprets the past" (in Roberts 1991, 37–38).

Notice the faintly biological sound: Memory is a need. Human nature abhors an historical vacuum. Does this imply a narrative gene whose demand for a morally acceptable past simply must be satisfied? If so, it is grist for the fallacy textbooks. As an empirical proposition, it presumes what it must prove. Or is Stürmer speaking figuratively about the power of primitive rhetorics? Perhaps he is thinking of the sort of rabble-rousing the Serbs have used to inspire ethnic cleansing. The Bosnian genocide is said to stem from grievances dating to the Battle of Kosovo in the fourteenth century. But who kept these grievances alive? One can't prove that they did not smolder in the collective breasts of an historic people, but one can say that the flames had ample fanning—by mullahs and priests, poets and playwrights, nationalist historians and a "virulently anti-Muslim" Belgrade press (*Newsweek,* 19 April 1993, 31)—an intelligentsia that has, it must be said, served a thuggish government well.

COMMUNITARIANS AT THE GATES

But the fact that grievance narratives sometimes succeed scarcely proves that there is an innate human yearning for historical identity. Not everyone, after all, is "going tribal." Poland and Hungary have listened more to other rhetorics; the Czech-Slovak breakup was at least "velvet;" and in Germany the primal appeals have thrived chiefly in working class neighborhoods of the late GDR. And the evidence is at best scanty that ordinary Americans are yearning for national-scale unity. The participation research suggests otherwise. And so does an argument communitarians often make. The argument is owed to Tocqueville who foresaw the retreat to privacy long before VCRs and CD-ROM—a world of consumers, not citizens, fixed on "the petty and paltry pleasures with which they glut their lives." Each is a stranger to the rest; his children and friends are for him "the whole of mankind." "As for the rest of his fellow citizens, he is close to them but does not see them; he touches them but he does not feel them; he exists only in himself and for himself alone; and if his kindred still remain to him, he may be said at any rate to have lost his country."

Hence the "social democratic ideal," something to get one out of the house, to get one "involved with mankind." The problem is that Tocqueville's couch potatoes are comfortably esconced. Left to their own devices, they will move only for beer and chips. *Habits of the Heart* thus speaks for the tradition: "on the basis of our interviews, and from what we can observe more generally in our society today, it is not clear that many Americans are prepared to consider a significant change in the way we have been living. The allure of the packaged good life is still strong, though dissatisfaction is widespread" (1985, 294). Notice again the take-off from evidence: The runway isn't the interviews but "what we can observe more generally," and nothing in *Habits* proves that "dissatisfaction is widespread."

Once airborne, we hear Livy's voice: "We have reached the point where we cannot bear either our vices or their cure" (ibid., 294). But who is we? Some communitarians attribute a vague disquiet to even the most self-absorbed homebody: Something is bothering him, though he may mistake it for gas. But *Habits* takes the more usual line: "as some of the more perceptive of the people to whom we talked believe, the time may be approaching when we will either reform our republic or fall into the hands of despotism, as many republics have done before us" (ibid., 294). So there it is: Gibbon in bell-bottoms. With despotism at the gates and a historical narrative nowhere to be seen, only a revival of the public—fueled by sports-scale adrenalin—can save the republic.

With this turn, the communitarian case is open to a criticism often leveled at advertising, that it creates wants, that it sparks artificial needs and desires by creating fantasy worlds. *Habits,* on its own account, wants to stoke a dying ember—a desire for finding the meaning of life in one's participation in the polis. It legitimates its aim by appealing to "more perceptive" people—just as advertisers appeal to "the discriminating smoker." And it uses fear appeals that are, if anything, stronger than the advertiser's norm. As the communitarian tells it, a fear of meaninglessness ought to be scarier stuff than, say, a vacuous fear of "ring around the collar." And it demands measures more heroic than a trifling purchase. If my life alone is without meaning, the solution must be a union of my identity and self-worth with my political involvements. This is a familiar tactic to students of persuasion. As one of the classics puts it: much as therapists must convince their clients that they are ill, political leaders create true believers by convincing them that there is something wrong with them, something missing in their lives (Hoffer 1951). Our lives lack meaning, says Ms. Clinton, we are "crippled by alienation and despair." Now that, as any huckster would say, is a hook.

THE LIBERTARIAN'S STORY

If you are profoundly unimpressed by this criticism, you have passed a litmus test: The progressive spirit is assuredly with you. Wyle and Croley knew that the moral equivalent of war is artificial demand. Their intention was to create it—to take Jefferson's rhetorical experiment a step further. If the melting pot is possible, then it should be feasible to create an ideal polity, one that does the right things for the right reasons. And as it is a nobler thing to crave an ideal polis than to crave one's MTV, the communitarians are surely embarked on a higher human calling than peddling frozen dinners.

But understood, then, as agenda-setting, as political persuasion, communitarianism's moral ground is inseparable from its rhetorical ground. This brings to mind Aristotle's warning that rhetorical means have side effects—that persuaders are liable for foreseeable outcomes. If you believe—intuitively—that the goal of turning consumers into citizens is not vindicated solely by its nobility, you have passed a rather different test; and assuredly a very different spirit is with you. For where the communitarian wants to know what is wrong with asking the public to aim higher, to become something better, the classic libertarian reply is that "the expansion of power feeds on the quest for community" (Nisbet 1990, xxi). The rich sentiments favored by communitarians turn virulent too easily and strengthen states too readily. What is benign locally turns malignant with scale: The language of camaraderie and neighborliness—joined to the apparatuses of modern states—has a totalitarian potential that Nisbet called "the most profound threat to freedom in human history" (Schambra 1990, ix).

This is a venerable argument, at least as old as Montesquieu's critique of despotism. Even Tocqueville fretted about the tyrannical potential of majority opinion. And in what Mussolini called "the fascist century," the brutal facts—Stalin, Hitler—demanded an Orwell and a Huxley, who gave us the striking image of tyranny with a benign face. To Orwell and Huxley, the languages of kin, friendship, and fraternity were objects of alarm anywhere in the vicinity of modern states. The discourse of intimacy is transformed on a mass scale, much as gene-splicing spawns bizarre mutations. A small community's DNA molecule spliced to a state's yields a despotic hybrid.

Of course this argument is as susceptible to arm-waving as the communitarian view. Orwell's fears were framed in a world patterned by states. Totalitarianism needs sealed borders. But though the age of the nation-state is by no means past, states do seem to be evolving to meet the demands of interdependency. Albanian-style borders are both passé and bad economics. Moreover, though we still have Pol Pot, the skinheads, the Aryan Nation, and any number of authoritarian theocracies and social movements, the domino-like collapse of the Stalinist police states does suggest that the totalitarian experiment is, if not finished (Moynihan 1993), at least in disrepute. And, it bears saying, no matter how hard one squints at Ms. Clinton, she doesn't remotely resemble Joe Stalin. Nor do any of the communitarians. They want no race wars. They plan no Orwellian horrors. They want gentle virtues writ large: fraternity, civility, the "we-ness" people feel with their neighbors, a common purpose to good ends.

But libertarian minds want to know: How do gentle virtues and familial feelings get writ large? Social engineering is a matter of harnessing the mundane details of policy, organization, and administration to goals and ideals—and weighing the odds that one's vision will be distorted as it is translated into organizational imperatives. As the libertarian sees it, the paving on the road to hell doesn't matter. Good intentions or bad, the mechanics are everything, and it is the mechanics of national-scale community that libertarians fear. So if our lives lack meaning, what is the remedy and how does it work? We know how Dior does it, but how, short of putting us in uniform, does a state give meaning to our lives?

The libertarian's answer is that when states are asked to give meaning to people's lives, they respond with practical organization. They do what organizations do. Put in charge of identity, they identify; they classify and distinguish; their categories harden into institutions that perpetuate themselves through enforcement.

These organizational bents make libertarians especially distrustful of appeals for unity. Mass community, they suspect, is a creature of limited means, for there are only so many modes of effective mass identity. Community is a relational idea (McKiernan 1989), a feeling of belonging to families, gangs, or movements. It involves identification, a merger, to one degree or another, of self- and group-identity (Kelman 1961). Personal feelings of this sort may enrich local relations, but they are not easily extended to a mass scale. The chief vehicles of mass camaraderie have been appeals to race, ethnicity, religion, and nationalism, and these appeals in mass politics have often needed a rhetorical boost of an especially repellent sort. Let's call it the politics of invidious contrasts.

Contrasts are to some degree inevitable. Even local unity entails distinctions and boundaries; to pull together with some people is to pull away from others. The invidiousness comes from the need to heat up the distinctions. Mass unity is hard to come by in complex societies, and because heterogeneous masses are most easily consolidated against something, rhetorics of inside and outside threats become increasingly important.

The libertarian fears that once the personal rewards of identification are heightened by a contrast with outsiders, the chief beneficiaries are states and mass movements: Vehicles of mass unity create emotions that can find outlet only in institutionalized channels. And the results, I would add, are rarely conducive to world peace. If we consider the track record of ethnic nationalism, as I propose to do now, there are grounds for a gloomier prediction. For it isn't inconceivable that a world of communities will be Beirut writ large.

NATIONALISM

The libertarian fear takes the form of a slippery-slope argument, and as with all such things, there can be disputes about the slipperiness and steepness of the slope, and about the degrees of slipperiness or steepness that are tolerable given the magnitude of the risks. The libertarians' strong suit is the magnitude of the risks, so it is with the potential for national symbols to become "beacons of death" (Snyder 1976) that I will begin.

I have nothing original to say. My intuitions are stitched on the samplers of more gullible eras: Johnson called patriotism the last refuge of scoundrels. Pope called a patriot a fool in every age. Denunciations of nationalism are arguably a genre that includes Mark Twain's "War Prayer," Dominique Behan's songs, Dalton Trumbo's plays, W. H. Auden's poems. Around nationalism, aphorisms buzz like flies. Poets throw everything they have at it.

Then there is Tolstoy's haunting split-screen picture: on one side a mob of good-natured oafs, gaping like children at the uniforms, leaders, and waving flags; on the other side a desolate plain—a tableau of hunger, misery, blood, agonies, rotting corpses (Snyder 1976, 47). Nationalism, Tolstoy believed, had turned Europe into a charnel house. This is a pre–World War I picture, mind you, by an author who had not seen Gallipoli, or for that matter Hiroshima and Nagasaki, landscapes in 1945 thought to be an improvement on World War II. But Tolstoy would know the post-Stalinist world—the race wars, the headlong rush of some of the historic peoples of the East back to the nineteenth century because, thanks to an Orwellian time warp, they were denied the lessons of the twentieth.

Among these lessons is, arguably, the mother of all cautionary tales. It describes a road to hell paved with a number of intentions, but it begins with communitarian intentions. It begins, indeed, in the eighteenth century with a student of Kant's, the philosopher-poet Johann Herder, who proposed that the need to belong to a *Volksgeist* is an instinct as irresistible as the needs for food and security. One's self-identity is inseparable from one's social identity. Cut off from one's own kind, one feels lonely, adrift, and nostalgic. The *Volk,* Herder believed, was a genuine expression of living social traditions. It differed in kind from the modern state, which reflected only the contingencies of aristocratic power struggles. These pseudo-states would never achieve world government, but if each *Volk* could be restored its place, the result would be a peaceful pluralism.

This peaceable kingdom became a garden of earthly delights by taking a modernist turn. Herder was vague about how one restores a *Volksgeist* in a cosmopolitan world, but operational definitions are the sort of thing modernity does well. If something simply had to have the natural right and responsibility to realize the *Volksgeist,* G. W. F. Hegel had just the thing. You will find it in his *Philosophy of Right* and *Philosophy of History,* and it is, I submit, one of the worst ideas humans have ever had: Human meaning and spiritual worth come "only through the state." The state is an "end in itself," "a secular deity," "the march of God in the world"; Truth is "the Unity of the universe and subjective Will; and the Universal is to be found in the state." This vision mingled easily with the *Volk* mythology, for as Hegel, and later Heidegger saw, the basis for unity needed to be an aboriginal people.

To see why, one must appreciate the romanticism at the heart of the *Volk* movement, its hatred of cities and idealization of peasants. Imagine a people whose blood pulses to the rhythms of mountain streams and dark forests (Johnson 1988, 118), a *Volk* rooted in a place, a land where the values of the past have soaked into the soil. They re-emerge—apparently in one's Müeslix—to nourish the *Volk* with natural, pure, and pastoral myths and images. This food chain has been corrupted by modernity, by cities, where the rumble of street cars muffles the murmur in the blood. But, many historians insisted, the people were indestructible. They might be dulled and warped by city life, torn from their roots in the forests and fields, but their truth coursed in their veins. They could recover their souls by purifying their society.

Alfred Rosenberg, the architect-turned-Nazi-philosopher, called this a "rebuilding of the soul cells" (Cohen 1972); *Mein Kampf* called it a return to health. But to see it at work watch Leni Riefenstahl's *Triumph of the Will.* Just after the Junkers tri-motor descends from heaven and the triumphant motorcade, we get a pastoral scene that brings the gloomy, brooding city to life. We see costumed peasants eating their evening meal. The camera moves from face to smiling face, then lingers on a scene of boyish innocence—shirtless young men playfully wrestling and blanket-tossing. The camera moves among them, catching beaming faces, cheerful horseplay. The effect is insidious: These might be boys from any home town; they seem guileless and likable. So it is a stunning moment when, as if on command, the young men turn from their play, don their crisp, clean brown shirts, straighten their swastikas, and line up in smart formations. Right before our eyes, natural purity fuses with the discipline and hard virtues of the totalitarian state.

Hitler did not invent these "splendid predatory beasts." Nor did Goebbels hatch the obsession with racial purity. The *Volk* was a cause célèbre on German campuses long before 1935: "The jurists and teachers of German literature and language were stridently nationalist. The historians were the worst of the lot. . . . The academic community as a whole was a forcing house for nationalist mythology" (Johnson 1983, 125–126). The result was a ready-made propaganda package—a mythic vision so idealized, so pristine, that only a totalitarian state, and nothing short of a holocaust, could redeem it.

So in August 1945, the Enola Gay dropped from her bay doors what might be called the end of community, or the end, at least, of its most malignant kind. The poisonous mix of race and nationalism in Germany and Japan had spawned a collective psychosis, complete with homicidal rages and killing sprees. In its stead, the Enola Gay inaugurated an opposite extreme: Mutually Assured Destruction. MAD was a community. It obliged the superpowers to make their behavior mutually intelligible and predictable. But it was also alien and hermetic—a technical discourse. "Strangelovian" logic for limitless stakes was not the world community most people had in mind.

Nor were the technical discourses that flowered with the growth of multinational business and interdependence. The idea that technical discourses have impoverished public life is now a central communitarian theme. Habermas, for instance, reiterates Max Weber's fear that administrative and economic rationalities have distorted the broader spheres of life that ought to be cultivating their own rationalities for "forming a collective will." There is "a greater need today for types of relations within which more subjectivity and more sentiment can find expression, in which affective conduct is taken more into account" (in Dews 1986, 64).

Presumably he means benevolent sentiment and affect. If he is proposing a nationalism at all, it is one based on Enlightenment claims to reason. The goal, presumably, is to steer a middle course—to find a form of community more humane than MAD and more benign than the toxin of the 1930s. But this, one would think, puts a premium on the nuts and bolts of doing it. If one's call is not for just any affective conduct, then how do we guard against uglier varieties? In fairness, Habermas's claim was published three years before the Berlin Wall fell; reunification was then inconceivable; and a generous social welfare system was straining but nonetheless working. One could scarcely have predicted "the largest spree of racial violence in Germany since the early Nazi era" (*Newsweek,* 29 July 1991, 34), or that the beatings, murders, and firebombings would continue through 1994, or that racial purity would become a global theme—with 48 full-blown ethnic wars going on and a combined death toll so far in the millions (*New York Times,* 7 February 1993, 12). One is almost nostalgic for the good old days of the cold war.

But with the wisdom of hindsight should come a certain impatience with vagueness. Given the mercurial potential of social movements, the persuasion theorist wants from the communitarian something like an environmental impact statement—enough details about engineering the gentle virtues to reassure us that more volatile sentiments are safely contained. The libertarian sees gremlins in any proposal to galvanize mass unity. This stems partly from a distrust of anything that feeds state power, but it stems too from the suspicion that there are no moral equivalents of war, that left to state apparatuses, community is nationalism's disguise, its most readily available mass vehicle.

This, I submit, is an eminently debatable proposition. The libertarian fear turns on the difference between calls for unity and the dirty details of engineering it. If we treat this fear as a concern that may be allayed or confirmed on a case-by-case basis, we form the basis for a possibly instructive debate: The merits and risks of mass unity may sort themselves out in the give and take. The libertarian, for instance, may have to narrow the sweep of her generalization, conceding, for example, that the Peace Corps achieved a relative mass unity for good ends and that Americans got through their Bicentennial without redeclaring war on the British. But it is harder to say how the communitarians will fare, and the reason why brings us to what is perhaps the heart of the matter, for if the communitarian case is not your proverbial knockdown argument, neither is it one of the best-laid plans of mice and men. In fact rarely is it a plan at all.

MODERATION-BY-FIAT: SOCIAL PLANNING WITHOUT A PLAN

Habits of the Heart is essentially a plea. It presents neither a detailed argument whose call for unity would rouse the potatoes from their couches nor a consideration of the kind of mass appeals that might. The risks of community-gone-awry are simply invisible, and this, I submit, fairly characterizes the communitarian tradition. One doesn't know what the authors would say about the resurgence of nationalism. One can only guess that, preoccupied with good sentiments, they might say of bad ones: "I'm not talking about that, I'm talking about this."

Oddly, this guess is confirmed by communitarians who explicitly acknowledge the extremes to which community may veer. One might expect this acknowledgment to prompt detailed proposals for avoiding the extremes, but in fact it prompts stipulated distinctions. Alter (1994), for instance, simply lays out a distinction as if it is a difference in natural kinds: good versus bad community. And Nodia (1994), without saying how, argues that though nationalism is "less than fully rational," it can go hand-in-hand with liberalism.

This is not a mode of arguing we would admire in other advocates. The Chamber of Commerce would be greeted by derisive snorts if it came out for monopolies—"only the good kind." And no one, I imagine, is much impressed by the distiller's unctuous pleas for "responsible drinking." But why, then, do communitarians feel so free to call for community—"only the good kind"?

"Only the good kind" is the cornerstone of what might be called "the social infrastructure" view of community, which sees nationalism as a tool for central planning, a "dynamic principle capable of engendering hopes, emotions, and action; it is a vehicle for activating human beings and creating political solidarity" (Alter 1994, 21). This thinking entered the mainstream in the 1960s, as scholars focused on the politics of developing nations. The idea is that "nationalism awakens a people by stirring its patriotic sentiments, by calling upon the past to aid the present, and it has a thousand wise uses" (Maier and Weatherhead 1964, 10).

Not quite, perhaps, a thousand: Indeed in the infrastructure literature I see just two: fighting communism and bolstering states. Many saw the latter chiefly as a means to the former, but others had a modernist vision of states as instruments of progress. Progress meant infrastructure; and that, as a rule, meant central planning. States are incomparably better than tribes or clans at building railroads and highways, so the idea was to create general interests that would work against feudal and tribal interests.

It should have been easy. Even allowing for Winchian-scale cultural differences, it is not, one would think, an insuperable challenge to argue the benefits of, say, plumbing over cholera and river blindness. But the idea of arguing supposes a measure of mutual respect. It is not the mode of discourse one chooses if the problem is to civilize hearts of darkness and enlighten savage minds. If tribalism seems to draw its power from the backwardness of primitives, then the antidote must be a rhetoric that trades upon that backwardness, that turns the primitive way of thinking to good uses. And it needs to be potent stuff. If the problem is to raise primitives to higher allegiances, the solution, as every demagogue knows, is to put hope in their hearts, fire in their bellies, and goose bumps on their arms.

The phrase "nationalism awakens a people" is presumably a loose expression, perhaps meant to evoke gentle virtues. But why use a loose expression to denote a nation-building technique central to one's program? And why so primitive an image? To awaken is to stir, rouse, kindle; to awaken a people suggests an aboriginal identity to be roused much as spirits are summoned by sorcerers. Such talk has a seamy history, though one wouldn't know it to read *Webster's*. As the *Tenth Collegiate* tells it, atavism is a purely biological phenomenon. "Reversion to ancestral type" means the recurrence of traits or inherited ailments. Ethnic nationalism isn't counted among these traits, and there is no hint that it ever was. But, as Gould (1981) reminds us, Lombroso's criminal anthropology ranked-ordered races by their proneness to criminality, and one notable mirror of that nature is *Mein Kampf*, which portrays atavism, in that quasi-biological patois the Nazis used, as a reversion to racial type. No nature-nurture controversies here, just a convenient scam: The *Volk* is a natural category, with a hard-wired destiny, a force, as it were, lurking beneath the surface ready to blossom at dramatic moments.

So Mr. Webster take note: Atavism is also a persuasive strategy, an invitation into a world, or fantasy theme (Bormann 1972), designed to convince people that they have an obdurate nature that links them with others of their kind. The strategy depends on defining a natural category—a people—and contrasting it with outsiders. It achieves unity by vivifying contrasts; and the contrasts heat up as needed, for if unity proves elusive, then the basis for mass unity becomes increasingly primitive. Atavism, in other words, reverts to rhetorical type. For the most politically viable languages for describing aboriginal identities are the languages of race and religion.

But what was bunkum in Rousseau's day hasn't improved with age. Rousseau thought that when it is right with nature, the state represents reality—as opposed to the appearance of will manifested by what people say; thc statc is a single mind, a godlike voice that silences factions by bringing individual wills into compliance with the general will. Of course, in the developing world, the general will is often the General's will. And the most convenient cover for thuggish intentions is a rhetoric of authenticity boosted by a common threat. It taps a fear of disorder and uncertainty. it enjoins a sheeplike followership, and it is, above all else, xenophobic, for when the need for national unity is great, the rhetoric takes a racial/religious turn. This is a mixed blessing even for regimes, for strong states set their apparatuses in concrete. As they become more authoritarian, they become more set in their ways, resistant to critique, and thus more incompetent. Their intransigence forces their opponents to opposite extremes, whose strategies of community also inhibit critique and reconstruction. The first victims are tolerance and moderation, and the next victims are the innocents caught up in mercurial movements or police roundups.

And if, after all the tub-thumping, states seem less like natural entities than like modern weapons, then the Idi Amins of this world see quickly enough that state institutions can be turned to tribal purposes. This too has an ugly track record. From the Congolese civil war on, tribal competition for state power has been brutal. Lately, for instance, the Tiv and Jukun in Nigeria, the Kasai and Katangans in Zaire, and the Tamils in Sri Lanka have rivaled the Serbs in body counts. And the Hutu have upped the stakes in purging their Tutsi neighbors: 100,000 may have died in Burundi in a span of months (Associated Press, 10 March 1994); 500,000 may have died in Rwanda in a two week pogrom (CBS, 3 May 1994). As I write this, the horror there is still unfolding, with cholera and starvation thinning the ranks of refugees numbering in the millions.

One could dismiss the social infrastructure view for its Victorian paternalism. At its worst, it is a rationale for trading on and bolstering the backwardness of primitives. Such cynicism, if warranted, really ought to have a better track record. And one could say that nationalism, in an interdependent world, is a needlessly narrow vision of rhetorical possibilities. The language of sovereignty and inviolate borders is a "feel-good" rhetoric for people in subsistence circumstances. But it is a self-defeating vision of economic development. At best it sparks Bismarckian foreign relations

—a politics of winners and losers in zero-sum games. And at worst it sparks the sort of jingoism whose track record we are considering. But it is the social engineering without a blueprint that should prompt the most skepticism. For the sheer scale of ethnic warfare around the world suggests not that the slaughter is an aberration but that there is something intrinsically malignant about the mix of nationalism with aboriginal awarenesses.

From Killing Ground to Common Ground (and Back)

Perhaps there is something better. Some communitarians focus less on the politics of identity than on the grounds for cooperation in heterogeneous societies. The goal is common ground—a basis for compromise, bargaining, and mediation that needn't, in principle, imply shared identity. But whether common-ground communitarians are open to nationalist risks depends very much on what they mean by common ground, and this is not always easy to fathom. The idea is often left vaguest by those who use it most; it often crops up in political discourse as a vague, approving label for centrist positions, and it is sometimes used as a label for confederations of strange bedfellows. For instance right-wing Catholics and evangelicals have lately claimed to have found common ground—by which they mean a coalition against the left. Common ground thus seems to function much like the word "Heaven": Everyone is in favor of it, but nobody knows what it is.

Perhaps the least equivocal vision of common ground is found in rhetorical theories—which stress stylistic appropriateness and audience-adaptation. In antiquity rhetorics were often handbooks of commonplaces—common topics appropriate for general audiences. The idea was that it takes agreement to get agreement. Aristotle thus saw common ground as shared opinion, the underlying unity that makes enthymemes possible. Enthymemes are rhetorical syllogisms trading on the listener's ability to supply premises to a speaker's claims. The common ground between speaker and listener is a cognitive unity: The said calls up the unsaid, and together the speaker and listener create a common syllogism.

Aristotle had a thoroughly materialistic view of perception (the image in *De Anima* is of a signet stamped on wax—form molding matter), so common ground was literally a matter of sharing the same opinion. The point of coincidence between the speaker's major premise and the hearer's minor premise is a syllogism, a common ground structured by logical form. As a matter of logical form, similar beliefs become functionally the same beliefs, for syllogisms and enthymemes get their validity from the arrangements of terms in their premises, and it is the arrangement of terms that explains how people come to common conclusions.

Kenneth Burke (1969) gives a Catholic twist to this thinking. *Communication* (from *communicare*) means "to share." Persuasion is thus *identification,* a commonality, a *consubstantiality,* meaning a "common substance," which is dialectically achieved by resolving linguistic differences, dichotomy by dichotomy, back into the "great molten mass" of meaning. This is a linguist's version of realism: It is meant to be a description of the world as it is, namely, as constituted by language. But the idea that *A* and *B* can achieve a unity in substance, that two people can become one, bears an eerie resemblance to practices found in the "imagined worlds" of science fiction. As mind-melds go, consubstantiality is pretty potent stuff: It is not unlike a state of bliss for Braden (1969, 184), who sees ethos as something on the order of a spiritual communion. In a similar vein, and bearing in mind that every star ship worthy of the name has a computer that translates all known idioms and dialects, Katz (1971, 41) speaks of a "common core of psychological reality" transcending linguistic differences and of a need to find common understandings to translate "the problems of one group into the functional language of another." And finally, if ever an idea had pointed ears it is the vision of oneness achieved through a shared objective reality. Hikins and Zagacki (1988, 224), for instance, speak of a common ground "in objective reality" uniting rhetoric and philosophy.

Guilty, we might say, in three degrees: Braden's image is ethereal—and more than a little theological in tone; Katz's view focuses on translation into a common commensurating discourse; and Hikins and Zagacki seem to be thinking of commonality based on realism. Despite surface differences in beliefs, humankind is ultimately one, either in spirit, language, or a mirror of nature.

Not all rhetorical theorists, when they speak of communication as sharing, mean anything so expressive. Indeed few see communication as nothing but a process of revealing inner realities; it is commonplace to see conventions and rhetorical creations as common ground. And they certainly know that rhetoric is more than a vehicle of unity. One might study the organization of discourses in order to undermine them or, as with the rhetoric of science, to better understand their epistemic makeup. Still, communitarianism to some extent comes with the territory. The very idea of rhetoric implies concerted action: It deals with problems individuals cannot solve by themselves, "issues that require shared attitudes and cooperative action for their resolution" (Campbell 1972, 3). Without some unity, nothing will happen, and since rhetorical studies often focus on how rhetorical processes constitute societies and on persuasion as a social binding agent, they often conclude that the solution to problems is more unity. One fears that without community, reasoned discussion is futile, so, the more being the merrier, one is tempted to seek increasingly powerful unifying values.

Unfortunately appeals for community are advanced chiefly as remedies to social upheaval. Theologians have produced the biggest communitarian literature, in which crumbling institutions are objects of alarm, rampant individualism is a disease. Comte saw cohesion as a definitive symptom of social health, and Durkheim thought that suicide varies inversely with the degree of integration of religious, domestic, and political societies. This way of thinking pathologizes pluralism; it favors integration over everything else.

More unfortunately, solutions to fragmentation often come down to special pleading. Hauerwas (1981) thus wants to recover the grounds of a Christian community that can express itself intelligibly to outsiders. But in forming and clarifying the boundaries of this community, he sets it against others—the sharpest split being with the political sphere. His point is that Christians have lost the abortion battle by letting the enemy pick the argumentative terrain. And his remedy is a withdrawal from the general into the local.

One more discourse might be scarcely noticeable in a world of balkanized groups. Unity, bought at the price of isolation, may prompt the discourse to turn inward and become increasingly self-confirming and provincial. But it is in precisely such remote soil that certainty takes root, zealousness blooms, and xenophobia blossoms. If one adds political ambitions to this pot, the provincial vision may take on that tinge of manifest destiny true-believer discourses so often have. Competitor discourses will seem transient or of less weight; the local will, it will seem, simply must be the general will; and if one can (on one's account) adjudicate among competing positions, render verdicts, then isn't one morally obliged to do so? Add to this "white man's burden" the self-righteousness of humble servants of the truth, and you have the classic imperialist's rationale—and the sort of gunboat epistemology that characterizes intellectual traditions at their worst.

But if the idea of common ground does not, as it stands, lay the libertarian's fear to rest, this needn't be the end of it. For there is still a way to give the communitarians something of what they want without threatening the functions of common ground libertarians want to protect—cooperation, mediation, and compromise. Admittedly, in the argument to follow, it may seem that the communitarian stands to lose more than the libertarian. There is a perverse feel to an argument that endorses what many take to be the worst side effects of mass culture. Still, I ask communitarians to bear with me, for however odd it may seem, the "imagined world" I want to defend is a community of sorts; and perhaps the gentle virtues can be writ large within it.

RETHINKING COMMON GROUND

Melting pot anxiety is not groundless. Senator Moynihan may be mistaken in saying that the melting pot never melted; but he does point to ethnic identities and differences that seem to have persisted. Schlesinger points to a number of writers who do seem to be encouraging *Volk*-like revivals. And both underscore a divisiveness in public life that can scarcely be denied. Fragmentation is ubiquitious. Brute confrontations are too much the rule. The melting pot does seem fragile—and alarmingly dependent on economic prosperity.

These concerns are especially plausible if we doubt that the melting pot is an overwhelming force—fused Marxist-style with capitalism's inexorable consumerist culture. One may wonder whether the authors surveyed in chapter 1 live in the same world as Moynihan and Schlesinger. But still, if the authenticity view is as inflated as I claimed, then it won't do to say that the melting pot is an all-encompassing, undefeatable superintelligence.

But the pot has one source of resilience that Moynihan and Schlesinger have overlooked: It is not simply an ethnic mixture. It includes a bewildering array of incidental identities and unities of popular culture. Incidental unities form, inter alia, around commodities, life styles, and entertainment. For instance, Knicks fans are a public in Dewey's sense—and perhaps more of a community than many publics: They number in the millions; they are joined in common enthusiasm, purpose, and subject matter; they are as loyal, and fickle, as people in other communities; they are enthusiastic, at least occasionally; and their unity is reinforced by regular gatherings, either in Madison Square Garden or via television.

We have, remember, only the communitarians' word for it that such faux unities are less satisfying than more "authentic" ones. And for some communitarians, the menace of popular culture lies precisely in its attractiveness. There are, I am told, true-believer Trekkies; many writers have noticed the religiosity of physical fitness movements; and others have noticed that fandom, in various mutations, can be every bit as involving as racial and ethnic identities. It is this attractiveness that has sparked the ethnic and racial revivals that Moynihan and Schlesinger fear. At least some people find it intolerable that "authentic" identities are no stronger than incidental ones.

These movements do attract followers. Italian Pride Days—hatched by a Mafia *Capo*—sparked turnouts in New York. Schlesinger paints a grimmer picture of separatist movements bent on undermining the *unum* in a desperate scramble for identity. But these movements are struggling, in their different ways, in an environment rich with competitors. And perhaps that richness bears a closer look: The melting pot's apparent weakness may be its strength. Perhaps it gets its vitality from its vagueness and is able to dilute identities precisely because it is itself an amorphous, all-things-to-all-people idea. In a world where people may change identities by changing logo shirts, one's newfound ethnic identity—assuming these movements are successful—will still compete with one's identity as, say, a Catholic, a Knicks fan, and a Trekkie.

And perhaps the image itself, the pot, isn't quite right. A pot creates a new hybrid by mingling everything simultaneously. A smorgasbord, on the other hand, is a linear, sequential progression of choices: One is a Catholic on Sunday, an entrepreneur on Monday, a Knicks fan on Tuesday, and so on. A smorgasbord appeals to a variety of tastes; not every dish on it is equally rich. And it presents, for all practical purposes, an infinity of choices: Given the hours in the day, one can be only so many things. This sheer number of choices may be important, for perhaps the Serb and the Croat can be neighborly in America not simply because their primal identities have been subsumed by a new mongrel breed, but because they can choose among so many identities and allegiances that it is easy to forget that one is a Serb or Croat, or at least hard to feel one's Serbness or what have you with the intensity one would have if one were only or essentially a Serb. On some nights, certainly, it is immeasurably more important that one is a Knicks fan.

Of course communitarians want citizens, not fans. They want the unity and enthusiasm of fans gathered behind progressive reforms. But the thing to consider, as nationalism rubs shoulders with Nikes in the marketplace of ideas, is that on the whole fans are less lethal than patriots; differences are easier to tolerate when trivialized; and primitive differences are the ones least conducive to cooperative ventures. If being a Knicks fan is a less intensely-felt identity than, say, being a right-to-lifer or an Aryan nationalist, then perhaps there are reasons to appreciate ties that only loosely bind. The very thing that makes lifestyle enclaves seem so unappealing in *Habits* makes them seem less coercive to libertarians; and in something of this spirit, it may be worth considering whether blandness is useful in managing differences across vast expanses of heterogeneity.

Consider one experiment in the management of differences that is now underway. Federated Europe is even now grappling with "aboriginal" demons, and its ally, "Euroculture," is arguably the newest variation on the melting pot. Federalism, I submit, is the most interesting—and fragile—rhetorical experiment in recent memory. The "bland Eurocrats in Brussels" (George Will's dismissal) speak of community in the blandest imaginable way. It is a drab, uninspiring term for a trade federation—with all the hair-raising drama of Local 631. But it is just this blandness I want to defend.

BLAND NEW WORLD

Community can be seen as a conventional matter of rules, roles, and relations—the stuff of etiquettes and protocols, what we have when you and I know that red means stop and green means go. And, of course, community can be seen as something people create, for instance, identities and situations that promote cooperative ventures, much as the Federated Europe movement is trying to create a nonnationalistic alternative to sovereignty. Federalism, I argue, is a rhetorical strategy designed to create a legal (conventional) entity.

Alongside the evolution of federalism is the cosmopolitan blend of style and attitude called "Euroculture." This label is not always a term of endearment. Some malign it as a synonym for Americanization—over the emphatic objections, of course, of Europeans (meaning the champions of Euroculture). Still, Euroculture is a melting pot of sorts. Like its American counterpart, it is a smorgasbord of lifestyle enclaves, art, architecture, clothing styles, and travel patterns. It is a point of view one hears expressed at cocktail parties: a cosmopolitanism, a transnationalism, a tolerant pluralism. It is a bit more sophisticated than taking the pledge to become an American. It assumes that people can manage multiple identities—that, for example, one need not be any the less Dutch as one becomes European.

This identity is not entirely new. The excesses of European nationalism have always prompted proposals for a European identity. Herder was reacting to some such identity in the eighteenth century. So Euroculture—like federalism—has evolved glacially, with many setbacks. This incrementalism may seem mysterious to infrastructurists, but, judging from their track record, one can only conclude that melting pots can't be engineered. They have to just happen. Peter the Great was able to build St. Petersburg, but not a westernized population. Stalin's Russification turned basically on mass slaughter—and lasted, as we learned in 1989, exactly as long as the will to enforce it with brute military power. But Euroculture seems to be just happening—much like its American precursor.

The American pot was largely a creature of circumstance, an accident of immigration, a side-effect of cosmopolitan growth and frontier expansion. No one would call the founders' social engineering utopian. Federalism had all the idealism of a real estate deal; it was the founders' vision of the best that could be done with the situation as it stood. Since becoming an American was thought to be a rational change of mind, and since in those days it took luck, an iron constitution, and a certain willfulness to arrive in one piece in the new world, the founders were largely content to let Darwin (so to speak) do his work.

Of course this laissez-faire cookery didn't last. The Americanization movement tried some ugly recipes during World War I, and many of Jefferson's successors have seen themselves as chefs, selecting only the finest ingredients for the pot, or as Millard Fillmore might have said, "keeping the undesirables out." Still, quota periods have waxed and waned, so it would be stretching things to claim that the current makeup of the pot reflects anything like a plan—which is why I used the word "incidental" to describe the unities and identities that lie along the American smorgasbord.

If Euroculture is just happening in a similar way—coincidentally with growing economic, social, and intellectual interdependence—then infrastructurists will need to restrain their impulses to help it along. Indeed the new federalists are taking care to avoid any appearances of social engineering, and their rationale is worth a closer look.

When Geertz (1988, 147) argues that the future use of ethnographic texts "will involve enabling conversation across societal lines—of ethnicity, religion, class, gender, language, race—that have grown progressively more nuanced, more immediate, and more irregular," he passes too quickly over "Esperanto-like culture, the culture of airports and motor hotels." He seems to want something deeper. Perhaps he assumes that intelligible discourse on a world scale will be earnest and piquant, infused with a Greco-Roman nobility. But the political rationale for Esperanto's blandness is worth recalling, for the blandness of airport culture enlarges the possibilities for discourse. Bland contexts submerge differences; they offer no distractions from the business at hand. It is no accident that the United Nations Lobby looks like an airport, or that the design principle for mass media content is inoffensiveness. Nor is it surprising that English has become a de facto Esperanto, for as languages go it is rather like an airport. It has no *Académie française* to keep it pure, so it is a loose collection of "jargots," so to speak. It adapts as easily to the arcane codes of business and industry as to mass entertainment.

American culture is often likened to fast food—and thus seen as a menace. Its melting pot sameness, proletarian triviality, and infuriating popularity evoke both disdain and fear from defenders of local cultures. If the Paris papers in 1992 were any indication, the arrival of Euro-Disney was the greatest threat to French life since the plague.

It is hard not to sympathize. Respecting culture, our aesthetic sensibilities lead us astray. As with food, we may prefer rich to bland. We resist homogenization; we sometimes feel obligated to our histories; and being empathetic to this need in others, we want to preserve unique cultures. Thus Kaplan (1961, 10–11) fears that the "rich diversity of the world's cultures is rapidly giving way to an empty sameness." "I do not look forward," he says, "to a state of society in which all men espouse one world philosophy, but rather to a state in which each man espouses his own philosophy, but one in which he can live at peace with all the world."

But what sort of philosophy is so unthreatening in a world of scarcity, religious and cultural rifts, and competing interests? Call it the airport philosophy. It must be vague enough not to clash with a range of tastes and interests. It must be eclectic—with a contrived depthlessness, a shallow quotation of its competitors. It must leave me free to have whatever beliefs I like as long as I move in an orderly manner through the airport of life. It must be, in other words, like the jingle on a Disney ride: "It's a small, small world."

The closest geo-political parallels to the letter (not the spirit) of the jingle are the new consortia. The Japanese are finally achieving their "co-prosperity sphere" in the Pacific Rim. North America is gradually coalescing into a trade bloc. But the most immediately interesting experiment is in Europe, where federalism is continuing the trends set in motion by the old European Economic Community. Much of the unity is bureaucratic and economic—an attempt to bolster interdependencies by reducing border formalities, trade and employment restrictions, and bureaucratic redundancies. But the federation is unprecedented in its reliance on formulae by which states negotiate away their sovereignty. This softened sovereignty seems to have co-evolved with the interdependencies among multinational firms and consortia, and with common currency, a common military, legal uniformity, and academic uniformity will come still more joint projects made possible by pooled resources. And Europe is now a public sphere—competing for cognitive space and time with every other public sphere.

This captures Rorty's (1982, xxx) intuition that "the quest for a universal human community will be self-defeating if it tries to preserve the elements of every intellectual tradition, all the 'deep' intuitions everybody has ever had. It is not to be achieved by an attempt at commensuration, at a common vocabulary which isolates the common human essence of Achilles and the Buddha, Lavoisier and Derrida. Rather it is to be reached, if at all, by acts of making rather than of finding—by poetic rather than philosophical achievement." This poetic isn't the earnest humanism of traditional rhetorical theory: "The culture that will transcend, and thus unite, East and West, or the Earthlings and the Galactics, is not likely to be one which does equal justice to each, but one which looks back on both with the amused condescension typical of later generations looking back at their ancestors" (ibid.).

This is right, but too flippant. The condescension needs to be kept under wraps, for it is the federation's Achilles' heel. The point is to avoid emotional factors that harden disputes and intensify differences. Culture is a chip on a group's shoulder, so smart cosmopolitans watch their manners. The federation movement has taken care to seem unthreatening to local cultures. Its government is strictly bureaucratic. The point isn't to resolve differences but to ignore them if they don't affect joint projects. So there is no rhetoric of revolution, with bold proclamations about the end of sovereignty. The rhetoric, rather, is the curiously bland discourse we might expect to arise if a new multinational airport were proposed.

Federated Europe bears a family resemblance to a more global society—the air traffic control (ATC) system. The ATC system exemplifies the sort of concrete project that defines a public interest of world scope. It is a world society meshed with other global institutions—weather bureaus, airline schedules, reservation systems, supply networks (for parts, fuel, trained personnel), and other technical domains. Like the telephone system, the ATC system exploits an agreed-upon project with a technical language fitted to the concrete specifics of the project and a functional language that is fully global, namely, English. There are no local culture-honoring exceptions: Air traffic controllers speak English not for its cultural heritage but because, after 1945, it was the most readily available Esperanto. Thanks to British colonialism, the allied war effort, and the fact that the biggest pool of available airline crews spoke English, the biggest airports happened to speak English. In much the same way, and because English is the Esperanto of the international business world, English may be the de facto Esperanto of European federalism. Scholarly exchanges, especially in engineering and the sciences, are already dependent on English, and despite multiple translations of all documents, much of the public discourse resorts to English.

Environmental protection may be a similar, though politically more volatile, project. Its actors are multilingual, but nitrogen and sulphur oxides, hydrocarbons, and pesticides speak Esperanto—SO_2 is SO_2 is SO_2, as Gertrude Stein might say—so its technology will become a lingua franca. Selling environmentalism to poorer countries requires more blandness than the air traffic control system did: Developing nations want the fruits of industrialization and see environmentalism as a new technological variant of imperialism (Rosenbaum 1973). This conflict of rich versus poor may be bypassed by environmental disaster, but it is more likely to be smothered beneath a bland surface of rationales. Abatement technology may become the new start button for foreign aid—packaged in a language of helping and caring and frosted with a rhetoric of shared risk.

Federalism has always courted nationalist backlashes. Margaret Thatcher once dismissed it as "airy-fairy nonsense" on grounds much like Kaplan's, that European nations should try to speak with a single voice, but without a dilution of sovereignty. Sovereignty, markets, and culture may be separable issues, but the issue for Thatcher was whether there will always be an England. Milder versions of this distress are undoubtedly shared by many, and it is hard not to sympathize. No one loves Euroculture. It is a tofu culture with no taste of its own: it is French here, Italian there, and "Euro" when it concerns lifestyles, tastes, fashions, and products. Federationists are identifiable chiefly by T-shirts, bumper stickers, and flags with a circle of yellow stars on a blue field. These trivialities are distressing to those who fear that their cultures are disappearing into an empty sameness. That fear led Danish voters to reject the Treaty of Maastricht and has fueled oppositional movements throughout Europe.

But Euroculture's empty sameness has its reassuring side. A transcendent culture needn't be richer or more satisfying than local cultures. Air traffic control, pollution abatement, and multinational consortia require the airport aesthetic—neutral, functional, and polyglot. Just as airports won't replace museums, Euroculture won't obliterate local cultures. It will blur them, and perhaps convince the people who define their lives as expressive of a culture of the menace in their feelings. Pride is prone to fierceness; otherwise why have it? And this, of course, keeps the bayonets at the ready.

The New(est) Colossus?

Euroculture will probably thrive, not because it is an all-consuming culture, but because it will Americanize (meaning trivialize) Europe's ancient demons. The new *Lebensraum* will be the living room, the coffee shop, and the café (and, to be sure, the golf course, the shopping mall, and the sports arena). As national identities blur, national borders may fade in importance; as interdependence grows, workforces and economic interests may become increasingly cosmopolitan. The result may be an empty sameness, but as the Bosnian Muslims know, there are worse panoramas.

And the sameness may not be entirely empty. Little Italy doesn't remotely resemble Chinatown; Miami scarcely duplicates Boston; and no sentient person would mistake Kansas City for Kansas. Euroculture will nestle, like fast-food restaurants, among greater differences than these, for unless one falls in a canal, one wouldn't mistake Amsterdam for Venice. At best, the new lingua franca will resemble the odd utopia envisioned by Esperanto advocates a century ago. Differences in language, architecture, and local customs will remain, but everyone will have a second language, and no matter how cosmopolitan that language may be, it isn't likely to be an empty sameness. It will be, as English now is, a loose collection of jargons, slangs, idioms, and dialects.

But if Euroculture won't be the empty sameness communitarians fear, neither will it be as powerful. For it, like its American cousin, is frightfully dependent on prosperity. The fortunes of American demagogues have largely co-varied with the business cycle: the Know-Nothings in the 1840s, the Populists in the 1890s, Huey Long and Father Coughlin in the 1930s. The 1990s recession spawned a Ku Kluxer and a primitive nationalist seeking the presidency—and a neanderthal broadcaster whose audiences are treated to a daily diet of Japan-bashing, isolationism, and calls for immigration restrictions. Privation in Russia has spawned the specter of Mr. Zhirinofsky, who garnered 20 percent of the vote with a scale of demagoguery that would make Huey Long blush. So it is scarcely surprising that hard times in Western Europe have fueled Le Pen's National Front in France, Haider's Freedom Party in Austria, the Flemish Bloc in Belgium, Alessandra Mussolini and the neo-fascists in Italy, the Republikaners and German People's Union in Germany, and overt Nazi revivals in the late German Democratic Republic. All of these movements have anti-immigrant, nationalistic, and racial purity themes; and for all, the federation is a convenient whipping boy.

It would be foolhardy to predict how these cases will play out, but I do venture this: These movements are largely creatures of the un- and underemployed; race-baiting and hypernationalism are entertainments chiefly of people with nothing better to do. Prosperity will weaken them politically and, if not silence them, reduce them to the most ignoble status imaginable—namely, like the Aryan Nation in the United States, they will become lifestyle enclaves. Ugly ones to be sure, minority voices to be sure, but voices we are unlikely to hear in all their authentic richness; for if all goes well, they will be drowned out by other voices—just as *Federalist* 10 predicted.

CODA: THE WORLD TURNED UPSIDE-DOWN

I appreciate the size of the camel I am asking communitarians to swallow. There is a sticky, republican feel to the praise of weak unities, and a tinge of capitalist apologism in the view that people are best united by no nobler a motive than consumerism. But let's get this camel's identity straight: My argument has been about mass scale. It doesn't proscribe clubs, churches, and professions, or friendship, neighborliness, and the amity that makes social life tolerable. The argument, rather, is that the definition of identity is not best left to states and mass movements, for it creates a kind of unity that benefits only states and movements.

Communitarians, of course, want to benefit their movements—and to strengthen states only in the interests of reform. But the grace of good motives scarcely vindicates the realism strategy. Community—seen as an irresistible force—is a potentially lethal rhetoric that feeds political despotism by validating the true believer's vision. It runs the risk of being a self-fulfilling prophecy, or a license for suppression, for the recurring theme in demagogueries of race is that a reality that can't be denied is being suppressed.

So communitarians should be careful what they wish for and should hesitate before saying things they would hate hearing from the propaganda apparatuses of modern states. Community is a flawed solution to differences, for local visions often masquerade as global solutions. These appeals strike at our fears that, as Geertz says, we can't keep out of each other's way. But they should also engage our skepticism, for totalizing visions are corruptible and imperialistic. Community stifles rather than transcends differences. Governments should not traffic in activities and icons best left to restaurants, museums, and tourist stands.

The same holds for world community, which I think is best kept bland, technical, and (in popular imagery) trivial. Blandness isn't more pleasing than rich cultures. Airports aren't prettier than monuments. The case for blandness, for the dullness of federated Europe, lies in its safety. It is better for bridging cultures because it is unthreatening. This view may seem perverse to those who lament the erosion of culture by the blandness of mass society. But as we've seen, Kaplan's good-natured concerns in Mrs. Thatcher's voice became a primitive drumbeat we know all too well.

THREE

Commensuration and Unificationism

This chapter continues the disease-masquerading-as-diagnosis theme. Here the poseur is a fixation on relativity—the diagnosis that public life is decaying for want of a commensurating philosophy. One source of this view is epistemology, whose vocabulary has seeped into the humanities and social sciences. Another, perhaps, is a philosophical impulse behind the very idea of criticism. But whatever the reason, critics in many fields are making claims that seem epistemological: They are foundationalistic; their focal syndrome is relativism; and they are often couched in a pontifical style, *theorizing totality* in the Marxist argot. That style, I submit, is driving the arguments.

EPISTEMOLOGICAL NARRATIVES

The image of a center that doesn't hold goes back to John Donne, but it became popular after 1919, when the *London Times* (ignoring Einstein's protests) proclaimed that relativity had overthrown "the certainty of the ages" (Holton 1982, xii). In newspapers, magazines, popular science writing, political oratory, theology, and critical treatises, *modernity* came to mean epistemic and moral fragmentation. And this ominous rhetoric, I contend, is not merely still with us after all these years, it is positively blooming.

APOCALYPSE NOW: THE HISTORIAN'S NARRATIVE

Imagine two contrary images. One is of a central system in dramatic collapse, trailing wires and connections that pull satellite systems toward the debris in the center: human knowledge as black hole. The other is a big bang: A monolith has exploded. Knowledge is mimicking the universe's expansion, fragmentation, and miniaturization. The black hole tells a Camelot-like story: A city of truth (Toulmin 1976) flourishes, then collapses from within. The big bang proclaims the balkanization of knowledge: Unity becomes diversity; the central government falls; knowledge is atomized.

Oddly, these images lead to the same result. They seem to be simply different literary twists on the same catastrophe. And both are equally plausible. The twentieth century is seeable as a stage onto which struts a robust epistemology. As in Greek tragedy, the protagonist has too much hubris to see fate closing in—projective geometries in the nineteenth century, general relativity and quantum dynamics in the early twentieth. Until 1930, when Gödel presented his undecidability theorem, one would have been on orthodox grounds in many fields in thinking that the universe is a system whose laws are knowable and codifiable, that knowledge mirrors reality, and that the mirror is as holistic as the objects it reflects.

Little of this legacy remains. Its Cartesian base and Kantian superstructure (Nelson, Megill, and McCloskey 1987) are now so widely doubted that Baynes, Bohman, and McCarthy (1987, 7) call some versions of the *end-of-philosophy* position straw men: "Notwithstanding the repeated denunciation of philosophers who believe in a priori knowledge and self-evident givenness, in necessity and certainty, in totality and ultimate foundations, there are relatively few of them around today." This claim would be mistaken applied to the "theorists of totality," or the critical thinking movement, or to Habermas's felicity conditions of discourse, which certainly seem a priori, if not foundational. Still, the claim is suggestive: Allowing for Kuhn's Planck effect (old paradigms survive until their proponents die off) and assuming that the claim is half right about how things stand in philosophy, then evidently an erosion of foundationalism occurred after 1931 and culminated in the latter half of the century.

Rorty (1979, 9–10) argues that the Cartesian turn, based on the Greek metaphor of an inner mirror of reality was shattered by Wittgenstein, Heidegger, and Dewey: Each reminds us that "investigations of the foundations of knowledge or morality or language or society may be simply apologetics, attempts to externalize a certain contemporary language game, social practice, or self-image." The idea that we arrive at justified true beliefs by confronting reality is mistaken if our views of reality are socially grounded. The search for a privileged discourse has thus distorted epistemology (Apel 1980, Harre 1980, Hesse 1980).

"The cult of the system" (Toulmin 1972) self-destructed. The great systems floundered on their own assumptions. The euclidean symmetry and logical niceties of Cartesianism surrendered to the projective geometries. The formal systems that wedded mathematics to the revolution in logic at the beginning of the twentieth century were beset with paradoxes. Frege's axioms (and the consistency proofs in the *Principia Mathematica* and Hilbert's *Grundlagen der Geometrie*) were vulnerable to Gödel's proof. Mathematical logic was not to be the universal discourse, not because local languages couldn't be translated into it—that is a different problem—but because mathematical logic can't prove its own consistency. A privileged discourse mustn't itself start from undecidable formulae—ones that cannot themselves be proved or negated.

The quantum revolution forced a reassessment of physics, the Vienna Circle's candidate for the privileged position. Positivism didn't die—the vigor of the Popperian school attests to its resilience—but the idea that physics might be a final epistemic arbiter is now doubted. The Bohr-Heisenberg emphasis on the observer's position and the idea that otherwise perfect systems might be incommensurable yielded a powerful relativity (Heisenberg 1952).

Reductionism met a similar fate. The microanalysis in Wittgenstein's *Tractatus* seemed to authorize a hope to find commensuration in the structure of language per se. If philosophical problems stem from mistaken expressions, then disagreements can be solved by translating imprecise statements into logically acceptable ones, reducing them to the basics, to the language of nature. This language would be so securely founded that it could explain the formal structure of natural languages. By the 1970s, this theory had been supplanted by the language games view in Wittgenstein's *Investigations*. There was a black hole problem: No existing formalism adequately represented a natural language, or ever got close. And there was a big bang problem: Equally legitimate formulations of incompatible knowledge claims were possible. Logic thus seemed to be irrelevant to the study of substantive problems. Wittgenstein may not have meant the *Investigations* to be philosophically skeptical or relativistic, but his *forms of life* acquired lives of their own in the social sciences. The idea that society is divided into communities that play different language games sparked the evolution of sociolinguistics, ethnography, and a bewildering variety of social knowledge schemes.

So the historian's narrative ends catastrophically. The Enlightenment succumbs to *Balkanization*—an apt name for the twentieth century. *Balkanization* names the time when relativity prevailed, when antirelativists retreated into enclaves of selective ancestor worship. Inside this story, we can only regard the future with shame: Our progeny will blame us for fumbling humankind's most persistent ambition—the search for a higher criticism.

Quantum Politics: The Critic's Predicament

At first glance, rhetorical and literary critics are unaffected by the end of epistemology. The critic appreciates the theatricality of the historian's narrative, but is neither blinded or stunned by epistemology's quasar. The apocalypse is specific to epistemology. The critic who never believed that pragmatic questions of knowledge are connected to epistemology doesn't feel threatened by its collapse. Criticism needn't presuppose a Higher Criticism (Booth 1974). It only needs foundations in specific fields (*criticism* thus labelling a field's epistemic discourse). As long as foundationalism goes native inside localities and stays there, the claim that the end of epistemology threatens criticism is a red herring.

But this dismissal is more equivocal than it seems. Critics of public discourse are rarely content with local grounding, and they speak in what can only be called an epistemological accent:

> As the modern public expands, it shatters into a multitude of fragments, speaking incommensurable private languages; the idea of modernity, conceived innumerous fragmentary ways, loses much of its vividness, resonance, and depth, and loses its capacity to organize and give meaning to peoples' lives. As a result of all this, we find ourselves today in the midst of a modern age that has lost touch with the roots of its own modernity. (Berman 1982, 17; see also Mills 1963)

This *sounds* like the historian's narrative, complete with big bang criticism and Diaspora critics. And listen again, this time to a theologian:

> As the universe of discourse tries to extend its boundaries, it finds itself full of imitating and expanding systems, each pretending to complete worldhood, and the more it impresses the one on the many, the more it spawns new possible worlds, until discourse loses itself in an infinite anarchical many. . . . The little systems imitate the great cosmos without internal restraint or external restriction (S. Buchanan 1958, 6).

This image is neither a casual flourish nor a momentary lapse. For Buchanan, relativity is "Satan's work" (so quantum mechanics, one guesses, cannot be God's). And consistently, big bang images, of acceleration, expansion, and explosion, are interspersed with biblical allusions. There is a loss, a catastrophic fragmentation, and, as one closes Buchanan's pages, there is only one conclusion: Cosmology and epistemology are back, slouching toward Babel.

So we have a social critic and a theologian using the apocalyptic metaphor. But why? Foundationalists, of course, would say that if every body of knowledge is connected (in a great chain of being or Aristotelian hierarchy), then critics can't be nonchalant about epistemology's fate: The grounds of critical judgment *are* dependent on the status of epistemology. But I favor a vaguer explanation, namely, atmosphere (meaning milieu, ambience, deliberately vague terms that imply nebulous influence). Terms of art indigenous to epistemology have seeped into other fields and formed the "background awarenesses," as ethnographers say, in which knowledge is discussed. The seepage is partly attributable to border-spanning discourses, but the "patient zero" in my epidemiology is the Franco-German Sociology of Knowledge, which appropriated epistemology's language and much of its theoretical agenda, even while rejecting Kant's view of reason and of the sovereign subject (Baynes, Bohman, and McCarthy 1987). *Wissensoziologie* is now an historical curiosity, but its influence lingers, for while its fate was played out inside sociology, it also found niches abroad—in organizational studies, informal logic, information theory, rhetoric, and political theory—where the relation between social and conceptual systems is still debated in terms laid out by Znaniecki (1952, 1955). Because ideas become more powerful as they recede to the background (Kelly 1955), Durkheim and Mannheim have become more influential as they became more historical, for it is largely through them that criticism has become philosophy pursued by other means.

Chief among these means is the argument from imported authority. For instance Hartman (1980, 110), surveying criticism's loss of authority, quotes critics and philosophers interchangeably but gives greater authority to the latter. Cassirer, Derrida, Fichte, and Heidegger (among many others) are authorities against whom critics are measured. On Nietzsche's authority, for instance, Hartman wants to level the "Appollonian culture," dismantle it "stone by stone" till its foundations are visible (1980, 110). Criticism will transform rhetoric: The "coefficient of power" may become the enemy of power if the reader is infected with a "kind of stutter" (ibid., 32) that makes the grand narrative falter. Plainly, then, the images and goals of epistemology are alive and kicking.

Is it atmosphere or crumbling foundations? I think it is a little of both. My reason lies in an admittedly speculative vision of why interfield borrowing happens. This explanation is certainly incomplete, and parts of it are a bit wild-eyed, but think of it as politeness to an ancient mariner. Hear me out.

First, whether or not all bodies of knowledge are connected, and no matter the status of foundationalism in epistemology, most expert fields are to some degree foundationalistic. Normal science is the norm; and with normalcy comes a devotion to getting better. To some extent, the very idea of discipline requires a certain optimism—a whiggish telos, a belief in progress, and a hope of ideal completion. One pays the price of discipline—the loss of freedom, the narrowed vision—expecting a payoff in *warranted confidence*. One hopes for a greater virtuosity, coherence, mastery of detail, and consensus. Every epistemic field has a veridical/judgmental system for deciding what counts as knowledge and for adjudicating competing claims. These systems may vary in the degree to which they inspire confidence but they are sufficiently public and open to criticism that we see our confidence in them as being justifiable. One source of that confidence is the belief that the system itself is held accountable, inter alia to a continuing comparison of reach versus grasp; one expects, or hopes, to see some progress toward realizing the field's exemplars of excellence, its ideal types, its hopes and ambitions.

And from whence do these ideals come? The answer is step two in my argument: Self-appraisal is often a matter of comparison with other fields; epistemic ideals are most easily operationalized by other fields taken as models; and it is easiest for fields to visualize their interdependencies with other fields in foundationalist terms. Fields, in other words, often presuppose other fields. Their ideals are often embodied in a vision of another field. One wants the certainty or precision the other field is thought to have. So the other field becomes a vehicle for imagining the ideal completion of one's own field. The Vienna Circle looked to physics. So did experimental psychology. Argumentation once looked to logic, and the sociology of knowledge looked to epistemology. Now, psychology looks to physiology, genetics, and biology; argumentation has rediscovered rhetoric; and sociology looks to statistics.

Hierarchies of scientific precision are often status hierarchies. Fields rarely import ideas from "inferior" fields (Sherif and Sherif 1969). With every import comes the exporting field's authority, and Hartman, manifestly, is using that authority to settle things. "Guarantor fields," if I may call them that, are thus most likely to be least invisible in fields undergoing extended debates about their scientific stature. Sociology's progress from the Continent to the New World can thus be seen as a debate about scientific stature, which is to say imported authority embodied in a "standard view of science" (Mulkay 1979). Such altercasting reflects the importance of science as an exemplar. Fields whose self-definition turns on scientific stature prize hardness—precision, rigor, and technical control. These standards often make for an epistemic modesty—a rueful appreciation of current limits. To be modest is to see one's field as a "soft" version of some "harder" field:

> When I talk to social scientists they tell me that what they do is soft science and that the real hard scientists are the physical scientists. When I talk to . . . meteorologists or geologists they tell me that what they do is soft science and that the real hard scientists are the physicists. And so it goes. The experimental physicists, feeling a bit soft, point me to the real hard scientists, the theoretical physicists. The theoretical physicists point me to the mathematicians, where the linear algebraists, feeling a bit soft, point me to the hard cutting edge, the typologists, who tell me it's all very mystical and intuitive (Schweder 1986, 39).

The merest whiff of mystical underpinnings gives foundationalists the jitters; but it prompts, nonetheless, the third step in my argument. Though many cases of interfield borrowing are considered moves, wishful thinking isn't unheard of; and it isn't inconceivable that this classic distortion of logical thought sometimes transforms hopes for ideal completion into working assumptions about what stands behind claims.

First, it isn't unusual for the guarantor of a critic's claims to lie in an outside field. For instance, the critic who detects a fallacy presupposes the existence of some guarantor for the fallacy itself. Standing behind this fallacy is the idea of fallacies, a scholarly tradition capable of certifying a use of the fallacy as a standard, and a body of reasoning that justifies using the fallacy as a method of condemning the practices in its ambit. The critic needn't defend the fallacy from scratch; she presumes that someone could do so.

Guarantor fields may be appealed to quite explicitly and logically. But the trouble comes when what was once a considered move becomes a habit. Custom makes for implicitness; practice brackets skepticism (Rescher 1973), and fields in the habit of importing ideas grow accustomed to relying on outside authority. So the tentativeness of a field's links to another field may well be relegated to the background in daily practice. The result is a vague sense, an intuitive *unwarrantable confidence,* a blind faith, really, that *something* stands behind one's practices.

Let's call it *the daisy chain of being:* The connections are tangled and unclear, but one assumes that all is somehow well. Standing behind one's own system is another field, sanctioning its justifications, authorizing its methods, vouching for its assumptions, and certifying its claims. If pressed by a skeptic, one's work can be ratified by the more rigorous field.

Skeptics may push the critic back here and there, but to proceed with criticism is to believe to some degree in the ultimate triumph of justification. So if skeptics mount some final assault, the critic can scamper to some final, irrefutable ground, or has reinforcements in the wings, or the dispute will transpose into a higher order and ultimately settleable conflict on another field's ground, and so on. If we lack the time, resources, knowledge, or authority to develop our own rationale, we rely on an outside authority.

And it is not unusual to find a de rigueur disavowal of absolutism licensing a nonchalance about the authority of a critic's claims. Some, indeed, avoid explicit defenses of their standards, yet write *as if* some vaguely understood but fully accomplished field certifies their claims (e.g., Andrews 1983, 3–4).

But the failure of foundationalism, leaving epistemology as a continuing conversation or hermeneutic, removes the comforting backdrop against which criticism is sometimes placed. Criticism thus finds itself confronted with epistemic conditions more complex than a simple relativistic thesis implies. Criticism is in trouble with or without Higher Criticism. On my explanation, epistemology's failure removes a vague faith that insulates criticism from self-scrutiny and protects ambiguous knowledge claims. On the foundationalist's explanation, the end of epistemology is the end of criticism: If pressed by a skeptic, critics can't fall back on epistemology. There is an abyss at their backs, not a comforting structure.

The atmospheric explanation, to sum up, is that because public problems are often knowledge problems, the language and assumptions of epistemology have seeped into the discourses on public life. The apocalyptic scenario provides the catastrophic images; the critical scenario either dies by those images or muddles them. Relativity is the problem a public philosophy must solve. A public discourse must be in some sense a commensurating discourse into which local languages are translated. For reasons that will be clear in chapter 5, neither scenario is satisfactory. Relativity isn't innocuous, but it is only one problem among many.

Arguing by Totalizing

"The world is full of a number of things," Lewis Carroll's Walrus says—among them, presumably, people with different beliefs and ways of seeing things, different languages and ways of ordering things, different technologies and ways of doing things, and different priorities and ways of valuing things. There are also diverse circumstances. Humans have achieved "splendid local adaptations" (S. J. Gould 1980) to deserts, savannas, jungles, mountains, and islands, to Lilliputian plots and vast expanses, to factories, crafts, and executive washrooms. And there are diverse fortunes, for Chad and Bangladesh in the late twentieth century are not like Switzerland and Sweden. The Walrus, many would say, was belaboring the obvious: The only universal fact is differences.

But there is a way of putting things, a rhetorical style, that obscures these differences. Consider the last sentence in the previous paragraph: Skinner (1985) argues that in the wake of Mills's (1959) puncturing of the pretentiousness of grand theory, even grander theories have arrived to explain why there can be no grand theories. Lyotard's *Postmodern Condition,* for instance, depicts a shared condition, a holistic lack of holism. In rebutting totalizing views of reason, Lyotard (1988, 278) says "there is no reason, only reasons"—a claim that is also totalizing (Conner 1989). Relativity thus becomes absolute and universal. Difference is discussed so abstractly as to obscure real differences. As Wittgenstein (1953, 12e) says, "If you do not keep the multiplicity of language games in view, you will perhaps be inclined to ask questions like 'What is a question?'"

The style that obscures the multiplicity of language games involves a level of generalization, of panoptic, universalistic claims that permit speaking of complexities as if they are holistic unities. From Rousseau on, it has been commonplace to speak of the public philosophy as if the public sphere is a single place with a single pathology to be cured by a single, unifying discourse. So we have *The Civic Culture* (Almond and Verba 1963), *The Human Condition* (Arendt 1958, Giroux 1988), *The American Leviathan* (Beard and Beard 1930), *The Legitimacy of the Modern Age* (Blumenberg 1983), *The Dilemma of Modernity* (Cahoone 1988), and *The Logic of Modernity* (Galgan 1982). These books *can* be judged by their covers; their titles accurately label a way of putting things: A single real entity with a single pathology needs a single philosophy or discourse.

The classic, of course, is Adorno and Horkheimer's (1972) *Dialectic of Enlightenment,* wherein the postrenaissance world is of a piece. Observers of modernity across the centuries will see a unity—a mixture of instrumental reason and enlightenment self-negations extending intact from the seventeenth through the twentieth century. The hulking organizational monoliths of the nineteenth century have lumbered into the late twentieth intact, crammed to the gunnels with contradictions; and so we find ourselves in a postcondition. Modernity is "the related economic, social, scientific, political, and cultural programs of the Western world since the renaissance" (Cahoone 1988, 181)—an all-encompassing holism of art, architecture, politics, industry and services, agencies, urban planning, and indeed everything of importance in modernity.

Even in the abstract, this thesis can't be swallowed whole. It is merely original sin gussied up as world-historical determinism, and it shares four flaws with its religious ancestor. First, the claim that anyone working within the system is condemned to replicate and confirm it turns on the stance and argumentative ground of the claimant. Seers, as they denounce the blindness of others, must account for their vision. Priests claim to be pure; and the critical version of chastity is outsider status. One would think that outsider status would be hard to defend given the system's all-encompassing determinism. The solution is a rhetorical style that presumes the status, an oracular voice that summons attention, that leads readers into a world, rather as novelists do, and invites them to suspend their doubts. It is a style, in sum, so fervent in its witnessing that it prompts forgetfulness. The manifest truth of the author's vision makes arguments and evidence seem superfluous.

Second, there are logical reasons to be skeptical about the pervasiveness of the system's contradictions. Admittedly, cost-benefit analysis and other rationalities can yield distributive injustice, Auschwitz, nuclear winter, or environmental disaster. But I can't work the reasoning to get the same result from Rawls's justice as fairness to find the self-destructive seeds to turn his *original position* against itself to yield the same outcome as cost-benefit thinking. The original position might not succeed (see Daniels 1975), but it is not self-destructive.

Third, there are empirical exceptions to the Adorno-Horkheimer thesis. Rationalization has followed multiple paths, and, as we shall later see, organizations have evolved differently by adapting to different functions and environments. Organizations do act to preserve themselves, organization per se does pull the discourses within its ambit toward a governing telos, and some organizations do die because they can't adapt. But some organizations change dramatically, question their founding assumptions, and, in different ways, adapt to new conditions. Habermas may thus be right: Some rational creations are amenable to critique and reconstruction.

And fourth, totalizing labels like *the postmodern condition* seem theatrical, like an Aeschylus revival where one is more conscious of the performance's curatorship than of its verisimilitude. If there are differences between life in Bangladesh and Belgium, then it is dubious to impute a common condition to the world. Some societies are suspended between tribalism and nationalism; others—the theocracies—are suspended between medieval institutions and nineteenth-century hopes; the new Eastern democracies are caught between nineteenth-century nationalism and postmodern interdependence; and Federated Europe has a tenuous grasp on a postmodern future but must still deal with a modernist Realpolitik.

All four flaws are operating in Jameson's (1988) denunciation of postmodernity. Jameson's phlogiston is capital, and it is everywhere, shaping architecture, politics, literature, consumption, science, and all aspects of daily life. Apparent differences merely disguise the underlying unity. Postmodernity is an all-encompassing threat—multinational capitalism's disguise. This is a theory of everything—superstrings for humanists. But its holism is an artifact of the level of abstraction at which Jameson writes. For in that prose, as Montag (1988, 92) has pointed out, vast pluralism and local specificity collapse into "one blurred, harmonious totality." His mode of exposition presumes the existence of universal essences and that all knowledge can be integrated into a single closed system. This must be true because the only alternative is sheer heterogeneity and idiosyncrasy (Jameson 1988, 16; 1991, 1–25).

This is shaky reasoning (holism must be true because if it weren't, then it wouldn't be true). And it begs the question: It presumes—uses as premises and evidence—an unproved holism, common condition, and author's vantage point. Begging the question involves presuming what in fact must be proved. And arguing by totalizing is just what is in question. If my claims in chapter 5 are right—if competence comes with focus, if focus is an organizational feature, and if expertise is narrower than most problems—then competence declines with breadth of vision and *theorizing totality* will be hard to defend. It will thrive, indeed, where it is most taken for granted, in fields where evidence is the sparsest and the problem of competence is most invisible.

In modern rhetorical theory, as opposed to Ramist and elocutionist theories, stylistic devices are not geegaws. Style is intrinsic to ideas, not adornment. The reasoning behind this view is a kind of operationism. Ideas *are* their modes of expression. *Theorizing totality,* for instance, has the *feel* of systematic philosophy. It *sounds* like Hegel. It implies a span of vision that transcends particulars. It presumes a privileged position, a reflective mastery, an oracular, all-encompassing vision. It thus propounds particular claims. Partial consciousness is false consciousness; local knowledge is subordinate to universal knowledge. The authority for these claims lies not in logic or evidence but in the "blurred, harmonious totality," the panoptic span of vision whose only authority is the confidence in the author's voice.

Unificationism and the Realm of Reason

Arguing by totalizing is often linked to an awareness that might be called unificationism—a belief in or hope for oneness, unity, and foundations. Unificationism is sometimes defended explicitly (the realm of reason, for example, is advanced as a transcendental human reason that overarches localities), but I will consider it here as atmosphere, as a background awareness, a strong but vague value. Unificationism, I submit, permeates thinking about the public much as a church's rituals and architecture inspire piety or the ambience of a Marseilles dive inspires vigilance. It is an intuition about public life that acquires power when it is taken for granted. When it is inexplicit, we infer its presence much as astronomers infer the presence of a hidden planet by observing oddities in the movement of visible bodies that are explicable only as effects of an unseen body. The various theories of public discourse likewise have peculiarities that are explicable only if the invisible picture is being presumed.

Unificationism comes in at least three versions: a literal belief, a philosophical idealization, and a rhetorical idealization—suppositions, in other words, about a single place, a single philosophy, and a single discourse.

A literal unificationist thinks that the public sphere is a real place. The mass media are modernity's version of the public spaces of the eighteenth century. What happens there is shallower than (a romantic vision of) goings on in the Athenian agora, so current practices seem degenerate. Television's fatuousness and reduction of news to entertainment are seen as evidence that Tocqueville's nightmare—democracy sapped by individualism—has come of age. The hope, apparently, is that pluralism will dissolve in something just a little less breathless than McLuhan's tribal unity. McLuhan passed from favor as quickly as the Age of Aquarius, for the "cool iconography of the electronic scanning finger" was to yield tribalism, not Reaganomics. Still, even for critics who take care to avoid McLuhan's exaggerations, the idea of an electronic Champs de Mars is tempting: "By merging discrete communities of discourse, television has made nearly every topic and issue a valid subject of interest and concern for virtually every member of the public. Further, many formerly private and isolated behaviors have been brought out into the large unitary public arena. . . . The widened public sphere gives nearly everyone a new (and relatively shared) perspective from which to view others and gain a reflected sense of self" (Meyrowitz 1985, 309). Lest we doubt the epistemic import of this reasoning, listen again:

> The opening of closed situations is a reversal of a trend several hundred years old. As Michel Foucault brilliantly argues in *Discipline and Punish,* the membranes around the prison, the hospital, the military barracks, the factory, and the school thickened over several centuries. Foucault describes how people were increasingly separated into distinct places in order to homogenize them into distinct groups with single identities ("students," "workers," "prisoners," "mentally ill," etc.). The individuals in these groups were, in a sense, interchangeable parts. . . . But Foucault does not observe the current counterprocess. The old social order segregated people in their special spheres in order to homogenize individuals into elements of a larger social machine, but the current trend is toward the integration of all groups into a common sphere with a new recognition of the special needs and idiosyncrasies of individuals. (1985, 310)

If one thinks, however, that the current trend is toward greater heterogeneity, with the proliferation of magazines, the growth of new networks, the decline of broadcasting, and the explosion in home electronics, then it seems dubious to say that nearly every issue is a subject of interest to nearly everyone. Public issues may affect everyone: The acid rain and supercollider hearings had implications, certainly, that might have affected us all. And in some circles, admittedly, it is de rigueur to have opinions on the issues of the day: As Henry James would say, opinions, like cufflinks, are indispensable accessories for the well-dressed man-about-town.

But it would present something of an empirical challenge to claim that the people who express opinions can always defend them, or that they come by their opinions by reasoning from arguments and evidence. And it would be more dubious—indeed a caricature of real attention spans—to say that people who can argue some issues in depth can do the same across the range of the American issue agenda. If I can argue to a fare-thee-well about abortion, I am in all likelihood unable to do the same for gun control and taxes. I am far likelier to take the peripheral route or rely on opinion leaders (Petty and Cacioppo 1986). Ignoring the problem of knowledge entirely, there are simply too many issues on the American agenda for Meyrowitz's claim to be plausible. Not even the best-trained public actors or most highly engaged voters can take interest in all of them.

Meyrowitz also underestimates Foucault's view of language-as-prison. Foucault (1977) says that all forms of inquiry refer us from one disciplinary authority to another. Criticism is a delusion; critics are oblivious to their blindness. If he is right, a transcendent discourse (i.e., the public sphere) is impossible. But Meyrowitz doesn't do the archaeology needed to support his claim. Instead he gives a countergesture. The unity of the public sphere will bring disparate groups together. This conflates claims about popular and expert cultures and thus confuses public decision-making with mass life in general. As will soon be clear, it will take more than that to get around Foucault.

Literal unificationism may be a vestigial trace of theocratic philosophies. Rousseau and Cardinal Newman were the forerunners of a still robust theory of states. If you see the state as a religion's servomechanism, and shared religion as the basis of community, you will seek unity in your philosophy. Even your defenses of tolerance, if you bother with them, will flow from the single position. Literal unificationism may also stem from popular views of what one does when one thinks philosophically. We owe to Plato the preference for the universal over the local and the idea that states serve natural or divine ends. If one's mirror of nature is polished, humankind's reflected image is the perfect state. A properly justified state is like a fact of nature.

But except on a small scale, no such place exists. There is no single, distinctively public field of discourse with judgmental standards of its own. I become a member of a public by virtue of the people and events I notice—my entrance into a public being a shift in my psychological stance, a change in my field of attention. I also move among publics as I move from group to group, context to context. I am a Democrat at a 9 A.M. rally, a Rotarian at noon, pro-labor at a 3 P.M. meeting, and pro-abortion at 6 P.M. As I move across these boundaries, a single vision of the public may or may not undergird my discourse. But entering these publics isn't analogous to becoming a juror, where I expect to be educated in public rules and procedures. Instead I am likely to bring with me field-dependent standards I deem appropriate.

If one can't quite bring oneself to be a theocrat, the traditional alternative is a secular vision of the organizing intelligence of states. For many of the same reasons one can't be a theocrat, one intuits that there is such a thing as *human reason,* spoken of much as romantics speak of *the human spirit.* The stylistic model is Kant. A transcendental faculty, art, and discipline, a domain of reason (S. Buchanan 1958) or court of reason (Grootendorst 1989) is the kingdom to which states should aspire.

Thinking this way brings with it a proneness to capitalize the word *Reason.* One is dealing, presumably, with something more transcendent than the "small-*r*" reasoning of specific fields. Fields, one thinks, are Merton-like self-fulfilling prophecies. Their institutions and thought styles are self-confirming, protectionist. Reason (capitalized) is something more.

Again, one can scarcely challenge the decency of this thinking. Reason is generally better than violence among states and people. And Reason has indisputable emblematic uses. Pedagogy is largely a matter of paper-training the young, of convincing them, inter alia, that the brain might be counted among their useful organs. But beyond the admonition that it is best not to think with one's glands, what more should the young be told about the search for a transcendent Reason? That it has been successful?

It would be something beyond ironic if Reason functioned as a false consciousness. But consider a case that captures where the search for a transcendent reason stands: Even if Habermas finally convinces his skeptics, universal pragmatics can't settle substantive questions. Disciplines and expert fields have evolved as they have, and fill the niches they do, because they are successful. Their local hegemony is rationally and organizationally warranted. My argument later will be that transcendence is always local—a matter of particular border crossings. Beyond such regionalized successes, it seems to me, the theorists who defend argumentation principles as field-invariant have hitched their wagons to a black hole.

Unificationism as a philosophical idealization involves seeing the public sphere as a standpoint one may take, a counterfactual Newtonian center amid the quantum dynamics of argument fields. Perelman's universal audience is the paradigm case. It is vague, grandly synthetic, and functionally authoritative—a common denominator of substantive beliefs, and thus a standard for adjudicating interfield disputes. One determines the public interest by factoring out special or technical interests. Thus, "If thinking is disciplined to serve the interests of a particular individual or group, to the exclusion of other relevant persons or groups, . . . it is sophistic or weak-sense critical thinking. If the thinking is disciplined to take into account the interests of diverse persons or groups, it is fair minded or strong-sense critical thinking" (Paul, in *Critical Thinking,* 7:10).

Only the most obstinate Hobbesians can object to tempering the "blunt quest of advantage." But how many views must we consider? Are we accountable for the whole world? If so, how could we go about it and how would we know whether we succeeded? And if not, by what standard do we judge the sufficiency of our perspective? How do we know the difference between special and general interests? And how do we warrant rejecting the views of specific people and groups? Logical form transcends field boundaries but doesn't settle substantive disputes. Fallacy theory crosses field boundaries in the sense that equivocation is equivocation, no matter where. But one needs field-specific knowledge to know whether a particular claim is equivocal. The move from formal to factual considerations is a move into a field. So the recommendation that we take all diverse interests into account is easier to preach than to practice.

Another version of the philosophical idealization wants the public sphere to function as a broker discipline—an arbiter of interfield disputes. If the public sphere is an arena in which various constituencies compete for public power, and amid this relativity, technocratic hegemony over what counts as fact has co-opted the public's prerogatives for debating values (Wenzel 1982b), then the public needs a sovereign philosophy of its own—one that can authorize knockdown arguments against the claims of specialized fields.

The advocates of this view are mostly God-fearing secular humanists. They do not want theocracies or totalitarianism. But it is harder to say what they do want, for it is one thing to want to realize the realm of reason inside the Beltway, and quite another to specify what this would require. The sheer number of public issues and the diversity of arenas in which they play themselves out suggests that there is no single marketplace of ideas.

My rationale for this claim will gradually unfold. But the gist of it is this: To be an arbiter field, the public sphere would need to be an identifiable conceptual ecology with something like a governing economy. But theocracies aside, a governing public epistemology is infeasible. Its grounds can't be clearly defined; it can't get around the field ownership of facts; and there is nothing especially conceptual about its governing economy.

Finally, the rhetorical idealization is a vision of the Greek agora—a place, a forum where private concerns recede to the background in favor of common subjects. I don't know whether this reflects Rousseau's influence, but it is certainly his vision. Rhetorical unificationism thus matches the lone place to a single art appropriate to it: deliberative rhetoric. Rhetoric is thus seen as standing at the end of the road where theology once gave way to epistemology and epistemology is now surrendering to a single art that may "bring down needless walls between the human sciences" (Nelson, Megill, and McCloskey 1987, 16). This call makes rhetoric's renaissance seem like the next logical turn, just after the linguistic turn. Thus White (in Simons 1989, ix) suggests that rhetoric may provide questions and methods that will "enable us to move from one academic field to another and in so doing to unite them. . . . Rhetoric in the highly expanded sense in which I speak of it might even become the central discipline for which we have been looking for so long—which science has proved not to be—by which others can be defined and organized and judged."

I doubt that many rhetoricians of science would put the matter so strongly—or in the same way: The terms "defined," "organized," and "judged" imply epistemological authority. Since Aristotle, rhetorical theorists have seen rhetoric as a single art spanning all subject matters. But this doesn't mean that rhetoric functions everywhere in the same ways. A general rhetoric can encompass special rhetorics only by ignoring their content. An attempt to turn Rhetoric into a broker discipline to arbitrate or regulate interfield discourse "invites again the disaster that renaissance scholars visited on themselves. The effort is doomed to failure, and a good thing too. If it succeeded, we would push the foundationalist bully off the academic block at the cost of permitting an even less disciplined rhetorical bully to terrorize our work" (Leff 1987, 29). So the rhetoric of inquiry doesn't say that rhetoric will accomplish epistemology's commensurationist goals. Leff's essay appears in Nelson, Megill, and McCloskey, (1987), its presence suggesting that the editors see Leff's position as an internal check.

Axiology—Dressed to Kill

To many people, the language of negotiation, compromise, bargaining, and debate seems epistemically inferior to the language of certainty, precision, and logic. And the attempt to bring scientific discipline to the vagaries of government must be counted as among the most important developments in the twentieth century. The policy science movement was perhaps the most explicit; and its chief method, cost-benefit analysis, is the closest thing we now have to a public philosophy.

The "father" of all this technocracy is often said to be Fredrick Taylor (1913). This paternity suit is mistaken, I will later argue; but Taylor's *Principles of Scientific Management* did became something of a cause célèbre. Taylor's most devoted reader, ironically, was V. I. Lenin, who turned a modest proposal for shop management into a totalitarian blueprint. The irony in this was less impressive than the results. Before Stalin hit his stride, Huxley's (1932) *Brave New World* had described a tyranny of positive reinforcement. But by the late 1940s, Orwell, who, it is said, kept a picture of Stalin in his room while writing *1984* (1949), described a form of dictatorship unique to the twentieth century (Friedrich and Brzezinski 1965). Societies of vast scale would be as neat and orderly as Taylor's shop. Governments were "theorizing totalities" and thus intervening, brutally, ruthlessly, in all aspects of life. Totalitarianism of the right or left was thus to be, as Mussolini said of fascism, "a synthesis, and a unit inclusive of all values" (in Christenson et al. 1975, 50).

Popper (1950), conversely, saw totalitarianism as an ancient evil going back to Plato, whose guardians were the forerunners of Himmler's SS. All the Platonic themes—the public sphere is deteriorating, the people are degenerating into freedom and pluralism—are integral to totalitarianism, Popper argued, and he saw these themes in the "shallow cant" and "mystery method" of Hegel whose veneration as a great thinker, Popper held, was a public relations scam. Schopenhauer had called Hegel an "illiterate charlatan," but Popper was, if anything, less generous. This venom may be one reason why *The Open Society and Its Enemies* is not, so far as I know, read much today. This is unfortunate, for if one cuts through the fulmination, one will find a sound argument that Hegel's ideas heightened the evil in Plato by harnessing it to the apparatuses of modern states.

And one will find a convincing argument that Stalinism was the logical result of Marx's historicism, essentialism, and totalism. Governance, Popper argues, can't be harnessed to the belief that all change is decay without totalitarian results. This applies, I submit, to more recent theorists of totality. It is no accident that authenticity, common ground, and commensuration bear a family resemblance to epistemological foundationalism. A belief in the unity of knowledge easily transforms into a belief in the unity of people and to equations of consensus with substantive agreement, community with sameness, and communication with authentic representation of cognitive perspectives. A disaffection with relativity leads to a desire for solidarity, unity, and unanimity. As a Bulgarian educator recently argued: "The totalitarian reality demands *one* point of view, *one* truth, *one* way of talking and writing, *one* type of behavior" (Popov 1990, 4). These, it seems to me, are the stakes in asking states to achieve unity and commensuration. When nation-states are thought to serve philosophical ambitions or embody philosophical truths, they become vehicles of unity and oneness; they are expected to solve disputes, to commensurate differences, to act as instruments of community.

CODA: THE EXXON VALDEZ OF DISCIPLINES

The starting point was something of a toxic spill: The language of epistemology has seeped into the arguments of critics, theologians, social theorists, and rhetorical theorists. Its chief symptom is a way of putting things, an oracular style, a panoptic vision. That stentorian, authoritative voice is a textbook case of begging the question: It presumes its own authority. And its resemblance to systematic philosophy comes from its realism strategy: Argument by totalizing gets its rhetorical power from its expressive sincerity.

But if argument by totalizing is nothing but a rhetorical ploy, then history is in one's premises, not coursing through one's veins. One would not write about history as if one is talking about genetics, or claim to see realities—other than earth, air, fire, and water—that cross time intact. One would read the realism strategy antagonistically—putting a stammer in any narrative claiming or presuming a basis in atheoretical facts.

Rhetorical theorists should be stingier with their endorsements of the epistemological style and not slip too easily into thinking of rhetoric as epistemology's successor. Foundations imply ground, and ground implies locale. Because many fields are foundationalistic, foundationalist imagery easily worms its way into our thinking about the makeup of fields. But in the form usually given it, rhetoric is unifying, not foundationalist.

And rhetorical theorists, perhaps more than anyone else in the academy, should be skeptical of the impulse toward unity. They know this rhetoric well as it crops up from dirt road demagogues, but seem to see it less clearly closer to home. Calls for spiritual revivals and unity of purpose are humanism's reactions to the business cycle. They peak in good times, for prosperous people prefer shopping sprees to pogroms, and thus need to be preached at for their shallow consumerism. And they bottom out in bad times, for privation and dislocation may create common causes no humanist could applaud.

FOUR

Foucault's Trap

This chapter is about exaggerated determinism. The next is about inflated freedom. Their joint aim is to give an Ionesco twist to a Sophoclean standoff. The chorus—heard here—is fatalistic: We are playthings of social structures. The protagonist—in the next chapter—defends an heroic vision of free will and rational mastery. This is, I argue, a clash of caricatures; and some tinkering with both sides may make for a better debate.

I will ignore the issues that animated Greek fatalism, or Aquinas and Duns Scotus, or Brand Blandshard and Percy Bridgeman. Beyond kismet, divine order, or Newtonian causation are some empirical claims that social structures determine thought and action—the Franco-German sociology of knowledge and its offspring: overdetermined views of thought collectives, institutions, and gestalts.

These views share a predicament I will call *Foucault's trap*. The most familiar version of the trap is Foucault's diagnosis of the modernist's plight. Intellectuals are trapped in their fields, doomed to a faux critique that merely affirms ruling paradigms. Foucault is often said to have caught himself in this trap. The rhythm and architecture of his early work strangle the revival of agency in his later work. But the real trap, I submit, lies in exaggerating the self-confirming nature of discourses. One concludes that critique can only come from outside, yet on Foucault's reasoning there is no outside. Critique is either futile or a brute confrontation of one total institution versus another.

Foucault the Modernist

I will begin by sketching my version of how Foucault is best read. This is admittedly a rash venture. His friendliest commentators have noted his Delphic ambiguity and apparently shifting stance; and there is little agreement in a now-sizable literature about whether his views evolved or were deliberate explorations of tensions. Still, a powerful explanation of reflective thinking is at stake in reading Foucault. So, risks and all, here is my sketch.

Foucault is making a case for ambivalence. His point "is not that everything is bad, but that everything is dangerous" (1984, 343). Every method has a price; every rule and role, every way of doing things carries a trade-off. So *ambivalence* means *taking care*—in the sense that we are careful with power tools, in the sense that tools may draw us into their realities, and in the sense that some tools become more powerful as we use them. Disciplines, for instance, entail *discipline*—a term that once connoted the hermetic regimens of medieval monasteries and now suggests the canons of professions and disciplines. On one hand, professions institutionalize expertise through credentials and licensing. They finance and organize media for disputation and package knowledge for pedagogy. Disciplines get the advantages of professionalism plus the blessings of specialization—adeptness, sharp critique, economy in communication. Their heuristic effects are so great that it is hard to imagine intellectual life without them. But discipline also means constraint, loss of freedom. One must abide by the rules, use the recipes. Professions thus exert an inertial drag on innovation. They politicize and bureaucratize conventions. They draw boundaries, define what is focal and marginal, and invoke sanctions against transgressors. They make "narrowly technical proficiencies the badge of the fully licensed professional," and develop idioms "by which professionals recognize one another and for the lack of which they stigmatize outsiders" (MacIntyre 1971, 105–6). So we should have mixed feelings about professions and disciplines. We want their benefits, not their drawbacks, so we want the reflective control Habermas seeks.

The dangers are *power without a subject,* power exerted by organizations, not individuals (Foucault 1980); *normalization,* a loss of self in organizational imperatives; and *governmentality* (Foucault 1991a), a "mentality" that causes individuals to internalize public disciplines and order their lives harmoniously with organizational goals. They purchase upward mobility at the price of their freedom, and in the bargain, ironically, become mixed blessings. For their organizations, the price of loyalty is entropy. Too much harmony yields a closed system—the self-confirming, inflexible behemoths often criticized in the organizational literature. So organizations and their actors have a stake in maintaining a tension between loyalty and dissent.

To weaken governmentality, Foucault proposes a method called *eventualization* (1991b). Eventualization is a recovery of lost moments—moments buried in time and literatures when people had choices. The idea is to capture these moments in all their uncertainty, to expose their parameters, in order to call current inevitabilities into question. If the reifications of the past prove to have been avoidable, their determinism can be broken.

One can point to studies that succeed with something like eventualization. Fleck's history of syphilis (examined below), Toulmin's (1990) reconstruction of the Cartesian quest for certainty, Habermas's (1987) tracing of Hegel's turn toward the absolute, and Janis's (1983) postmortems of decision-making fiascoes all capture turning points at which options were closed off. They are chronicles of closure in which the uncertainties of one moment are submerged too resolutely, thus shaping the inevitabilities of the next. Foucault's histories of madness, sexuality, and penology are eventualizations of this sort. So is Hacking's (1992) debunking of the realism behind demographics. These studies stress the political effects of notational systems seen as reflecting authentic realities. They suggest strategies for questioning suppositions and debunking claims to objectivity. Eventualization thus does for history what Kelly's (1955) view of freedom does for people who have reached cognitive dead ends. For Kelly, freedom and determinism are features of one's thinking, of the extent to which one takes things for granted. Theories are interpretations of events. To explain is to control, so determinism waxes in the implicit and wanes in the explicit.

What is needed is a "detachment or suspension of judgment that opens new possibilities for thought and action" (Bernstein 1992, 161). This skepticism may liberate individuals, but it also serves organizations by balancing the tensions between their needs to serve current interests while maintaining their capacities for innovation. Skepticism about the former may enable the latter. It may be subversive—sabotaging the organization, empowering subaltern groups—but it may also benefit organizations by increasing their adaptability.

This, at least, is my reading. Its modernist tinge echoes Habermas's (1986) view that Foucault, after a long haul, finally found his place among modernity's therapists as a pragmatist. It echoes McGowan's (1991) division of Foucault's thought into early, middle, and late periods, the latter centering on the problem of agency. Its corporate strain has Foucault moving from a critique of the total system and the Cartesian knowing subject toward the view that disciplines, despite their despotism, provide the basis for reflective discourses. On this reading, Foucault's insistence that one can't brandish truth in the face of power is analogous to Dewey's objections to the quest for certainty. His denunciation of metanarratives and hegemonic systems is one more assault on the epistemological search for a universal standpoint.

THE TRAP

The chief obstacle to this reading, of course, is Foucault himself. As his critics often point out, his early works debunk not merely humanism's heroic agent but the very idea of agency. His stance is so individualistic, so oblivious to corporate possibilities, that his case for ambivalence may justify little more than a mood. Foucault the archaeologist, it seems, has dug a deep hole for Foucault the modernist.

The digging begins in *Naissance de la Clinique* (1963), *Les mots et les Choses* (1966), and *Histoire de la folie* (1972b), where we first meet the "total institution." Prisons, hospitals, and asylums are Sapir-Whorf-style *prison-houses of language*. They organize time and space so as to dominate the humans inside. Their normalizations are comprehensive. They circumscribe all thought and speech. They manipulate the human body to fit organizational structures. The container force-fits the things contained, turning its victims into *docile bodies* (1977, 138), more like airline passengers than decision-makers.

The digging escalates in *L'Archeologie du Savoir* (1969), where the macro-structures of Levi-Strauss are replaced with micro-structures. These *discourses* are linguistic structures, discursive or enunciative regularities (1972a, 61–65). They circumscribe all thought and speech on a preconceptual (1972a, 62) with uniform anonymity (1972a, 63). They are visible only as points of divergence in groups of concepts (1972a, 72).

As *The Archaeology* tunnels into the little prisons, it becomes clear that the site of the dig doesn't matter. Foucault the archaeologist exhibits artifacts but doesn't say where they were found. There are few footnotes. Ideas exceed names in the index. And names figure as manifestations of ideas, not originators: "Mais ces regularites—on y reviendra par la suite—ne sont pas donnees une fois pour toutes; ce n'est pas le meme regularite qu'on trouve a l'oeuvre chez Tournefort et Darwin, ou chez Lancelot et Saussure, chez Petty et chez Keynes" (1969, 189–90). The same "regularities of discursive practice" are not to be found "at work in" these authors (1972a, 145). These regularities come from decisions buried in history. Now the ideas are working themselves out in ways dictated not by the efforts of authors in framing their arguments, but by the enunciative field, which determines the statements that can be made by defining a priori the "pure experience of order and of its modes of being" (1970, xxi). The field "never sleeps." Any "statement—the most discreet or the most banal—puts into operation a whole set of rules in accordance with which its object, its modality, the concepts that it employs, and the strategy of which it is a part, are formed" (1972a, 146–47).

Total institutions are self-confirming, not self-correcting—just the point of Lowi's (1969) iron law of decadence: Organizations subordinate everything to self-perpetuation. They achieve nothing but normal science, whiggish progress, and confirmations of ruling paradigms. The modernists are thus victims—trapped by totalities whose normalizing power comes from the nature of language. They are naive about power, for to define critique as a completion of the project of modernity is to become entrapped in its institutions.

This is arguably the bleakest portrait of human agency since Sophocles. It is "profoundly pessimistic" (Said 1986, 151), even neoconservative (Habermas 1985). It doesn't lack an alternative to current disciplines (as Habermas says), it forecloses alternatives. "There is no freedom in Foucault's world, because his language forms a seamless web, a cage far more airtight than anything Weber ever dreamed of, into which no life can break. The mystery is why so many of today's intellectuals seem to want to choke in there with him" (Berman 1982, 34–35). Thus Bové (1988, xi), in an ironic preface to Deleuze's (1988) hopeful reading of Foucault, argues that humanists often misread Foucault to blunt his effect on their own fields.

So we have a world-scale mesh of maximum security prisons—and an answer to Bernstein's (1992, 158–59) question about the claim that "everything is dangerous." Dangerous to whom? he asks; from what evaluative stance are these dangers dangerous? Foucault's answer is an intense individualism: "My problem," he says, "is my own transformation" (1988, 14). It is a feeling of powerlessness: "I know very well that knowledge has transformed the world," but "if I refer to my own personal experience I have the feeling that knowledge can't do anything for us and that political power may destroy us. All the knowledge in the world can't do anything against that. All this is related not to what I think theoretically (I know that's wrong), but I speak from my personal experience" (1988, 14). So the archaeologist's silent partner is an individualism tinged with a romanticism worthy of Keats. Despite his hostility to humanism, Foucault's personal dilemma outweighs his case for ambivalence; his driving concern is for the endangered individual, namely himself. And since a lone individual can't reflectively master vast organizational spaces, any try at reviving agency will land Foucault squarely inside the trap.

WHAT IS TO BE DONE?

The first step in getting Foucault the modernist out of the trap is to notice empirical exceptions to the self-replicating system. Fields do change their minds—and not always by consolidating past truths. There are Kuhnian gestalt shifts: relativity and quantum dynamics, perestroika and glasnost; American Marconi became RCA by deciding that the "problem of broadcasting" (everyone can eavesdrop) might have commercial possibilities. There are also innovations. Heisenberg invented matrix algebra to bypass a roadblock that arose in arguments with Bohr and Pauli. There are protracted struggles: The S-O-R behaviorists decided to open the black box partly because S-R puzzles ceased to be interesting, partly thanks to Chomsky's revolution in linguistics; yet they kept behaviorism's determinism, and thus found themselves beset with attitude-behavior problems, dissonance about cognitive dissonance, and a twenty-year rearguard march toward the proactive agent of current cognitive response models. And, of course, there is the proliferation of schools of thought, which either thrive as small enclaves at the outer edges of larger fields or find larger audiences, as chaos physics did (Gleick 1987). Their actors are scarcely "docile bodies." They argue and advocate, adapt and innovate. They seize on new ideas, sometimes from scratch, sometimes importing them from other fields and transforming them to fit local needs.The transportation of ideas across intellectual borders is so widespread that the lines formerly dividing many disciplines are blurring (Geertz 1980). So who are all these people and why are they free of Foucault's trap?

The answer is that the trap is a sham, like the conspicuous booby-trap that lulls the soldier who finds it and thus disguises the real trap. The stage setting is an exaggeration of the total institution. Foucault takes the behavioral rehabilitation model at its word, much as Anthony Burgess did in *A Clockwork Orange*. But though prisons and asylums may entail "civic death," they are not nonsocieties. Inmate cultures are quite complex (Clemmer 1940, Jacobs 1976). And rehabilitation (surely the paradigm case of a Foucauldian power technology) has proved less decisive in reducing criminality than passing the age of forty.

Nor are total institutions typical. Much as Freud was criticized for building a psychology on observations of hysteria, Foucault can be criticized for generalizing from extreme cases of civic quarantine to schools, agencies, factories, and academic fields. Giddens (1984, 154–55) thus prefers Goffman's view "that entry to prison or asylums is demonstrably different from moving between other settings. . . . 'Total institutions,' by virtue of their all-embracing character, impose a totalizing discipline upon those who are placed within them." That discipline is not as effective as Giddens thinks: It is a bromide in criminology that inmate cultures are more influential than official cultures. What prisons chiefly produce is criminals. But management in, say, businesses and schools involves more leadership and cajolery, and its practices, functions, and aims differ in kind from prisons and asylums.

The trap is also an artifact of literary insularity. Foucault ignores how ambivalent many fields are about their nature as double-edged swords (Taylor 1986). They see the dangers of discipline; they take reflective critique seriously; they protect dissent and tolerate peripheral movements. They can and do change their minds. Yet to hear Foucault tell it, there are only mysterious disruptions in the textual flow.

This puts one to thinking about the meanings of an author's silences—the things left unsaid. And to appreciate Foucault's most striking silence, read, say, Blumer (1964) alongside *The Archaeology*. Two jarringly dissimilar worlds appear: Blumer's "actors" interpret, think, negotiate realities, and bring social structures to life; Foucault's "containers" squeeze and mold their contents. So is Blumer delusional? This, one would think, is an argument Foucault should have made. Symbolic Interactionism was then a prominent and substantial research tradition. Its ideas have since guided many studies that confirm the importance of concrete practices (Knorr-Cetina 1981, 1982, 1988, Knorr-Cetina and Mulkay 1983). Yet it is invisible in *The Archaeology*.

The result is a world that is nothing but texts. History is the interrogation of documents (Foucault 1972a, 6); it aspires to archaeology (7), to becoming a way of reading that disrupts the taken-for-granted worlds standing behind documents (26–27). One maps the dispersion of points of choice by tracing the emergence and disappearance of concepts (35–37). One describes a discourse by noting its successive arrangement of statements into wholes, and how its ways of recording observations recreate a perceptual process—a "relation and interplay of subordinations between describing, articulating into distinctive features, characterizing, and classifying" (57). The practices here—seeing, writing, describing—are symptoms, not causes, so it is only from documents that the archaeologist can recover lost moments of uncertainty.

But can an interrogation of documents recapture moments in all their uncertainty? Documents may conceal just the uncertainties Foucault wants to expose. They are marked by silences and ambiguities, question-begging, and equivocal links to other documents. They are tidied for company and often deliberately obscurant. Their justifications are scrubbed and polished, their positions poised to meet public scrutiny. Grant proposals mask defects and exaggerate linear rationality (Redner 1987a); revolutions masquerade as normal science (Campbell 1989); and to cut through all this, the interactionist would say, documents must be contextualized within the practices that produced them.

Foucault would not have reduced discourses to documents had he engaged his opposition; similarly, he would not have reduced intellectual change to normal science. To explain epistemological breaks he (1972a, 4) quotes Bachelard, not Kuhn. Bachelard sees conceptual revolutions as consolidating past truths—the new theory being a more comprehensive covering law. There is no hint of Kuhn's emphasis on the ways normal practices reach points where dissonance becomes noticeable. And this silence is retrospectively incriminating: The Kuhnian revolution has been so ubiquitous, and inspired so much subsequent work, that it is not merely a counterdoctrine to hold that ideas are brought to life by the arguments, debates, shenanigans, and chit-chats of field actors. If conceptual change is not purely a literary phenomenon and Foucault's Trap is, then the better analog for Foucault is with an archaeologist who does his digging in museums.

This failure to engage the opposition makes *The Archaeology* seem insular—oblivious to an outside world that says otherwise. Its view of discourses as epiphenomena requires its view of texts, and the fixation on texts obscures the importance of practices. And it ignores peripheral and interfield discourse. It depicts fields as single-cell organisms and thus as hermetically sealed and deterministic. It doesn't see that a field's innards may be diffuse, with a periphery filled with enclaves of competing views.

So the second step in getting Foucault out of the trap is *shallow quotation*—an idea I will defend more fully later. For now suffice it to say that authors needn't be swallowed whole. Their positions needn't be seen as holistic systems to be accepted or rejected wholesale. The problem is to know the point at which many of an author's ideas must be jettisoned, that one might more profitably read someone else. To save *power without a subject,* for instance, it might be easier to read Sennett (1980) on *autonomous power.* Still, Foucault is open to selective reading: Each lacuna, ambiguity, and apparent contradiction provides a footing for creative reading, and Foucault the modernist is worth the effort. He sets the interdependence of individual and organizational interests at the center of things. He challenges Habermas's claims about a priori universals and impartial standpoints. He contests the efficacy of Rorty's conversations. He challenges the belief that consensus is the sine qua non of organizational life. And he makes a powerful case for valuing dissensus (Willard 1987a) and protecting peripheral communication.

But here is the obstacle: Power, for Foucault, is like an Anne Rice demon. It may be attacked, even set back momentarily, but it never weakens "power can retreat here, re-organize its forces, [and] invest itself elsewhere" (Foucault 1980, 56). Like a mirror-opposite of the writers who see order giving way to chaos, Foucault's omnipresent threat is order, a penchant for organization.

But we can coax a reading out of *The Archaeology* that jibes with Foucault's claim that actors can constitute themselves "as agents, not victims" (in Hacking 1986, 235) if we ask why he bothered to write it. *The Archaeology* isn't an anguished cry. Nor does it read like a prison diary or an archaeologist's field notes. It has all the appearances of an author marshalling his case. Its argument is sustained, complex, even tedious. It is laid out in a rather conventional way, as if it is is addressed to somebody who is meant to follow it. And we can follow it "only if we have not been completely normalized" (Hoy 1986, 14). *The Archaeology* is about actions: observing, ordering, recording, engaging, and distancing. Preeminently, it is about the acts of writing and reading—goings-on that would make no sense without a proactive reader.

And nothing in *The Archaeology* contradicts the view that normalization is a double-edged sword, so we are free to reread it as saying that individuals and organizations may have equal stakes in resisting normalization. In vast organizational spaces the obstacle to reflection is a lack of omniscience. The actors affect the field without knowing what their long-term effects will be, often with the effect of random mutations. So systems, thank goodness, are imperfectly self-confirming. There are strange attractors in the corridors of power, people, groups, local motives. Their dynamics are nonlinear. The best-laid plans suddenly veer, policies mysteriously dissipate. This perhaps explains why chaos metaphors are becoming popular in the organizational literature, and why it is a bromide that organizations, however despotic they want to be, are often incompetently so.

What has to go is the individualism. It is the image of the manacled self that lends hyperbole to the total institution. Most organizations are not designed to promote self-development; and it ought to be an open question whether self-development should lead every list. Intellectuals expect their jobs to mimic the self-expression of medieval crafts. From Adam Smith on, intellectuals have expected to find workers alienated from their work. Workers, on the other hand, have presented a mixed picture. Later on, we will meet some assembly line workers who, without a whiff of false consciousness, endure bad jobs for good wages. So if self-development is seen as *sui generis,* then other collective goals can be judged on their own.

And the text-fixation has to go. If texts display deliberate and inadvertent obscurant effects, they cannot be the only evidence for eventualizations. This is a challenge to those who hope to find a logical progression of ideas in literatures. They want (and sometimes find) a linear rationality, a tidy, whiggish progress guided by a clearcut telos, but are often frustrated by inexplicable shifts whereby things that were previously unknown or controversial are suddenly taken for granted. Foucault the archaeologist saw the importance of those disruptions and lacunas, but Foucault the modernist came to appreciate the barriers to reconstructing them. *Archaeology* became a term "I no longer use" (Foucault 1988, 31).

What we are chiefly keeping, then, is the ambivalence. The idea that the current state of a field's knowledge might be governed or touched by accident should keep organizational actors on their toes. Whatever the limits of individualism (lone-wolf archaeologists may get lost in their diggings) organizations are no more omniscient than individuals. Their only epistemic advantage is their division of labor.

FOREIGN AFFAIRS

Now for the real trap, the belief in outside criticism. To see the trap, one must realize that once the total institution is taken as a paradigm case, Foucault and "Foucauldians" often part company. If one ignores aspects of Foucault's work, such as his main point, one can read him as saying that, though critique is futile inside fields, it is possible from outside. One thus reads Foucault as meeting Nietzsche's summons to aestheticize and stand outside dominating discourses (Habermas 1987). We couldn't know that "we are difference," and "our reason is the difference of discourses" (Foucault 1972a, 131), unless "the archaeologist stands outside all discursive formations" (Dreyfus and Rabinow 1982, 87). And it is here that Foucault's trap—the real one—springs shut.

"There is no outside" (Foucault 1977, 301). "Power is coextensive with the social body; there are no spaces of primal liberty between the meshes of its network" (1980, 142). There is nothing outside an iron cage except more iron cages, more local nodes of a world-historical grammar. And this grammar, it turns out, is an entelechy without a plan. The relation of macro- to microstructures is accidental or circumstantial—a matter of chance and local adaptation. However odd it seems, Foucault is both a structuralist and a metaphysical nihilist. The microstructures are dissimilar and incommensurable. They may have plans—organization per se always comes up with something—but the only big picture is order itself, language and, in later works, *power* or the penchant for organization.

This aimless entelechy explains why Marxists call Foucault a poststructuralist. There is nothing "post-" about the structural linguistics. Even friendly commentators call the grammar of enunciative regularities "quasi-structuralist" (Dryfus and Rabinow 1982). But Foucault suspends the question of the relation between macro- and microstructures, and dismisses (with extreme prejudice) the Marxist belief in totality. So we have here a falling-out among determinists. Hall (1980, 71) sees Foucault as "constantly falling into the pit which he has dug for himself." Because he stresses the noncorrespondence among practices, "neither a social formation, nor the state, can be adequately thought." But this is Foucault's point, not his weakness. If the present is caged in an all-encompassing, aimless system, it is pointless to use cultural totalities (world views, ideal types) "to impose on history, despite itself, the forms of structural analysis" (Foucault 1972a, 15).

Power, for Foucault, is all-encompassing, monolithic, and ineluctable. It permits no possibility of criticism unfettered by injunctions and interests. The iron cages are closed language games (Deleuze 1988)—hermetically sealed, self-confirming. They permit no genuine engagement with the other, with anything alien enough to spark insight, reflection, and freedom. So "critique" must be enclosed by scare quotes. Inside fields, it is delusional, and outside, it is only a confrontation between total institutions (Fish 1989).

Geertz thinks that Foucault is caught in this trap. The closest he comes to freedom is that the prisoners want to escape (in Hoy 1986, 25), but Foucault does better than that. He points to an exemplar—himself—of an old, familiar idea: the *marginal man*. Much like Erasmus, who thought that scholasticism was obsolete, but decided to work within it, Foucault's marginal is no outsider. Marginals are simply less house-broken, less convinced. Thus, Foucault says (1988, 6), his vague status in the *Hôpital Ste Anne*—the lack of a clear, organizationally defined role—was his leverage for insight into the total institution, and because Mendel was not *dans le vrai* "within the true" of biology, he was able to envision alien objects and methods (Foucault 1972a, 224).

This vision of a not-entirely-convinced actor, a faint believer, so to speak, is entirely plausible, though scarcely new. Interactionists have long seen reflective thinking as a matter of standing back from the stream of events. But the theories discussed below turn Foucault's skeptical insider into an enigmatic and scarcely credible outsider. Their marginal man, I argue, is largely gestural, a deus ex machina, a contrivance by which determinists exempt themselves from their own theories.

THE OUTSIDE TRAP AS A COMPETENCE PROBLEM

I later argue that interfield discourse breaks both traps. Expert fields are rarely hermetically sealed, single-cell organisms. They are amalgams of subfields; their outer borders are complexes of overlapping border fields that capitalize on hybrid ideas and cosmopolitanism. Porous borders and peripheral discourses make local transcendence possible, so a strict inside/outside dichotomy is untenable and outsiderness is a matter of degree. But the idea of local transcendence suggests limits: We move most easily among nearby discourses and less readily into more alien ones. So I will venture here an alternate version of the outside trap—one that suggests the upper limits or ultimate constraints on one's freedom to move among discourses. For there do come points, surely every academic has stumbled on them, where one feels either like a bumbling tourist or that one is lost in a swamp.

Outsiders are to some degree incompetent. They lack the native's expertise, bona fides, and legitimacy. If they come from too far afield, they are like tourists. If I visit France but speak no French, I may glean some insights into French life unnoticed by natives, but no one would trust me as an ethnographer: I must have most things interpreted and I am incompetent to evaluate my interpreter. This is, to various degrees, the predicament of the cross-field reader. Writing, like speech, observes the quantity maxim; it is enthymematic, indexical to background awarenesses, and embedded in a retrospective-prospective sense of occurrence (Cicourel 1974). Insofar as economy is an editorial virtue, writing is a matter of picturing what one's readers needn't be told. Writers thus take for granted events, assumptions, methods, and arguments made elsewhere:

> I think that analytic philosophy culminates in Quine, the later Wittgenstein, Sellars, and Davidson—which is to say that it transcends and cancels itself. These thinkers successfully and rightly blur the positivist distinctions between the semantic and pragmatic, the analytic and the synthetic, and linguistic and empirical, theory and observation. Davidson's attack on the scheme-content distinction . . . summarizes and synthesizes Wittgenstein's mockery of his own *Tractatus*, Quine's criticisms of Carnap, and Sellars's attack on the empiricist "Myth of the Given." Davidson's holism and coherentism shows how language looks once we get rid of the central presuppositions of philosophy. . . . On my view, James and Dewey were not only waiting at the end of the dialectical road that analytic philoso-

> phy traveled, but are waiting at the end of the road that, for example, Foucault and Deleuze are currently traveling. (Rorty 1987, 32)

This passage presumes a certain literary virtuosity. The reader presumably knows the names standing for positions, their surrounding literatures, and whatever conventional wisdom about them is in the air. Such shorthand is common in specialties, but the passage appears in two books (Nelson, Megill, and McCloskey 1987, Rorty 1988) whose readers span multiple fields and may differ in their ability to unpack and expand economical expressions. The degree to which one can analyze Rorty's reasoning (say, discuss in an informed way whether he shortchanges Sellars) is the degree to which one can determine whether his claims are warranted. Nonvirtuosos may be influenced by the authority, turn of phrase, or tone and coherence of the essay. For them, the pragmatist revival may be a fait accompli whose origins are invisible. In this case, interfield discourse isn't a matter of one system butting against another. It depends, rather, on the degrees of success readers have had in their continuing struggle against literary isolation.

It also depends on the division of labor in border fields. One can't read everything; but sometimes one needn't, for the public life of a field—not merely its journals, but its talk, its forums and seminars, lectures and chats—fill perhaps more lacunas than we realize. This is a mixed blessing. Talk is less disciplined than print, so mistakes are likelier and harder to weed out. The corrective power of print is uncertain both because essays respond most readily to other essays and because readers bring their preconceptions—right or wrong or muddled—to the printed page. I don't pretend to know how many misunderstandings start in Hilton corridors and end up between the lines, but I offer this suggestion to more imaginative researchers: Study protracted disputes—the ones characterized by "is-not, is-too" posturing in which the same arguments keep recurring. You will find, I predict, "de novo" essays (whose authors seem to have discovered the issue on their own), "eureka" essays (whose authors seem aware of only a small fraction of what has already been written about it) and "once more, dear friends" essays (whose authors seem to have found a second wind). The source of all three, I predict, will turn out to be actors grouped into like-minded enclaves, egged-on by nods of agreement in Marriott meeting rooms, who keep reinventing their own and other peoples' wheels.

My version of the trap doesn't mean that the sham trap is innocuous or that some theories might not impale themselves on both traps at once. To illustrate this double whammy, I need to briefly describe the twentieth century's most peculiar incident.

WISSENSOZIOLOGIE

Following Curtis and Petras (1970), I will use the term *Wissensoziologie* to distinguish the views of Mannheim and Durkheim from modern sociologies of knowledge. *Wissensoziologie* emerged in the 1920s coincidentally with the erosion of idealist epistemology. It was meant to be a relativity without regrets, a way of saving epistemological intuitions by explaining relativity deterministically. The determinate thread unifying disparate societies and cultures is found in the relationship between social structure and cognitive processes. Relativity thus threatens nothing important. Group differences are surface appearances, momentary impediments along a positivistic road to discovery.

The standard historical narrative has it that *Wissensoziologie* died from a self-inflicted wound. The existential determination of thought was a caricature—whose successive narrowing parallels to a striking degree the disintegration of formalism. First came "grandiose hypothetical schemes," sweeping universal claims of the sort common to nineteenth-century historicism and positivism (Curtis and Petras 1970). Then came a skeptical critique. The vast brushstrokes were soon riddled with exceptions, and *Wissensoziologie*'s determinism, idealism, and nominalism ultimately faded beside symbolic interactionism's claim that groups exist in and through the interactions of their members. This narrative is a cautionary tale for Foucauldian trappers: Expositional conveniences are not mirrors of nature; prose techniques are not natural categories.

Wissensoziologie got its determinism from Marx. It saw the existential determination of thought as an "emotional-unconscious undercurrent" that invisibly governs the impulsive, irrational features of group life. This "collective unconscious" (Mannheim 1936) is *ex hypothesi* false consciousness. It lends stability to groups by masking real conditions and ensuring the preeminence of ruling class interests. Scheler ([1916] 1973, xxiii) saw *Wissensoziologie* as the anthropological basis for a "rigid ethical absolutism and objectivism." His (1924) "codetermination" idea stipulated the primacy of ruling class interests as the source of individual beliefs, though it exempted the content and validity of the intellectual's ideas from the existential determination of thought. Intellectuals are coerced by intuitively knowable knowledge principles, reflective thinking thus being the other side of the coercive coin. One is either pushed by history, pulled by ideology, or coerced into belief by knockdown arguments. Argumentation is thus less an avenue to freedom than a process of being battered into justified true beliefs.

This determinism didn't travel well. Imported into the U.S., *Wissensoziologie* was transformed by pragmatism to square with the Dewey/Mead emphasis on situated action, functionalism, and the centrality of communication. It was open to this transformation because "total ideology" was something of a double threat: impossible to operationalize yet possible to falsify. No one, Mannheim said, perfectly or totally represents a thought system; people vary in competence, specialization, and participation, yet ordinary people, the pragmatists claimed, routinely do what *Wissensoziologie* says is impossible: They calculate, innovate, and adapt. They are "multivalent" (Lee 1966): they participate in multiple, overlapping, even competing groups; they select among cognitive options and thus shift allegiances and modulate their commitments. The pragmatists, indeed, noticed that people shift etiquettes, move from one set of rules to another to adapt to social conditions. Thus one can reason now within the institution of cost-benefit analysis, later within Rawlsian distributive justice, and still later like a rule utilitarian. One isn't, by these shifts, successively possessed by three spirits, each successor exorcising its predecessor. One is simply perspective-taking.

There was also the problem of imputation. Ideological imputation works best for groups that have deliberate ideologists and least well for classes, societies, and cultures (Child 1940–41a, 1940–41b, 1941–42, 1943–44). Differences within such units preclude anything more than innocuous abstractions about the bourgeoisie or British society. The fact that people have different abilities and opinions, pursue independent lines of action, and rebel and complain as often as they acquiesce is a deep intellectual problem for the determinist. Once the door is opened to individual differences, rebellion cannot be equated with deviance. And if one finds *groups* of deviants, it takes a certain single-mindedness to save the meaning of *deviance*.

It might be objected that the existential determination of thought was not as clear as I am making it. Mannheim rejected "mechanical cause and effect," but failed to provide a clear substitute (Hartung 1970). But this makes the existential determination of thought unarguable. To fit ideas into world views is to make empirical claims that presumably square with evidence that a group's members act in thus and so ways and thus can be said to hold thus and so beliefs. The proof is in the pudding. But to impute interests and ideologies to a group regardless of whether its members accept these characteristics is to claim special privilege, as in the *Eighteenth Brumaire* and *Manifesto,* where false consciousness causes workers to stubbornly resist their best interests, or as in Mannheim's *ideal type,* which he admits is solely the researcher's creation. With this turn, rational argument is foreclosed. The position is self-sealing; its enabling condition is protected from critique. False consciousness has become phlogiston—everywhere and everything—and thus irrefutable.

The idealist sees no need to distinguish among the kinds of commitments people make. Group allegiances are beyond rational consideration. The social and the rational are dichotomized, and because social life is irrational, rationality must be nonsocial. Thus arose *Wissensoziologie*'s two most influential ideas: the free-floating intellectual and the distinction between social and scientific reasoning.

Hartung (1970, 693) argues that *Wissensoziologie* was a plea for the employment of intellectuals. He (facetiously, I think) credits this plea to *Wissensoziologie*'s emotional undercurrent and analyzes Mannheim's thought as the expression of a collective unconsciousness infused with class needs and insecurities: *Ideology and Utopia,* he says, could not have been written anywhere except in Germany between 1919 and 1933, and this, perhaps, explains the hole at the center of the theory.

That the hole is there is part of the standard narrative. *Wissensoziologie* had a necessary but infeasible condition: Mannheim's free-floating intellectuals. The free-floater was necessary for *Wissensoziologie* to be able to explain its own existence. The existential determination of thought coopts self-awareness, so the platform for exposing determinism had to be a privileged position exempted from the laws of group life. Justifying this exemption should have been a matter of proving that the intelligentsia differs from other groups or (perhaps) that intellectuals are protected by their estrangement. Neither argument would have been easy. The whole point of the existential determination of thought was to prove that differences among groups are surface appearances, but the hole in *Wissensoziologie*'s project isn't that the arguments are flawed, but that they are invisible. The free-floater is simply presumed.

Why would a necessary condition be taken for granted? Perhaps because the free-floater is as old as Socrates. Philosophy is the examined life; society is the genesis of error; the whole point is to cast off the idols of the tribe, to stand apart. *Wissensoziologie* may thus have been a botched version of the examined life, its blunder being the acme of all ironies. It took the examined life for granted.

The distinction between social and scientific reasoning was born of the same necessity: The irrationality of the social made it imperative that science not be social. So Speier (1970) wanted sociologists to study the extent to which scientists leave "immediate partisan interests behind them." If science is free of ethos, the "basic emotional structure of value preferences" (and repugnances) that manifests itself as institutional pressure through which a particular reality is objectified, then relativity applies only to social life. The result is a relativism "without philosophical repercussions." "It does not encroach upon reason and upon reasonable action."

Parsons (1951b) pressed a distinction between science as a mirror of reality versus society as a mirror of sociopolitical and ideological forces. He saw society as an ordered set of components. Cultural systems inform social systems that inform subsystems that inform individuals. The mandates of these concentric levels are embodied in norms and roles. A "fundamental unity of human culture and of the conditions of human orientation to the world" yields "universal criteria of empirical validity." The scientific community's structure (he singularizes it) is comparatively nonsocial. As one moves from the inner core of science to other social groups, one finds increasingly powerful strains between objectivity and social forces. Sociology, then, is to study the selection of problems in societies; epistemology is to study science as the ideal toward which all knowledge should aspire.

Merton (1970) focused on scientific ethos. Science is a priesthood because scientific practice is ennobling (Barker 1979, Mitroff 1974). A human priesthood, to be sure: Merton distrusted the *Naturwissenschaften* piety; he thought that practices intermingled with ideas in the natural sciences as much as the social sciences. Still, the priesthood is a telling analogy. Scientific ethos is a readiness to appreciate knowledge, but is irrelevant to its creation (Merton 1973, 270, Mulkay 1979, 24–26).

The "demarcation problem," as it is often called, is by no means settled. Though social studies of science are proliferating, many people still doubt that science is social in any important way. Because the competing camps have their own journals, they often ignore one another, and this, perhaps, is for the best. The worst that can happen is a debate of caricatures. The social camp might impute a hyperrationalism to their opponents: Intellectual growth isn't rational unless one can trace every step in an unbroken epichireme; irrationality has crept in if one spots a single leap of faith, follower effect, argument-from-authority, Planck effect, or opinion drift. There can be no punctuated equilibria in the texts: it all must be there, not retrospectively but in proper sequence, like a logic of discovery; and the consensus must have evolved just as we reconstruct it. This opponent is ripe for plucking, but only the "archest" arch-rationalists actually go this far.

Rationalists might concoct their own easily defeated caricature, much as Kuhn was once accused of reducing science to "mob psychology." They would have the social camp saying that everything is a deception, all change is organizational momentum, and all practices are shaped by organizational structure. The result will be an an "is-not, is-too" debate that will make it harder to think clearly about the degree to which intellectuals are able to conquer human and social frailties and the degree to which disciplined discourses, for example, are less impulsive or better at self-criticism than ordinary groups.

A better debate is possible if the rationalist can concede that procedures are part of a science's rationality, that aspects of that rationality may be invisible in a field's texts, and that a field's intellectual progress rarely follows a single thread of thought. Differentiation makes for equifinality and redundancy. So in big fields (consider the paper tonnage conjured by the expression "current sociology"), the march of ideas may be indefinitely describable because different groups follow different paths; individuals pursue lines of action that may or may not touch, cross, or parallel one another.

It should be possible to argue concretely that expert fields are epistemically better than ordinary groups; that they are more self-consciously critical, or that they argue more rigorously. If fields are social orders whose practices and concepts are bound together, they are not thereby irrational. The linkages of practices and concepts may embody rationalities worthy of study, especially if we think that scientific concepts are distorted by pragmatic practices or that policy-makers distort technical claims. If NASA is prototypical of modern knowledge use, then the Challenger disaster can stand as the archetype of its pathologies.

If *Wissensoziologie* got the worst of both traps, the fate of other theories suggests that the sham trap alone can be fatal. The existential determination of thought can undo otherwise insightful theories—a process worth tracing, for when a theory brimming with good ideas lurches toward systems-theoretic *seppuku,* it presents a cautionary tale worthy of notice. It is to such a tale that I now turn.

THE BAD SEED: FLECK'S THEORY OF THOUGHT COLLECTIVES

Ludwick Fleck's *Genesis and Development of a Scientific Fact* ([1935] 1979) is more than a history of syphilis; it is a broadside against epistemology that, though it was written in the thirties, might have been written in the eighties. But there is an extraordinary tension in Fleck between a powerful structuralism and a strikingly modern view of the social bases of science. It is rather as if Durkheim and Kuhn have co-authored a book without checking one another's work.

SETTING THE TRAP

Fleck builds on three themes. First, he argues, epistemology is "empty word play," "egocentric" and "naive." Without historical and comparative investigations, it glances off surface impressions, the popular culture vision of science. Second, Fleck snipes relentlessly at psychologists and dismisses all talk of individualism and cognitive styles. And third, he presses an incommensurability thesis turning on the differences between our language of microbes and protozoa and medieval science's animistic, demonological language (period paintings show tiny devils spewing from a sick man's breath). Medieval chemists used the names of Greek gods; anatomists see a body full of spirits and predilections, biles and humors; anatomical illustrations are built upon ideograms. These alien styles were as systematic in their own way as modern science; they make statements as complex as our own, but they refer to a reality either baffling to us or fathomable only as metaphor.

This incommensurability is heightened by a structuralism drawn from Durkheim. "Thought collectives" envelop one in a "thought style," the carrier of a field's historical development and stock of knowledge that "provides the context and sets the limits for any judgment about objective reality" (Fleck 1979, 39). It is a gestalt, a "readiness for directed perception" (142) that resists change by assimilating ideas into its systemic imperatives. Specialism and focus yield centripetal force, a "thought nexus." A field's habits seem natural, inevitable. "No further thinking about them is even possible" (107). The individual is like a soccer player, the thought collective like a soccer team, and cognition like "the progress of the game" (46). Once in the game, one's "mind is structured"; one can't think "in any other way." The individual "is never, or hardly ever, conscious of the prevailing thought style which almost always exerts an absolutely compulsive force upon his thinking and with which it is not possible to be at variance" (41).

MARGINAL MEN AND SCIENTIFIC PUBLICS

The hedges "almost always" and "hardly ever" suggest that there can be anomalies in "the average mood of the collective." The "marginal man" doesn't amount to much in this theory, but he is the *only* bridge between Fleck the determinist and Fleck the interactionist.

The latter Fleck infers from the history of the Wassermann reaction a thoroughly social vision of intellectual change. A thought collective is "a community of persons mutually exchanging or maintaining intellectual interaction" (Fleck 1979, 38). Community enables indexical speech: Every word presupposes a surrounding circle of the unsaid, every claim a bigger claim, and every bigger claim a still bigger corpus that gives it meaning, vouches for it, and makes elided speech possible. Cognition is thus a social activity, for "the existing stock of knowledge exceeds the range available to any one individual" (ibid.).

Think of a scientific community as a Ven diagram—an array of intersecting, variously-sized circles. One may belong to several big (exoteric) circles but "only to a few, if any, esoteric circles" (ibid., 105). Esoteric actors relate to exoteric actors as elite relates to mass, as teacher relates to student, and beyond that, "the elite panders to public opinion and strives to preserve the confidence of the masses" (ibid.).

At each circle's center, organizational conservatism resists change. Once an idea gets agreement, the community's rituals, propaganda, authority, and solidarity come into play to defend it. The carnal scourge thus resisted new ideas by a proactive process. Contradictions to the system seem unthinkable; anomalies are either invisible, kept secret, or explained in ways that corroborate the system (ibid., 27).

Change may occur by virtue of a communication accident. One invents an idea; it passes along person to person, changed a little with each transmission: "A set of findings meanders throughout the community, becoming polished, transformed, reinforced, or attenuated. . . . After making several rounds within the community, a finding often returns considerably changed to its originator, who reconsiders it himself in quite a different light. He either does not recognize it as his own or believes . . . to have originally seen it in its present form" (ibid., 42–43).

And there is the *marginal man,* whose effects are analogous to cross-pollination by honey bees. Marginals are not sociologically secure at the center of a field, so they are able to transport ideas from one field to another. They pale in importance beside team players, but they act as media for whom thinking and reality are not fixed and absolute. They can discover new facts because they can think in new ways (ibid., 50–51). This is possible because communication isn't simply the translocation of rigid bodies in euclidean space. It involves transformation, a stylized remodeling that achieves intracollective corroboration and thus change (ibid., 111). New ideas may change the importing field; new environments may transform the imported ideas. Both cause shifts and changes in the currency of thought. "The change in mood during the intercollective passage of ideas produce[s] an adjustment in this cash value across the entire range of possibilities, from a minor change in coloration, through an almost complete change of meaning, to the destruction of all sense" (ibid., 109). Thus, as the syphilis idea moved from one community to another, "each passage involved a metamorphosis and a harmonious change of the entire thought style of the new collective arising from the connection with its concepts. This change . . . offers new possibilities for discovery and creates new facts" (ibid., 110).

A third source of change is the public. Multiple publics surround esoteric domains, like concentric rings. A biochemist communicates her findings outward to a more general thinker, who interprets it for a wider audience, where it is taken up by a still broader thinker and interpreted for the popular scientist (e.g., general practitioners), who then interpret it for the lay public. It is in the popular realm that revolutions get noticed, crises of confidence seem urgent, and the effects of new ideas are first seen. Exoteric knowledge arises from the esoteric domains, exerts popular influence, and in turn influences subsequent esoteric thinking. "Popular science is a special, complex structure" that addresses an educated but amateur audience, omits the detail of controversies (making knowledge claims more certain than they are in the expert domain), and through simplification creates a vivid picture.

Each stage of translation from esoteric to exoteric requires new simplifications and metaphors. Intellectual histories become smooth narratives of rational progress that blur over the stages, metamorphoses of thought styles, disruptions, and choices actually made in expert domains. The knowledge becomes holier, more trustworthy; the story of its creation becomes inevitable and rational. It acquires a pictorial quality, that the expert hopes will make an idea intelligible. "But what was initially a means to an end acquires the significance of a cognitive end. The image prevails over the specific proofs and often returns to the expert in this new role" where "it provides the background that determines the general thought style of the expert" (ibid., 117). This is sometimes "no more than an exalted feeling about the solidarity of all human knowledge," or a belief in "the possibility of a universal science," but, "owing to simplification, vividness, and absolute certainty, [popular knowledge] appears secure, more rounded, and more firmly joined together. It shapes specific public opinion as well as the *Weltanschauung* and in this form reacts in turn upon the expert (ibid., 113): "Certainty, simplicity, vividness originate in popular knowledge. That is where the expert obtains his faith in this triad as the ideal of knowledge" (ibid., 115). When economists speak of the economy as an organism, or when organizational theorists speak of systems, or biologists speak of syncytium, they are importing popular knowledge concepts into their fields (ibid., 112).

The Trap Closes

But Fleck's debt to Durkheim squelches his interactionism just when things are getting interesting. His marginals, indeed, are so trapped within self-confirming thought styles, and so rarely effective, that it is inexplicable how they are ever effective. They are, apparently, deviants of some sort, but deviance itself is a puzzling miracle. Out of the blue comes "a unique mono-collective," a lone wolf dialoguer, a multivalent participant in multiple collectives (Trenn 1979, 160) whose powers come, apparently, from another planet.

Fleck's predicament has modern parallels. Douglas (1986, ix) likens the social control of cognition to Fleck's thought style and argues that institutions prefer determinism. Institutions can't think ("Only individuals can intend, plan consciously, and contrive oblique strategies" [ibid., 92]), but they do have minds of their own. They systematically direct memory and channel perception. They infuse projects with moral unction, wrap themselves in self-affirming rationales, and transform problems into their own terms and techniques. If an institution depends on participation, it will reply: "'more participation!' If it is one that depends on authority, it will only reply, 'more authority!' Institutions have the pathetic megalomania of the computer whose whole vision of the world is its own program. For us, the hope of intellectual independence is to resist, and the necessary first step in resistance is to discover how the institutional grip is laid upon our mind" (ibid., 92). Successful institutions veil their influence. Determinism inheres in what is obscured; freedom arises from critique-as-Habermasian-transparency.

But what permits critique? Not one's discipline on Douglas's account. She quotes Fleck (1979, 103) and might well be quoting Foucault: "The general structure of a thought collective entails that the communication of thoughts within a collective, irrespective of content or logical justification, should lead for sociological reasons to the corroboration of the thought structure" (Douglas 1986, 18). One can't resist the classifying pressures of one's institutions without an independent classificatory exercise. But "all the classifications that we have for thinking with are provided ready-made. . . . Our minds are running on the old treadmill already. How can we possibly think of ourselves in society except by using the classifications established in our institutions? (ibid., 99).

The trap springs shut: The scientists' minds are "deeply in thrall. Their subject matter is cast in administrative categories, art separated from science, affect from cognition, imagination from reasoning" (ibid., 99–100). Classification serves existing institutions. "There is a feedback of Robert Merton's self-fulfilling kind. The labels stabilize the flux of social life and even create to some extent the realities to which they apply" (ibid., 100). Institutions harness everything to the task of reinforcing themselves (ibid., 102). They block curiosity, organize public memory, and "heroically" impose certainty on uncertainty. In marking their boundaries, they "affect all lower level thinking, so that persons realize their own identities and classify each other through community affiliation"

One way to temper a claim is to call it a metaphor. The gestalt (we will see) became less literal when applied to social processes. Its determinism got diluted as it became unfashionable to see cognition and communication as epiphenomena. But the total institution can't be diluted in this way. Its whole point is the determinism of the container to the things contained. Inside a field, one's choices are either-or: One acquiesces or leaves. This seems dramatic vis-à-vis broad categories (society, class, culture), but less so if the individual's world is seen as a quantum domain, filled with choices for which partial inclusion is an option. Even cognitive prisons have escapees, dissident subcultures, and merely compliant members. The libertine priest lives a secret life; the Thugee informs on his friends; and even in dramatic attempts at isolation—the mass suicide at Jonestown, for example—some people fled to the jungle; others were murdered. The interesting question concerns the differences between the rebels and the sheep, which probably range from the psychological to the rhetorical, from feelings of self-worth to the architecture of the joint reality created by a group's members. The total institution, even as metaphor, paints over these differences.

Douglas's solution to repression and deadlocks is the creation of new communities (ibid., 102–3). But she leaves unexplained how reflective breakthroughs or breakups are possible. Like Foucault, in making the case for reflection urgent, she makes it too hard, so her solution is largely gestural. The result is arm-waving, which is what people do when caught in Foucault's Trap.

What Is to Be Done? Part 2

I have lingered with Fleck because his comparative epistemology is a nascent field theory. It captures the importance of the relations between esoteric and exoteric knowledge; and it problematizes translation across codes of different complexity. All that is needed to turn Fleck into a full ally of epistemics is a reading that dilutes his determinism. Instead of likening the individual's epistemic importance to an ant's importance to an anthill, we might agree that cognition is "socially conditioned" (Fleck 1979, 42), but interpret it, à la Dewey, (1920) as meaning that the individual isn't a given, that mind arises from communication, and that communication is an emergent, negotiated process. Structuralism may be true for the cognitively lazy, but reflective thinking is possible. This makes Fleck's view similar to Kelly's (1955) claim that unexamined ideas are "hostages we give to fortune." Reading Fleck this way, that is, turning him into a symbolic interactionist solves the mystery of the marginals by transforming them into peripherals (chap. 7).

Fleck's view of communication may also fare better if we change his way of putting things. He speaks of the thought collective as a single universal; one size fits all. Science, religion, and the general public are monolithic entities—all equally resistant to change. Conceptual change is a single drama playing itself out before a constant audience. Epistemics, conversely, will emphasize interfield differences and problems of scale and literary density that preclude seeing big fields as common audiences and single stages.

Force Fields

For many fields, the search for scientific respectability is a familiar story. Between 1850 and 1957 (that is, between Comte's *Positive Philosophy* and Skinner's *Verbal Behavior*), realism and operationism were "in the air." Scientism was an ideal, not an epithet. So the most famous version of this story, behaviorism, answered Carnap's call to reduce psychology to physical terms. It was premised on a literal realism (the Sherringtonian reflex was not a metaphor); and it created an experimental methodology to fit the idea of a closed system.

Lewin's (1935, 1951) force field is less famous. The "father of group dynamics" is most remembered as a pioneer in leadership studies, and many would dismiss his grand paradigm as scientism at its worst—precisely the spiritless *Zeitgeist* one expects from an operationalist crusade. But the force field is more than an historical curiosity. It parallels the structuralism in Foucault and Douglas and poses a clear inside-outside trap. It is, indeed, au courant in organizational studies where the logic of self-referential (closed) systems is called *autopoiesis* and social systems are seen as consisting solely of "recursive self-reference" (Luhmann 1990, 113). And the force field has found new life as a metaphor for the "new constellation" of modernity/postmodernity (Bernstein 1992).

The force field also illustrates an effect of time lags in interfield discourse. Ideas may become famous after they have been changed inside their originating fields. Lewin's vision was purely Newtonian, and in the 1930s, he was not hitching his wagon to a star. Long before the physicalist frenzy peaked, physics had begun undercutting the realism psychologists wanted. Einstein saw the application of physical models to human affairs (by Eddington and Bohr) as reprehensible—*not* because relativity undercut established order, but because it described a reality incomprehensible to lay people and irrelevant to their affairs. "Contrary to the entrenched faith in the ultimate continuity between the common perception and the scientific construction of reality, Einstein insisted that the very concept of reality that permits universal agreement between scientists and laymen is a constraint on the advancement of knowledge" (Ezrahi 1982, 256). Einstein took this view believing all the while in geometric order. God doesn't play dice; particles behave themselves. Quantum dynamics, however, could not be assimilated to Newtonian intuitions (Heisenberg 1958). Where nonphysicists may have erred in thinking that relativity had any bearing on commonsense reality ("The people writing the articles did not understand the physics" [Dirac 1982, 80]), they were apparently oblivious to the quantum revolution. Thus Lewin, as late as 1951, published his merger of Maxwell's electromagnetic field and Newtonian intuitions about systemic wholeness.

Lewin's (1947) force field was meant to operationalize personality and group dynamics. His personality theory resembled *The Authoritarian Personality* (Adorno et al. 1950). The force field joined to the Freudian psyche described a total ideology and a view of personality types ("central tendencies" such as authoritarianism or racism). The result was a cultural determinism: A kiss-up, kick-down culture perpetuates itself by raising little Prussians.

Closely allied to the cultural determinism was a gestalt view of perceptual organization—the field being a "dynamic whole," a system of causal dependencies. Where Kohler's neuropsychology linked visual fields with electromagnetic fields in the cortex, Lewin applied this picture to psychological and sociological fields. The result was a series of mathematical formalisms, each expressing the "force" of such demographic categories as age, sex, religion, experience, and intelligence. One's "life space" is an interplay of forces, a force field that functions like an auto-pilot. Thus attitudes, beliefs, interpersonal relations, and motivation are drivelike, consummatory action fitted to the larger, self-regulating field.

If one can find the universe in a grain of sand, then the cosmology to be inferred from Lewin's view of mind is his group theory (1948). Bodies emanate force—attraction or repulsion. As bodies move in and out of each others' force fields, zones of tension like rival magnetic fields are created. These tensions push and pull, altering the bodies, their outer boundaries, or their positions so as to achieve equilibrium. The result can be characterized as *absolute space* for minds and groups: Everything—gestalts, race, and ethnic groups—has a natural state to which it will return if left undisturbed. Disturbances prompt countervailing forces throughout the system, for every element of the whole is interdependent with every other. Their relations lie in the ratio of strength between them. Conflict occurs among equally powerful individuals and groups. Persuasion occurs when a persuader's force exceeds the persuadee's resistance. People and groups have "stable conflicts" when they have inescapable regions of tension. Inescapable conflicts spark aggression, apathy, frustration, or anomie. Thus, for instance, racial aggression can be plotted and predicted by joining the mathematical formulas for each racial group to create equations for the conflict of forces between them. The result is as determinate as astronomers' measurements of gravity.

From this view of groups flows a purely demographic marginal man—a person straddling racial, ethnic, religious, or generational boundaries: The marginal man "stands on the boundary between two groups, A and B. He does not belong to either of them, or at least he is not certain about his belongingness. Not infrequently this situation occurs for members of an underprivileged minority group, particularly for the more privileged members within this group" (Lewin 1951, 143–44). The "characteristic symptoms" of marginals are emotional instability, sensitivity, unbalanced behavior, and hostility to people of lower status (1951, xi). Marginality, one infers from the clinical terminology, is a disorder, a loss of equilibrium. Marginals are rootless, homeless, and dispossessed. They are victims of a pathological syndrome—*role conflict.*

Taken literally (there is not a whiff of metaphor in Lewin) the force field is a normative horror. It underwrites every status quo, a point Habermas (1971) raises against systems theory. Its scientism joined to its determinism create an ideology favoring current states of affairs. It is worse than conservative and apologetic, for it actively discourages critique. The demographic equilibria are atavism in another language, and one could justify apartheid if the sum of repulsions exceeds the sum of attractions. Moreover, the pathologizing of marginality is an invitation to dullness. It stigmatizes cosmopolitanism and underwrites provincialism. At worst, it stamps ethnocentrism and a Bismarckian vision of power balances with a scientific imprimatur. If marginality is a disorder, then there must bc a preferred state of nature (or a tradition or culture so strong as to be functionally equivalent to absolute space). So the zone of tension between Belgrade and Zagreb must play itself out; Beirut is a stable conflict.

Fortunately, the force field is untenable. Like the "system" of systems theory, the force field assimilates everything toward equilibrium and thus flies in the face of innovations and adaptations organizations in fact achieve. The effect is analogous to seeing only the default settings in a computer program. And consider the implied view of communication. If knowledge is mental representation, and representation is a simple link between distal and proximal stimuli, then languages can't be seen as pragmatic activities or meaning as a cooperative adaptation to situations. Coordinated social life, the mutual adjustments actors make to facilitate common action, is simply an effect of force fields bashing against one another. There is no place in this thinking for communication to be emergent, negotiative, strategic, adaptive, and cooperative. If exogenic causes and processes mirror endogenic causes and processes, then conventional communication is an epiphenomenon (loud thought) and the rhetorical possibilities for the creation of situations and selves are beyond imagination. At best, Lewin's view is solely of expressive communication. I emit force by dumping the contents of my head into yours; you then "feel the force," like Luke Skywalker, and resist or acquiesce depending on your own force fields.

Where the problem of agency is pivotal in debates about systems theory in Habermas's debates with Luhmann and Foucault, for instance, it is inconceivable in Lewin. Cognitive choices are symptoms of competing forces. But how, then, do people make mistakes? How do they distinguish between the vital and trivial, exigent or remote? And how (and why) do they change their minds? Though Lewin discusses situated action, his theory denigrates its importance. Situations are places where cognitive forces and tensions play themselves out. Situated reasoning is like Cleanth Brook's definition of poetry: "patterns of resolved stresses."

Systems theory is often criticized for its inability to coherently explain boundaries. Borders just are; their origins are invisible and inexplicable. And open systems theory is unclear about how borders come to be open. Adaptation just is; its origins are invisible and inexplicable. The force field is open to both criticisms. If each field's shape is an effect of being squeezed into existence by the larger system, then what explains individual differences? And if border-crossings are empirically more common than the theory permits and these cross-pollinations prove to have effects, then the force-field is unsalvageable.

If one simply must have physical metaphors, the better analogue is gravity—which waxes up close and wanes with distance. Gestalts are thus like black holes: Close to the center, nothing escapes them, but their pull ebbs at the periphery, perhaps influencing the tides here and nothing at all there. Fields with porous borders don't have either-or choices between internal and external ideas; some ideas seep further in toward the center than others; the activities of subfields at a field's periphery are thus divergent from, but not necessarily incommensurable with, the ruling paradigm at the center. Thus, by importing outside ideas, fields change their minds, but if the gestalt is seen as assimilating everything in its ambit, like a whirlpool pulling debris toward its center, then the transformational possibilities of idea importation are nil.

Can the Force Field Thrive as a Metaphor?

One often needs further information to know what a theorist means by calling something a gestalt. For instance, it isn't especially informative to hear that switches in visual gestalt are elementary prototypes of scientific revolutions (Kuhn 1970a, 111–12, 116). We only know that prerevolution ducks become postrevolution rabbits. One normal science tradition replaces another by a shift of vision; one changes paradigms and acquires a new perceptual readiness. We don't know whether these shifts are irrevocable, or whether different gestalts are incommensurable. The determinism depends on the theorist's views of rational mastery, organizational effects, institutional closure, and circumstances. The more pessimistic the theory, the more literal the gestalt; the more optimistic the theory (the more open the question of agency), the more the gestalt becomes a loose intuition about the cognitive effects of social worlds (Hanson 1958).

The need for optimism is epitomized by Bernstein (1992), who draws his view from a commentary on Adorno by Jay (1984). Bernstein's force field is a "relational interplay of attractions and aversions that constitute the dynamic transmutational structure of a complex phenomenon" (Jay 1984, 14–15). Modernity/postmodernity thus form "a new constellation—a juxtaposed rather than an integrated cluster of changing elements that resist reduction to a common denominator, essential core, or generative first principle" (Bernstein 1992, 225). The contradictions between them are not resolvable in a Hegelian synthesis—though Hegel's master trope of rupture and reconciliation is a part of the force field. "Contradiction," Hegel says "is the root of all movement and vitality; it is only as something has contradiction within, that it moves, has an actuality" (in Bernstein 1992, 315). Modernity/postmodernity is thus a standoff of explicit arguments nestled in attractions and aversions; it is a *Stimmung,* Heideggerese for a mood that is "amorphous, protean, and shifting but which nonetheless exerts a powerful influence on the ways in which we think, act, and experience" (ibid., 11).

At first glance, Bernstein seems to be flirting with Foucault's trap. His only hedge in quoting Adorno authoritatively is to call the force field a metaphor, though he seems to mean it literally. He says that "philosophers are parts of history, caught in its movement" (ibid., 29) and attributes the influence of Lyotard and Kuhn to the fact that their ideas are "in the air" (ibid., 12). He portrays a discourse with dialectical dynamics that *reflect* real paradoxes in modernity/postmodernity; and the writers he reviews are, if not forced, at least being nudged toward a confrontation with praxis. Heidegger, Derrida, Foucault, and Rorty are gravitating "more and more to confronting the ethical-political consequences of their own thinking" as a "dialectical consequence" of the questions they raise (ibid., 11).

Still, Bernstein (1968, 1983) is a Weberian ideal type among modernity's therapists. He sees the determinist's risks and reviews Habermas's (1987) point that totalizing critique (which undercuts its own grounds) leads to "performative contradictions." He wants to explore the modernity/postmodernity constellation because, while something like Adorno's logic of history is working itself out "behind our backs," the question of critique keeps resurfacing. To explain its resilience, he asks his readers to "relentlessly pursue" the questions Derrida and Habermas's positions raise about each other.

This pursuit scarcely needs the force field. If literatures are as big as I will claim, *most* things are going on behind our backs. Field affairs are quantum, not holistic, which suggests, to me at least, that concrete projects take precedence over grander standoffs—and, in turn, that the risk of Bernstein's metaphor isn't Foucault's trap so much as that the force field has become (to use Bernstein's own phrase) an "impotent, vague abstraction."

CULTURE

"Wherever you find a culture, kill it."

This slogan is about corporate cultures. Its sentiment is common in the organizational and business literatures. *Culture* is shorthand for *unity*—which muffles dissent, obstructs adaptation and innovation, and promotes groupthink. Cultures close the system, and it is a bromide in those literatures that closed systems are doomed. The solution is to weed out the indolent, interrogate their habits, and reflectively monitor the costs and benefits of their conventions. Agency, in this literature, is a solution not a problem.

Of course, this optimism can be as much a caricature as the determinisms just discussed. Still, readers who are persuaded that fields change their minds more often (or more rationally) than they should if Foucault's trap is genuine may want to consider a link between the business world's optimism and more academic views of culture. That link, I argue, is culture's function as an argument.

First an obvious point: Some views of culture are deterministic enough to fall into Foucault's trap. Among its many meanings, culture has been seen as innate, racial, and as a matter of national character or personality types. The Freudianism of *The Authoritarian Personality* is now less popular than the modal personality—a typification of statistical data gathered by polling. Culture is thus operationalized by the answers people give to questions. Others say that culture is most apparent in nonverbal behavior: It "is not innate but learned; the various facets of culture are interrelated—you touch a culture in one place and everything else is affected; it is shared and in effect defines the boundaries of different groups" (Hall 1977, 16). Others define culture as patterns and models for behavior and thought statistically typical of a whole society, including an individual's psychology as well as the collective orientation of a whole people toward their institutions (Rosenbaum 1975). These diverse views share two traits. They stress culture's pervasiveness—it is everywhere, affecting everything. And they stress its nonconscious operation (ranging from the collective unconscious to the dim-but-analyzable awarenesses stressed by ethnomethodologists).

Ironically, perhaps, culture also arises as a reflectively considered claim in theoretical discourses. It is most often conscious, considered, and controversial—the opposite of the reality the cultural theories describe. The various theorists may not agree about what culture is, but their theories have, so to speak, the same illocutionary and perlocutionary force. Hall (1977, 14) says that to study various models of culture is to discover more about the theorists who propose them than about culture. He means that researchers impose their favored categories on objects of study, but I would carry the claim further: Culture is less an invisible force than a line of argument favored by intellectuals: The reactionary sounds the alarm about barbarians at the gates; the anthropologist queries the natives and paints a portrait of a milieu; the pedagogue presents the society's ideal types. In each case, culture is a theoretical construct, a point of dispute.

Omnibus and deterministic definitions of culture ought to be evaluated occasionally as messages directed to a general public, for this displays their functions in regime rationales. Since most anything can be justified in the name of cultural preservation, cultural theorists ought to hesitate before saying anything they would hate hearing from a state's propaganda machine. The message of the determinist theories is: Culture can't be understood, only lived; it is central to identity, but invisible, so "know thyself" is merely an invitation to demographic pigeon-holing, and reflective thinking is at best the culture working itself out. This, it seems to me, applauds Foucault's trap, underwrites it, and uses it as an instrument of social control. It turns the trap into (in Berman's phrase) a world historical alibi, for a nonconscious, all-encompassing force relieves people of the responsibility for historical inventory, for considering what is good and bad in their cultures, and for deliberating about its importance.

CODA: PERESTROIKA FOR FOUCAULDIANS

Determinisms are best kept in permanent tension with the evidence that says otherwise. Fanatics and sycophants are rarely in short supply, but there are too many rebels, critics, and expatriates—and too much adaptation—for the determinisms to be convincing. Neither the inside or outside trap can explain why we find rebels squabbling with sheep in the same communities. Clearly, the field isn't the sole source of influence. The victims must help. Persuasion is cooperative (the persuadee must actively participate), so there will be psychological variables that, contra Lewin, influence how people construe their cognitive options, and social variables that affect the incidence of fanatism, obedience, and provincialism. There will be peripheral fields, sometime-rebels, and sporadic cosmopolitans, and thus interruptions of normal science.

Determinisms at their worst are primal howls of powerlessness, bleak portraits of the predicament of intellectuals. And critique, a euphemism for the intellectual's contributions to society, seems to be (in early twentieth-century imagery) a tiny voice drowned out by the thunder of factories or (in late twentieth-century imagery) a murmur lost in a Babel of competing tongues.

But the ultimate mystery is the marginal man. Whether a happy accident, anomaly, or triviality, the marginal is the determinist's ground. Yet (with apologies to Marx) all that is marginal melts into air. Inside Foucault's trap, we can't imagine how criticism and cosmopolitanism are possible, or how theories come to be written. The *Wissensoziologisten* at least felt obliged to proclaim the viability of their stance, though they had no arguments to defend it, but more recent macro-determinists (see the glaring case in Graebner 1987) have no outsiders to call upon, for they envision an all-encompassing system against which there is no outside. Having no visible means of support, and no solutions, their conclusions are so pessimistic one can only offer sympathy. This is the real trap: There is nothing more to be said.

FIVE

Pluralism, the Public, and the Problem of Knowledge

The problem of knowledge is best introduced by two men who believed they had solved it. The passage is from the Jefferson-Adams letters: "I agree with you that there is a natural aristocracy among men [of virtue and talent, not wealth]. . . . May we not even say that that form of government is best that provides the most effectually for a pure selection of these natural aristoi into the offices of government? . . . On the question, what is the best provision, you and I differ; but we differ as rational friends, using the free exercise of our reason and mutually indulging its errors" (Jefferson, Letter to Adams, October 28, 1813). They hardly seem like revolutionaries: Two old "cocked hats," keeping the conversation going, tempering their antagonisms with gentility. Not once in 150 letters do they grouse about a betrayed revolution. If anything, they brim with satisfaction and a contentment with leaving their disputes for the ages. One can't imagine Robespierre and Danton going on this way, agreeing to "differ as rational friends." And real revolutionaries, surely, would not have lived to ripe old ages and died in their beds (Kristol 1983, 83).

But the preference for checks and balances over final solutions is arguably still a revolutionary idea. If "liberty is to faction as air is to fire," then the price of liberty is tolerance. So instead of guillotines, the founders created institutions that reflected the substance of their disputes—ones designed to modulate the stresses and strains of permanent tensions. Indeed their deepest dispute inspired their most revolutionary creation.

Democracy, they believed, would always straddle a tension—an emotional cleavage between two intuitions. One might be called the *republican instinct*—the feeling that governance is best left to "the best and the brightest." The other can be called the *populist instinct*—the feeling that governance is best judged—and perhaps best done—by ordinary folk. These instincts are about *the public*. They evoke powerful images. Jefferson's *the people* versus Hamilton's *great beast,* Dewey's *public* versus H. L. Mencken's *booboisie.* And they reflect different intuitions about—or caricatures of—human nature. The vox populi is either a heavenly choir or, as Mencken said, a "simian grunt."

The republican instinct was a gourmet blend: a pinch of patrician vanity, a smidgen of natural rights (those who own a country, Adams said, should run it), and a hefty dose of social Darwinism: Life is a Hobbesian battlefield, Madison argued, a greedy scramble, each against all. Wealth is the scrambler's reward and, because it stills the predator's hunger, his bridge to virtue. Altruism being an acquired taste, only the wealthy can envision public interests.

The spice was a premonition of the Jacobin terror. Hamilton's beast was no figure of speech to these wealthy men. They doubted that laborers would be happy with their lot—much as Adam Smith feared that workers might be alienated by repetitive labor. So they were not squeamish about using false consciousness as a tool of social control. They had read Plato, whose philosopher kings determine the Truth and then use rhetoric to dupe the degenerate Athenians into behaving well, and Rousseau, who wanted a hidden hand to spin illusions of self-government to socialize citizens into the collective will. So "if the people think they govern," William Penn intoned, "they will be governed."

The populist instinct is often credited to Jefferson, who did indeed rail against the "*faux aristoi.*" Being an observant man, he doubted that wealth confers an immunity to greed. Being a generous man, he saw that the public had stakes in the public interest. And being a dyed-in-the-wool Aristotelian, he believed that truth had a natural tendency to triumph—and that the public, warts and all, had a mystical knack for sorting through factional spats to arrive at wise decisions. Tocqueville thus called him "the greatest democrat."

But Jefferson was not a "Jeffersonian democrat." No modern Jeffersonian would endorse his "natural aristocracy" or the educational system he proposed to nurture it. The system would teach the three Rs to everyone, then select the best students to "receive, at public expense, a higher degree of education at a district school; and from these district schools to select a certain number of the most promising" for universities (letter to Adams, October 28, 1813). The cream, in other words, would rise to the top—just like the second and third presidents.

They were, you see, their own ideal types: When they talked about a natural aristocracy, they meant people like themselves—"Harvard men," the best and the brightest. They believed they knew the world in all its complexity, and that their comprehensive intellectual mastery could be passed onto the next generation. Adams thus held that education should furnish the public with a general knowledge, to which government should ensure access for even the lowest ranks of society. The public could then serve as one of many checks and balances among republican and egalitarian institutions. This government-by-Aristotelian virtue would be a meritocracy checked internally by rival institutions, existing alongside a genteel realm of elections and referenda. The people would have the wisdom to vote for their betters if demagoguery could be kept to a minimum.

That *if* must have kept them up nights. The highlight of the 1804 social season was a duel between a vice president and a general. *Federalist* 10 lamented the "vicious arts" that decide elections. And there was the spectacle of a patrician president campaigning against his populist opponent's wife—not George Bush but John Quincy Adams, whose attacks on Andrew Jackson's spouse were so vicious that Jackson believed they caused her death (Hofstadter, Miller, and Aaron 1964, 119).

The Jacksonian era brought tobacco stains to White House carpets and a meaner kind of populism. To put it mildly, the republicans were demonized; the French revolution was sanitized; and the "common man" was canonized. American politics had become, in Mencken's words, "The Greatest Show On Earth": "Democracy is that system of government under which the people, having 35,717,342 native born adult[s] to choose from, pick out a Coolidge to be head of state. It is as if a hungry man, set before a banquet prepared by master cooks and covering a table an acre in area, should turn his back upon the feast and stay his stomach by catching and eating flies" (1958, 213). The public reaps the leadership it sows, Mencken believed, and everywhere there is "the mark of the savage," the taboos and shibboleths, the "anthropoid fears and rages," the "implacable hostility to every novel idea and point of view" (1955:101). Ku Kluxers and Know-Nothings exist everywhere, but only in America are their mean-spirited imbecilities "accepted gravely as logical ideas." The result is an "astounding and unprecedented swinishness." "Here," he wrote, "the buffoonery never stops." Here we take seriously "the ribald combats of demagogues, the exquisitely ingenious operations of master rogues, the pursuit of witches and heretics, the desperate struggles of inferior men to claw their way into Heaven" (ibid., 121).

This from a man who never heard of Willy Horton, the Nixon White House, or televangelism: Mencken's "clown dynasty" was an assortment of Mullahs, Methodists, and Know-Nothings. Their "clown prince," who for forty years tracked "*homo neandertalensis* with coo and bellow, up and down the rustic backways of the Republic," was William Jennings Bryan, "the most sedulous fly-catcher in American history" (Mencken 1990, 162). The Great Commoner's sin was not his "invincible disdain for ideas." That would merely make him a journalist—journalism being a "vast and militant ignorance," a "fathomless prejudice against intelligence" (1958, 218). His sin was a preference for the plebeian: "The simian gabble of the crossroads was not gabble to him, but wisdom of an occult and superior sort" (1990, 163). "His career brought him into contact with the first men of his time; he preferred the company of rustic ignoramuses. It was hard to believe, watching him at Dayton, that he had travelled, that he had been received in civilized societies, that he had been a high officer of state" (ibid., 164). Bryan's sin, we might say, was democracy's original sin: summoning a public for whom the differences between crackpots and experts are too unwieldy, impolitic, or even impossible to articulate.

The founders called this incidental equalizing "leveling" (Le Bon 1879, Martin 1920). One can impugn their motives: They used the word to label most any threat to their purses or privileges. But they also held that a society with no distinctions among citizens substitutes arbitrary authority for merit. A discourse unable to distinguish among the credibility of claimants levels everything to the lowest common denominator.

Mencken saw no limit to how low that denominator could be. Imagine, he might say, that astrologers demand that their "science" be taught in the schools. Their demand would not be self-evidently lunatic. If polls can be trusted, 52 percent of adult Kentuckians believe that astrology is a science (Louisville *Courier-Journal*, 3 September 1993, B2); and scientific illiteracy, by all accounts, is as American as apple pie, not only among the 90 million functionally illiterate but among college graduates who can't answer rudimentary questions about science (Hazen and Trefil 1991). So the only certainties are that scientists will rally against the threat, the matter will end up in court, and American journalists will report the story objectively—meaning fairly. Each side will be given equal time or space; the bona fides of the players will be impartially mentioned (setting "Dr." Jones against Dr. Smith). If the astrologers argue for *fairness*, for teaching astrology alongside physics as an alternative view, their plea may play better in Peoria than an insistence on scientific purity. And if astrology is easier to cast into a popular idiom than the scientific theory, popular opinion may favor the pretender over the unintelligible (often arrogant) scientist, while legal opinion, because it too is professionalized, will side with the scientist.

If this scenario seems far-fetched, consider a hair-raising study of *McLean v. Arkansas*. Taylor and Condit (1988) argue that the scientists were rhetorically inept in translating their arguments into a popular idiom. The creationists' plea for fairness squared with the journalists' populist visions, so the distinction between scientists and ministers became invisible: A commitment to objectivity "produced a journalistic leveling which rhetorically transformed competing discourses into equivalent ones" (Taylor and Condit 1988, 293). In the court of law, the scientists carried the day. Professional courtesy, so to speak, preferred the claims of an arcane discourse. But in the court of public opinion, "as the story evolved in the mass media, creation science appeared as the equal competing theory to evolution that the creationists claimed it to be" (ibid., 306).

"Only in America," Mencken would say, where most people believe that the sun orbits the earth (Louisville *Courier-Journal,* 24 October 1988), and a president (the protagonist behind the most massive union of government and science in history) has admitted to consulting astrologers. If we really had democracy in America—and thank God and Henry Ford we don't—creationism, astrology, and heaven knows what else *would* be taught in the schools.

And that, in letter and spirit, is the pluralist's case for meritocracy. Complex issues do not belong in public. To expect wisdom from the public is "preposterous" (Schattschneider 1960). The idea of majority rule is a carelessly held dogma protected from criticism by a "mystical doctrine of equality" (Lippmann 1925, 1965). A political expedient is "hallowed by an altogether adventitious sanctity due to an association of ideas with a religious hope of salvation" (Lippmann 1963, 11). Majority rule is simply the rule of force. The only difference between 51 and 49 percent is that 51 is bigger than 49. So public participation is best kept as innocuous as possible, governed ideally by "the manufacture of consent."

The best to be hoped for is a weak check: A small politically active elite, perhaps the 8 to 10 percent of the populace that actually tracks public issues (Neuman 1986, 6), might choose among options formed by experts. This public would be more appreciative than activist—onlookers, as it were, to the competition among elites in the marketplace of ideas. And to the familiar objection that this arrangement isn't very democratic, that voices worth hearing don't get heard, the pluralist replies that opposition among elite factions ensures that most views get aired. *Pluralism* is thus the pluralists' word for the democratic state of affairs—a tolerance of diversity within unity, a free competition and as much democracy as a democracy dares allow, for ultimately the sort of knowledge needed to run a complex civilization can't be democratized (Schumpeter 1942). A technocracy (Galbraith 1971) or elite oligarchy is inevitable.

Pluralism, then, is the power elite thesis (Mills 1956, 1963) sans apologies. And some readers, I imagine, will be surprised to learn that it *is* a school of thought, as opposed to a distant evil, like famine in Somalia or the Reagan White House. Outside political science, pluralism is as alien to democracy's critics as physics to Zande witchcraft. Instead of denouncing the power elite, it wallows in it. And instead of a world in crisis, it describes a world that is muddling along, getting by. Not the best of all possible worlds, mind you, but every day, in at least some ways, it is getting better and better.

DEWEY-EYED PRAGMATISM

Dewey is the famous exception to this laissez faire. He was a pluralist, certainly: He championed the rule of experts and wanted to put science—the most consistently reliable form of knowledge—to work for democracy. But he also believed that democracy needed an empowered public, to promote reform, help the melting pot melt, and serve as a check. He believed that a public could be created from the common experiences of Americans and that it would be rational and benevolent if the Jeffersonian promise could be redeemed. The means to that end comprise his most famous legacy—the focus on liberal education as a means of enfranchising the general public.

Part of this legacy is the modernist's belief in empowerment—a vision of epistemic mastery that, from the 1930s to the 1990s, has been the dialectical opposite to postmodern powerlessness. "Knowledge is power," the saying goes, so the modernist seeks to critique and reconstruct systematically distorted communication so as to attain an encompassing and reflective epistemic mastery—a position of autonomous judgment, a reflective awareness of how institutions function. Habermas thus demands that we acquiesce only to fields whose epistemic operations are transparent. Determinism is the spawn of unexamined ideas; to explain is to control, so the truth, as another saying goes, shall set us free.

This thinking is open to a pluralist reading. One could put the onus for critique on an elite—and hope that Neuman's 8–10 percent might benefit from trickle-down enlightenment. *The Public and Its Problems* (Dewey 1954) is vague about how big the public might be. And deliberately so, I think. Benign pluralists with populist hopes don't parade their republican reservations. Empowerment is a matter of degree, so the best course is to posit an ideal, be vague about who might meet it, and hope for the best.

This vagueness permits the more usual, exuberantly populist reading of Dewey, which sparked several educational traditions dedicated to democratizing the Adams-Jefferson vision of general knowledge. Pedagogies in argumentation, informal logic, critical thinking, and many visions of humanism and liberal education hope to produce a "renaissance citizen," so to speak. The goal is an ecumenical competence, a field-spanning practical wisdom that may find a unity of reason and praxis. It is typified, I submit, by the following passage:

> While submitting to the authority of what has been attained and established by scientific enlightenment—the formal and technical disciplines—the person should reach through education, a level of understanding, independent judgment, and creativity, at which the scientific-technical values and norms are established. Only at this level the person can become competent to understand the rules, and their embodiment in concrete social life, and be in a position to pass an autonomous social judgment and engage in a free debate. (Mickunas 1987, 336–37)

Guiding this judgment with the gentle nudges of rationality will be—in one view—the leadership of "social science as public philosophy." The key to this kingdom is a panoptic span of vision. "Knowledge of society as a whole involves not merely the acquisition of useful insights from neighboring disciplines but transcending the disciplinary boundaries altogether" (Bellah et al. 1985, 300).

With this claim, the rhetoric is in full blossom—with a fulsomeness that blurs the renaissance citizen and social-scientist-philosopher together. Both have field-spanning vision, positions of autonomous judgment. And this, for me at least, prompts one of those startling moments where one starts to question a whole line of thinking. As one follows a line of thought, one may agree here, have a qualm there, but generally nod along until there comes a sudden skeptical shock that prompts a reassessment of one's earlier agreements.

Leaving aside the question of what the renaissance citizen can do, *can* the social scientist-philosopher achieve knowledge of society as a whole and transcend disciplinary boundaries altogether? Or is this merely ex cathedra humanism—another revival of Mannheim's free-floaters? Nurse this suspicion a bit and another question suggests itself: How sound is the very idea of general knowledge? Indeed what would happen if we take the populist ideal—the vision of knowledge thought to be attainable by the public, and then ask whether this ideal can be met not by the public but by pluralist paragons, the most splendidly-trained public actors?

The result, I submit, should rouse the pluralists from their dogmatic slumbers. For as intellectual conceits go, pluralism is no more tenable than populism. Or that, at least, is my claim here. My proof will lie in some sketches of what I take to be the epistemic predicaments of expert fields. I will describe a family of problems—relativity, de facto divisions, literary density, authority-dependence, and organizational scale. Any of these problems alone might obstruct individual mastery, but this is a Eugene O'Neill family: Each problem worsens the others. And this synergism, I submit, is a basis for doubting the very idea of general knowledge.

PROBLEMS OF KNOWLEDGE: EPISTEMIC INCOMMENSURABILITIES

Calling these problems "incommensurabilities" runs a risk of confusing epistemics with epistemology. But we run this risk anyway. If the terms and images of epistemology have spread as widely as I claim, then possible confusions are best kept at the center of attention. And doing violence to incommensurability's logical roots may be profitable. One can, after all, make too much of the fact that disputes are resolvable in principle. Most disputes can be resolved by cost-benefit analysis, if we are not too squeamish, but if this prospect seems appalling, then the disputes are not resolvable in principle.

Public knowledge, let's say, concerns the management of competing positions. Public problems arise from obstacles to viable agreements. Viable means feasible or serviceable: A viable agreement permits further cooperation. It is a footing for action. Incommensurabilities are thus stumbling blocks—impediments to cooperative action. And it is with the most famous of these impediments that I will begin.

RELATIVITY

Relativity *is* the case. Our world is riven by unbridgeable cleavages, of culture, state, and belief. There are intransigent disputes about abortion, equal rights, free speech, sexual mores, and poverty. Add moral and religious quarrels to this litany and the social fabric seems like shreds joined only by bureaucracy. Sovereign fields that left alone might go their own ways are pressed into public conflict. Their advocates trade shots from privileged sanctuaries, demanding public acceptance, acknowledging no allegiance to the commonweal.

These disputes do not necessarily turn on mistakes. Some of the divisions that torment society arise from competing positions that make claims coherently indexical to expert fields; their truth depends on field-dependent assumptions. Consider some examples of what I (1983) call closure—retreating to one's field when challenged, closing the gates, refusing to stand on any ground other than one's own. Closure may be a cagey dodge. One ducks scrutiny by standing on convenient principles. But it may also be a respectable epistemic move, made sincerely, and based on conventionally correct premises.

Along with law, cost-benefit analysis is the closest thing to a public philosophy we have. It is a universal, commensurating discourse—a theory of rationality for states and organizations. It is also a hermetically sealed argument field (Willard 1982). The cost-benefit analyst is at risk only to objections couched in fiscal terms, and thus is invulnerable to moral critique (Goodnight 1987c). This gives cost-benefit analysis a position of special privilege vis-à-vis competing values.

According to cost-benefit analysis, for instance, a zero-defect air travel system is too costly. Some fatalities are inevitable. The cost-safety tradeoff means that airliners are lined with fabrics and plastics that emit toxic fumes when burned. Other materials are heavier and weight equals fuel consumption. Since retrofit costs exceed damage awards, passengers are not given shoulder harnesses (though seatbelts are less effective) and redundant systems on some airliners abut, so that damage to one may threaten the integrity of the others. The ceiling on the value of safety is reached when safety costs exceed the expenses incurred by lost lives, the latter being determined by court awards. These settlements are themselves fixed by cost-benefit analysis, so the value of lost lives is lower than the innocent passenger might think.

Facing criticism, the cost-benefit analyst takes refuge behind the ledger. Ledgers have no columns for hunches and intuitions. They allow value considerations *if* the values are cast in monetary terms that permit a "rational" comparison with other values. Thus inside cost-benefit analysis, one can't argue that nature should be valued not for its utility to humans but for its own sake (Tribe, Schelling, and Voss 1976). And in the airline case, equity issues such as racism and sexism can't be put into fiscal language. As the courts tally the cash value of corpses, white male breadwinners with four dependents and high anticipated life incomes will have more value than black female breadwinners with four dependents and lower anticipated incomes. And safety tradeoffs will pit profit against safety as equally legitimate competitive interests, thus precluding innovations that would marginally reduce fatalities. Against the cost factor, we are preordained losers. The fix is in. The result is like a Rawlsian original position in which the participants choose distributive justice, but must do so in a language that predetermines the distribution. Because cost-benefit analysis is a commensurating discourse and a litmus test of rationality, it is a "principle of attention" (Willard 1983) by which a field maintains openness or closure by deciding which ideas merit attention. The cost-benefit analysis principle of attention insulates it from critique not by proscribing value claims but by stipulating the forms they may take.

Creationists, in a similar way, risk losing arguments only if they make a strategic error—leaving the grounds of creationism. Insisting on "creation science" opens the door to outside criticism, for even diverse sciences agree on a general public position for representing science to nonscientists. Against this standard, creation science is perhaps as tenable as phrenology or astrology (Hayes 1983, Kitcher 1982). But creationists are unbeatable on their own grounds: Personal revelation can rarely be undone by logic or evidence (Jacobs 1983, Jacobs and Laufersweiler 1981). So as a doctrine competing for public acceptance while avoiding scientific critique, creationism has done rather well and presents something of a challenge to advocates of democracy by polling. For the majority of Americans, to hear the polls tell it, believe that creationism should be taught in the schools.

Nuclear power technologists have similarly refused to be accountable to any standards except those of nuclear engineering (Goodnight 1982). To hear them tell it, only nuclear engineering can credential arguers to speak about nuclear safety; only a consensus in that field can evaluate the adequacy of evidence; the decision-makers are thus to take the proclamations of the field as arguments from authority. They are to lay aside their doubts, where certainty is impossible, in much the way Catholic theologians of the twelfth and thirteenth centuries laid aside their doubts by appeals to final earthly authority.

Such retreats to one's field may be rational moves made from conviction, not deviousness. Indexical claims imply ground. Challenged speakers go to ground. They seek proof where they expect to find it: in authoritative fields. They confront their interlocutors with facts and assume that refutation must comport with the standards of their own not their interlocutors' field. They assume this not from fear of criticism but from a kind of self-righteousness born of competence: I'm right; my opponent is wrong. This closure thwarts discourse with outsiders. It precludes agreement (that isn't surprising) but its worst political effect is that it obstructs disagreement: It makes argument untenable by undercutting its necessary conditions. People don't need to hold the same beliefs to argue, or to achieve decisions and execute policies. They need only reach agreement on a viable measure of their differences that permits working agreements, compromise, and consensus.

Interfield relativity, in sum, includes obvious disputes: *A* says *X; B* says *not-X*. These claims may be competently indexical to authoritative fields whose grounds are so different that *A* and *B* may be unable to argue. Their differences needn't involve incomprehension so much as an inability to conceive common projects. When such differences move onto the public stage, decision-makers often settle them by appealing to the commensurating discourses—cost-benefit analysis and law, for instance. This is a case-by-case sort of thing. Public decision-makers are not falsifying or confirming thought systems. They can be content with purely local successes. One can obey the rules and abide by the outcomes of any number of decision scenarios, but then use different scenarios for the next decision.

But it is a mistake to assign decontextualized importance to relativity. The relativist's diagnosis is at best a partial picture. It implies a clear problem set on a clean stage: Diversities in beliefs, values, and practices clash; arguments occur; decisions are made. But there is more to it than that, for differences become apparent in contexts where other human and institutional problems are also operating. There is, I will now argue, a synergism among them: Unmanageable literatures heighten authority-dependence, which aggravates problems of scale, which heightens conflicts, and so on. The result is a family dynamic of incompetence.

De Facto Differences and the Luxury of Indifference

Incommensurability needn't involve explicit dissimilarity. The folk beliefs one might discover at a cockfight in the American South might or might not be different from the beliefs one would find at one of Geertz's Balinese cockfights. But locals by definition don't travel. They go their own ways, mutually unconcerned and unaware. The most energetic anthropologist may fail to rouse their mutual curiosity. This provincialism has parallels in the de facto divisions among expert fields that stem from focus and specialism. Like all complex organizations, professions may contain overlapping, redundant, and competing subfields. These subdivisions get the advantages of smallness and specialization: Their actors become adept at catching errors in each other's work (Faust 1985) and more likely to achieve mastery of the relevant literature. Competence and deftness come with focus. So does holism, for innovations may shake each strand of small corporate webs, though they are unnoticeable in bigger ones.

But the density that makes for local success may impede communication with broader publics—making it hard for one to explain or even see the relationships between one's work and work in other fields. The problem isn't necessarily incomprehensibility. There may be folk to whom the goings on in a physics lab are as alien as those in a Balinese cockfight, but insularity is a personal predicament, not an organizational imperative. The deeper problem is focus. It isn't that a high energy physicist and an Italian renaissance scholar might as well talk to a Balinese cockfighter as to each other but that they are unlikely to talk at all.

Cardinal Newman's "university community" has given way to discourses in niches in ecosystems. Specialism and expertise require focus. Research traditions proceed unilaterally—divided less by disputes than by preoccupation and indifference. Chaos physics goes its way; particle and atomic physics go theirs; Freudians go their way; constructivists and behaviorists go theirs; and so on. Overt conflicts are rare and newsworthy —witness the cold fusion wars of 1989. More often, fields touch one another by the incremental seepage of ideas across borders.

Often the only contact among insular groups arises with conflicts over scarce resources.This may yield a commensurability of sorts. We sort through intransigent differences; and what's left may be enough ground to permit compromises. Zero-sum games require compromise among competing positions, not their integration, so the management of differences is often seen as a justification for states—witness Tocqueville's admonition that states prosper only when the citizens are rallied around predominant ideas. Conflicts must be solved as they arise—treated as momentary lapses in an otherwise harmonious system.

Academics may not be so sanguine about the intellectual world. They may speak abstractly of the scholarly community, or contrast academe with the world of commerce, but more or less ignore such abstractions in their daily work. Except for general education debates, Aristotle's goal of integrating all departments of knowledge, and Cardinal Newman's belief in a common language enabled by a shared religion, aren't so much rejected as ignored. They are irrelevant to normal work. This is a de facto relativity: The expert fields are pragmatically segregated.

Notice the difference between a landscape dotted with tiny confederations and the grosser lumping of learned activities into humanism versus science. This venerable dichotomy is a field theory of sorts. It suggests distinctive methods, problem foci, beliefs, and attitudes toward consensus—differences that seem as incomparable as Edgar Snow's two cultures. Humanism and science are still important labels in some fields; and they still sometimes provoke powerful emotions and holy wars. But the two-cultures hypothesis is a limited polemical device, good for budgetary spats and the occasional creationism trial, but beyond that largely irrelevant to the specialism that splinters the sciences and humanities alike (Ozick 1987, 3).

So many differences are de facto accidents of time, place, and focus. They needn't in principle be solved, bridged, or transcended. But the twin of focus, alas, is provinciality—an isolation amid a fine-grained, cluttered environment of nooks and crannies into which data runs, as Ozick says, like quicksilver. The conflicts that do flare up play themselves out like infantry battles in jungles; partly seen and heard, mostly obscured by the surroundings; one can't get the whole picture. This is scarcely an attractive situation: The uncertainties of partial pictures make for anxiety, and spark either an urge to keep one's head down (one does one's work and leaves the big picture to others) or one succumbs to a temptation strikingly analogous to a lifestyle choice (and ominously analogous to General Gavin's Vietnam era enclave theory). If one's center isn't holding, one finds one that does, however provincial it might seem to others. Comfortably cocooned, one becomes an old buffalo, a defender of paradigm cases, an enforcer of standards, who is happiest, on the whole, hunting relativists and skinning skeptics.

One can sympathize, certainly. Clear-cut opponents are better than anxiety; and for reasons that will soon be clear relativists can almost always be fought to a standoff. But if de facto differences alone justify the image of a chaotic jungle battle, they are not the worst of it. For they are not alone. My point, remember, is that epistemic problems are synergistic; and it is time now to turn to a crucial reinforcer of focus, literary density.

THE IGNORANCE OF THE SPLENDIDLY EDUCATED

Many authors argue—with convincing statistics—that too much is published; however, they also claim that most published work is incompetent or worthless (e.g., Broad and Wade 1982, 221). I have always found this second claim less convincing: It is too sweeping; its defenders never seem (to me) to have read the material being dismissed or to have the credentials for making the judgment; and I have often thought that I saw defenses of the censured work to which its critics seem oblivious. Here is a typical example: The Institute for Scientific Information counted the number of times papers published "in the top 4,500 of the 74,000 science journals had been referred to in later papers. The findings: 45 percent of these supposedly top quality papers, published between 1981 and 1985, received not a single citation in the five years afterward. The implication is that nearly half the scientific work in this country is basically worthless" (*Newsweek,* 14 January 1991, p. 44). The last sentence is splendidly illogical. If these were the top 4,500 journals, the uncited articles presumably passed peer review. Conceding the usual criticisms of that institution, we still don't know that the uncited articles are worthless, for we don't know that anyone but the peer reviewers read them. We do know that editors cut footnotes and bibliographies when space is at a premium. So how many of the uncited articles were replications, the easiest things to cut?

I belabor this both to give the reader another look at general knowledge in action and to distance the claim I want to defend from this familiar argument. My claim is not that too much is published. How could we know whether a subject is getting enough attention? And my claim is not that most of it is trivial or bad. Doesn't any such claim imply that one has read it all? My claim is that Sisyphus had it easy: The sheer enormity of what is published creates a macro-incompetence for competent disciplinary actors.

Others have noticed this. Decades ago, Rogers (1958) predicted that the Yale library circa 2040 A.D. would contain 200 million volumes on six thousand miles of shelves (the card catalogue lying in 750,000 drawers occupying eight acres of floor space). Moore (1972), still well before the era of data bases and the World Wide Web, argued that the doubling rate of knowledge "has been reduced from millennia to around a decade." And Michel Serres predicted that the new architectonic field would be library science (in Fuller 1988).

This is a striking proposal in a consensualist world. Consider the annual publishing figures for books. The separate science and technology categories in Bowker's *Library and Book Trade Almanac* each have between 2,000 and 3,000 books published annually from 1978 through 1989. The sociology and economics category ranges from 6,465 in 1978 to nearly 8,000 books in 1989. The philosophy and psychology category shows between 1,000 and 2,000 books per year, and the business category hovers around 2,000 per year. The smallest reading load was in philosophy: *The Philosopher's Index* lists 15,000 articles in U.S. journals, 12,000 English articles published abroad, and more than 5,000 books published between 1940 and 1976.

These numbers mean little by themselves. A chess position may admit of untold permutations, but a smaller number of serviceable moves and still fewer good moves. So the fact that one has not read 99 percent of what is published is less a disaster than a pressure toward specialism: "The marketplace of scientific ideas is so crowded that most scientific papers are ignored; most are seldom, if ever, cited. . . . In chemistry only one paper in a hundred is cited more than ten times" (Gilbert 1976, 294 and Small 1978, 330, in Gross 1987, 494). One might like to think that this selective citation reflects a qualitative winnowing, perhaps an invisible hand at work, thumbing through all these pages, or at least a law of diminishing returns. But the sheer paper tonnage suggests, I think, that one's "general knowledge," one's general mastery, that is, of a specific field, is likely to be much narrower and sketchier than "generalists" expect: If something on the order of 200,000 theorems are proved annually in mathematics (Ulam 1976), "no one is surveying the mass as a single conversation" (McCloskey 1987, 486).

Perhaps it *isn't* a conversation and would require entirely too much rhetorical creativity, or too much effort, to become one. Keeping the conversation going is an invitation to civility, certainly, but a field's consensus of the moment may not be the outcome of a single conversation, or a fully coherent one. It may be an accidental side-effect, a bibliographic artifact, a matter of fame or of a statistical drift in a community's awarenesses and fascinations of the moment (Fuller 1986). And border-spanning topics merely make matters worse. Confronted with multiple expanding literatures proceeding along multiple paths, one never knows whether one has fully heard a position out, or seen it in its best form. There is always more to read.

Public actors are more vulnerable in this regard. They are less competent than experts to translate disciplinary content into less arcane languages. Like Fleck's general practitioners, they are ignorant masses to the specialists, and often find themselves on the business end of a paternalistic relation—kowtowed to, led, and cynically manipulated. Public actors do not master or use bodies of knowledge, they use testimony—positions maintained by authoritative emissaries of knowledge domains who presumably bridge the gap between their disciplines and public decision-making. These bridges are contained in positions that interpret expert knowledge and suggest policy applications. They are packaged in language and images strategically selected for an audience. Some of these strategies are credibility-using (e.g., claims of objectivity). Others are credibility-enhancing (e.g., testifying about a subject that has not been subjected to the rigor and care normally associated with one's science or giving advice on matters irrelevant to one's disciplines) (Albury 1983). Both effects leave decision-makers in the position of either accepting or rejecting testimony wholesale.

THE PROBLEM OF AUTHORITY

My claim here is that public decision-makers and expert fields are authority-dependent, especially when claims cross field lines. Their dependence may differ in degree, but their predicaments are of a piece. For they face a dilemma: While it is presumptively rational to acquiesce to authorities, such deference forecloses debate. And, I will argue, individuals cannot respond to the dilemma by achieving epistemic mastery of complex fields.

PUBLIC DECISION-MAKING

No one doubts that governments and corporations are major employers of scientists and technologists. They are enormous epistemic bureaucracies riddled with study groups, research staffs, advisory boards, and consultants (DeSario and Langton 1987, Nelkin 1981). But does this mean that the Beards' expression, "the rule of experts," should be taken literally? Leiserson (1965) says that every aspect of government is expert-driven. Habermas and Goodnight claim that the technical sphere dominates public discourse because government agencies have institutionalized the modernist fallacy.

Pluralists, however, wish that this were so, or at least more so. And the decision-making literature often points to the amorphous power of politics to bend and twist pretty much everything. On this view, authority-dependence is a saving grace: The problem of rational policy-making is to get elected officials to listen to experts and to do as they are told, for it is the nature of the political beast to listen to experts only when convenient, and to distort expert testimony to serve partisan agendas.

The difference here is about who *should* be in charge, not who *is*. But the better question is: Who *can* be in charge? We might concede the Habermas-Goodnight point that professional and political legitimacy differ in kind, but to what extent can we assume that expert knowledge can be translated into a commonsensical parlance and thus judged by nonexperts? Is the rule of experts to some degree dispensable, or is authority-dependence largely inevitable, even for the best trained, most public spirited decision-makers?

Consider two examples of what might be called pragmatic incompetence: One is a city council member weighing pro and con testimony about a proposal to build a recombinant DNA lab. The other is a senator considering funding for the late—in some circles lamented—supercollider. Both are typical public actors: They are demographically typical elites: wealthy, college-educated males trained in business or law. Their attention spans are framed by their daily agendas, which move from topic to topic. Next week they will need knowledge of economics, business, sociology, and engineering, but now the subjects at hand are molecular biology and high energy physics, and the issues at hand are cost-benefit and risk-benefit calculations. Since predictions of costs, benefits, and risks depend on specialized technical knowledge, the counselor and the senator will turn to experts.

The experts present the counselor with a mess: The pro-experts paint a picture of scientific necessity, of the possibility of dramatic breakthroughs in vital areas including cancer research. The anti-experts paint a doomsday scenario: cancers crossed with virulent viruses—malignancies as contagious as the common cold—escape by unforeseen routes into the general population. The counselor is thus confronting two sorts of relativity—the dispute among the experts and the incomprehension that divides him from both camps. The former forces him to adjudicate among the experts; the latter ensures his incompetence to do so.

The senator's predicament is somewhat different. The supercollider was the most ambitious high-tech engineering project in history (Trefil, 1989). It was to consist of multiple superconductive, supercooled tracks—56 miles in circumference. Along two tracks, protons will race in opposite directions. After millions of revolutions, the protons will be traveling at nearly the speed of light and be diverted onto a collision course—thus reproducing "the temperature that existed in the universe when it was 10^{-16} or 0.0000000000000001, seconds old" (Trefil 1989, 44). The pro-experts argued that this replication of the stage setting of the big bang will confirm a "theory of everything" that unifies force, time, and matter. The anti-experts questioned the theory's value—to physics and to society at large, and they weighed against it the "little science" projects, whose theoretical and social utility are equally promising (and/or unknown), that might be starved by a project whose projected cost grew, Pentagon-like, from a modest $4.4 to $10 billion. As one Nobel laureate put it, "science in the United States is dying of giantism" (in Trefil 1989, 46).

Let's say that our senator sets pork barrel interests aside. She wants what is best for the country, for science, and for physics, and she is prepared to rank priorities, which any organizational and management textbook will tell her she should do. She wants to know, and needs criteria for deciding, whether the supercollider is more cost beneficial than, say, the human genome project, the space station, AIDS research, or many modest programs spread across a range of fields. This is a challenge of considerable magnitude—one that most academic experts, including science-policy experts, shy away from: "the idea of [the National Academy of Sciences]—or any group—actually trying to rank priorities makes them nervous, particularly if that means comparing one field to another" (Cordes 1988, A24). Our senator, in other words, will be on her own.

Both cases require adjudication among pragmatically incomprehensible options. This needn't mean total incomprehension. Counselors and senators presumably know something about disciplinary arrogance, human frailty, and about how arguments are put in formal testimony. They can presumably read essays in the *Atlantic, New York Times Magazine,* and *Omni.* Perhaps they can even read trade paperbacks about biotechnology and physics. And perhaps they have been tutored by research staffs so that they can read executive summaries in technical reports. But even if they are conversant with the contents of many books and reports, they are not on an equal epistemic footing with the experts, and reading a hundred more popular books won't improve their positions, for there are only so many slogans, metaphors, and images appropriate to popular audiences and the specialized knowledge. So the counselor and senator are prepared only for the mode of testimony they are likely to receive and only for the task of choosing among authorities. In the most optimistic case (see chapter 11) the experts will frame their testimony in a language fitted to the decision-makers. In the more usual case, the experts will cast policy recommendations in the language of progress, falsification, and objectivity that has become the coin of governmental discourses. They will be deliberately arcane and heavily reliant on their ethos as scientists.

The counselor can only hope that there are more laureates on the pro than on the con side (as it turned out, there were), and the senator can hope for a clear-cut consensus among physicists and perhaps to seize upon a catchy slogan (the "theory of everything" *is* good public relations). For they have no options beyond nose counting; they cannot assess an expert's virtuosity or inspect the evidence for themselves.

My picture of the senator's problem is based on an essay that illustrates the limits of popular writing. Trefil's *Beyond the Quark* (1989) is a splendid instance of popular science writing—an exemplar of the art and of its limits. Given the limits of the medium, it is hard to imagine how Trefil's essay can be improved. It lays out the issues, defines obscure terms, and does justice to the disputes:

> [T]he interactions between these basic constituents of matter [quarks and leptons] are not nearly as complex as they were believed to be. Physicists have known for a long time that whenever anything happens in the world it does so because of the action of one of the four different forces acting in the universe. These are gravity, electricity/magnetism . . . and the so called strong and weak forces which act inside the nucleus of atoms. It is the strong force that holds the nucleus together, and the weak force that is responsible for the process of radioactive decay. But physicists now believe that these four forces are simply different aspects of the same force, which operated in its pure form only at the beginning of time. It is the deeply held belief among physicists that the key to the universe lies in understanding the one fundamental force that underlies everything. The search for a so-called unified field theory, which would show that two (or more) forces can be thought of in this way, dates from Albert Einstein's attempts in the 1920s and 1930s (Trefil 1989, 27).

That, I submit, is as clear as it gets. Nonphysicists may comprehend claims, but not the reasoning and evidence behind them. So Trefil ultimately rests the matter on his own authority. A fair gloss of his conclusion is that authorities *X* believe *N;* authorities *Y* believe not-*N;* I conclude that the preponderance of evidence favors *N*.

The fallacy theorist might say that Hobbes foresaw this predicament. There is a simple difference between accepting a claim on its merits and accepting it because of its advocate's merits. Professional authority, unfortunately, is meant to glitter; hence the eleventh-hour stratagem of sending seven Nobel laureates to Washington in April 1993 to save the supercollider. Manifestly, the argument might go, ethos was being substituted for good arguments and the mantle of cutting edge science was being used to obscure the advocates' interests and goals.

But we are looking at decision-makers who can't judge claims on their merits. They can't assess every claim by the niche it occupies in an ecosystem, or by the degree to which it fits with the veridical apparatuses of the relevant field, and they certainly can't evaluate those apparatuses. If deliberation should be fueled by facts, the facts in these cases can't speak for themselves. They must take their intellectual authority from the professional legitimacy of their advocates. This puts a premium on the grounds of that legitimacy; and even allowing for considerable political mischief, it puts the onus for good decision-making on the expert.

The Expert Fields

Conceding that intellectuals may be more reflective than ordinary folk and that expert fields have unusually stringent checks on authority, do experts nonetheless share the authority-dependence of public policy-makers?

Consider Haskell's (1984, xi) claim that we believe in evolution "not because we have in mind the evidence and experience it would take to envision the process and grasp it in a fully rational way, but because we trust biologists." I might prefer the Darwinian to the biblical narrative because I have examined the fossil record for myself, analyzed the details of Darwin's arguments, and followed the debates that led to the present version of the theory. But, Haskell says, failing to one degree or another at any or all of these tasks, I prefer the Darwinian narrative because I accept the conclusions of experts. Given the enormity and complexity of the technical literature, I accept expert testimony in lieu of inspecting evidence or hearing the arguments out.

This example arguably typifies the academic's "general knowledge." Ecology is a widely-used metaphor in history, mathematics, law, and most of the social sciences. And it is used in much the same way as metaphors (and substantive claims) drawn from quantum mechanics, big bang physics, biology and systems theory, psychology, ecology, and jurisprudence.

Consider too the statistical perspective, which infuses most of the sciences, governs every level of decision-making in business, industry, and government, and has seeped into mass political discourse. Indeed most public knowledge is in statistical form: business cycles and forecasting, environment and health, budgets, the cost of living index, capital investment and inventories, the balance of payments, risk assessments, and public opinion. But the decision rules of inferential and descriptive statistics may be invisible but authoritative. Their formulae are operations whose innards needn't be fully understood or even known. Multiple regression "just works" once we plug in variables and directions, and with SPSS, we need only learn managerial commands. The rest is not unlike magic. Our computers, for all we know, wave talismans at data to create facts.

Deference to authority also arises as an expositional accident. Consider, for instance, the side effects of the APA citation style—as in this made-up passage:

> Argumentation causes a Socratic effect (Colt 1945) and cognitive rehearsal of counterargumentation (Mauser 1977). When people believe they are being "argued to," they become more alert and critical (Smith and Wesson 1988).

Notice that the parenthetical citations stand in place of definitions, which puts the burden of intelligibility on the reader's familiarity with the cited literature. The arguability of the passage, its openness to questions or disagreements, depends on the reader's mastery of the cited work. The citations function emblematically as proof in much the way that nonverbal communication fuels ethos. Amid swelling literatures, the parenthetical citation is an unexamined presumption of proof whose pragmatic power comes from the size and scope of a field's issue agenda and the size of the literatures relevant to the claims at hand. Big agendas and reading loads may discourage readers from investigating citations unless suspicions are aroused. The power of this presumption is proportionate to one's reluctance to read still more. Consider a real example:

> Practical studies of interesting cases of appeals to expert authority in argumentation in Woods and Walton (1974), Woods and Walton (1982) and Walton (1985), indicate six requirements to be met for an appeal to expertise to be reasonable. (Walton 1989, 60)

Next come the six requirements, stated briefly *as if* fully defended. And later, in defending the usefulness of the logic of expert systems as ways of avoiding improper uses of authority, Walton (1989, 69) argues this way:

> [A]nalogy is extremely important in expert reasoning, and is equally important in understanding many kinds of reasoning in informal logic. But as indicated by Eliot (1986), current research in AI is tackling the problem of analogical problem-solving as a form of reasoning in expert systems.

Walton is arguing in a perfectly conventional way, but the effect is not without irony. He is quoting an authority (just as I quoted Haskell) to make a point about authority. Nor is it without risk. Both Walton and I are arguing in a way that makes literatures accident-prone, for even when scientific reports are retracted for fraud or validity reasons, they continue to be cited (Pfeifer and Snodgrass 1990; see the special issue of the *Journal of the American Medical Association,* 9 March 1990).

STILL FALLACIOUS AFTER ALL THESE YEARS

Now the dilemma: On one hand, arguing from and accepting claims on authority are the twentieth Century's definitive epistemic methods. On the other hand, the medieval logicians' chief reason for seeing the argument from authority as a fallacy still holds: To invoke authority is to abort debate.

Neither horn of this dilemma can be dismissed. In a consensualist world, the consensus in a field is relevant to the truth of a claim. It is neither practical nor possible to evaluate all epistemic claims that engage our attention, so it is presumptively rational to acquiesce to a disciplined consensus. This authority-dependence is more noticeable in ordinary discourse. In a complex world, the nonexpert's deference to authority is presumptively rational (Stich and Nisbett 1984)—routinely the prudentially, morally, and legally preferred course. Fallacy theorists thus no longer argue, as Hobbes did, that the subordination of logic to sociology is the intellect's treason against itself. Instead they have expanded the range of cases in which it is sound to argue from or acquiesce to authority. Ignoring or disregarding experts is now the fallacy, not the reverse.

The other horn of the dilemma is just as sound. We still attach importance to keeping the conversation going. With only a little stretching, three familiar ideas can be cast as versions of the authority-fallacy. There is the Rortyian fallacy (cutting the conversation short), the Habermasian (keeping the dominated conversation going), or the Foucauldian (keeping the dominated conversation going without realizing it, thus making delusional claims of critical mastery). Arguing from and acquiescing to authority may violate any of the three standards, for authoritative intervention in any deliberative context is meant to be a turning point; getting one thing settled, the process moves on.

Most organizations rarely straddle this dilemma. They are impaled on the first horn and simply lucky that authority-dependence is often for the best. Their actors are reluctant to straddle both horns because they do not want endless conversations. Critics straddle both horns, believing that organizations benefit from critique and reconstruction, that authority works against interrogations and interventions, and that the more that is known about how fields legitimate their authorities, the less trustworthy authorities will seem. These beliefs may lure organizational actors onto both horns, for they do explain the sort of organizational stupidity corporations spend fortunes (on consultants) trying to avoid. And most organizations grapple with coordination problems—fitting different modes of expertise together. No organization, if it is thinking straight, wants to fool itself. Reflective moments are supposed to be serviceable for longer range interests.

So with a little coaxing, most organizational actors may be persuaded that authority-dependence is a dilemma, not a frailty or skill deficiency. For now I will leave them straddling both horns. The critics most likely to coax organizational actors into the dilemma—the ones who make the most powerful and eloquent cases for acquiescing to or interrogating authorities—are not necessarily the best guides for dealing with the dilemma. The determinists are too fatalistic; and modernity's therapists are too optimistic.

ORGANIZATIONAL SCALE

Big policies in big contexts aren't easy to discern. Knowledge claims may arise in organizations whose expanse precludes Olympian intellectual mastery. Complex organizations have multiple channels and projects. Policies can play themselves out along an embroidered fabric of detail and overlapping venues, which heightens authority-dependence. If it is hard to weigh expert testimony in simple cases when the expert's intervention between a discipline's facts and interpretations and recommendations can be evaluated only by other experts, this effect will be multiplied as organizational complexity makes for enhanced specialism.

This complexity creates a managerial predicament for organizations that want to be authoritarian (with all authority and control flowing downward from the CEO at the top. With apologies to LaPlace (whose words I am changing ever so slightly) we can call this CEO the "demon miscalculator":

> A CEO knowing, at any given instant of time, all forces acting in and on an organization, as well as the momentary positions of all employees in the organization, down to the mailroom clerks, would comprehend the actions of the biggest departments and those of the lowest wage slaves on the food chain, in one single formula, provided it were sufficiently powerful to subject all data to analysis. As there is no such formula, and the CEO sees only chaos and quantum weirdness, consultants will be hired to whom nothing is uncertain, both future and past are present before their eyes.

LaPlace's demon calculator was a reductionist theory of everything (Davies and Brown 1988). It knew everything so it could predict everything. Systems theory tried to duplicate this omniscience in complex organizations—justified by Hegel's concern for totality and Lukacs' belief that partial perspectives are false consciousness (see Eagleton 1991, 99). The result was a theory authorizing management-by-megalomania.

Searches for public agreements likewise occur in complicated tapestries of activity—often ones that cross multiple organizational lines. Inside organizations, disputes may not consist only of confrontations of competing beliefs. Competing beliefs often can be kept under wraps. But lines of action intersect, diverge, and clash. Big projects make for cluttered environments in which claims, arguments, and whole positions are easily lost.

MISUNDERSTANDINGS

"Incommensurability-by-spurious-agreement" is Fuller's label (Fuller and Willard 1987) for protracted yet undetected misunderstandings. Some misunderstandings are obscured beneath literary density and field complexity (Shotter, in press), but hidden differences may remain even after much effort at creating commensurability between positions. Consider views of justice from Plato to Rawls: Do we find diverse answers to a single question or different meanings that have been attached to justice and its allied terms?

> [T]he evidence for there being severe misunderstanding is exactly the same as for there being a genuine "conversation of mankind," namely, a uniformity in the surface structure of the discussion. One telling feature is that after an issue like justice has been discussed for awhile, new problems are generated that render the issue more difficult than initially suspected. Is this a sign that the depths are being plumbed or simply that we have confused ourselves? . . . [One] has to entertain that the possibility that disputants are using language, yet their utterances are not completely translatable into our own—if only because they speak as if they were talking about the same thing, even though *we* can show that their pattern of usage indicates confusion. Thus, when rendering the dispute in our own terms, we must decide whether to suspend some of *their* presumptions about the nature of the dispute or some of *ours*. (Fuller and Willard 1987, 319)

This doesn't include anthropological contrasts that oblige westerners to make charity-like moves vis-à-vis primitive utterances. At least some differences are vouched for by disciplines whose members know what their words mean and who would emphatically deny that their terms are primitive versions of ours.

The bigger and sloppier the ideas, the more plentiful the hiding places for undetected differences in meaning. The terms of political discourse (Connolly 1974) are at least as porous as *justice* and have the added disadvantage of arising in time-constrained contexts. It may not be disastrous if academics misunderstand common uses of justice. After a century or so, things may clear up. But the environmentalist who speaks of resource management (and thereby seems to have arrived at common ground with governmental agencies and developers) may find herself locked into irreversible policies—fully co-opted in a short time.

Klein (1990a, 127) sees these risks in interdisciplinary research: "Team members think they are speaking the same language when they are really not." She points to a study by Luszki (1958) of mental health projects involving psychiatrists, psychologists, and sociologists who agreed on common terms too quickly. They thought they had a common view of aggression, but after analyzing their data discovered that the only thing they could agree on was that aggression is a "nice word" (ibid., 150–151). They avoided "creative problem-solving conflicts" by "ignoring the depth of their differences and jeopardizing work at larger stages" (Klein 1990a, 127).

The Rest of the Family

Some other epistemic problems need to be mentioned. They are, so to speak, organizational and individual frailties; and they pose special challenges to the pluralists' illusion of control.

"Policy freezes," for instance, are dogmatism for organizations. Good ideas at one stage of decision-making become bad ones at other stages. When one moment's expediencies become a successor moment's hard and fast rules, deliberative discourse is skewed. Socolow (1976) argues that environmental cost-benefit calculations are often based upon golden rules and numbers gilded not by merit but by the inertial weight of precedent. The prescriptions and routines followed at first—no matter the reason—become minimum guidelines for subsequent proposals. Thus, if a preliminary analysis divides a problem into three parts, this becomes a hard and fast standard—for example, the basis for perfunctory rejection of three proposals, each solving one of the three problems, or a proposal solving only two, etc. Golden numbers work the same way: "To hallow any [number—in this case, minimum water flow] is to skew the discourse. Whenever a ground rule of discussion is that some standard or guideline is to be accepted as an on-off number, above that there is 'safety' and below that there is 'peril,' two vital kinds of discourse become illegitimate: discussions of acceptable damage and discussions of damage limitations" (Socolow 1976, 8).

So one of the most powerful incommensurabilities arises from what may be the most commonplace practice of regulatory rule-making. There are minimum occupational safety standards (measurements of contaminating parts per million) for exposure to thousands of toxic gases, metals, and chemicals, carcinogens (asbestos, vinyl chloride, and dyes), heat stress, vibration, and ultraviolet, infrared, and ionizing radiation (Ashford 1976). There are at least as many on-off numbers measuring permissible pollutants (Davies 1970). These golden numbers make it hard to argue that pollution/exposure threats interact, that carcinogens are synergistic (asbestos exposure plus smoking plus air pollution), and thus that current on-off numbers are too permissive.

The adage that one cannot be reasoned out of a position one has not reasoned into applies to regulatory agencies. The Challenger calamity, for instance, came about partly because the luck of previous launches affected the probability calculations for the next—like a pyramid scheme for inferences. Expert objections to the last launch got reevaluated in light of outcomes in such a way that good fortune was transformed into future probability. When positions and proposals are ruled out (or as in this case given weight) in advance of any defenses that might be entered, an incommensurability is created.

Alienation may be an effect of policy freezes. The skeptical decision-maker often finds not the clamor of competing fields but the insistent voice of a single discipline—against which there exists no alternative. Cost-benefit analysis has dominated environmental discourse (Frost 1971, Goldman 1968, Irvin 1978, Layard 1972) and other planning domains (Blumstein 1968, Bruce 1976, Capron 1968, Conley 1976, Cook 1978). Criticisms of cost-benefit analysis most often focus on its reductionist ideology and effects (Tribe 1972, Williams 1973). But consider it for a moment as an unopposed decision-making model, for cost-benefit analysis is hegemonic in some domains.

Perhaps the most puissant incommensurability is the gap one feels between one's skepticism and the public institutions to which one conforms.

Because cost-benefit analysis ropes environmentalists into positions not of their own making (Socolow 1976), it yields feelings of bad faith. One is prevented from expressing what one cares most about while being forced into conventional institutions that contradict one's private beliefs. One feels soiled by participation—about legitimating the dominating discourse by playing by its rules—but lacks the rhetorical resources for seeing oneself as playing (or forced into) a role. Cynicism and alienation thus supplant public spiritedness. One doesn't just suspect the results, one devalues or disengages from the decision-making process.

A faith in hidden mistakes explains why we find people of good will behaving as if their interlocutors are mistaken. The assumption, from Aristotle on, has been that when sincere people disagree, at least one of them had to be wrong. Disputes, if we scratch their surface, stem from mistakes. Study a dispute, find the mistake. Fix the mistake, end the dispute. This is Russell's theory of descriptions transformed into a critical principle.

But as we saw, some incommensurable views can be come by competently. Academic disputes may turn on positions achieved competently and vouched for by different fields or research traditions. Public disputes may equally engage advocates functioning competently within their frames of reference.

Intransigence makes everything else worse. We applaud people having the courage of their convictions, but condemn intolerance and closed-mindedness. The list of pejorative labels for adamant advocates is long and ugly. They may be obstinate, stubborn, recalcitrant, rigid, bull-headed, and inflexible—or seem this way to others but see themselves as circumspect, prudent, and conventional. Adamancy, it seems, is a virtue only if one is right.

Mulishness is pathological joined with vehemence, and argument seems to be the matchmaker. There is something about disputation that brings the passion out and converts personal frailties into public threats—which is why most people profess to dislike arguments. Academics who study argument have largely ignored this problem, focusing instead on logical and procedural rules. There might be profit in studying etiquette and protocol (Whittenberger-Keith 1986). If the rationality of argument is protected not by rules but by decorum and propriety, then a society's codes for maintaining civility—and a knowledge of how they succeed and fail—are pertinent to the study of argumentation and decision-making.

And to field discourse, though to explain this I need to introduce a distinction between professionalization and professionalism. Professionalism is an interesting mix of etiquette, law, and culture, perhaps only a little better than Amy Vanderbilt. Intransigence, after all, is not unknown in the expert fields, and zealots are not unheard of in university faculties. So if professional discourses do argue more productively than less disciplined ones, what aspects of professionalism and discipline get this result? And if professionalism and discipline do no better in suppressing intransigence and fury, can they be improved? Can they, for instance, offset the intransigence that expert fields, to some extent, authorize? Disciplinary actors needn't be true believers to be committed actors. Fields are going concerns because people believe in them. They vie for political power because their actors believe that they work from a correct position. Their arguments are essentially arguments from authority. They assume the validity and cogency of the standards that credential them. Such arguments are authorized by the field's practices, traditions, and pieties. These, in turn, are legitimated by the faith and trust of field actors. So the retreat to one's field is the natural outcome of sincere arguers making true claims.

Critiquing Ourselves to Death: A Second Look at Autonomous Judgment

Given these epistemic predicaments, *can* we acquiesce only to epistemic domains whose operations are transparent? *Can* we submit to authority yet achieve a position of autonomous judgment? Or do modernity's therapists need to narrow their slogans?

One slogan could do with some trimming, for the truth may only bog us down—in data bases and libraries. The National Archives, for instance, reportedly have 325 million pages of classified documents (*Washington Post,* 15 May 1994, A-12)—a figure that doesn't include more current classified documents kept by various federal agencies. So assuming for a moment—and this is quite an assumption—that these documents are self-evident truths, needing no explaining, then what would it take to meet the journalist's goal of "getting the information to the people"?

And *is* knowledge power? Why should we think that an awareness of the basis of authority will weaken rather than heighten authority-dependence, or that experts who give public testimony somehow violate their fields' rules, or that we become autonomous by catching these mistakes? The defenders of autonomous judgment assume rather than argue that we know the proper balance between authoritative and public prerogatives, that we are able to concede to technical discourses the authority due them and to integrate their testimony into a sovereign argumentative ground. But the ground differs from case to case between, for instance, engineering equations assessing the soundness of a bridge and a nuclear reactor or between an economist's estimates of short- and long-term costs of a bridge and reactor. There are differences in the kinds and numbers of experts whose testimony must be balanced in public issues: Expertise in measuring low level radiation isn't equivalent to expertise in measuring the incidence and demographics of leukemia; and neither expertise bears on reactor design. And there are differences in the degree to which decision-makers rely on translators. The move from esoteric knowledge to policy may be simpler for a capital gains tax than for an income tax, and for psychiatric predictions of defendant dangerousness versus assessments of rehabilitation. There may be cases in which most or all of the steps from esoterica to policy are expert-driven—monetary policy, military uses of space. But if the autonomous judgment view might be strongest vis-à-vis concrete examples, its advocates rarely argue it that way.

What, indeed, is autonomous judgment? Do individuals stand alone against an expert field like a showdown in a spaghetti western? If decision-makers acquiesce to the epistemic hegemony of nuclear engineering vis-à-vis technical questions of nuclear safety, how do they then pass judgment by virtue of understanding the ways technical competence is valued? Estimates of low-level radiation, long-term exposure, and long-term health effects all depend upon the interpretation of esoteric evidence.

And finally, if public discourse is as organized and technical as I claim, the modernists are not simply exaggerating the possibilities for epistemic mastery, they are pursuing the wrong therapy. By individualizing knowledge and critique, by demanding of individuals a panoptic span of vision, they overstate our abilities and misstate the problem of authority-dependence. The unity of reason and praxis may be quite technical. Expert discourses are unities of reason and practice. They are "splendid local adaptations" (Gould 1980) whose evolution reflects their problem-adaptedness and local successes.

CODA: A MODEST PROPOSAL

From democracy's oldest dispute, one gathers that the intelligence of democracy poses a Hobson's choice: It either relies on experts, and isn't very democratic, or relies on public opinion, and thus isn't very bright. But the choice, I submit, is nowhere near that attractive. For there are reasons to doubt that we purchase competence at the price of democracy. The rule of experts has scarcely perfected the welfare state. Drug wars and crime waves, disemployment and homelessness do not inspire confidence in the pluralist's credo that democracy "somehow works." The best, as David Halberstam might say, isn't all that good; the brightest aren't all that bright. So if we simply must have a crisis of liberal democracy, the problem of competence will do.

Pluralism's delusions of adequacy have seemed plausible only because the renaissance citizen has seemed so implausible. But fixed on democracy's original sin pluralism has ignored its own, for the renaissance expert is no more plausible. The Adams-Jefferson vision of general knowledge is untenable. Specialism and focus exacerbate relativity and literary density, all of which, in turn, worsen authority-dependence; and so on. This synergism is bad enough for experts, but worse for public actors whose problems often span many fields. What is enervating locally is doubled in crossing two fields, trebled with three, and so on.

So I suggest a moratorium on all talk of omnicompetent public actors, whether social scientist–philosophers, splendidly educated senators, or Neuman's elite citizens. It may be more productive, or at least entertaining, to ask how, in concrete cases, field actors in fact confront problems of competence. Competence, after all, isn't unheard of, even in the Congress. And NASA now and then gets something up. The interesting question is how—and it is, I submit, quite a concrete question, a case-by-case sort of thing, and not the sort of question best addressed by grand gestures.

The populists do have a point (Parenti 1983, Reiter 1987). An elite oligarchy will always smack of class without merit; technical discourses will always be tyrannical enough to justify a Foucauldian ambivalence. But the populists are, nonetheless, guilty of the grandest gesture: They are defending a caricature of what general public knowledge might be and of a citizen whose competence is unavailable to the best trained elite. They assume the existence of a viable general discourse—an ecumenical language in which public affairs may be discussed by nonspecialists. Later I will argue that this assumption is (to use Schattschneider's word) preposterous. But even so, it is an open question how much Neuman's 8 to 10 percent might be enlarged. Perhaps some issues—if not the supercollider, something—can be discussed by nonspecialists. But if the populists are to find a nonspecialist issue agenda, like the pluralists, they are likeliest to succeed by arguing concrete cases. Instead of asserting that technical issues can be translated into a mass public discourse, they might try doing it. There are precedents for this: Science writers, for instance, though they raise authority-dependence to a near-religious level (see chapter 11), might be an instructive starting point, for science writing *is* an experiment in translation.

But whatever their result—and there is no reason not to wish them well—the populists need to distinguish between the rudimentary missionary work needed to redeem Bubba and the rather higher-toned claims they make about the renaissance citizen. And they need to lower their expectations for the latter, for the upshot of what I have had to say can be captured in a hypothetical question.

Assume for a moment that the populists succeed beyond Dewey's wildest dreams: 250 million citizens end up with Ph.D.s, C-Span goes interactive, and the public sphere becomes—this scene is not for the squeamish—a faculty meeting writ large. Will the mass plebiscite improve on the rule of experts? Madison might say so: *Federalist* 10 argues that mass scale is a safety mechanism ensuring that no one faction gains supremacy. Of course Madison was willing to let factions bog themselves down or burn themselves out in continuous combat. Instead of a thousand flowers blooming, imagine a thousand weeds choking one another. But the populist wants to inform the people, then hear them out. So what would they have to say? More of the same, only louder? The problem of competence suggests that it would be more of the same, and the prospect that it might be louder is the subject to which I will now turn. For the issue is not solely what intellectuals ought to be saying about democracy; it is, more fundamentally, how they might best make their cases.

SIX

Democracy in America: A Thought Experiment

Liberalism's idée fixe is that everything of importance about democracy stands or falls with claims about the public. The public is a potent symbol: It evokes strong attitudes, extravagant rhetorics, and has lent color and choler to democracy's oldest dispute. This debate has been largely an "is-not, is-too" affair—a battle of intuitions and dueling pieties. And the problem of competence, I contend, has fallen through the cracks.

But perhaps a better debate is possible. Perhaps indeed this is one case in which gut intuitions can be transformed into clear argumentative faults. A sharper picture might let us hear the truths each side has to tell yet allow us to catch all three in common mistakes. Then, at least, the three sides might make their cases differently. But a change of subject is also needed, and, as with all such conversational turns, it must happen slowly. The subject of competence must credibly insinuate itself and the heat of the debate must cool. For only with a change in mood can a cooperative agenda suggest itself.

THE THREE FACES OF LIBERALISM

ZEPPO: *Sire, the masses are revolting.*
GROUCHO: *I know they're revolting; I've seen 'em eat.*

Imagine a massive Bauhaus building, an ugly, mean-spirited brute: the Sears Tower, the Tour Montparnasse, or most any building in downtown Houston. It is modernity without mercy: spare, functional, and cold, a thing that dwarfs and diminishes the people around it.

Imagine that people put off by this austerity attach to the cold surfaces a rococo-baroque facade—Italian-style loggia here, Florentine Romanesque there, statues and sculptural groups everywhere, and some gargoyles and flying buttresses thrown in to give it substance. Raise Garnier's Paris Opera eighty or ninety floors, gussy it up, and you have the idea—a busy facade cloaking a utilitarian monolith.

The next step is a bit fanciful, but if you got the Opera up to nintey floors, you can certainly handle this: Imagine a Mary Shelley plot twist—the science-gone-awry theme in B movies: "It's alive!" The marble for the facade has been irradiated by a nearby fast breeder reactor. Once hanging on the building, the facade comes to life. The winged cherubim (et al.) believe that they are supposed to help hold the building up, so they reach inward and attempt to fuse with the underlying structure. When they succeed, the result is a bizarre mix—load-bearing gargoyles, flying foundations, trilobate-arch ductwork, and bas-relief conduit. Understandably, the inner structure resists the invasion, not wanting function to follow whatever form it finds. But as it isn't designed to resist its decoration, the result is a building at war with itself: Everything works—but oddly, incoherently, badly.

The thing simply must have a name. "Metaphor" seems drab. "The discourse of liberal democracy" seems pretentious. Walt Kelly might call it "The allegory of the swamp." But I prefer something simpler and more expressive, and on those criteria, only one name will do. Call it *Leviathan.*

Now the thought experiment: How will pluralists, postmodernists, and modernists read Leviathan? The answer, I submit, is within three distinct gestalts. They are separate enough to be dysfunctional. They lie in hermetic literatures, their advocates largely ignore one another, and the result is much like a multiple personality disorder. Admittedly, the trauma that sparks the disorder is only an extravagant ideal punctured. Given a utopian view of a rational public, democracy has a bumblebee flaw: It can't possibly fly. However much a caricature, this "paradox" is liberalism's adolescent trauma, the stammer in its narrative.

THE CONNOISSEURS

Pluralists at their worst might be called *connoisseurs,* for they appreciate virtues wrung from necessities. They contrast the lay public (the "simples" to Occam and the Scholastics, hopeless savages to the sociologist Sumner) to an elite—the sheep and the shepherds (Bell 1964). To seek knowledge in the sheep is to dilute wisdom. The sheep are educable to a point, beyond which elite authority fills the void. The "natural aristocracy" is racially inevitable to the statistician Galton and the craniometrist Broca (Gould 1981), a matter of refinement to Edmund Burke and Lord Acton. The aim of public education is to prepare the elite for leadership and the public for followership. The public, Mill says, "that miscellaneous collection of a few wise but many foolish individuals," should follow the lead of the wisest people (1956, 26).

The connoisseurs have a point. One can, with grounds, revive Aristotle's pessimism about the "depraved character" of the Athenians. These grounds are often called the "Lazarsfeld tradition" (Lazarsfeld, Berelson, and Gaudet 1968, Lane and Sears 1964, Dahl 1956, Key 1961), a body of research that improves the odds on Mencken's wager that nobody goes broke betting on the ignorance of the American public. Using research methods likely to understate citizens' flaws (Neuman 1986), it reports irrationality, frivolousness, primitive passions, infantile reasoning, ignorance, and an attention span that can be likened to Hobbes's view of life: brutish, nasty, and short.

This is why politics in America is professional wrestling pursued by other means. Mencken's circus of oompah bands and rottweiler rhetoric is a discourse that has found its level. Advertising and public relations techniques dominate political life because they are rhetorically appropriate to their audiences.

But connoisseurs go well beyond noticing democracy's susceptibility to hoopla. They want to insulate elite governance from the storms and rages of public life. For them, populism is synonymous with demagoguery (Hofstadter 1960, 1967). And inevitably so, for it is the irony of democracy, remember, that the vox populi may be undemocratic. To capture the flavor of this reasoning, I have patched this passage together from some elitist classics (Michels 1962, Mosca 1939, Ortega y Gassett 1950, Pareto 1966, Schumpeter 1942). None says it exactly like this, but all say it something like this:

> Fortunately, most citizens are politically apathetic. All vital functions are performed by elites. And should be, for no serious question could be debated before, or decided by, a mass public. The political reasoning of even well-educated citizens is primitive and infantile. And the instincts of the least educated are authoritarian, illiberal, and barbarian. Given full voice in a free and open plebiscite, the American public would divide along homicidal lines, of race, ethnicity, and religion. It would abolish most of the Bill of Rights and trample the most fundamental democratic values. Tolerance, charity, and equity—and preeminently the idea of protecting minorities—are not virtues that have welled up from the people. They are ideas that have come from elites.

Hence the connoisseurs' fear of leveling. Given power, the mob will trample the very values that justify giving it power, which is why the founders invested government with an inertial sluggishness resistant to the passions of the moment. Expanded suffrage risks majority despotism, so much as software manufacturers turn glitches into advertising coups—"it's not a fault, it's a feature" (Scriven 1989)—connoisseurs see political apathy as a good thing, a buffer against populist excesses (Berelson, Lazarsfeld, and McPhee 1954, J. D. Peters 1989, Huntington 1974). Where Madison trusted only the tensions between competing factions, connoisseurs appeal to something like the invisible hand in Adam Smith's market: Democracy, they say, "somehow works."

Not that America has broken the poverty cycle or offset the side effects of capitalism. The idea, rather, is that we are muddling along. To borrow from Li'l Abner, "the country's in the very best of hands"—which is to say *not* public hands. And this fixation on the public's defects is why the problem of competence is invisible.

As the connoisseur reads Leviathan, we have Plato with a vengeance: Realpolitik, Leviathan's foundation and structure, is purely an internal affair. The facade is but extra weight. "The central fact of American politics is the behavior of the political elite. Washington is everything" (Robinson in Neuman 1986, 1). "Washington," here, means professionals, omnicompetent insiders, the meritocracy. Competition among elites ensures that the marketplace of ideas is a level playing field; the voices worth hearing get a hearing. The expert fields settle the issues, the professionals consult the experts, and then create rationalizations and agendas to preoccupy mass discourse. Political campaigns and mass communication in general hang on the structure but help it only by disguising it. The more innocuous the ballyhoo, the better; the more candidates are pushed toward centrist positions, the better. The illusion of participation isn't a fault, it's a feature, and as gargoyles elect gargoyles, the ideal is Potemkin leadership.

One can distrust the invisible hand because one doubts that any market, including Adam Smith's, actually has one. Unlike a faith in the afterlife, which at least has the grace of nonconscious falsifiability, the belief that democracy somehow works butts up against evidence to the contrary. One wouldn't shout this belief near Cabrini Green, or mutter it under one's breath while dealing with a bureaucracy. It would scarcely pop into one's head while watching a political convention. But the more telling objection, I submit, is that the hand is quite visible—and much shakier than connoisseurs think.

Connoisseurs trust institutions—experts, professions, and disciplines—because they are less mysterious than people. They expect the expert fields to formulate public options, to represent the inarticulate, and to canvass public opinion honestly (Frankel 1967:88). But studies of professionalization describe a monopolizing drift (Freidson 1986). To protect their turf—a jurisdiction from which state power helps them fend off competitors—fields cloak their achievements, disciplines, and techniques in mystery (Abbott 1988). And studies of disciplines and of how arguments work in organizations (the studies likeliest to reveal the invisible hand) do not salvage the connoisseurs' intuitions. They largely confirm the populist's fears: They underscore the conservative weight of prevailing views, the despotic effects of discipline, the weight of momentum, and a pathological preference for agreement.

And if the Latter-Day philosopher kings are inept, authority-dependent turf-tenders, neither are they immune to public rhetorics. The rhetorical environment of the cold war gave us the containment doctrine, both as public ballyhoo and as an idée fixe deep within the corridors of power (Halberstam 1964, 1969). And the degree to which science is a mirror of the whims and agendas of funding agencies is surely an open question. From foot-dragging on AIDS research to the unseemly scramble for coins that surrounded Star Wars, science in America has not presented an unalloyed spectacle of Parsonian purity (see Redner 1987a).

And as experts mingle with gargoyles, the subtlety and refinement of expert discourses may not be simply lost, but foreclosed. In public life the temptation to turn one's back on the discourse refinements and principles that protect one in the expert sphere is strong. Inside technical discourses, for instance, environmentalists won't always carry the day; they won't win every argument. Slogans and banners get results. The constraints of discipline may seem like excess baggage in a social movement. So expert and public domains cannot be separate but equal. The latter will co-opt the former.

ORACLES

The next group doesn't frequent the same clubs as connoisseurs. In their most fulsome moments, they might be called *oracles*. They claim to see what is invisible to others: the side effects of capitalism, distributive inequality, all masked by a false consciousness fueled by a running-dog lackey mass media (Chomsky 1988b). The oracles, indeed, may be as puzzled as the connoisseurs that I have called Leviathan a metaphor: The duality of structure and legitimizing facade is just the reality dominant ideologies mask.

The language of interests, history, power, and ideology dominates this discourse (Aaron 1950, Birnbaum 1960, 1962, 1971, Blackburn 1972, Hamilton 1975, Hunter 1953, 1959). Where others see constraints—a welfare state in receivership unable to cushion capitalism's side effects without sabotaging the civic virtue it needs to govern humanely (Connolly

1977:76)—the oracles see contradictions (Kolko 1962, Lindberg 1975, Weisskopf 1978, Wolfe 1977).

The oracles, too, have a point. It is Foucault's point: In a world patterned by complex organizations, no epistemic theory can ignore the cooption of individual reflection by systematically distorted communication: Organizations *aim* to make practices square with overriding goals. As this effect also sparks conservatism, resistance to innovation, and obduracy, actors and organizations alike have a stake in critique and reconstruction.

The oracles are blinded to the problem of competence by their populism. Take, for instance, their reasoning behind the economic critique of the mass media. The media seem public but are in fact private, compromised by their ownership and thus keeping vital information from the public (Demac 1984, Elliott 1982, Entman 1989, Hocking 1947). Elites are information-rich, monopolizing expensive information sources and jealously hoarding their data bases. The masses are information-poor, reduced to fatuous entertainment and appealed to as consumers rather than as citizens (Schiller 1986, Bagdikian 1971, 1983). Abrams (1983) attributes this to a conspiracy—the power elite actively connives to marginalize the public. Negt and Kluge (1979) prefer a Lukacsian class thesis—mass apathy and obedience reflect the architecture of class consciousness. And Chomsky (1987) advances something of a structuralist thesis—no conniving is needed; capitalism's very structure ensures the public's marginalization.

But all of them see citizen participation as the solution to elite oligarchy (Bachrach 1967, 1971, Balthrop 1989, Barber 1984, 1988, Marger 1987, Verba and Nie 1972, Verba, Nie, and Kim 1978). Populism is thus anti-elitism, typified by Chomsky's claim that what the Trilateral Commission calls "the crisis of democracy" is really the fact that citizens participate in politics:

> That report reflects attitudes that go way back. Even the mainstream democratic theorists have always understood that when the voice of the people is heard you're in trouble because these stupid and ignorant masses, as they're called, are going to make the wrong decisions. So, therefore, we have to have what Walter Lippmann . . . called "the manufacture of consent." We have to ensure that actual power is in the hands of what he called a specialized class. . . . The Founding Fathers had very strong feelings in this respect. The Federalists, for example, were very much afraid of popular democracy. . . . [The point, then, is to marginalize the population, reducing] them to apa-

> thy and obedience, allowing them to participate in the political system, but as consumers, not as true participants. You allow them a method for ratifying decisions that are made by others, but you eliminate the methods by which they might first, inform themselves; second, organize; and third, act in such a way as to really control decision-making. (Chomsky in Moyers 1989:40–41)

Notice Chomsky's view of public knowledge: "Compared to intellectually complex tasks [it] is pretty slight. It's not like the sciences where there are so many things you have to study. . . . By and large, what happens in political life is relatively accessible. It doesn't take special training or unusual intelligence" (ibid., 54).

But how sound is this claim? For instance, what would a senator or citizen need to know in order to assess a proposal to reduce the capital gains tax? A rational decision, Solow (1990, 9) reasons, would have to rest on an estimate of the pattern of losses and gains to the Treasury, a demographic understanding of how the effects of the tax change would be distributed across the population, and a sense of the tax's effectiveness in stimulating capital investment and research and development—"exactly the stuff of academic research papers and Ph.D. theses," media riddled with technical jargon, arcane assumptions, and mathematical procedures. One would think "that a body of interpretive economic journalism would fill the gap and mediate between policy-oriented research and policy-interested citizens. There is indeed some . . . [but] there is not nearly enough serious economic journalism and the average quality is pretty poor."

Criticisms of this sort are often calls for experts to be clearer. It is the expert who has the technical wherewithal to translate specialized into general parlance. And science writing, we shall see, is almost always expected to be an accurate mirror of authoritative knowledge. So the onus here is on economists, not journalists. But it is one thing to say that economic journalism should have a respectable and important berth in economics, and quite another to say how the writing can be improved. Consider some good economic journalism, for instance, the *Newsweek* essays of the past twenty years or so. Written by Paul Sammuelson, and later by Robert Sammuelson and by Mr. Solow, they are arguably exemplars—splendidly written, as a rule, but also arguments from authority, as a rule, especially as they turn from politics to matters of economic fact. For they have the unmistakable mark of the opinion piece: They make claims without fully surveying the evidence, reasoning, and state of authoritative consensus behind their claims.

They also presuppose a fairly sophisticated reader: Judged by squint-of-eye, their usual prose level is just below a university textbook, though some essays have strayed well above that. These vacillations likely reflect different translation problems. Some technical issues are tougher than others, and the essays likely reflect editorial struggles to find the simplest prose into which the knowledge can be translated. Space, I imagine, is the final frontier: One can cram only so many explanations and definitions into forty column-inches. So though they vary, the *Newsweek* columns are by no stretch easy going.

Nor are they only about economics; and therein lies another tale. The *Newsweek* columns meet a genuine need, certainly. They hold Capitol Hill shenanigans up to the light of cool reason; they critique or applaud the FED; they counter demagoguery with facts. And in so doing, they illustrate perhaps better than anything else the degree to which economic facts do not stand alone in policy debates. To judge by the arguments the columnists have made over the years, measuring the recovery from a recession is as much a matter of polling as of housing starts, inventories, and retail sales. And one gets the impression that economic policy issues are every bit as technical, and span as many field boundaries as policy issues in general.

So Chomsky has it backwards. Public policy issues are more intellectually challenging than specialized ones. They are more complex, they span broader ranges of relevant information, they demand coordination among different specialties, and they often require adjudication among competing specialists' claims. So if all that information now said to be suppressed is made public, it will be unmanageable. There is too much of it. It may be uninterpretable—too specialized and recondite. And it may be ambiguous—open to expert dispute. The public will thus be at least as authority-dependent and inept as elites, and arguably more prone to reject authority wholesale.

The key to the oracles' mistake is the grain of truth in their class-wealth-milieu view of elitism (Burch 1980). The founders are unquestionably open to Beard's economic critique; and one can scarcely doubt that Mills's (1956) inbred power elite does dominate corporate boards, presidential appointments, and state governments. As this aristocracy confirms a gut demonology, the populist recoils in horror, thus missing the merit in Lippmann's view, not as he defended it, but as it must be defended now. An idealized completion of the most utopian meritocracy, with not a whiff of class or milieu, will be as incompetent as the status quo.

MOURNERS

The next group might be called the *mourners,* for they are heartbroken by Leviathan. They mourn the loss of civic virtue. They fear the connoisseurs are right, that the facade can't be made less grotesque. But they share Dewey's hope for a competent public. Their ranks are swelled with refugees from the Progressive era—liberal democrats who share Dewey's belief in competence, specialism, and rational control and who want to recover the ideals if not the details of the Greek *polis* (Arendt 1958, Bell 1976b, MacIntyre 1981, Unger 1975, Wolin 1960). And even some pluralists want to use mass education to wean the state away from elite oligarchy (Dahl 1967, 1971, 1982).

The most noticeable mourners are journalists who see themselves as caretakers of the public sphere, guardians of the public interest, stewards of public knowledge (Chafee 1947, Commission on Freedom of the Press 1947, Cutlip 1985, Hennessy 1970, Hocking 1947, Hohenberg 1971, Meiklejohn 1948, Seibert, Peterson, and Schramm 1956). Carey (1992, 11) calls the public "the god term of journalism—the be-all and end-all, the term without which the entire enterprise fails to make sense." There are connoisseurs in the journalists' ranks—preeminently Lippmann. And Mencken, we saw, is a mourner in connoisseur's clothing. Cynics do not devote whole careers to denouncing the state of public life. Wounded, he bleeds printer's ink. The legendary wit is grim and purposeful, unrelieved by a twinkle in the eye. Perhaps a mourner has turned connoisseur out of despair. Or perhaps it is a rhetorical ploy. One way to galvanize popular participation is to rub the public's nose in the alternative. Most mourners would prefer this reading: They see merit in the connoisseurs' stance but are loath to wholeheartedly endorse elite oligarchy.

Also prominent in the mourners' ranks are Dewey's field troops, whose pedagogical mission is to enfranchise the general public with the skills and knowledge needed for political participation and for entry into the elite ranks (Blair and Johnson 1980, Pateman 1970, Pranger 1968, Ward, 1883). They are not blind to the shenanigans in the facade, but Mencken makes them wince, not laugh: They fear that democracy will die without competent citizens. And they often adopt the oracles' language when they speak of participatory democracy, critical thinking and argument skills being techniques for penetrating systematically distorted communication. The deficiencies of the public are symptoms of public inequities, not of an inherent failing in ordinary folk. The better educated the citizenry, the healthier the polity.

There is a difference—but no explicit debate—between mourners who see the fatuous state of mass discourse as reflecting the deficiencies of the mass public (the latter causes the former; every rhetoric reflects its audience) and those who see a circular relation between discourses and their publics (every discourse presupposes a view of the public that affects the self-image of a public). In the latter spirit, Goodnight (1982b:10) says that "it is difficult for a people to be more than their various forms of address ask of them. By uncovering and critiquing the implied visions of the public in what takes upon itself the name of the public, the critic may be able to discern what the American people are conceived to be and thereby circumscribed from becoming." Goodnight thus sees the demise of the Progressive era as an effect of the communications industry. "Crusading journalists found in the exposé a righteous cause and a means of selling more papers. The more titillating the scandal, the more degraded the social condition exposed, the more exotic the scientific solutions, the more papers sold" (ibid., 6). The gargoyles and cherubim on the facade learned the lesson: The guise of the reformer, no matter the facts, was the easiest path to power. The public and the public interest became platitudes.

The mourners are blind to the problem of knowledge because they straddle a tension between two values. On the one hand, they value participation. They want to enfranchise the public; they see critical thinking, argument skills, and subject matter competence as paths for redeeming the Jeffersonian promise; their pedagogy seeks to democratize the mastery of public issues taken to be the mark of competent citizenship. But mourners also believe in the improvability and recuperation of discourses and have fallen in with Habermas's search for a reconstruction of the public sphere. This goal seems complementary if one thinks that a more critical public will demand a public discourse of greater refinement and subtlety. But subtlety requires expertise, and expertise disenfranchises by exclusion. As specialism and complexity flourish, the democratization of competence becomes more distant, like an ever receding goal we run toward in a nightmare. For against every claim about public knowledge is a counterclaim about the requirements of competence. The disciplines are our models of competence. Our benchmark for assessing economic argument, for example, is the degree to which it mimics the technical discourse of economics. The better we want public argument to be, the more disciplined we will make it, and thus the less publicly accessible it will be.

This tension is magnified with lay audiences, for whom the marketplace of ideas is so vast that it may be misleading to call it a market at all. No greater irony is imaginable than a Rawlsian original position in which the conditions of free decision-making are met but the options are incoherent to the actors, or a Habermasian discourse in which every voice is heard, but in which the speakers are inarticulate or inane—free to speak, but nothing to say. Because the mourners are committed to the broadest possible view of general competency, they are beset by the biggest possible paradox. Their proposals for improving public discourse, the democratization of competence, egalitarianism, and the idea of reflective epistemic mastery seem like empty slogans, and their nostalgic calls for revivals—of the *polis* or some other idealized vision—seem both romantic and "sociologically naive" (Alexander 1991, 161).

The mourners rarely go as far as Chomsky does. The view that most anyone can handle public decision-making doesn't last long as one confronts the critical skills of heavy-breathing sophomores. But to have a viable pedagogy, they must resist the claim that decision-making is too hard, and their solution, on the whole, has been to focus on deliberative skills more than subject matter expertise. But the lesson of the incompetent elites should make us doubt that skills alone are enough. General rules of consistency, organization, coherence, and persuasion may cross subject matters at a rudimentary level, but at higher levels of sophistication, deliberative principles are inseparable from subject matters. Equivocation and consistency are general principles, but determining whether one *is* inconsistent or equivocal depends on substantive, technical judgments. The standard solution is a quasi-specialism for quasi-experts: Public decision-makers are to know as much as possible about subject matters. Leaving aside the question of whether knowledge at this level can be conveyed by mass media, the importance of subject matter knowledge brings us back to the subject of elite incompetence. For if the goal is increasing refinement, the emphasis on skills merely reinforces the paradox.

NOBLE SAVAGES

A fourth character is omnipresent. Connoisseurs, oracles, and mourners build their arguments by imagining people who see no difference between the facade and the building. If there really are such folk, let's call them noble savages. They are Rousseau's citizens in the state of nature—earnest, gullible, and thoroughly fooled by the facade. The connoisseurs want to exploit them, the oracles want to drop the scales from their eyes, and the mourners want to enlighten them.

This is as clear as it gets. The noble savage comes from Romanticism—the literary revolt (Wordsworth, Blake, Keats, and Shelley) against the Enlightenment's scientism and mechanical worldview and political rebellion

(Rousseau) against urbanization. The label "noble savage" is at least as clear as "proletariat" or "working class." These blurry labels are often used to avoid the technical discourse of demographics, defining a class, for example, by income, housing, and education. Such concreteness might restrict the level of abstraction patrons of the noble savage want to maintain. The oracles and mourners would not want a computer program to translate a statistical average into a single image. Their vision is better captured by the Frank Capra film *Meet John Doe* in which glitzy urbanites seek out the paradigmatic "average man" and find Gary Cooper who turns out to speak truths in a plain, candid way. Primitives and peasants, it seems, are close to nature and so have natural feelings. Because government by plain truth has been lost, the path to redemption is to listen to the common man.

But oracles don't care to hear everything the common man has to say. On their view, the noble savage has been corrupted. The corporate mass media have distorted his true nature by imposing various forms of false consciousness, including, apparently, some of the more colorful opinions and practices to be found along America's back roads. Along with snake-handling, cat worship, and some intensely nursed ethnic grievances, the media are apparently to blame for a breathtaking naiveté. Oracles thus lay out their theories as answers to the noble savage's ingenuous belief that Norman Rockwell's idealized town meeting is in fact how democracy works. Against this gullibility, Dye and Ziegler (1981), for instance, rush to expose Satan's work.

This is less credible than most straw-man arguments. It is an ancient cliché that Americans are cynical about government, leadership, and mass communication (see Merriam and Gosnell 1924). This cynicism, joined to the emergence of alternative methods of influence, has caused a decline in the importance of elections (Ginsberg and Shefter 1990). To hear the polls tell it, U.S. public opinion in the 1990s is reminiscent of the populist oratory of the 1890s: America is run by "the interests," the "wolves of Wall Street," and big corporations (Kimbell 1972, Levin 1960). If the mass media are purveyors of capitalist ideology, they are uncommonly transparent. Even young children are skeptical of advertising (Lowery and DeFluer 1988). So the oracles are laboring, arguably, to expose a reality that most ordinary people already profess to believe. And though it isn't deliberate, I'm sure, they are open to the charge of pandering, of telling people what they want to hear.

The noble savage is a vague, romantic idealization, a creature of gut intuitions, about human nature, character, and values. As these intuitions differ, the noble savage sparks the value disputes in which the connoisseurs, oracles, and mourners most irritate one another. At their worst, the connoisseurs infuriate everyone by qualitatively ranking people; the oracles claim to know what the people really think, or would think freed from dominating discourses; and the mourners claim to know what the people should do, that if they deliberate rationally, they will embrace the goals of equality and justice.

When topics bring out the worst in arguers, it is often wise to change the subject. The noble savage gave Romanticism its melancholy, and it is having the same effect now. Where the oracles (and some mourners) stress the noble, the connoisseurs (and some mourners) stress the savage to get a mirror-opposite caricature: A beastly human nature is tamed or suppressed by civilization. This makes for shouting matches, so all three camps might profit by dispensing with the noble savage. A change of subject is possible, for the connoisseurs' chief concern can be shared by mourners and perhaps some oracles. Bracketing questions of human nature, there are reasons to fear crowds.

I will call this new topic "Le Bon's nightmare." To introduce it properly, I will explain it as an occupational hazard. I teach persuasion—the war college of the social sciences. As a subject matter, persuasion is partly theoretical—Aristotle on rhetoric, Fishbein on attitudes, Weaver on ethics—and partly case studies—how the Nazis did it, how advertising works. This is, if not the guiltiest praxis, certainly a compromised one. As an art and science, persuasion is a Kantian bête noire—it treats people as means. And it is an exemplar among double-edged swords: Methods that promote affiliation can be warped; we sow community but reap xenophobia; rhetorical successes prepare the way for stronger control; every audience is potentially a mob.

As the persuasion theorist tells it, the demagogue is democracy's analogue to cancer, and the premalignancy is the crowd. Thus much of the subject matter of persuasion consists of case studies of crowd contagion, diffusion of responsibility, and self-persuasion. The persuasion theorist's deepest qualm is embodied in the crowd in the French revolution. Summoned by bells, whipped into furies, and cynically manipulated by spellbinding orators, the crowd became an end in itself and a symbol for the worst outcomes of mass persuasion. To draw crowds, the persuasion theorist would say, is to draw blood.

Le Bon's nightmare is a potent image in our own time. If there is a single picture that bedevils our century it is the memory of Hitler's crowds—the sea of faces and raised arms, the flags, torches, and movie-prop emblems of the Goebbels-Speer high modernist spectacles. This image colors how we see modern parallels—from Armenian nationalists to Iranian fundamentalists—and inhibits our approval even of crowds we agree with. Just as animals become jittery before earthquakes, connoisseurs and mourners dread crowds. Connoisseurs see the crowd through Le Bon's lens; mourners see a risk that the ironist's view might be right. Preferring discipline to unbridled emotion, they want to ensure that audiences never become crowds.

Connoisseurs and mourners might agree, then, that the worst imaginable belief the noble savages might adopt—the most debilitating mass political doctrine—is a Rousseau-like idealization of communication as expression and, thus, an idealization of mass politics as authentic expression. Like those who expect organizations to have human characteristics, those who expect mass politics to express their personal feelings are bound for alienation—or martyrdom.

I will return to Le Bon's nightmare at the end of this book, for the success of my postmodern alternative—the field of epistemics and its political model, federated Europe—ultimately rides on the differences between crowds and organizations.

A Suite for Three Voices

Perhaps by now Leviathan doesn't seem so fanciful, even the part about the marble coming alive. It is an argument in the liberal style—except that it is about how the three schools of thought argue. The three gestalts are instinctive abhorrences, not positions arrayed in a lucid debate, so my aim has been to make the debate clearer than it usually is. I will leave it to the reader to decide whether I have lined up a reductio ad absurdum of each, or, as I prefer to think, I have shown the ways in which expansive rhetorical gestures drive the arguments.

At the end of the day, what the connoisseur most basically has to say is that the populist case is untenable. What the mourner has to say is that it is better to do the right thing—redeem Dewey's vision. And what the oracle has to say is that false consciousness is possible and that the welfare state has failed to offset the side effects of capitalism. All three have more to say than this, but these ideas are a footing, at least, for reading all three sympathetically. It involves some gestalt therapy, so to speak—building a new gestalt within which the three views are not mutually exclusive. For if the meaning of our allegory is that the requirements of expertise preclude popular decision-making, perhaps it *should* evoke all three emotions. By getting in touch with its feelings, liberalism may be able to hear all three voices, thus preserving some of the intuitions of modernists and postmodernists while accommodating to modernity's needs for competence.

The trick is in how we pitch the voices. If they all sing full blast, we will have a crisis of liberal democracy! And a multiple personality disorder: three distinct realities preferred to outside rhetorics segregated not by lines of dispute but by a theoretical apartheid. A trio, conversely, is an interweaving of three voices, not a multiple personality disorder. That we can hear these voices is a refinement; we have developed an ear, not a pathology. To let the three voices mingle is to let each tell its truth. Though they have politically incompatible programs, their differences aren't contradictions—even the ways oracles and connoisseurs value the obscurationist effects of the facade.

Fearing expressive politics, we still need the oracle's voice speaking for modernity's victims. This voice needn't threaten the connoisseur. Connoisseurs don't assume that poverty is good for business; they largely agree with the oracles that disemployment is both cyclical and a continuing adaptation effect. The better questions are whether their greed precludes their sympathy—as the oracles charge—and whether their sympathy might translate into humane policies.

So instead of seeking a higher synthesis of the three views, or attempting to defeat them, we can see them as forming a kind of hermeneutic circle around the building and its facade. As they are aesthetic reactions, they are, in a fundamental way, part of the building's reality. Neither the underlying structure or the facade can be understood apart from the beholder's valuing of them.

Preeminently, the three orientations are not fixed points in an historically constant environment. The modernity of the late eighteenth century isn't the modernity of the late twentieth; the technical discourse that Vico feared isn't equivalent to our technical discourses. The metaphor does reinforce Nietzsche's point about the importance of aesthetic values to the evaluations we make in the political world. So the metaphor is unfinished and will remain so, as the relation of praxis to practice evolves its way toward unimagined permutations. The question is how the epistemic scholar can participate in this evolution.

We have a place to start, for we have caught all three in common mistakes—their dichotomies of rhetoric versus reality, elites versus masses, technical versus public, economic versus public discourse—and at least one failure of imagination, their single-mindedness about *the* problem of *the* public sphere.

THE REALISM STRATEGY REVISITED

Connoisseurs and oracles alike claim to see what others do not. Both see Leviathan more as a photograph than a metaphor—a reality veiled by rhetoric—and thereby claim a position of epistemic privilege, a Realpolitik, a discourse shorn of humbuggery and pretense. Both see rhetoric as the antonym of reality: The connoisseurs want to use it to keep the masses happily impotent; the oracles want to cut through its deceptions to expose the truth.

A Barbara on both their houses:

> MAJOR PREMISE: All claims to privilege are rhetorical.
> MINOR PREMISE: Realism is a claim to privilege.
> CONCLUSION: Realism is rhetorical.

How good is the major premise? From the divine right of kings to elder veneration to the beat cop's daily apple from the street vendor, claims to privilege demand, insist upon, or request the acquiescence of others. The privilegee is empowered, entitled, and sanctioned—three distinctively social effects that require assent or compliance from others. If the word rhetoric has no other uses, it applies to claims of privilege.

Is realism a claim to privilege? One is claiming that the world is as one sees it, that one's ways of seeing are unaffected by one's ways of thinking, speaking, and listening. One claims to be privy to realities, and thus makes truth claims, not in the abstract but in pragmatic circumstances. The policy scientist claims to have bare facts, the cost-benefit analyst claims to have advice untainted by human frailty, the Marxist claims to see a reality invisible to others, and one makes such claims to others, implying that others must set aside their own defective views. If the word rhetoric is to have nothing but invidious meanings—humbuggery, pervarication—then realism is arguably its paradigm case.

This doesn't mean that any particular claim to Realpolitik is mistaken—only that Realpolitik is as rhetorical as image politics. Positivistic claims to rationality and realism (claims to be nonrhetorical) are as functionally persuasive as a candidate's claim to be a "man of the people." They are birds of a feather. And arguably, the claim to Realpolitik is the worse of the two, for it heightens the devaluation of opponents, short-circuits controversy, and claims a presumption in its favor that entails no burden of proof.

Max Weber brings a more rhetorically sensitive reading to Leviathan. Weberian organizations have rhetorical momentum, which is why they sometimes seem deterministic, hermetically sealed, and thus why Foucault's trap seems plausible. So Leviathan isn't a reality covered by a rhetoric; it is a fusion of two ways of seeing, thinking, feeling, and speaking. And this is why the ornate facade and the discourse beneath it fuse. Competing discourses clash, repel, and compromise; they merge piecemeal, sloppily, situationally. Elites and politicians are forced together by occasions and by common agendas. Both seek adherents, and both have vested interests in demeaning the other.

The mourners have the best ground here—not in redeeming a transcendental reason or saving logic from rhetoric, but in tracking the intersections and conflicts among rhetorics. They are not ideologically committed to an inside versus outside dichotomy, so they are more likely to see discourse domains as made up of multiple architectures, with different effects, and complex intersections with other discourses. As we shall soon see, treating argument fields as rhetorical structures opens the door to seeing them as diffuse, complex ecologies. Instead of seeing fields as state-like, separated by Berlin wall borders (within which Foucault's trap springs shut), the mourners can stress the permeability of field borders—their fuzziness, vagueness, imprecision.

The Language of Class Warfare

To hear Tocqueville tell it, the problems of democracy can be summed up as threats to the public sphere, especially the sapping of public spiritedness by privatism. Tocqueville understood that a dissolute aristocracy could leech onto a commonwealth abetted by the obscurant effects of ideology. But his aim wasn't, as Gladstone said, to back the masses against the classes. He didn't prefer proletarian to aristocratic values, and he saw the need for competence. But he also doubted that wealth immunizes against greed and that only elites could manifest public spiritedness, and he distrusted trickle-down benevolence. He saw democracy's promise as a matter of spreading ability and responsibility. Fueled by prosperity and infinite natural resources, the democratization of competence seemed limitless. The educational prerogatives reserved for the rich in primitive societies could be extended to whole populations, transforming a *faux noblesse oblige* into a true public. Thus Tocqueville more than Dewey fathered the "rhetoric of mass enfranchisement."

Many people believe that Tocqueville's answer holds good today. But they miss his claims about competence by emphasizing a different nineteenth-century image: Aristocrats-as-predators. Bram Stoker made his vampire a count who preys on peasants; and for oracles and many mourners, the term *elite* is always malignant, its contrast with the masses always invidious—the former bleeds the public sphere for private gain, the latter is democracy's lifeblood, its whole point, indeed, the embodiment of the word *public.* The elite versus mass contrast thus includes rich versus poor, insider versus outsider, strong versus weak, and private versus public. Merit, in all this, is oligarchy's mask (Domhoff 1971).

But even if capitalism is marked by concentration of wealth and organizational control, it is worth questioning the usefulness of the elite-versus-mass contrast and the language of class conflict it invokes. My objection to class is not just that it is phlogiston, but that it confuses otherwise plausible arguments. Consider, for instance, Ginsberg's (1986) claim that the public sphere was created by elites to suppress opposition. The modern state, he argues, arose at a time when there existed no public or public opinion. "Popular consent has become politically important, at least on a routine basis, only in modern times" (ibid., 7). The upper and lower classes in the late seventeenth century were kept separate by the exigencies of daily life, so public ideas were upper-class ideas. Though the European bourgeoisie did much of the work in the eighteenth and nineteenth centuries in constructing voting and parliamentary apparatuses, it was indifferent or hostile to enfranchising the lower classes. The upper classes took the initiative to extend popular suffrage—not from altruism but to circumvent more dangerous forms of rebellion and to dilute the power of the middle class. The growth of the public sphere was to be an innocuous legitimacy. After all, free speech is easiest to defend when one is confident of winning all the arguments; the right of free speech isn't much of a gift to the inarticulate, so the marketplace of ideas would be free, but purely a sellers' market.

This market, Ginsberg fears, is prone to state monopoly, which masquerades, in an Orwellian way, as public instruction. Government, in this view, uses public relations to sell its services. The forerunner of this trend was the Committee on Public Information created to promote enthusiasm for World War I. This committee, Ginsberg believes, remains the model for all governmental agencies, which now use polling to guide their public relations. And as citizens adopt these visions and become increasingly reliant on government services, the result is enhanced state power.

Like most libertarian arguments, this one might be easily overblown. But Ginsberg doesn't flatly say that any state rhetorics are pernicious. He might even applaud (say) the surgeon general's public information campaigns about smoking, AIDS, birth control, substance abuse, and prenatal care. His point is about side effects: We should temper our enthusiasm for government propaganda we approve of by remembering that state power grows with use.

But Ginsberg's diagnosis overpowers any solution. He insists that upper-class interests shape media content rather than the reverse and that the lower classes are molded by exposure to television. The power elites dominate the marketplace of ideas (there is just one); their victims are powerless. But there are reasons to doubt the first premise: Content Analysis studies of entertainment programs suggest that corporations and business people are routinely portrayed as villains; Daddy Warbucks long ago gave way to J. R. Ewing. Also, much of Ginsberg's diagnosis depends on the belief that high socioeconomic status people watch news and public affairs programming and that the content of this programming has been adapted to suit the audience; yet his analysis of how the lower socioeconomic status people get their false consciousness assumes that they are watching and being influenced by the same programs.

A mourner would say that a lack of education is a lack of immunity to ideology, but Ginsberg cannot deploy this strategy, for he also argues that education is an ideologically charged medium of class suppression. Jefferson and Lippmann would say that education is supposed to housebreak the young into the folkways of the power elite. But this is Ginsberg's point: The rhetoric of mass enfranchisement dilutes lower socioeconomic status rebellion; it coopts the discourse by pushing a value structure advantageous to elites.

Ginsberg is half oracle, half mourner, and all populist. He can be seen as, razor at the ready, warily circling the connoisseurs—especially Lippmann—and reserving a special scorn for Locke's proposal for weighted voting. His exposition turns on a nineteenth-century view of class, and it has more a religious than scientific tone. Indeed his causal reasoning contradicts his picture of class effects. He argues that lower class people are under the spell of media content and so have no class identity to speak of. But here the priest-role of the oracle gets the upper hand, for Ginsberg sees an underlying reality that may unify the voiceless working classes regardless of their thoughts. In the same vein, Garnham (1986, 44) charges that Negt and Kluge's (1979) view of the public sphere collapses to a "mysticism that attempts to ground its universality not in a consensus reached after rational debate between competing interests, but in a Lukacsian notion of an imputed class consciousness which is inherently universal."

Privileged visions are often self-sealing arguments. Oracles dismiss, for instance, the differences among the beliefs held by African Americans, say, versus Ku Klux Klanners as symptoms of a reality only oracles see. And in much the same spirit, oracles insist on pathologizing plebeian tastes. The pabulum on television doesn't just reflect the fact that people prefer it. It must be an effect of the connoisseur's machinations, a plot that Birnbaum (1988), who can fairly be called a Great Books Marxist, describes as "the cretinization of the public."

At this point, the oracle is a sitting duck for the ironist's artillery. The issues that would unite the lower class—race, nationalism, war, and religion—are just the things oracles fear. But why use this line of argument? The oracle wants to convince capitalism's victims that they are victims, that their participation in democracy is emptier than it seems, that they should see past the vacuous entertainment on television, and that they can build political action around points of agreement (the poor African American shares poverty with the Ku Kluxer). Outsiderness, in other words, can be seen as an argument, not a mystical state. What the oracle needs to do is figure out how to make equality and justice outweigh race and nationalism.

It is odd that the connoisseurs share the oracles' penchant for speaking of elites and masses as distinct, homogeneous groups. Dye and Zeigler (1981) say that elitism (the theory) groups elites by wealth and a fundamental consensus on values (they disagree only about tactics). Oracles have a theory-confirming interest in sweeping generalizations about class, but connoisseurs, one would think, have an interest in noticing the rough-grained texture of organizational structures—governance and power so multilayered as to be effectively invisible. Hence the second economy: Specialized expertise has created so many strata in complex organizations that the idea of class seems extraneous. Any organization driven by technologies, facts, and programs is reliant on experts. The possession of knowledge or technical proficiency is thus functionally analogous to the possession of wealth.

A general elites-masses contrast seems less useful than one between specialists and governing elites, the former regarding the latter in much the way elite theorists say elites regard the general public or in the way Fleck says that esoteric specialists regard general practitioners. The oracles can still speak for the disenfranchised and still point to inequities of wealth and power; the connoisseurs can still insist on the importance of excellence—the value of elitism, if you will. But if both stop talking about the masses, they will see the predicament of the elites.

TECHNICAL VERSUS PUBLIC AND *ECONOMIC VERSUS PUBLIC* DISCOURSE

Since the 1930s, the claim that technical discourses are co-opting public discourse has been commonplace. It is typified by Habermas's denunciation of the modernist fallacy—cloaking decisions and policies in counterfeit technical justifications. Matters that are not technical are made to seem technical. A scientistic ideology thus masks cynical strategies. It is fitting to call this a fallacy. Fallacy theory stresses spurious resemblances: Flimsy reasoning masquerades as sound argument by donning the mask of authority. Thus, if a psychiatrist can be hired to prove almost any claim in court—the defendant is (is not) dangerous, is (is not) schizophrenic, etc.—then forensic psychiatry's "scientific" status needs puncturing.

In this vein, Goodnight (1982, 1989) distinguishes between *public* and *technical* discourses and reserves *rhetoric* for distinctly public matters: "Rhetorical argument addresses those topics that extend beyond individual concerns and reside outside the margins of technical reason. Its forum, the public sphere, is comprised of a community of nonspecialized interlocutors who participate in ongoing discussion, debate, and decision-making about common rights and duties, matters of collective preference, contingent choices, and responses to events that could come out this way or that" (Goodnight 1987b, 139). Technical discourses, in other words, are nonrhetorical, and with this claim, I think, a mistake has crept into the modernist fallacy. To say that technical discourses are not rhetorical is to play into a self-defeating language game: Goodnight's distinction strengthens his enemies: It confirms the self-definitions of the prime villains—cost-benefit analysis and policy science—and endorses their claims to special privilege. One takes the logical positivist at face value and is left holding the rhetoric versus reality bag. Goodnight can as easily take the opposite tack: To see the sciences as rhetorically constituted debunks their aura of invincibility.

It is plausible to see technical discourses as rhetorical, as using argument, debate, and ethos, and sometimes succumbing to social contagion. One can read the rhetoric of inquiry and social epistemology literatures very skeptically and still conclude that the sciences are rhetorically constituted (Fuller 1988, Lyne 1989, 1990a, 1990b, Lyne and Howe 1986, 1990, McCloskey 1983, 1985, 1987, Mulkay 1979, Nelson 1983, Nelson and Megill 1986, Nelson, Megill, and McCloskey 1987, Weimer 1979, 1984, Whitley 1986, Zaltman 1968).

And why insist that public issues are not technical when it is so easy to point to genuinely technical questions—ones that don't fit the modernist fallacy? For instance, risk arguments arise in debates about the environment, disarmament, nuclear power, forensic psychiatry (predicting the dangerousness of defendants); indeed there are few public issues for which risk assessment is irrelevant. Risk arguments characteristically involve technical measurement and political argumentation: One defines the risks and says what levels of risk are acceptable (Hynes 1987). Environmental and energy arguments are thus measurement-dependent (how does one argue properly that fossil fuels are harmful without drawing inferences from SO_2 and SOX emissions?).

Nor is this mingling of technical and political rhetorics harmful. Think pedagogically: The disciplines are our benchmarks of competence; it is hard to describe competent public discourse in any other terms. Imagine, for instance, that you set out to refute my earlier claim about the vacuous state of public discourses. You would go about it by arguing from example: "here is Senator *X* making economic arguments; she isn't as inept as Willard claims; her points are well-proved, she makes the right claims; and her inferences from evidence seem sound." These judgments imply technical standards from economics and argumentation, against which the senator's performance is weighed. They imply that sound public discourse to some extent mimics the relevant technical discourses. The mourners' program, it seems to me, turns on such "disciplinization."

Goodnight presumes that the electronic agora will have a discourse expressing human concerns that differ in kind from technical concerns, that, freed of technical claims, a genuine public consensus is possible. But how will he measure it? In a democracy of 250 million, how can a consensus emerge except through demographic statistics, polling, and perhaps interactive cable? This is technical discourse par excellence. Given Ginsberg's (1986) claim that polling creates its own realities (indeed that public opinion is an artifact of polling techniques, and often a sham perpetuated by pollster-advocates), the measurement of public consensus is as open to abuse as cost-benefit analysis, but potentially worse because it "covers its own technologies" (Beisecker 1989, 69).

Mourners and oracles are drawn to the technical versus public distinction by their concern for unity. They attribute democracy's disintegration to loss of shared purpose. They want equality and justice to function as grand, unifying abstractions. They have lost the Dewey-Lippmann faith in science but want the "moral equivalent of war" to be a rhetoric of equality and justice, and they think that technical discourses are about means while (genuinely) public discourse is about ends.

But the means-ends distinction obstructs their argument. A rhetoric of equality and justice that is not largely a technical discourse will be mostly arm-waving. Argumentation about poverty, homelessness, inequality, and injustice is more competent when linked to measurement. Arguments about solutions presuppose claims about causality and magnitude that would be empty bombast without evidence. So what counts as evidence is central to determining what the achievement of equality and justice in society would mean. And if the bad guys are skewing the statistics to paper over poverty, etc., one exposes the lie by engaging the measurements.

So the problem of authority goes deeper than the modernist fallacy. It is a genuine dilemma. Authority-dependence allows technical discourses to dominate public life and deprives public actors of a basis for distinguishing fallacious from sound authority, yet most public questions are technical or symbiotic with technical questions. We often *should* rely on authority. Specialism and disciplines are indispensable, so acquiescence to authority is more often than not the rational thing to do. So what the modernist fallacy needs, I should think, is to be divorced from vague visions of general discourse and related instead to the intervening variables between local realities and general discourses, namely, modern organizations, the subject of the second half of this book.

Now let's consider the technical versus public distinction, its Marxist ancestor, economic versus public, and its critical theory cousin, private versus public:

> Within the political realm the individual is defined as a citizen exercising public rights [debating, voting] . . . within a communally agreed structure of rules and towards communally defined ends. The value system is essentially social and the legitimate end of social action is the public good. Within the economic realm, on the other hand, the individual is defined as producer and consumer exercising private rights through purchasing power on the market in the pursuit of private interests, his or her actions being coordinated by the invisible hand of the market (Garnham 1986, 46).

What the critical theorist wants to say is that the values of the latter have infected the former. Advertising and public relations appeal to consumers, not citizens. Publics should seek nobler ends than self-interest because there is no invisible hand to make countless acts of Hobbesian greed sum up to benevolent utility. As opposed to the utilitarian's rational actor, citizens value justice, fairness, equity, tolerance, and freedom—the public values (Reich 1988) that make public spiritedness a kind of altruism.

Unfortunately, what critical theorists do say is that the distinction between public and private is a feature of the discourse itself. Habermas holds that his felicity conditions are wired into the essence of communication. Garnham doubts this claim (as do, so far as I know, all communication theorists), but he argues that the public sphere is different from the private on economic grounds. His goal is to recostume the liberal theory of the press to grapple with "the fundamental contradiction between the economic and political at the level of their value systems and of the social relations those values support" (ibid., 46).

This thinking can be made less a matter of essence than of linguistic imperialism and a side effect of practices. The reasoning is similar to my earlier claim that taking Positivism at face value plays into a self-defeating language game. First, one concedes that people translate value preferences into utilitarian terms. The recurring complaint in the organizational literature is that corporations cast everything into cost-benefit language, and environmentalists argue that defining nature by its utility to humans makes it impossible to express what we most care about (Tribe, Schelling, and Voss 1976). But this translation doesn't occur because greed and altruism differ in kind. Utilitarian thinking is simply easier.

My corridor colleague Shirley Willihnganz has pointed out that it is easier for banks to make loans on purely economic grounds (the applicant's debt, liquidity, etc.) than to ask harder questions: Is the proposed project socially worthy? Does this loan create a competitor who may harm other loans we have made? Should we make this loan because it helps a disadvantaged minority? If greed and altruism are oil and water, we would always find greed triumphant. But some banks in fact ask the harder questions. We ought to wonder how and why.

Corporations are widely thought to behave benevolently for a bad reason—public relations, putting a happy face on Hobbes. Behind this demonology is an expressive view of communication: Organizations should be like honest human beings earnestly expressing public concerns. Still, public spiritedness creates binding conventional contracts. Once the avaricious corporation commits itself to a public relations stance, it can be held accountable in new ways, and the tendency of fiscal thinking to translate everything to its own terms is but one face that can be put on it. Not everyone dichotomizes greed and altruism. Organizational theorists, public figures, and even corporate executives often make arguments for tempering greed. From a rhetorical perspective, the fact that they take these positions at all is sheer possibility.

None of this is to deny that organizations and people are often reckless and greedy. The question is whether a case for public spiritedness can be made that transcends the devil on one shoulder and angel on the other. This dichotomy plays into the hands of the greedy by feeding the prejudice that the opposite view can't be expressed rationally. But environmentalists have gotten around this to a degree: Their shared risk arguments play well, even in corporate America.

Garnham's thinking provides the segue to the next mistake: the assumption that the public sphere is a town meeting writ large. The search for what is left after "a rational debate between competing interests" supposes that the public sphere is an argument field. Thus "public opinion is distinguished from mere opinion as presupposing the existence of a reasoning public" (Garnham 1986, 42). The legitimation of the modern state, à la Habermas, "lies in its role of guarantor of the public sphere through law" (ibid.). But where, I now want to ask, will we find the public sphere? And in a world of 500 channels, what will the public sphere look like?

AUTHENTICITY REDUX: THE ELECTRONIC AGORA

The subject of television brings connoisseurs, oracles and mourners together like strangers at an accident scene and has provoked, as we have seen, more fulminating prose than any of the subjects we have considered. And of all the high crimes and misdemeanors of which it stands accused television's worst offense is that—Mitroff and Bennis (1989, 19) interrupt our regular programming with this bulletin—"What we see on TV is not 'the real thing.'"

In other words, Geneva's First Citizen is back, bristling with indignation, hoping to inspire an "informed, moral outrage" (ibid., xxv) and to save the people from their trifling amusements: "A pervading, powerful sense of unreality infiltrates the land." "TV not only defines what is reality, but much more importantly and disturbingly, TV obliterates the very distinction, the very line between reality and unreality" (ibid., xxi). If "the fact of the matter is that the U.S. today lacks a true purpose to give meaning to people's lives, [then] great, true leaders and myths are therefore necessary to stem the tide" (ibid., 193).

The merry old Calvinism behind this thinking can be appreciated by noticing that television is only one of the barbarians at the gate. Amusement parks are also Lucifer's handiwork, and from what one reads in the papers, reality has had a narrow escape in Virginia, where the Disney company hoped to build a glitzy variation on Colonial Williamsburg—an amusement park featuring American historical themes. The threat was thwarted by a number of factors, including a parade of eminent historians who condemned the unreality of synthetic history.

An amusement park, I should think, could be inauthentic only by virtue of being unamusing. The Disney parks notoriously promote a whiggish technology worship, though it has all the subtlety of North Korean propaganda. So what is the illocutionary force of denouncing an amusement park? Why do prominent historians bother? Do they want Brugges or Colonial Williamsburg, for example, to be more accurate mirrors of medieval and colonial life, complete with sewage in the streets and costumed actors condemned to short life spans? Disney could no doubt design a ride in which people would actually get bubonic plague.

But if, as I prefer to think, verisimilitude of this sort isn't quite what the critics want, then what do they want? The answer admittedly is between the lines, but as one reads the dozen or so most recent books by television's severest critics and the various denunciations of amusement parks, one finds that authenticity is code for a more primitive intuition. What the champions of authenticity want is good-old Calvinist seriousness. The mortal sin of popular amusements is, quite simply, that they are amusing.

Consider, for instance, America's most famous one-man Pantheon. One would scarcely call the Lincoln Memorial amusing. There is nothing frivolous about standing in awe of monumental greatness. And standing in awe, as any connoisseur would point out, is the whole point. Monuments are supposed to humble us into citizenship, to infuse us with the myths that Mitroff and Bennis think we need. And verisimilitude, of course, is not the point, for so far as I know, no one has ever attacked the Lincoln Memorial as synthetic history, though more literal minds might point out that Mr. Lincoln wasn't really that large and that the Gettysburg Address wasn't really cast in bronze.

But there is, or used to be, another Lincoln memorial, at Disneyland, of all places. The attraction involved being seated in a replica of an old-fashioned lecture hall and watching an automaton Lincoln rise from a chair and deliver the Gettysburg Address. This is synthetic history, certainly. For authenticity, the speech would need to be delivered out-of-doors and be inaudible to two-thirds of the audience. But the marvel, of course, was the technology, how lifelike this simulacrum was. Not, mind you, how Lincoln-like it was, though I can report that the question of verisimilitude did come up. I once sat through this presentation with a ten-year-old who asked, as we walked out, a question that fairly captures the stakes in the authenticity issue: "Did he really sound like that?"

Inquiring minds, apparently, *do* want to know; and this question, to be sure, can spark a moment of Baudrillardian panic. If one sees history—à la Foucault—as an interrogation of documents, and expects the documents to authentically recreate the experience of the Gettysburg Address, then one might well get caught up in "a pervading, powerful sense of unreality." What with the real Mr. Lincoln being dead and all, we cannot recapture his cadence and kinesics, the timbre of his voice, the shifts of his gaze. All we have is Raymond Massey and his replicant, the Disney automaton. They are hyperreal—more real to us, as a moving, speaking human, than the real Mr. Lincoln.

Perhaps we should amend Disney's warning signs: "This ride not recommended for pregnant women or persons prone to motion sickness or Baudrillardian panic." People prone to the latter are better off on the Dumbo ride where—one hopes, at least—verisimilitude is not an issue. But if, as I imagine, the champions of authenticity wouldn't be caught dead on the Dumbo ride, not because it is an unreal recreation of the *actual* experience of riding a flying elephant, but because it is undignified, then we have a glimmering of what is at stake. No one, I submit, of any age, has ever left Disney's Lincoln under the impression that they have seen the real Mr. Lincoln or heard the real Gettysburg Address. But one does leave the Lincoln Memorial under the impression that one has experienced something very deep and real. So when proponents of the latter sort of experience denounce the former, the issue is what Lord Byron called the "evil of pleasures and the pleasures of evil." The point—it is a musty old point—is that "the happiest place on earth" needs a new motto—perhaps a yellow public health notice with Seneca's words: "the evils of idleness can be shaken off by hard work."

Those who wouldn't be caught dead on flying elephants often have the same attitude toward television, which leads me to a more serious argument. For as one reads television's severest critics—I encourage you to check me on this—one gets the distinct sense that they don't watch much television. For out of the 60 or so channels currently available, they focus on the ones most suitable to their blanket dismissals, namely "the networks," whose programming seeks the widest possible audience.

This focus on mass programming has a certain ideological value to oracles, who attribute television's fatuity to the machinations of the connoisseurs. With this expectation and demonology, calamity-howling comes easy, for mass programming predictably fails the test. And as the networks are owned by the wealthy, the demonology is confirmed.

But mass programming is a notorious sitting duck: It requires sparse codes; it prefers narrative and pictorial images—communicative modes that disprefer rational argumentation. It favors goose bump events: disasters, rescues, wars, and ceremonies. And ultimately, though many hope to improve the quality of *infotainment,* most print journalists would say that the networks are what they are. There are upper limits to what they can be, not, as the usual criticism has it, because of the nature of the medium, but because they seek the biggest possible audiences.

If the focus on mass programming is uncomfortably analogous to denouncing the Dumbo ride for its lack of informational content, it is also quite misleading, for there are 55 or so other channels, not all of which can be dismissed as, to use the famous (thirty-year-old) phrase, a "vast wasteland." *Cardiology Update* on Lifetime can scarcely be dismissed as infotainment; and it would be interesting to see how the arguments would go to condemn as wastelands the Discovery Channel, for example, or the Learning Channel, Arts and Entertainment, or the "regionals," the new all-talk and all-news networks.

Indeed I suggest an experiment: Spend a full day, if you can stomach it, watching CNBC or C-SPAN. During commercials, or lulls, read Postman (1989). And then at the end of the day, hold Postman's book in your hands and ask the ten-year-old's question: Is this what television is really like?

Of course there is also the question of what television ought to be like, and many oracles and mourners focus less on authenticity than on idealizations of what television might accomplish. It might, for instance, be the vehicle for an earnest political community—the global village as town meeting. Whether we would *want* this is an open question: A study of a small Vermont town by Mansbridge (1976) suggests that town meetings can be dominated by cliques and characterized by considerable inequality. But to my mind, the decisive question for television's severest critics is this: If C-SPAN, CNBC, and CNN do not realize the electronic agora, then what would?

One can only speculate about what the world will be like once five hundred channels and the new viewer-demand technologies are up and running. Tocqueville's couch potatoes will have, no doubt, a more expansive menu of "paltry pleasures," and market segmentation, in all that expanse, will likely follow profits. The result in some respects will be more of the same—more QVCs and shopping channels, more sports channels, and—

Heaven help us—more religious channels. But "more of the same" is likely subject to diminishing returns, and in the long run, whatever turns a coin will find a niche. So if we now have a science fiction channel and four (that I know of) adult channels, can other genres be far behind? Mystery, war, and romance channels are already in the works, and by some reports, networks are being planned for bikers, travelers, hunters, joggers, and paramilitarists.

Whether this plethora will equal, or even surpass, magazine publishing in sheer numbers may be a technological question. To start up a magazine, one needs enough venture capital to pay for presses, paper, content, and distribution. To start a network one needs only a modicum of equipment, so the unknowns are the costs of the content and the space on fiber-optic cable. But the greater unknown is—as with magazines—how small a network's audience can be and still be profitable. For that, I submit, will determine the degree to which the electronic emulates the specialization of magazines.

Nonetheless, the standard prediction is that we will have five hundred channels, and the question, it seems to me, is where, amid all this, will we find Dewey's public sphere, and what will be on it? I don't think the answer is more of the same. CNN and C-SPAN can be endlessly cloned, but they already serve relatively narrow audiences. So the likeliest outcome is a relatively modest proliferation of more specialized news and public affairs channels targeted to relatively narrower audiences. It is a virtual certainty—like taxes and potholes—that every state legislature will find its mini-C-SPAN. City and county commissions in some places already have them.

These channels, I predict, will be watched chiefly by journalists and elderly farmers—people devoted to complaining about the government full time. But it isn't inconceivable that something of quality will turn up—perhaps the Progressive Channel; and it's entirely possible that its content will be more of the same, only more so—more news, debates, congressional hearings, and discussions. It will appeal to a very narrow audience—the people who actually track public issues. And it will do about as well as can be expected, which is to say it will utterly falsify the liberal theory of the press. For one network won't do to get "the information" to the people. Assuming seven or eight networks devoted exclusively to publicizing government secrets, a like number devoted to publicizing the contents of corporate data bases, and another ten or so networks devoted exclusively to deliberating about the meaning of all that information, the result might well be the numbing of the American mind. And that is the least of it, for the liberal theory of the press expects citizens to track whole discourses and to integrate all that information into an ecumenical general knowledge.

Intellectuals will never, I suppose, get entirely weaned away from denouncing popular amusements. Harrumphing at the peasants for not bettering themselves is the sort of thing teachers are given to. We come by it naturally. And in this spirit the improvement of television is a perfectly worthy goal, as long as it doesn't interfere with the trash I like to watch. But television is arguably an empty ritual kill, and a rather misleading one. It is a straw man—that has been my argument here. And it is an empty gesture, for assuming that the electronic agora springs fully to life, no one has a clear idea of what its content will be. And that, as the second half of this book will argue, is another story.

CODA: A TIMEOUT FOR THE DISCOURSE OF LIBERAL DEMOCRACY

So liberalism is of three minds—three emotional *Gestalts* that color three much too distinct theoretical positions and thus very different versions of the crisis of the public. These dueling demonologies have made for a dysfunctional discourse—a battle of expansive calls, ringing denunciations, vapor-ware proposals, and poor listening habits. Admittedly, in modulating the three voices, I have likely manhandled the reasons why people find holding these views satisfying. The connoisseurs are left with a Pyrrhic victory over the populists; the oracles have given up their most rhetorically effective contrast (indeed the Marxism that remains seems to owe more to Groucho than Karl); and the mourners are left with the uncomfortable suspicion that their pedagogies are largely following a connoisseur's path. To all three, perhaps, the surrender of realism may seem a high price indeed for embarking on a not-entirely-attractive joint venture.

But think of it this way: Your decision to follow me into the second half of this book will scarcely disturb the universe. All three discourses will keep going, in all likelihood, at full tilt. The most that will happen is that a few in each camp will be persuaded that the discourse of liberal democracy needs a different way of thinking about knowledge problems. The most unrepentant connoisseur can entertain the possibility that she needs a way to think about authority-dependence, fragmentation, unmanageable literatures, and so on. And the most zealous oracles and mourners can still entertain the proposition that many problems of liberal democracy call for more, not less, expertise.

The question isn't whether one class or another is better suited to govern. As Lord Acton said, "every class is unfit to govern." Nor is the question whether corporate power dominates political life. Of course it does. The question I want to pose is quite a different one. For if modern democracies must to some extent be elite oligarchies, can they at least be made to function more competently than they do—and perhaps a bit more democratically?

PART II

Discourse across Differences

Conflict, Dewey said, is how a democracy thinks. By give-and-take, argument and counter-argument, concession and compromise, a democracy reasons its way across time—existing less in its formal institutions than in the communicated experience of its citizens. It survives by protecting the public spaces where reflective self-monitoring flourishes, and it matures by nurturing its critics. The intelligence of democracy thus lies in the quality of its conversation, in the expertise, temperance, and precision of its discourse.

Whether this vision should inspire confidence—or panic in the streets—depends partly, I suppose, on whether pragmatist virtues can be made of federalist necessities. In *Federalist* 10 the virtue of size is that no single faction can fully triumph. The virtue of uncertainty (about whether good decisions will be made or capable people will be elected) is that it points unerringly to the one thing that can be trusted. The virtue of opposition is that it checks power even assuming the worst. Assuming no self-restraint or civic spiritedness, factions will either wear themselves out or sort things out, much as predators and scavengers sort things out over a carcass. To govern such goings-on, the only necessities are the coercive power of law and decision-making procedures braced, as it were, for total war.

But Dewey, let's say, was more optimistic. He envisioned a malleable future, indeed a creative, progressive discourse. He saw conflict, "the gadfly of thought," as an indispensable spark for reflection and inquiry and as a method for testing and improving ideas. In government and science alike, contingencies and indeterminacies spark discussion and debate. And out of the clash of ideas emerge stronger ideas—ones that have not merely escaped falsification but that have adapted to the opposition and thus changed for the better. "Warranted assertability" was thus a corporate achievement, and if it had a certain Darwinian ring—suggesting, so to speak, the survival of the fittest ideas—it was unquestionably a gentler vision than Madison's. And it is this spirit of things—that dead ends are invitations to creativity—that I have tried to capture in arguing that democracy's critics should try not to want total victories, that they needn't behave like lawyers locking horns.

But it remains to be seen whether there is a principled difference between tinkering with other people's ideas and manhandling them. And it is an open question whether Dewey's pragmatism offers anything better than the pluralists' invisible hand. For Dewey asked philosophers to leave comprehensive intellectual mastery to the future. He promised no rose garden, certainly, no final truth. But he argued that the future would be better than the past, that each generation's confusions would give way to more interesting ones. So even though individuals neither can nor should seek comprehensive epistemic mastery, there are grounds for optimism: Something will turn up.

This faith comes easy *if* one trusts the intellectual institutions of modernity. Listen, for instance, to an eminent organizational theorist:

> Knowledge is a collective, social product only imperfectly represented in any one mind. Therefore, properties of a field such as its theoretical power, record of verification, and integration are social products that are imperfectly represented in the work of any one scientist (Campbell 1969).
>
> If I cannot see the coherence in organizational theory, and neither can Whitley (1984), McGuire (1982), or Astley (1984), that does not mean it is not there. Coherence may exist collectively even though our limited rationality may not grasp it. If individuals can never know their field in its entirety, then theorizing boils down to an act of faith that collective omniscience is significant and growing. (Weick 1987, 118)

Weick is proceeding as if his field *somehow works*. Mastery is sharpest locally and fuzziest globally. Local horizons compress one's field of vision, so one can only hope that collective omniscience will eventually compensate for the confusions of diversity. And the truth, by implication, won't literally set us free, "not because there is no truth or freedom to be had, but because the two are not integrally involved with one another: truth is too unwieldy to be practical, and practicality is too local to encompass the whole truth" (Steve Fuller, private correspondence).

This *invisible mind* is more premise than promise. Weick is gesturing to mystery not to explain how his field works but why actors within it should continue to work. Surrendering the conceits of individualism, accepting one's finitude, that one's Cartesian ego can be crammed with only so much holistic knowledge, one makes a Pascal's wager, as it were, on one's field—a decision to tend one's garden while betting on the growth of a collective omniscience one can't fully see.

But I would not bet the farm on organizational studies—not, at least, if growing omniscience is understood to mean the assimilation of more and more cases into a single theory. Organizations grow, we will see, by adapting to endlessly diverse circumstances. So it isn't inconceivable that Weick and his colleagues can't see the collective coherence of their field because it isn't there.

And if one distrusts one's intellectual institutions, if these collective arrangements seem dangerous in a Foucauldian way, one may doubt the likelihood of progress, and wonder whether the problem of knowledge will turn out to be just another crisis, one more intractable predicament to add to the frustrations of history, legitimacy, and identity.

Still, one can say of organizational studies (and of many rational enterprises) what individualist treatises often say of "Man": Fields know, and know that they know, and wonder how they know. They try not to leave their reflective thinking to chance or individual minds. They may get lost in their literatures, but instead of pushing on resignedly, they sometimes search for new ideas; they travel abroad to sample wicked delights and alien heresies. And travelers, I submit, leave trails. They cross borders; they make customs declarations. And when they return with souvenirs, they are sometimes greeted in well-documented ways. If they are noticed, and not met with indifference, they spark unusually explicit greetings. For alien ideas, whether greeted by confrontations or warm embraces, prompt moments of reflection, points at which fields are most on guard against Fullerian opinion drift. At such moments, the persistence and change of ideas is rarely left to an invisible mind. The field, to some extent, "shows its hand."

The study of such moments won't complete each field's history, filling in all the gaps and thus producing an unbroken rational train of progress. It may soften or enrich textbook certitudes by appreciating the uncertainty within which knowledge is created (Latour 1987) and the importance of working certainties (Weick 1987). Not knowing how things will turn out, one hopes to get lucky. One provisionally trusts one's technology; one takes data on faith, on the ethos of other scientists. Such risk management, and roads not taken, may be indistinct or invisible in the historical record. Decisions may thus seem inexplicable or, with the wisdom of hindsight, inevitable.

But as people struggle with the legitimacy and fitness of particular ideas and policies, they deploy strategies for managing knowledge problems, and there is much to be learned from their successes and failures. If meaning and truth lie in their effects on situated action, then they are to some extent determinate, analyzable features of real discourse in real organizations, and among such concrete affairs, the situations that spark the most explicitness may prove to be the most instructive and perhaps the most reassuring to Foucauldians.

This proposal depends on a division of labor, indeed a sizable expert field. And this field, I contend, is already forming. Epistemics, of course, stems from an old intuition, that the departmental lines subdividing the humanities and social sciences are purely bureaucratic, but it involves a new modesty. Scholars are behaving as if other fields can problematize their knowledge, as if disciplinary sovereignty is an impediment. They are invoking other fields' ideas, citing outside authorities to solve internal problems. They are avoiding mainstream journals by publishing in alien fields or creating new journals. And they are doing all this, some of them at least, without the humanist's faith in general knowledge.

So what sort of field will epistemics be? Does it seek covering laws, falsification, letting a thousand flowers bloom, or keeping the conversation going? The first two may happen locally, and there is nothing wrong with the latter two, but epistemics is chiefly interested in the movement of influence across borders, in the ebb and flow of consensus as a special case of persuasion, and in the losses that occur as knowledge claims are translated across different levels of discourse complexity.

In describing any field, the thing to avoid is an "over-psychologized" picture. Communication scholars use this expression to describe theories that make individuals so cognitively unique as to preclude communication. Similarly, the way analysts and field actors describe a field's internal organization circumscribes what they are able and prone to say about discourse at its borders. If it is seen as a closed system, it will seem to have centrifugal force. The paradigm cases at its center will be immunized against outside ideas; peripheral discourses will be marginalized and stigmatized. The field will seem autistic: Locked in its private world, it can conserve but not innovate.

But if a field is seen as a living environment, a synergism of people, practices, and ideas engaged with local realities defined as much by its interactions with neighbors as by its internal structure, then peripheral discourses will seem pivotal to innovation. So chapter 7 introduces epistemics by looking first at its communication practices. Then, much as we impute inner traits to people on the basis of their behavior, we will work our way toward the field's innards and discover therein a way to describe differences that doesn't preclude discourse across differences. The enabling assumption is that size makes for complexity: Big fields are mélanges.

As their myriad subfields grind through normal science and butt heads in overt competition, peripheral fields multiply, sometimes with only tenuous links to the professional identity holding the big field together, and often with stronger connections with other peripheral fields. They function rather like synapses: Information passes, so to speak, from the axon of one border field to the dendrites of another. They are gateways for alien ideas that sharpen the tensions between conservation and innovation. For diffusion makes some yearn for a center that will hold, yet sparks in others the delights of novelty—hence the jostles and jolts among locals and cosmopolitans.

Chapter 8 proposes the "argument field" as a unit of analysis. By argument I mean polemical conversation, disagreement, or dispute, which I take to be the principle medium by which people maintain, relate, adapt, transform, and discard ideas (Willard 1989a). People make their cases. They take positions (public stances rigged for conventional battle). The claims in positions are grounded in particular discourses; so a field description is a template we create to aid the scrutiny of disputes: We interpret advocates' positions by inferring the backgrounds they presuppose—the traditions, practices, ideas, and methods of particular groups. The *field,* then, is a social entity defined as much by its disputes as by its agreements. And if this seems sociologically quirky, as it plainly is, we have the word *community,* remember, for groups with more agreement than disagreement.

Chapter 9 argues that fields are organizations, not impersonal bodies of knowledge: They are animated by practices, harnessed to mundane realities. Organizations are explicit attempts to fit intentions to practices. Their rationalities lie in concrete cases in which knowledge is created, used, and changed. They differ because they are functionally fitted to different aims, methods, and contexts. But in one sense or another, each field has its version of "laboratory life" (Latour and Woolgar 1979).

Once you have heard me out on the possibilities for studying the organizational bases of knowledge, you may wonder whether the spirit of rhetorical disarmament has been carried too far, whether a fixation on the intelligence of democracy is ignoring, at its peril, certain habits of the heart. If the melting pot culture is as powerful as Marxists say, do liberals dare surrender their rhetorics? Won't the search for distributive justice lose its voice? And if, on the other hand, the melting pot is as fragile as Senator Moynihan believes, then if we cease to speak of states and civic life as if they are surrogates for the *meaning of life* and *human condition,* haven't we left democracy vulnerable to zealots?

Democracy will always be vulnerable. Demagoguery has a virus-like quality: It can't be killed without killing the host. The best to be hoped for is symptomatic relief. And though Moynihan and Schlesinger may have overlooked some of the pot's strengths, I did not, remember, accuse them of calamity-howling. Still, I would venture the bold suggestion that results might count for something. Most liberals, surely, would be encouraged—and even libertarians might pause to gape in awe—at the spectacle of a welfare state actually producing some welfare. The tragedy as I see it isn't a *heartless system.* From the New Deal, to the Great Society, to even the stingiest Republican administrations, the system has pumped billions into trying to be a welfare state. Its successes and failures will be debated endlessly no doubt; but no one counts high-rise ghettos and family assistance programs that destroy families as crowning successes of social engineering; and no one, so far as I know, has declared victory in the War on Poverty.

It would be wrong, certainly, to blame experts alone: From the 1960s on, old-time puritanism, howling in from the hinterlands, has ensured that government would throw only slogans at the problem of teenage pregnancies, thus perpetuating, in large measure, all the ills of the poverty cycle. This failure has fueled the political right's penchant for demonizing big government as a miasma of pork barrels, corruption, and waste. And as there has always been an uncomfortable grain of truth in that critique, it is scarcely surprising that Mencken's "mean-spirited cruelties" are once again being "discussed gravely as logical ideas." As I write this, orphanages are back, Big Bird is an endangered species, constitutional amendments are queuing up like welfare recipients, and a perfectly scandalous demagoguery is passing as commonsense economics. One senses at such moments that expertise plays no role at all.

But if I have succeeded in demonstrating that democracy's critics can be rhetorically distinguishable from Mencken's circus, it remains to be seen whether expertise can function as an alternative to it. So the immediate question is whether epistemics has anything of value to say to the welfare state. Call it bleeding heart pluralism if you must, but on this topic, epistemics does have something to say.

It will seem modest and technocratic. Chapter 10 reopens the question of how expertise can best mingle with policy-making by focusing on procedural principles. It argues that the traditional views of presumption are Enlightenment dinosaurs. The conservative presumption (things should stay as they are unless a burden of proof is overcome by the advocate of change) and the liberal presumption (things as they are reflect past expediencies, so in cases of doubt we should prefer change to preservation) are pieties masquerading as principles. They rule out the epistemic presumption, that all expertise is piecemeal, that no expert's span of vision is likely to encompass the whole of a public problem, and thus that no single expert should dominate any deliberative stage.

This conclusion is not new, certainly. It is a commonplace of the antitechnocracy literature (e.g., Fischer 1990). But that literature, having made the case that specialism by its very nature makes one incompetent in policy matters, then characteristically gestures to the public, or to the best and brightest among them who are elected as representatives. Democracy is thus expected to triumph over expertise, to govern its discourses with a value-laden practical knowledge that is commonsensical, accessible, and teachable. But the devil, as usual, is in the details. Government by phronesis is arguably an emptier gesture than the pluralists' invisible hand; so chapter 11 centers on the problem of evaluating expertise and on the obstacles to translation across differences in discourse complexity. It argues indeed that a new expertise must be invented and that both scientists and journalists are overly optimistic in thinking that this expertise already exists.

Chapter 12 compares liberalism and epistemics as models for newly emerging democracies. It muses about federated Europe's tenuous grasp on a postmodern future and the coexistence of nineteenth-century and twenty-first-century ambitions. Nationalist revivals, big and small, mean that the shallow quotation of nationalisms will be tricky going. Beyond that, there is the question of what ought to happen whenever nascent democracies turn to mature democracies for advice. The sudden collapse of a police state forces a nation to redesign its domestic and foreign affairs simultaneously. At such critical moments, the last thing in the world such nations need is identity politics—or the message that the transnational organizations vital to their futures are beyond critique and control. They need, rather, a way to think about civic rights and interdependence.

There will not, incidentally, be even a whiff of utopianism in the pages to follow. My arguments will not suppose organizations to be more principled than states. And there will be no *end of the state* bravura. Though global interdependencies may change postindustrial states, my arguments will assume that the welfare state, be it republican minimalist or Great Society colossus, will always be with us. Epistemics is the study of rhetorical possibilities, but the art of the possible begins with constraints. Argument fields, and organizations in general, are conventional structures whose inertia and momentum resist precisely the rhetorical achievements that would be most beneficial to organizations: controversy and open borders. So the tensions between expressive, conventional, and rhetorical resources will flare up once again at the end. For standing against organizational solutions is the primitive and romantic expressive, the originator of the themes with which this book began and the antagonist in a melodrama with which it will end.

SEVEN

Epistemics

Some time ago, Geertz (1980, 168) claimed that "a radical alteration in the sociological imagination" was underway. A blurring of genres was reconfiguring the social sciences, "not just another redrawing of the cultural map . . . but an alteration of the principles of mapping. Something is happening to the way we think about the way we think" (ibid., 166). Social scientists, it seemed, were putting the social back into the science. They were abandoning the natural sciences as ideal types—debunking claims about moral neutrality, objectivity, covering laws, and unified science. And they were replacing Cartesian individualism with a focus on group rationalities, on knowledge as group property. The new analogies were the *game* (owed to Wittgenstein, von Neuman, and Goffman), the *drama* (owed to Turner and Burke), and the *text* (owed to Gadamer and the hermeneutic tradition). And the new allegiances were to isms that crossed many of the old-time borders. Social scientists were borrowing ideas, methods, and techniques from one another; border-spanning work was blossoming; new audiences were coalescing; and new organizations and media were forming to serve them.

This thesis was perhaps overstated. Academics then and now are roughly as cosmopolitan as their funding and personnel committees allow. One can scarcely say that professionalization never restrains cosmopolitanism or that the academic reward structure never punishes marginals. One still hears the classic objection to interfield work—that the contents of two fields can be joined only by reducing both to their lowest common denominator. It is not unheard of for people with career stakes in the mainstream to denounce ideas that jeopardize conventional wisdom. And still, years later, many literatures are more provincial than not: On the topics of groups, organizations, and decision-making, for example, psychologists still cite mostly psychologists, sociologists cite mostly sociologists, and so on.

Nonetheless, it is my contention that the blurred genres thesis has, if anything, improved with age. The trends Geertz discerned have continued. The chinks in professional and bureaucratic borders have proliferated—and some, once erratically scattered, have formalized, localized, and professionalized in ways that protect peripheral discourse.

My evidence is admittedly anecdotal. A proper proof, I suppose, would be something on the order of the human genome project: a study spanning all of the social sciences and humanities. But there are some robust local signs. One is the recent cosmopolitanism of rhetoric: Seen as the theory and practice of persuasion, or the analysis of language and media, rhetoric is now seen as important to the creation, maintenance, and change of knowledge (Brown 1977, 1987); knowledge acquisition is now seen as a kind of socialization (Shotter 1984); and one of rhetoric's most familiar species, argument, is now seen as central to securing expert consensuses (Lyne 1990b; McCloskey 1985). Epistemics, I contend, is the part of rhetoric's renaissance that confirms the blurred genres thesis in its most interesting form: Not merely is a new field coalescing, but a new kind of field—reflecting, as Geertz says, an alteration of the principles of mapping.

Much of what I will say about epistemics might as easily be said of several up-and-running fields. There is considerable redundancy across the rhetoric of inquiry, social epistemology, and policy analysis. But my argument is not that epistemics subsumes these fields or is their evolutionary successor. People in these fields interact to some extent across many genres. They read widely because they see blurred boundaries as opportunities, and most of them, I imagine, would regard a debate about which fields subsume which as medieval.

Still, it may be useful to consider whether a new field is emerging. A field description is like a temporary position fix: We take our bearings in a sea of literatures. We inventory our assets and requirements and identify allies and opponents. The emergence of a new field is a kind of evolution whose course we can chart and steer. Embryonic fields are ripe with choices; their principles haven't become doctrines, their methods are not set in concrete. So I want to precipitate debate about the content and contours of this field.

Fields are best described by their metaphors, methods, problem agendas, and competitors. The metaphors capture the gut intuitions; the methods describe the tools at hand; the problem agendas describe what the field does; and the competitors describe the outer boundaries. Here I will focus on one metaphor and one method—not because these exhaust the possibilities but because they best capture epistemics' stance toward knowledge.

The Ecological Metaphor

> From Hobbes to Marx and beyond, political theory has largely been written in national and international terms. Our reflec-

> tions on the order of society, as well as nature, are still dominated by the Newtonian image of massive power, exerted by sovereign agency through the operation of central force, and we have lost our feeling for all the respects in which social and political achievements depend on *influence* more than on *force*. For the moment, the varied political relations and interactions between transnational, subnational, and multinational entities, and the functions they can effectively serve, still remain to be analyzed, by an 'ecology of institutions' that has as yet scarcely come into existence. (Toulmin 1990, 209)

An ecological way of putting things would differ, certainly, from Foucault's reflections on the order of things. It would put us to thinking about orders still unfolding, about living environments, about synergisms among people and practices, role-players and niches. Ecology is the study of interrelationships, of interdependencies among environments. An ecology of institutions thus suggests not iron cages or self-replication but cross-pollination, movement across borders, and actors occupying multiple niches. *Life,* we might reword Foucault to say, "can retreat here, reorganize its forces, [and] invest itself elsewhere" (1980, 56). Substituting *life* for *power* (as one can often do with *power is everywhere* arguments) brings the problem of explaining stability and change to center stage—and thus fixes our attention on the interplay of adaptation and influence.

Adaptation and influence suggest movement—birds cross from wetlands to prairies, bees buzz from flower to flower. Travel, inter alia, is what birds and bees do; it is not incidental to their nature. And since practices, following their own logics, may exceed any one system's spatial dimensions, border-crossings are inevitable. For no ecosystem is an island—everything abuts on something, which abuts on something else, and so on. So interdependencies are pivotal, not ancillary to the ecological way of putting things.

Witness the vocabulary: Where ecosystems abut, flora and fauna adapt to the tensions along their borders, creating smaller ecosystems called *ecotones.* Ecotones are junctions, crossroads, places where cosmopolitans mingle. They display the *edge effect*—more density and variety in life forms. And they develop *edge species*—hybrids and crossbreeds unique to the ecotone.

Are there such things as intellectual ecotones? Certainly there are names that suggest hybrid fields: American studies, area studies, behavioral medicine, biochemistry, biophysics, biopsychology, cultural ecology, cytology, environmental engineering, environmental studies, environmental psychology, forensic medicine, geochemistry, immunopharmacology, physical chemistry, political geography, political sociology, psychoanthropology, psychobiology, psychopharmacology, psychiatric sociology, public health, rhetoric of inquiry, social psychology, women's studies, and urban studies (I am embroidering Klein's [1990a, 42–44] list).

Of course names can be misleading. Sociobiology, judged by its cover, suggests a merger of evidence and methods, not a reduction of sociality to biology. Criminology seems like a narrow specialty, until one notices that criminologists graze widely in the social sciences, with occasional forays into law, psychiatry, and philosophy. And social epistemology suggests polemics from the periphery and the importation of something hitherto excluded from epistemology. But the label is only faintly suggestive of the edge effects one in fact finds: The journal *Social Epistemology*, for instance, has included essays on urban knowledge, feminism and hermeneutics, scarcity in economic thought, government research funding, artificial intelligence, experimental studies of science, genetic epistemology, education, relativism, progress, language, pornography, think tanks, business ethics, ethnocentrism, textual studies, cognitive science, pathologies of science, political inquiry, the sociological problem of levels, and Finnish sociology.

Accentuating this topical variety is the terrain that unfolds in the authors' footnotes. Footnotes are rather like trails one follows to learn where authors have been; and one can track social epistemologists across most of the noticeable borders in the social sciences. The philosophers among them are omnivorous grazers, and perhaps a genuine edge species—distinguished from other philosophers not only by their argumentative motifs and styles but by the breadth, size, and content of their bibliographies.

Of course flora and fauna occupy niches for survival—not curiosity, taste, power, prestige, and fame; they don't cross boundaries for instruction or influence; they don't try to keep their thinking consistent or their behavior conventional; they are not curators or political activists. And scholarly quests for dominance are arguably subtler than a Lorenzian territorial imperative. Humans put their scent markers on ideas by professionalizing—by rhetorics of specialist prerogatives. But they defend their turf selectively, or interfield discourse would be impossible. The ecosystem thus emphasizes the effects of proximity—focus, attention, and perhaps conformity—but not the effects of personal and institutional ethos, credibility, contagion, timidity, and the structure of movements, rhetorical strategies, and appeals whose success depend on the variables affecting all persuasion.

Literary density is the likeliest parallel to an ecosystem's geographical expanse and topography. Population isn't irrelevant, but a field's terrain lies largely in its paper tonnage and word counts. Its "semantic space," as it were, is distributed across regions that are relatively accessible or inaccessible, oft-visited or seldom-visited. We thus might imagine a field's commonplaces as distributed on a series of concentric circles, as in Fleck's theory. The paradigm cases are at the center where normal science is the rule, resistance to change is conventional and institutionalized, and a single conversation is feasible. But as one moves away from the center, the pull of the paradigm cases wanes: One finds border-fields, cargo cults, and interest groups—multiple conversations wherein outside ideas can get a first toe-hold (Cambrosio and Keating 1983, Collins 1975, Darden and Maull 1977). For instance, findings in genetics about the molecular structure of a blood protein were kept at anthropology's fringe—indeed lunatic fringe—before finding their way into the center as the Eve hypothesis. Chaos and superstring theories first thrived in tiny settlements in physics' outback. And the rhetoric of inquiry is a fringe movement in several professions.

With scale comes complexity. Whether authoritarian hierarchies or loose confederations, complex organizations are layers of overlapping venues; their physiology lies in the intersections among their practices, in the multiple local connections among their subdomains. Each locality is tied to *some* others just as actors normally criss-cross *some* boundaries. But cosmopolitanism is comparatively local: Many people cross some lines; nobody crosses all lines.

Suburban sprawl makes for diffusion. Diffuse fields have diverse media and big literatures, so peripheral discourse may not radiate inward. This is perhaps why falsification doesn't always bring theories down—and why Kuhn's Planck hypothesis is plausible: Ideas may survive until their proponents die off because, the more diffuse the field, the greater the division of labor; the greater the division (and the bigger the literature), the greater the likelihood that a field's paradigm cases will remain unaffected by (and their guardians innocent of) peripheral happenings. Systemic holism, then, may wax locally but wane globally. Contra Quine (1960), the greater a field's diffusion the less we would expect its knowledge to meet experience as a corporate whole or new findings to reverberate to all elements.

Of course some ecologists emphasize systemic holism. And biology textbooks are not above the occasional queen of the sciences argument: Everything being systematically related to everything else, ecology becomes the *real* unifying science. But holism of this sort make sense in the social sciences only at a level of such abstraction that human ideas and practices disappear. Witness Hawley's (1986) revival of human ecology—a proposal that at first seems to be inventing epistemics.

Ecology, for Hawley, is a synonym for organization. Adaptation is a group achievement; innovation comes from adaptation to outside influence; organization evolves through interdependence; and specialization sparks subdivision, greater complexity, and more communication channels. This seems to be the missing link in Giddens's structuration idea, an explanation of how practices change social structures and why structuration is not a single process. Adaptation means extreme sensitivity to local conditions. "Of necessity," he says, "we live close to the ground" (Hawley 1986, 9).

But Hawley is lined up on the grand theorist's runway and is planning high-altitude maneuvers. He aims to consider the system qua system, to "deal holistically with the phenomenon of organization" (ibid., 7). He wants a macro-level account of "unit character," of frequency of interaction within obdurate structure. So he adopts a level of abstraction at which ecosystems seem holistic—their boundaries concretely identifiable and their effects describable as covering laws. Equilibrium, he argues, is the chief stabilizing mechanism, and adaptation, organization, and specialization are ancillary to unit character.

It might seem that as Hawley emphasizes structural determinacy, the idea of ecology becomes increasingly literal. But his aims are no more metaphorical than those of human ecology in its first incarnation (Park 1936), which was a focus on the spatial organization of cities that helped establish sociology's scientific credentials by "biologizing" its subject matter and methods. Hawley wants Popperian credentials. Bioecology is "the parent discipline" (Hawley 1986, 3). So the metaphor here is not in its death throws; it is dead on arrival.

The result, if such a thing can be imagined, is a general systems theory with people in it. Of course Fleck imagined such a thing. So does open systems theory. And Hawley shares the family predicament. To explain unit stability and to keep his boundaries clear, he needs Lewin-strength force-fields out on the periphery—precisely where he least expects to find them: "A field of forces such as a community is certainly dense at the center and thins out with distance away from the center" (ibid., 27). He emphasizes the "frayed edges" of big systems and stresses the interactional importance of border fields, which he calls "ecumunes." But he insists that a system's openness is negligible compared to the unifying force holding it together. And to explain this force, he resorts to what he calls "a heuristic fiction" (49).

Equilibrium has been called worse names—voodoo, for instance (Fuller 1989). But I prefer to think of it as a grizzled old deus ex machina to be trotted out whenever systemness is the topic at hand. It enters stage left and casts a spell: All activity is suspended; the Darwinian commotion freezes. Disturbances, from without or within, have brought defensive mechanisms into play; the system has acted to restore a *state:* The system is, if not inert, at least fat and happy; nothing much is happening. Equilibrium, indeed, designates whatever state one finds after something has happened. No matter what it is, or what it looks like, Hawley is going to call it *equilibrium.*

Fortunately, discourse and influence are not in harm's way. Though we might infer that they are reduced to epiphenomena, they are in fact invisible and apparently irrelevant. There is no talk of thought systems or of ideas and practices arrayed in the equilibria of self-regulating systems. And it is worth pausing a moment to count this blessing: For applied to thought systems, equilibrium is indistinguishable from the hobgoblin of little minds. And on this subject, Hawley would have found it inordinately hard to stay consistent. For in the clearest-cut cases of thought systems, consistency isn't an automatic, self-calibrating mechanism. It is a fragile quality to be protected by ideologues conscientiously minding the store. Cardinal Ratzinger thus runs his litmus tests, roots out the occasional Köenig, and generally worries for a living about the system's well-being.

Religions and other flag-bearing isms get their systemness partly from their compactness. One can track the arguments, the paper tonnage problem is manageable, and there is a center that holds no matter what. God doesn't play dice with such universes of discourse, so new ideas are greeted with all the warmth Mark Twain associated with small southern towns: They are either made to fit in or booted out.

But it would be a trickier thing to stand guard in this way over bigger isms. Neo-Marxism, say, or symbolic interactionism would pose both paper tonnage and diffusion problems (de facto differences, disputes, essential tensions). And when the latter reach critical mass—when the field comes to life, so to speak—the word *equilibrium* might apply best to battle lines. Or it might become a misty aspiration like "ideal completion." Consistency makes sense in this role: It prompts the conservators in intellectual fields to perform their indispensable function—to greet outside aggravations by first trying to assimilate them, or by defending a presumption against threats to conventional wisdom. The conservators may allow for a Sorokin-style accumulation of small changes (systems must tolerate small changes or they would be destroyed by trivialities), but their niche, their function, is to keep things as evolutionary—and not revolutionary—as possible.

Incidentally, it doesn't follow from this reasoning that cognitive dissonance drives rebellion. Opinion drift and boredom with old puzzles aside, one gathers from the *Weltanschauungen* theorists that cognitive dissonance is like a nursed grievance: Aggravations accumulate; piecemeal adjustments no longer suffice; so finally, much as a pressure cooker bursts, one has an out-of-paradigm experience. But cognitive dissonance covaries with cognitive complexity: The greater one's complexity the greater one's tolerance for inconsistencies. Cognitive complexity is domain-specific, so *specialists* ought to be the most tolerant of inconsistencies and thus more open to change. Whether they are is an empirical question that may turn, for instance, on differences between scientists and ideologues. But it would turn on the preoccupations and proclivities of people, not on systemness.

The moral, then, is that an appreciation of border fields breeds an indifference to borders. An appreciation of adaptation, organization, and specialization doesn't suggest that they are ancillary to unit character but that unit character is an afterthought. Open borders and peripheral discourse make for complexity and diffusion, so the idea of equilibrium won't explain the rationality of both stability and change (Toulmin 1972). A complex field's resistance and openness to change may not involve the same people. Its stability and change may be happening in different subfields.

If the ecological way of putting things accentuates the fluid, emergent quality of local influence, it also suggests *competition*—an idea with multiple, and not equally palatable meanings. One expects, for instance, a certain savagery in rivalries over scarce resources. Big sciences tussle over the lion's share; littler ones scrounge for scraps. The competition grows no less fierce as the morsels get smaller, for from the scavengers down to the bacteria, from the social sciences, I suppose, down to the humanities, the stakes are approximately the same. But the degree to which this imagery prompts a certain embarrassment or regret is the degree to which the parallel breaks down. Predators, to twist Mark Twain, neither blush nor need to; yet even the advocates of the biggest projects pay considerable lip service to a concern for those lower in the food chain.

Competition also suggests *selection,* and in a meritocracy, presumably, a selection of the best and the brightest. How "natural" this selection should be is a political and moral question that should prompt us to remember Darwinism's checkered career as a metaphor. Spencer and Sumner gave us social Darwinism by twisting Darwin to fit their whiggish enthusiasm and Calvinist pessimism. And theirs is not the ugliest version of the republican instinct imaginable. If meritocracies blindly trust their selection processes, they may become smug about the rightness of things—and proportionately indifferent to the fate of those selected-against. Jefferson, remember, proposed a winnowing process: an educational system designed to usher the cream to the top. One can imagine the likes of Hamilton describing this winnowing as "selection of the fittest," and any number of the founders arguing that the system should begin with equal opportunities for all, yet have a rigorous selection process for moving upward. "And then," one can imagine them saying, "let Darwin do his work."

The social Darwinists, I suppose, will always be with us. They are certainly with us now, with a clear majority in the Senate and House bent on bleeding welfare dollars to build prisons—wherein Darwin no doubt *will* do his work. But this suggests only that ecology is arid grounding for altruism arguments: Nature has a lusty appetite for the unfortunate—which is why progressives, from Woodrow Wilson on, have used the imagery of rising above the brutes, of the welfare state as reflecting our better natures. That, of course, is another metaphor, and there is certainly room for it: Ecology has not masqueraded here as a theory of everything. So far, it has drawn our attention to the fluid, emergent qualities of local life, to the importance border fields and cosmopolitanism, and it has drawn attention to its own limits—and thus to the ambivalence the idea of selection ought to inspire.

But the metaphor does suggest that competition is the way of things—and that it is the the way things ought to be. It doesn't commit us to all of nature's little embarrassments: We can dismiss social Darwinism, for instance, as a moral failure or as a matter of taking things too literally. But the word *ecology* doesn't suggest peaceable kingdoms or the grandeur of nature, as romantic pantheists used to say. It suggests, rather, that competition is indispensable.

At first glance, this implication isn't so hard to swallow. In fact it is a bromide—Lippmann's "indispensable opposition," Dewey's "gadfly of thought." The source of all this is Aristotle's *Rhetoric,* wherein truth, with a little help from its friends, has a "natural tendency," to triumph over falsehood. But the two classic statements are John Stuart Mill's *On Liberty* and, in a very different vein, Georg Simmel's *Conflict and the Web of Group Affiliations.*

Mill argues that every truth should have its opponents, and if there are none around, "it is indispensable to imagine them, and supply them with the strongest arguments." A state sans opposition isn't and can't be healthy. The "peculiar evil" of suppressing ideas is that it robs us either of the opportunity to exchange error for truth or of "the clearer perception and livelier impression of truth produced by its collision with error" (Mill 1956, 21). Opposition thus keeps advocates on the epistemic straight and narrow: "Truth, in the great practical concerns of life, is so much a question of the reconciling and combining of opposites, that very few have minds sufficiently capacious and impartial to make the adjustment with an approach to correctness, and it has to be made by the rough process of a struggle between combatants fighting under hostile banners" (ibid., 58).

Simmel argues that conflict is the principle generative and regulative mechanism for change. A "centripetal and harmonious group, a pure 'unification,' not only is empirically unreal, it could show no real life process" (1955, 15). "The extent and combination of antipathy, the rhythm of its appearance and disappearance, the forms in which it is satisfied, all these along with the more literally unifying elements, produce the metropolitan form of life . . . and what at first glance appears in it as dissociation actually is one of its elementary forms of sociation" (ibid., 20). Cognitive dissonance theory is thus largely a fantasy: There is no such thing as a *drive* for consistency, and cognitive equilibrium is nothing like homeostasis. Indeed, cognitive processes are so complex and so riddled with ambivalence, mixed motives, and feelings, they can't be captured by any one psychological concept (ibid., 21). Indeed conflict waxes and wanes as people dicker and deal, adjust and compromise.

Let's call this point of view *the indispensable opposition.* And the first thing to notice about the indispensable opposition is that it faces substantial opposition, typified by Madison's claim that the rationale for government lies in "the primal task of overcoming conflict" (Dahl 1972, 14). The abhorrence of conflict is found in Plato, Locke, Rousseau, and the *Federalist* authors. And in popular parlance, unity means accord, harmony, rapport. Conflict means friction, strife, turmoil—all kissing kin to chaos and confusion. Among the most robust research findings in the social sciences are that people bond together on the basis of agreement; persuaders get high ethos when their audiences agree with them; groups get solidarity from their members' agreement; friendships are formed on the basis of shared beliefs and values; and people the world around profess to loath argument.

All this opposition to opposition sparks a certain faintheartedness in its advocates. For Mill and Lippmann, conflict is indispensable as a *means,* not as an end in itself. And for Dewey, the gadfly of thought is a genuinely curious creature. If conflict really is how a democracy thinks, Dewey devotes a surprising amount of effort to engineering unity. Perhaps, as I speculated, he is not the populist he is made out to be. But if we read him as a populist, we are presented with the fascinating spectacle of progressivism shooting itself in the foot—of working to create a want that is the last thing in the world it should want. I accused the communitarians, remember, of manufacturing wants, much as advertisers do, of trying to persuade Americans to yearn for community by telling them that they already do. But communitarians rarely claim to value disputation and argument. Progressives, on the other hand, envision a creative discourse—an ongoing clash of ideas out of which something will turn up. But what turns up from unity, chiefly, is more of the same—and therein lies a case for what I call *valuing dissensus* (1983).

Valuing dissensus is a shameless argument for demand creation—and quite possibly as quixotic a quest as the communitarians' quest for unity. It has, I admit, all the appearances of a "crackpot scheme," to quote Sally Jackson; and the Devil, certainly, will be in the details. Nonetheless, here is my reasoning: Organizations and people are hypnotized by an "ethic of completion." Success and failure are understood on an horizon analogous to the Protestant work ethic. One thinks of discrete tasks—load the hay onto the truck, clean the floor—and uses this simple vision as a basis for understanding complex projects. The completion ethic thus puts a premium on completing tasks, and on Weberian instrumental rationality, the fit of utilitarian calculi to goals.

Inside this ethic, disagreement is thought to be valuable yet menacing. The *indispensable opposition* thus permits idea-testing and a reflective evaluation of alternative means. Yet organizational stability and interpersonal cooperation are seen as precarious and fragile. Disputation is hazardous, threatening—the proverbial bull in a china shop. Since people loath contentiousness and disagreement in their personal affairs (Benoit 1983), they generalize this preference into a demand for harmony. Disagreement is thus viewed with the mixture of need and distrust with which military commanders sometimes view psychotic soldiers. Argumentativeness becomes a "thin red line" to be crossed only occasionally, only for dramatic purposes, and only by arguers capable of returning to sanity or by expendable ones who can be set aside once mundane life resumes its normal course.

But an institutionalized preference for agreement can be pathological. It can prevent adaptation and innovation and lock decision-makers into reckless courses of action (Halberstam 1964, 1969). Groups "tend to evolve informal norms to preserve friendly intragroup relations and these become part of the hidden agenda at their meetings" (Janis 1983, 7). The group members' "strivings for unanimity override their motivation to realistically appraise alternative courses of action" (ibid., 9). Thus begins "a deterioration of mental efficiency, reality testing, and moral judgment that results from in-group pressures" (ibid.). Though not all fiascoes are due to groupthink, one nonetheless finds it in extended case studies—of Korean and Vietnam war planning, pre–Pearl Harbor decision-making, and the bay of pigs fiasco.

So valuing dissensus is meant to counteract the completion ethic, to compete with everything else organizations do—especially with their institutionalized need to complete projects. It is a competing value put up against strong forces already deployed against. So the trick—and it will take a book or two to do it (the first stab is Willard and Hynes 1991)—is to persuade organizations that it is in their best interests to institutionalize the competing value. The ecological metaphor, certainly, will be the heart of the rhetoric—the presence of opposition needs to be seen as the way of things, and a good thing too. And within this thinking, the management of disagreement will take center stage. Some agreement, after all, is needed to have arguments at all; and it is interesting per se how organizational actors are able to bridge disagreements on one level with working agreements that permit cooperation on another. But the centerpiece, I think, will be an etiquette. For the real stumbling block will not be convincing people that opposition is the way of things; it will be convincing people that they can live with the result.

SHALLOW QUOTATION

The case for methodological eclecticism and triangulation is a familiar one (Denzin 1970b), so I will take for granted that epistemics can use any methods that fit its purposes. I will focus here on one method that is both postmodern and perhaps unique. The stumbling block will be convincing you that it *is* a method.

"Shallow quotation" is a way of reading liberalism, or any incommensurable position, that resembles the contrived depthlessness of postmodern architects—much as the voices of the connoisseurs, oracles, and mourners were modulated into a trio. I will focus here on how the depthless quotation of positions and theories might help ideas across field boundaries. Later I will apply the same reasoning to more politically volatile ideas—history and race.

I call it shallow quotation because one meaning of shallow is superficial. "Shallow" alerts us to the fact that we are doing something risky—something, indeed, that we often encounter in mistakes. If someone says "Freud's 'Ego' and 'Superego' are the same as behaviorism's 'learned predispositions,'" being doctors of philosophy, we rush to make a sick philosophy well: "No, these ideas are only superficially similar; they are embedded in different theories, presuppose different realities, and require different methods." The risk, then, is the incompetence of the nonnative: One borrows an idea without understanding its context and thus misuses it. And as we saw, accident-prone discourses are ones that address exoteric publics using the expositional economies of esoteric circles.

Nothing I am about to say impugns the value of in-depth understandings. I am assuming that it is feasible to tell the difference between mishaps and intentional misappropriations. But accepting the in-depth meanings of ideas is not always good advice for interfield discourse. Just as not all communications are expressive of the internal states of speakers, cooperative projects may require agreements that submerge local details. If Foucault can be read as a modernist (by ignoring his theory of language and relaxing his total institution) then, similarly, a weakening of Marx's determinism allows the existential determination of thought to become the organizational equivalent of Kelly's (1955) "determinism of unexamined ideas." The two combine to say that we may be enslaved by the taken-for-granted, by what seems natural and given, but we may be freed by reconstruing our circumstances. We have made Kelly less psychologistic by stressing that inevitabilities may be organizational imperatives. And, though we are not being good Marxists, we have enabled the constructivist to read, for example, Bourdieu (1977) sympathetically as he argues that capitalism skews our vision of inevitabilities. One might *want* to read Bourdieu sympathetically because presumptions about inevitability powerfully elaborate Kelly's view. Shallow quotation has allowed us to capitalize on a team effort: Kelly gets the basket; Bourdieu gets the assist; and Marx has set the pick.

Also, themes may emerge that fit the thrust—but not the details—of the civic virtue theories (MacIntyre 1981, Connolly 1977). One thing these diagnoses share with the therapists and postmodernists is a concern for justice as the product of civility and altruism. A reading shallow enough to let this literature cooperate with the literatures on corporatism and elitism allows us to see liberalism as a program of expanding rational control over organizations of vast scale governed by a hope to temper rationalization with humanity.

Likewise, an idea like "polyphony" (Bakhtin and Medvedev 1985) may be shallow-quoted to explain not state-scale pluralism but the cooperation and conflict that makes up discourses. To let all voices be heard is less invisible a hand than pluralism: It suggests that multiple voices don't fuse into a single system so much as function at different registers and strike at different angles (Stam 1988). But where polyphony might be a sound constitutional principle, it is pragmatically either a bromide (one wants to teach the world to sing in perfect harmony) or a celebration of racket. Letting a thousand flowers bloom is a sublime impulse, useful for first amendment arguments, but less applicable to concrete projects.

Because he was a denizen of a police state and writing about state-scale discourse, Bakhtin sides every time with the disenfranchised and oppressed; the "official line" is always suspect (Stam 1988, 131). Bakhtin's interpreters, such as Stam, thus want to hear the voices of groups they admire in their "full force and resonance," but not, I imagine, the Aryan Nation or Total Woman movements. And polyphony applies less easily to smaller-scale discourses. Just as it is dubious to equate, say, high temperature physics with a prison, it is dubious *in principle* to side *in principle* against a prevailing consensus. Some lunatic fringers *are* lunatics. The point isn't to celebrate opposition but to protect it—on the assumption that it is unwise to side either with or against a prevailing consensus *in principle*. A consensus ought to be seen more as a default setting—sharing the strengths and weakness of that idea. So if, as Stam suggests, an over-robust consensus makes for "innocuous pluralism" or a pseudo-equality of viewpoints, then perhaps the remedy is an idealization of tolerance.

Organizations may achieve these goals if they can tolerate dissent, and dissent is more tolerable when it is moderated by cooperative agendas and by argumentation that avoids doctrinaire warfare. Shallow quotation may calm down "ists" and keep their "isms" from infecting attempts to adapt to problems. Imagine, for instance, that you are arguing with a Marxist about commodity fetishism. You don't agree with the determinism or that class is a useful construct, but you do see a point well taken—that oppression does not leave its fingerprints on commodities, that the complexity of modern life makes it too easy to remain indifferent to the hidden details, the economic and environmental side effects. This point-well-taken is an achievement: You and the Marxist may be disappointed about all the remaining disagreement, but this one agreement may permit common projects.

The jointness of these projects may be modest. If I quote Harvey (1989, 101) "we cannot tell from contemplation of any object in the supermarket what conditions of labour lay behind its production," I must specify how out-of-context I want this idea to be. I can't figure out how to shallow-quote Harvey's populism (he mentions the French revolution often but has nothing bad to say about it). I doubt that money is false exchange or that credit is false money. And I don't idealize medieval crafts and direct exchange. The caveats may be so cumbersome that it is easier to reword the idea to cleanse it of all of Harvey's intentions. But this solution patches with concrete what may have been a promising hole in the wall. However thin the alliance, it did achieve a joint concern for labor conditions.

Whether shallow quotation is advisable depends on the purposes at hand, the borders being crossed, and the realization that shallow quotation is a creation, not a distortion of reality. If experts from six fields must cooperate to solve a public problem, the discourse they construct is not inauthentic, though it may seem heretical to the folks at home.

Admittedly, shallow quotation runs the risk of spurious agreements. Recall Klein's (1990a) multidisciplinary researchers who, after wasted effort, discovered that all they could agree upon was that "aggression" was a nice word. It might seem that "satisficing" caused the trouble, where "optimizing" would not. Had the researchers meshed their respective theories in their entirety, or at least grappled with their differences at the outset, they might have avoided their dead end. Of course the project might have died aborning. Wallowing in differences is not the most propitious starting point for common journeys; so the question is whether a more astute team might have negotiated some theoretical heresy if the price were right. "Aggression," like anything else, can be operationalized in a number of ways that, though they violate the background assumptions of the home fields, might accomplish some valued ends. Such working agreements needn't be seen as lies or distortions of an underlying reality: they are new rhetorical developments adapted to particular tasks and justified by the fact that the contributing fields could not have accomplished the tasks alone. Their "deeper" disagreements, or the degrees to which the hybrid lacks fidelity to the more established bodies of thought, may be irrelevant. So this risk can be accounted for, and never forgotten, and still not proscribe cases of shallow quotation that create possibilities where adherence to local detail would not. The value of shallow quotation is the cooperative projects it makes feasible—interfield projects, reading authors sympathetically. But the question always to be asked is whether some land mine has been left to trip us.

THE AGENDA

Toulmin (1972) says that rational enterprises are founded on shared problem foci, and this, I believe, is a useful way of seeing common ground. A problem focus involves agreements and disagreements. It is a working consensus that a problem is legitimate, relevant, and worthy of study. The ecology metaphor suggests that the things worth arguing about are the ones that explain how knowledge moves within and across borders.

DISCOURSE ACROSS DIFFERENCES

Epistemics' aim is to explain differences and their effects. First, there are interpersonal differences. To study fields is to study people. No field study would be complete without an ethnographic look at concrete cases, so the question of representativeness is paramount: Are the people being studied competent and typical? Presumably people construe reality differently, have different attitudes, beliefs, and values; they participate (in various degrees) in groups that differ in focus, makeup, ideological content and strength, and closure against outsiders; they have different competencies and beliefs about communication; and they have different tasks.

Second, there are discourse differences—-not just different languages or specialized vocabularies, but different pragmatics: On the surface there are different purposes, tasks, subject matters, argumentative agendas, rules, and methods, and beneath the surface there are the tacit assumptions, the taken-for-granted givens that arguably are the defining characteristic of discourses. Cosmopolitanism—or bilingualism—is thus a matter of competently grasping what needn't be said as well as what must be said.

People *do* function in multiple discourses. Multivalence (Lee 1966) is a fact. It isn't enough that I master the arcane detail of my specialty; I must also negotiate with colleagues, write grant proposals, testify at congressional hearings, deal with my neighbors and family, chat with strangers, and so on. Thus the high energy physicist participates in the esoteric discourse surrounding her work and participates as well in different discourses with close-by and more distant colleagues. She communicates differently in writing grant proposals and differently in influencing governmental science policy and still differently in translating esoterica to other discourses. To one degree or another, depending on communication competence, everyone confronts different pragmatic contexts and moves among different conventions, which we can represent as variations in *publics* and the discourses appropriate to them.

Third, there are ability differences. Assume for a moment an omniscient communicative competence. Our physicist is fully in control of her movements among discourses. The demarcations of different discourses are as blurred or sharp as they need to be. Asked at a cocktail party what she does for a living, she adapts her reply to her questioner. For an uninformed questioner, she resorts to vague images—physics' public relations—perhaps saying things she would never say to colleagues: "We are trying to understand the laws that govern the universe."

But imagine that she changes her tune: "We are seeking the common, indivisible matter out of which everything else is derived; since the advent of quantum dynamics, we think that the common matter is energy." She is likely speaking not to another physicist (why belabor the obvious?) but to a fellow scientist nonetheless: Her utterance capitalizes on, inter alia, a presumptively common view of matter and energy—and perhaps the assumption that any natural scientist has some knowledge of physics. The two also share a vague background identity as scientists. This identity is sometimes useful (*scientists* can unite against creationists). But such issues as the nature of science may never arise in her specialty. She may speak of progress and the discovery of truth in some grant proposals and not others or may relegate such subjects strictly to mass consumption (by which she might mean any public outside physics, outside her esoteric field, outside the sciences, outside academe, or what-have-you).

People vary in the degree to which they fall short of this full reflective control because they differ in their abilities to see and capitalize upon discourse differences (Delia 1983). O'Keefe's expressives don't adapt to contexts because they assume that other people code reality identically. And most anyone can be overoptimistic about how much another knows or about how much others agree with one's views. Ordinary conversation prefers saying too little to saying too much because it is easier to repair the former (Jacobs and Jackson 1983), so spurious agreement are always possible—and often uncovered only retrospectively as the interactants try to explain a stumbling block or a sudden, apparently mysterious confusion.

Local Cooperation as Transcendence

Epistemics is not an arbiter field. Its aim is not adjudication or information brokerage. Its aim indeed is to replace the epistemological impulse with what Steve Fuller calls epistemic affirmative action. The assumption is that local knowledge is important. Generality is more analogous to local area computer networks. Everyone's knowledge to some degree spans multiple fields, most often the ones in closest proximity—which is why it is often easy to regard the social sciences as a discourse of sorts, a general intellectual milieu subdivided into domains. Since such generalizations succeed for certain purposes, we may infer that generality is a local phenomenon enabled by proximity and working agreements. Practices and competencies are local. Particular people, for particular purposes, achieve sufficiently complex agreements to permit border-crossings and coordinated action. So, however oxymoronic it may seem, transcendence is a local affair.

Some readers may see this epistemic modesty as conduct unbecoming a discipline—*discipline* here connoting something like the Calvinists' doctrine of the elect, and presumably denoting a field's exact rank in the academic food chain. On this view, any discipline worthy of the name wants (or lays claim to) something like Toulmin's impartial standpoint of rationality—a position that transcends field particularities, that yields, in some sense, universal judgments. To try not to want such a position may seem to be an abdication of every field's philosophical obligations—the need to dream, to speculate, and to generalize.

But though epistemics leaves such things to others, it is, withal, a perfectly respectable enterprise: Local successes are interesting in themselves. Universality is an inappropriate standard for judging them. In pragmatic affairs, people are notoriously unable to agree on universals. And the principles that do transcend all boundaries do so by being empty, that is, they can't function until tied to local content and situations. *Avoid equivocation* may be a universal, but to observe the rule or interpret its violations, one must know particular facts: One needs the facts of physics (or whatever) to know whether a physicist (or whoever) is equivocating.

One payoff for this modesty is that public knowledge will not be seen as a degenerate variation on an ideal: Epistemics studies disciplined discourse and public decision-making as aspects of a common agenda. Intellectuals and public decision-makers share a common predicament—which transposes into questions that bear equal import in expert fields and in public life. What are the grounds of a well-founded consensus?

When is acquiescence to authority appropriate? How does our knowledge of the sociology of expertise affect our beliefs about the reliability of epistemic claims? How can the claims of competing authorities be weighed? By what standards are public positions to be evaluated? One can pose these questions: (1) *sociologically,* as field theorists see a claim's epistemic force as inhering in its position in an intellectual ecology and in the authority or stature of its claimants; (2) *pedagogically,* in terms of packaging the principles of sound conduct, inference, and speech for pedagogy; (3) *pragmatically,* as one might focus on the structure of language, speech acts, or contexts; and/or (4) *analytically* as one might focus on the coherence of positions, claims, and audience adaptations.

Another payoff is an appreciation of rationality's rhetorical functions. For epistemics, the idea of *rationality* has two dimensions. The first is familiar to readers of Dewey, Pierce, and James: namely, Mead's (1954) view of sociality which locates rationality in one's capacity to cognitively represent the perspectives of others. Mind, on this view, is animated by interaction, by one's importation of social organization. It is a cognitive development involving increasingly complex communication processes, repertoires and abilities and thus an increasing ability to assess, adapt, and accommodate—epitomized by one's capacity to play games by knowing the roles and expectations of others and by agreeing to play by the rules. Thus, second, rationality is a term of art used to designate conventionally sound procedures and performances. A rational claim, on this view, presumptively merits attention; it is not *irrational* (presumptively unsound); it is worth arguing about (Willard 1983, 1989a).

Of course there is a value judgment operating here—namely, that *boundary spanning discourse is a fact, not a predicament.* Epistemics' interdisciplinary character is a goal. Its actors are not preoccupied with creating a field whose structure can, once perfected, professionalize and harden into hegemonic methods, historical narratives, and problematics. For their focus on the prospects and problems of interfield communication is, arguably, a permanently interdisciplinary subject matter. Epistemics needs niches abroad in order to flourish: Its economy is *intermestic,* as economists say; the line between its domestic and foreign policy has "completely evaporated," as President Clinton says. There is a symbiosis between its domestic and cosmopolitan lives, which suggests that external discourse is more than case-buttressing of internal theories. It *is* a source of case-studies, but it is also a source of criticism on which the field thrives. If such a field is possible, it breaks Foucault's Trap and forces a rethinking of marginality.

It also forces, as Geertz predicted, a rethinking of the principles of mapping. We don't just notice and name fields as if they are impersonal empirical happenings to be pictured by a *Tractarian* language and then taxonomized. The map implies fixed territory, the only changes in the pictured reality occurring over geological or, at most, political time. Going intellectual orders may be more fluid than this as they seek balances between stability and change. We needn't propose a hyper-Heraclitean flux (which Jesse Delia once characterized as being unable to step into the same river once) to be dubious about taxonomies. This doubt owes more to Heisenberg than Heraclitus: For observers can take an indeterminate number of stances, yielding an indeterminate number of observations, each possibly changing the nature of what is observed, just as each new spin on an idea may become part of the idea.

So epistemics is inherently interdisciplinary. It can be seen as a standalone field, but it is more analogous to networkable software, like the cosmopolitan disciplines just discussed. It occupies niches in a number of much older fields. Its dispersion is such that we can say of epistemics what Nelson (1988, 21–22) says of the rhetoric of inquiry: it is "something on the order of a new field" "scarcely more at home" in one's own department than in any other organized domain: "indeed it needs homes in all disciplines in order to flourish. Thus the new field is and must remain at once within but across every discipline. It is an 'interdisciplinary' field in the deepest and best sense of the word."

This agenda might be expanded, but perhaps enough has been said to clarify the main themes. The point isn't that everyone agrees about everything but that they agree about the rationality of discussing and studying them. Regardless of whether epistemics in fact solidifies, research traditions spanning multiple boundaries have created a common agenda—an interest in the constitution of and interplay among discourses.

Two Contrasts

It may be useful to notice some definitive argumentative fissures in and around epistemics. A field's innards are easier to see as battlelines than points of agreement. People organize themselves around disputes, their positional arrangements constituting the larger organization's central nervous system. And a field's borders are often cast into boldest relief by disputes. One reason why people take the trouble to define their fields—to reify or reinforce their borders—is to resolve ambiguities created by overporous borders.

As epistemics is now as porous as a field can be, I want to firm it up by sketching two external borders. My claims are that epistemics should be more like policy analysis than policy science and that epistemics differs in kind from epistemology. These contrasts may seem like straw men. Policy science and epistemology, it might be said, have bypassed the ideas by which they are defined here. Actors in both fields might disavow the views on which I am basing contrasts with epistemics and claim that many of the traits I impute to epistemics are directions they advocate for their respective fields. Some epistemologists use social analyses and examples drawn from ordinary discourse. And some policy analysts denounce the scientism of policy science.

Quite so. The boundaries have blurred. But this doesn't make the case for pulling the social epistemologist and policy analyst into epistemics a straw man. Blurred boundaries symptomize peripheral activities, and the developments I want to draw into epistemics are not mainstream in their home fields. Fuller (1988) would not call social epistemology mainstream. And Hawkesworth's (1988) contrast of policy analysis with policy science is based upon importing outside ideas into a field—the critique of positivism permits her to discard the fact-value dichotomy and to replace the rhetoric of science with the rhetoric of practical reason. Fuller and Hawkesworth may prevail in their respective fields. But if resistance is too strong, or change is too slow, peripheral discourses find one another by developing new ground. And new fields form.

POLICY SCIENCE VERSUS POLICY ANALYSIS

Policy science is the Dr. Strangelove specter Habermas and Goodnight have in mind—a full-blown expert field devoted to nurturing the modernist fallacy. Positivistic, technocratic, and scientistic, it replaces Plato's philosopher-kings with scientists whose value-free codifications of facts (Dye 1975) can check and redirect society's vague value preferences (see the critique in Dunn 1983). In other words, policy science is logical positivism for publics, and it is arguably the dominant public philosophy, or at least the closest thing we have to a public philosophy, in the United States. Its best-known discipline (cost-benefit analysis) and its topoi (value-free facts, transparent reality, additive knowledge) are fundamental to decision-making in law, legislation, and planning at all levels.

The literature denouncing technocracy is, by my count, the largest crisis literature in existence. Much of it reiterates Max Weber's concern about "rationalization," or what Habermas calls the "colonization" of the lifeworld. But nestled within this tradition is a critique of policy science that owes its political thrust largely to Marcuse. Hawkesworth (1988, 193), for instance, says that policy scientists "are deeply implicated in a political process that privatizes and depoliticizes citizens as it reinforces elite decision-making." And "the rhetoric of policy science supports unbounded confidence in the possibility of technical solutions for social and political problems. Systematic training in quantitative analysis without any consideration of the problematic positivistic foundations of the discipline reinforces belief in the feasibility of value-free policy prescriptions. Governments' demands for cost-benefit analyses provide the rationale for the certification of a cadre of experts who can perform a needed public service."

Hubris on such a scale was bound to spark an *embarrassment of poverties* literature, and it should come as no surprise that policy analysis (Garson 1986) gradually formed around points of opposition to policy science. The organizing project was a debunking of scientism and the fact-value dichotomy (Kramer 1975, Schoek and Wiggins 1960), and as the *Weltanschauungen* critique of positivism was, at the time, in the academic air, consensus theories came naturally. And so did a certain, faintly republican brand of populism.

Hawkesworth, for instance, wants an empowered public, chiefly, I think, as a rival force to deprive experts of "unwarranted" authority. Like Dewey, she leaves open the question of how republican this separation of powers must be. She seems perfectly aware of the tensions between democratization and competence, and she certainly doesn't argue that the public is more rational or democratic than experts. But, like Adams and Jefferson, she puts her trust, nonetheless, in a rhetoric of practical wisdom.

Behind this trust are two assumptions: that nonscientistic policy studies (1) are less likely to mask control motives and (2) run a diminished risk of depoliticizing the citizenry and reinforcing elite rule. Both assumptions, I think, stem from a fixation on the evils of ontological-style talk—on the latent coerciveness in positivism's bare facts—and thus from a certain blindness to the risks of the alternative. The term *influence,* after all, covers a multitude of virtues and sins, and many of the latter are hard to distinguish from coercion. The appeal to consensus, for instance, is often used to settle disputes—to end debate. Yet it is precisely amid such contentiousness that a state of consensus may be unintelligible, difficult to assess, or endlessly debatable. Ambiguity and unclarity in a field's mass communications makes for a vicious circle: The more strongly one appeals to a consensus, the more one is arguing from authority and the more the authority becomes self-perpetuating. So the appeal to consensus is scarcely a panacea. It has as much potential to disenfranchise the public as scientism, and perhaps more. Scientism at least has the virtue of blatancy, but the veneer of open discourse masks authority-dependence and perhaps contributes to a vague faith decision-makers may have that expert claims have been tested by rational debate.

This criticism, to be sure, is merely a housekeeping chore. Policy analysis and epistemics have more in common than not. Both see argument as the central process of policy analysis and decision-making (Dunn 1981); and both, thanks to interchanges with the rhetoric of inquiry, analyze expert claims as rhetorical strategies. Epistemics is less sanguine about what we will have once the scales drop from the public eye, and therein perhaps lies a promising line of dispute. For if there is a lacuna in policy analysis, it lies in the practice of merely gesturing to practical wisdom—and thus leaving unanswered a more pivotal question: How are we to know unwarranted authority when we see it?

Epistemics Is Not Epistemology

To some degree, I suppose, any field that curious about the creation, uses, acquisition, and evolution of knowledge will seem "epistemological." Even the most *social* of the social epistemologists, and more than a few rhetorical and argumentation critics, use the language of "universality," "relativism," and "skepticism," of transcendent critical principles, of "truth" and "justified true belief." The philosophical tone of this talk is so strong that a more than circumstantial case can be made that the toxic spill described in chapter 3 has happened: Epistemology's language has unquestionably seeped outside its borders. So the question is: Has epistemics stepped into it?

The evidence that it has not begins, I think, with a difference in field-defining goals. Epistemics doesn't seek—nor is it even about—a universal commensurating discourse. It fears totalitarianism more than relativity and, thus, cares chiefly about how discourse domains both maintain and interrogate their knowledge and authority and with how they behave in public places. It is curious about the ways knowledge and expertise are tied to the apparatuses of states and the sociopolitical contexts in which they function. It is organized around an interest in the conditions of justified assent and in Dewey's phrase "warranted assertability." For it is ultimately interested in competent deliberation, in the authority of knowledge claims, and their optimum uses in decision-making.

Nor is epistemics a relativ*ism.* It is not a defense of relativity or an attempt to engage epistemologists with relativistic claims. It assumes that heterogeneity and pluralism are empirical facts. Genuine disputes are possible. And relativity is a feature of perception and measurement (e.g., complementarity and uncertainty [Heisenberg 1952]), of differences in modes of argument (Gross 1987, McCloskey 1983, 1985, 1987), and of disagreements. But relativ*ism* is an epistemological position. It gets its meaning from the discourse in which it functions. Relativ*ists* are arrayed against absolut*ists* or universal*ists*. Their *isms* get their meaning from positions taken in disputes. Relativisms thus resemble (and are often joined with) *skepticism*. We know the skeptic and the relativist by their opponents. Skeptical claims get their force from the breadth and scope of the claims to which they attach. Big claims court big critiques; modest claims get modest challenges.

Conceptual relativism is an epistemological position. It holds that beliefs are relative to points of view or conceptual schemes (Feyerabend 1965, Kuhn 1970a, 1970b, Goodman 1978). Against the avowedly relativist (Feyerabend and Goodman) and putatively relativist (Kuhn) are arrayed those who argue that relativism is a self-contradictory position (Mandelbaum 1982) and that the idea of incommensurable conceptual schemes is incoherent, since to be able to define an incommensurability is to possess a common language to transcend it (Davidson 1982). These views are allied with a theory of language and referential semantics (Tarski 1956) that suggest that if the philosophical disputes are settled, the result is a discourse capable of adjudicating disputes or exposing their triviality (Quine 1960, 1969; cf. Fuller and Willard 1987).

But Davidson's case against Kuhn scarcely means that if ordinary disputes can be described they can be solved. Palestinians and Israelis, Tajiks and Uzbeks, pro-lifers and pro-choosers, pluralists and populists are divided more by the pragmatics of daily life than by incomprehension. And relativity, I daresay, is relative. Fields differ in their hermeticism, and relatively few are single-cell organisms, so my concern is with how differences affect argument practices—especially the movement of ideas across borders and the coordination of multiple discourses by complex organizations. The relativisms that turn on closed, hence deterministic, systems are an empirically defective message: public problems cross field lines; so do ideas; and both spark interfield discourse. So relativity, though scarcely a triviality, may be less important than authority-dependence, big literatures, and epistemic focus.

Also whether one is a relativ*ist* may depend on one's attitude. Relativists, to some extent, wallow in relativity: They applaud differences (e.g., Stam 1988). They see homogeneity as a restrictive conformity (diversity across and within cultures is to be prized, not solved), because they relish disputes with universalists or because they want to seal their field's borders and stigmatize outsiders. Epistemics brackets all these values but one: However tolerant one wishes to be, differences in beliefs and practices pose problems. Public life is a family of arenas where competing claims are weighed, where agents of different fields compete for power. To defend *public* relativity is to belabor the obvious, so the question is whether epistemological terms are germane to public discourses. The decision that they are may have no bearing on the case for or against relativism.

So the claim that interfield differences are important is not an epistemological claim. It isn't addressed to the discourse in which relativists lock horns with universalists. For epistemics, relativity is empirically the case no matter how epistemological arguments turn out, for "in principle" arguments do not defeat positions people actually hold. To discuss relativity nonepistemologically means to consider controversies in their rhetorical and political contexts. The epistemic path brackets the epistemological concern for a commensurating discourse and replaces it with a concern for community achievements and for the ways *particular* disputes might be resolved.

This contrast with epistemology may clarify the pedagogies of informal logic and argumentation—which still resemble Russell's view of descriptions too much to be plausible (see Naess [1966] on "precization"): Disputes stem from mistaken expressions. Find the errors, fix the dispute. One *finds* mistakes by reducing faulty expressions to more precise language. One *fixes* the disputes by teasing out the implications internal to the critical language. One's results always begin with mutatis mutandis: *X*'s claim, reduced and thereby corrected, is defective, despite its apparent validity in *X*'s subjective or community-specific terms. But students shouldn't be told that whenever serious people have earnest disputes, someone is mistaken. The divisions that torment societies are not always misunderstandings; sincere disagreements may be (judged by a field's standards) correctly stated and based on presumptively sound evidence and reasoning. The pro-life or pro-choice positions needn't be faux arguments, misargued positions needing correction and final adjudication. The environmentalist's belief that nature should be valued in itself does not misconstrue the developer's claim that nature should be valued for its utility. So once again, rhetoric must be something more than a "study of misunderstanding and its remedies" (Richards 1965). It must do more than enhance "the precision with which we vex one another" (Geertz 1973, 29).

So epistemics differs from epistemology but, as with all escapes from ideology, must work at it. To illustrate this therapy—and to reassure the reader who is skeptical about the extent of epistemological seepage, I now turn to a field that, depending on how we read it, might be an ecotone at epistemics' edge or an enemy camp.

INTERDISCIPLINARITY—THE QUEST

There already exists a field devoted to the study of interfield discourse. It has an improbable name—*Interdisciplinarity*—but comes complete with conferences, journals, and a literature. A recent book by Klein (1990a) has a hundred pages of bibliography—books, essays, conference reports, and position papers—many of its entries the work of people in other fields reporting on interfield borrowing in their fields. Klein's book and the literature she surveys will be indispensable in epistemics, so is epistemics redundant?

Not, perhaps, entirely. For Klein also claims that the chief impetus for interdisciplinary work has historically been a "synoptic quest for the unity of knowledge" (ibid., 53). Now I think there is substantial epistemological seepage here, but there is much in Klein's book that suggests otherwise. She endorses the blurred genres thesis, repeatedly underscores the need for multiple methods, and stresses that many field crossings are purely local—short-term solutions to concrete problems. Because social problems often cross traditional field boundaries, many interfield research traditions and projects are problem-focused, driven by the demands of government and industry. When grants are tied to problems whose scale transcends standard field boundaries, a discourse arises from many fields adapting to the new public. Environmentalism is a case in point. Biochemistry was a hybrid with strong interactions with immunology, endocrinology, bacteriology, pharmacology, and physiology. Other hybrids include "biophysics, physical chemistry, materials science, environmental engineering, geochemistry, psycholinguistics, sociolinguistics, psychohistory, psychoanthropology, psychological economics, political economy, political sociology, geopolitics, psychiatric sociology, sociobiology, ethnomusicology, economic anthropology, cultural anthropology, systems engineering, and American studies" (ibid., 43). She also stresses the portability of disciplines such as statistics, computer-modeling, and demographics.

But though her cases-in-point are local achievements, the local focus is not the main impression she conveys. The main idea is the "synoptic quest." Her most oft-used words are "synthesis" and "wholeness." Her recurring examples of interdisciplinarity are general systems theory and general education. And she argues that the ideas of interdisciplinarity "are in fact quite old. . . . The roots of the concept lie in a number of ideas that resonate throughout the modern discourse—the ideas of unified science, general knowledge, synthesis, and the integration of knowledge. Plato was the first to advocate philosophy as a unified science." (ibid., 19). Interdisciplinarity is thus rooted in the *systematic* philosophers: Plato, Aristotle, Rabelais, Kant, Hegel—all described as "interdisciplinary thinkers." In other words, with the growth of the *disciplines* in the nineteenth century, *something was lost.*

Incidentally, the claim that the ancients were interdisciplinary thinkers is plausible only if we think they possessed a modern view of disciplinary structure. But Aristotle was a monist; his departments of knowledge reflect the telos in the world. The subdivisions are linked genus to species: Psychology is a species of physics which is a species of metaphysics. Of course, Klein is reading alien texts in the standard way—making them comprehensible by ignoring their strangeness, filling in their silences with familiar, not alien assumptions. So modern fields seem like Aristotle's categories. The historical unity Klein gives to the problem of interdisciplinarity makes me wonder whether she really believes the blurred genres thesis, or sees a tension between local foci and the epistemological impulse. Her last line reads: "whether the context is a short-range instrumentality or a long-range reconceptualization of epistemology, . . . [interdisciplinarity is] an important attempt to define and establish common ground" (ibid., 196). This equivocal tone colors every mention of local focus, so it is hard to read the silences behind them except in the spirit of "the synoptic quest."

She is equally equivocal about the ecotone and edge effect (ibid., 89–92). She discusses them much as I just did, but again is most suggestive in an epistemological direction: The intersection of cultural and ecological principles "may one day lead to a truly general ecological theory, different from current formulations in both biological and cultural ecology. At present, however, none has been systematized or put into axiomatic form" (ibid., 92). This coda suggests that the ecotone and edge effect are cautionary tales—of a lack of communication between and within fields and the failure of borrowers to understand the logic behind a borrowed idea (the borrowers, e.g., ignored the continuum school's claim that ecosystems lack the distinct boundaries of cells). The two ideas were promising tries, but failures, and Klein doesn't mention them again.

Still, I prefer to think that Klein can be coaxed into epistemics. Her case studies are interesting in themselves, not as Hegelian syntheses, by aim or result, but as *working agreements*, local connections for concrete purposes (Cicourel 1974). There are no theoretical obstacles to continuing these studies—and no reasons to think that the recovery of Athenian wholeness is just around the corner. So while waiting, epistemics *is* something to do.

CODA: TWIXT AUFHEBUNG AND PANDEMONIUM

Pandemonium (the condition, not Senator Moynihan's capital of Hell) is often said to be the cost of suspending the quest for wholeness. But pandemonium is not quite what we have. There is order aplenty from locale to locale and nothing especially anarchic about overt competition among discourses. One finds bedlam, I think, only when one tries to take an impossible perspective: One hopes to do for the whole of human knowledge what Weick, remember, despaired of doing for his own field. The result is a condition one can only call *confusion without chaos*.

So epistemics proposes to focus on local discourse and especially on cosmopolitan practices. It studies the conditions of justified assent, with a confidence level falling somewhere between weather forecasting and structural engineering. And unlike policy science, it does not claim to bring an encompassing philosophy to policy-making, nor does it propose still another cadre of experts to save political actors from themselves. It proposes, rather, a way of thinking and talking about knowledge. The architecture of this way is perhaps a little clearer now, but we need, still, a unit of analysis that will simultaneously explain the stability of discourses, their openness to change, and the shifting grounds of their claims to expertise. And that is the subject to which I now turn.

EIGHT

The Uses of Argument Fields

The argument field is in some respects a familiar idea. It belongs to a known phylum, the social knowledge camp. It calls to mind such things as social systems (Cohen 1962, Ziman 1968), rhetorical communities (Farrell 1976, 1977), discourses (Gurvitch 1971), social worlds (Becker 1982), rational enterprises, (Toulmin 1972), epistemic communities (McKerrow 1980a), worlds and world-making (Goodman 1978), and scientific communities (Longino 1990). It suggests stratification and boundaries (Berger and Luckmann 1966). And it emphasizes local realities—the beliefs, fixations, and vernaculars idiomatic to particular practices.

What may be less familiar is the idea of grouping people not by their points of solidarity but by their positions in controversies. Argument fields are places where disputes happen. Their structures are filigrees of argument fissures along which arguers align. Alignment suggests both "with" and "against." One is allied with some and arrayed against others. The latter is as social a phenomenon as the former. An adversarial relationship requires mutually reciprocal attributions; it has identity effects; and it is the sort of affiliation one expects in expert fields. The sciences rarely value dissensus for its own sake and may hope for an ideal completion in which solidarity forms around final answers to all questions. But the road to completion is generally thought to be bumpy. One expects critique, analysis, and the occasional ad hominem. One expects more contentiousness in the social sciences, because they have fewer agreed-upon veridical standards, and still more in the humanities, where essentially contested concepts thrive like crabgrass.

Still, one wonders about so odd an ethnography. Granted that the social world can be segmented in an indefinite number of ways depending on one's aims, but why *this* aim? Why deliberately set out to catch locals, some might say, at their worst? And why would one want to explain how arguments are possible and how they work?

Rest assured, the purpose of the argument field is not to celebrate collegiality red in tooth and claw. The ecological way of putting things doesn't envision intellectual life as a series of death-struggles lit by the faint glow of professional civility. The idea, rather, is that the study of controversy provides an ethnographic entry point that allows analysts to see the assumptions and practices standing behind claims.

WHY ARGUMENT?

Arguments are unique discourse events—conversations involving disagreement. They display epistemic structure more vividly than normal discourse, for they bring to the surface assumptions that would ordinarily remain submerged. Normal conversation prefers agreement (Jacobs and Jackson 1982). It is restrained by a politesse that inhibits interrogation and confrontation. So the simplest case of argument is conversational repair.

But some conversations let disagreement flourish. Argument etiquette permits challenges and demands for clarification and support, and these in turn yield more explicitness. It is a bromide that we study collectivities by noting their taken-for-granted routines. But it is an ethnographic bromide that normalcy obscures its enabling conditions. For the foreigner, the more successful the routine, the more opaque the background; the more that is unproblematic, the more that is hidden. Focusing on the normal is thus like trying to see an alien city on a dark night: One can make out parts but not the whole.

Arguments are like lightning flashes that momentarily expand our horizon. They summon explanation and reason-giving, attack and defense, and thus provide glimpses of the tacit world behind the routine. If I operationalize intelligence as the amount of buckshot I can pour into a cranium, you will infer that I assume "the bigger the better." If you notice that I ignore counterinstances, fudge my data, or subordinate my science to my politics, you may infer that I have a racist agenda (Gould 1981). Explicit confrontation is more likely to bring such details into the open than any other form of interaction. Arguments spark interrogatory moves and counterclaims (Jackson and Jacobs 1980). And the expectation of challenge introduces listener-sensitive refutations (Delia, Kline, and Burleson 1979) and is arguably a powerful social governor in legal, political, and expert argument.

The *field*, then, is a way of operationalizing *intentionality*. Kantians use intentionality to say that ideas are about objects, but I use it here to mean the deliberateness of writers and speakers. Texts may be indefinitely open to interpretation (O'Keefe 1987), but we often need to decipher their silences by attributing identities and motives to their makers. This is often a matter of describing a culture, a background, a tapestry of assumptions behind the text. When one creates such a picture, one is defining a field in which an interpretation of a claim or position is plausible. These definitions may be taken for granted in the natural attitude (Schutz 1962) or reflectively contrived positions. In either case, claims and positions are understood as embedded in background. There is something behind them.

And we often need to know what speakers mean to be saying—not all the hermeneutic possibilities one can dredge up, but the meanings and acts they intend to convey and perform. If an utterance might mean a hundred things, it is of more than passing interest that speakers are able to harness their performances to their intentions. When speech is sincere, pertinent, purposeful, and competent, it is not indefinitely construable. Hermeneutics would be a social impertinence. No speaker would agree to be held accountable for every meaning that might be imputed to a claim. If I refer to the "freedom fighters in Nicaragua," you may wonder whether I mean the Contras or the Sandinistas, but I am within my rights in refusing to acknowledge that I mean both. Whether I am a member of the Eagle Forum or the Che Gueverra Action Commune, I presume that my affiliation speaks for me, that some things needn't be said, that listeners will understand (and hold me accountable for) my intentions—leaving me free to say with Prufrock, "that's not what I meant at all."

OBJECTIFYING

Of course Prufrockian self-absorption has limits. Subjectivity is largely a personal predicament, like nearsightedness, to be solved by intersubjectivity, social comparison, and often by conforming to group norms. Intentionality thus works in tandem with indexicality. Claims take their meaning and authority from the field in which they are conventionally constrained. Much as communicative acts imply social contracts (Jackson 1985), knowledge claims imply grounds. In making such claims, one enters the institutions in which they have meaning. These institutions circumscribe interpretive possibilities—their public disciplines working against the indefiniteness utterances might otherwise have. And many of them lay claim to judgmental jurisdictions—spans of professional authority within which specialists stand ready to denounce poseurs. If I claim to be a Freudian, you would be surprised to learn that I believe in operant conditioning and astonished to learn that I don't believe in the Id. You might conclude that I am speaking unconventionally, or worse, sailing under false colors.

"Objectifying" is a verb, not a Cartesian state of grace. It means "going public" (Polanyi 1958), which is what interactants do when they refer to the disciplines and conceptual ecologies standing behind their claims. It means aligning one's thinking or playing by the rules in a domain of objectivity. And to some extent it means bracketing one's doubts: Just as the descent to practice silences all but the most doctrinaire skeptics (Rescher 1973, 1977b), action demands a momentary suspension of doubt—which I call the As-If Maxim (Willard 1983). One proceeds as if one's assumptions are sound, as if one's field is an accomplished body of knowledge. One's Toulminean leap from data to claim is to some extent a leap of faith—scarcely feasible if one is paralyzed by doubt.

As verbs go, "objectifying" is as conventional as any but more rhetorical than most. It suggests that beliefs and practices have historical weight and magisterial authority. Science, for instance, functions, inter alia, as an ethos, a Goffmanesque mask, a face of rationality (Geertz, 1988). This mask has regulatory uses: One's identity as a scientist keeps one honest. It has polemical uses, from fund-raising to slug-fests with creationists. And it has reverential uses, as would-be sciences rally around the idea of earning the label. It would be surprising not to find these uses mingling with the mundane, daily life conformities of normal science. Parsonians will disagree, of course, but identity does affect conduct, persuasion often courts self-persuasion, and ideals do provoke struggles to achieve them.

RATIONALITY

With conformity to a field's disciplines comes its imprimatur: By proceeding in conventionally coherent, conventionally sound ways, one is taken seriously—and thus to some extent vouched for, endorsed, and authenticated. Rationality, in this sense, inspires Foucauldian ambivalence: It smacks of rationalizing, of the self-referential institution rewarding behavior that feeds its power. But being taken seriously isn't equivalent to being agreed with. Disputes happen as field actors find opponents worthy of the name—which is to say, worth taking seriously. And the thing to notice as opponents lock horns is that naturally occurring arguments do not become less social (or persuasive) as they become more rational. They become more constrained, more rule-governed, more professionally and procedurally reflective.

This is scarcely the pristine state of grace many people hope that rationality might be. But armchair virtues by definition arise in the absence of temptation. Rationality is more like Hemingway's "grace under pressure": most to be prized when it is hardest to come by. In the heat and bustle of real arguments, any semblance of the virtues of reason and speech, however modest, warrants esteem. If humans, being human, can't discard their prejudices and interests or ignore their social surroundings, yet are able, nonetheless, to behave well, and if experts, still being human, are able to further discipline their discourses, then sociality, rationality, and persuasion may be pragmatically symbiotic.

The idea of virtue under pressure suggests something of a critical mission, though plainly not judgments on a Matthew Arnold elevation. For epistemics, capitalizing the word "reason" is simply an interesting native practice. It helps us decipher local customs—privileged positions, free-floating critics, and impartial standpoints of rationality. But like ancestor worship, it is the sort of practice best left to locals.

Field studies, as I envision them, are largely descriptive affairs—a matter of explaining the genesis of arguments, how and why they flare up, and the grounds on which knowledge claims rest. It is a figure-ground problem—a matter of finding a context within which claims are intelligible and verifiable. And it is a problem faced by analysts and actors alike. For what most people most need to know is how to interpret and whether to believe claims. The rhetorical moments come, when they do, at points of impasse, or ennui. Claims are reinterpreted or recontextualized. The reflective actor envisions a possible world, an alternative field. Or the visiting analyst coaxes the natives onto foreign soil.

In either case, ingenuity begins with understanding. Opportunities aren't conjured from thin air. All fields, real or imagined, arise as analysts and actors try to fit their thinking to available data. So the next step is to specify the social realities the field idea might be used to map.

FACETS OF THE FIELD IDEA

What follows has a pedantic air I find embarrassing but hard to excise. It reads like Aristotle's *Parts of Animals*. But the field is an artifice for naming real entities—the perspectives, relationships, groups, organizations, movements, and expert domains pertinent to interpreting the claims people make and the positions they take. This is expansive territory, and since the vocabulary of the social knowledge camp is so variable, it seems wise to purchase some precision at the price of a dogmatic tone.

PERSONAL PERSPECTIVES

People have fields of attention. They notice some things and not others. They anticipate events and construe their options; they interpret and decipher; they accommodate their actions to the perspectives of others; and they frame their communications within their intentions. These moves aren't always interesting: It is often more useful to interpret actions in a purely conventional way. But intentions are sometimes important—for disambiguating messages, contextualizing actions, framing replies, and for assigning praise and blame.

Indeed to study organizations (or function within them) is often to study people—to impute meanings to their actions, to make inferences about their beliefs, feelings, and intentions. It is often imperative to know what they mean to be doing, how they expect to be seen by others. How else, for instance, could we say that some modes of organizing are relatively free and open and that others are more ideological or prone to fanaticism? Ideology and fanaticism don't invariably leap out of enthymemes, fangs bared. Systematic distortion worthy of the name is at least veiled, if not invisible. So to know the iron cage, one must know something of its prisoners—their beliefs, feelings, and cognitive strategies (Davis 1968, Dixon 1980). To unpack the silences behind their utterances, one must know how they process messages. For only on some such evidence could we say with any confidence that they are prisoners.

And it is sometimes informative to read texts in light of their authors' behavior. For instance, one might not know from texts alone that the claim to outsider status is a privileging tactic. The claim to unequal status often lies between the lines, in things left unsaid, or in the tone of confidence in an author's voice. The devaluing of opponents emerges face-to-face along office corridors and at academic gatherings—and becomes admissible evidence, I submit, pertinent to interpreting a literature's silences and ambiguities.

And finally the question of how fringe ideas move into a field's mainstream often turns on the rhetorical skills of (and obstructions to) peripheral actors. Indeed, knowing the difference between geniuses and cranks sometimes demands outside help. Oliver Heaviside's work on operators in physical mathematics was vilified by "rigorists" and redeemed only when quantum physicists and electrical engineers began to use it (Hunt 1991). Rigor was a form of gate-keeping meant to shut the door on the idea that mathematics is empirical.

ENCOUNTERS

Still at the small end of the continuum are conversations: "A thought collective exists whenever two or more persons are actually exchanging thoughts" (Fleck 1979, 102). The sparsest conversations may be among strangers, but strangers at an airport might find that they are NBA fans and thus have a common subject matter.

Encounters are interesting cases of knowledge use. Because knowledge claims are indexical, their operation in arguments displays a field's function as a basis of social comparison. And encounters reveal how actors are socialized into fields because socialization is embodied in conversation, argument, and instruction. "The initiation into any thought style . . . is not merely formal. The Holy Ghost as it were descends upon the novice, who will now be able to see what has hitherto been invisible" (Fleck 1979, 104).

A failure to appreciate the field-constitutive role of encounters can yield dubious distinctions, for instance Goodnight's (1982) contrast between the personal and technical spheres. Goodnight's spheres are groundings not of claims, as in foundationalism, but of arguments, and his objection to a focus on encounters is that it ignores differences in how encounters and disciplined arguments are grounded. Personal argument is created in a durational time dimension: "Points at issue can be dropped, appear again years later, be returned to, or entirely forgotten." But a technical field "more or less objectifies time insofar as common procedures, schedules, measurements, and argument/decision/action sequences are set up by common agreement" (1982, 223).

Perhaps expert fields wish they were so objectified. But they do drop and later resurrect ideas (self-similarity in physics; rhetoric in philosophy); they do have lapses (recall my little history of *Wissensoziologie*), and they are scarcely immune to forgetfulness and strategic recall (witness the longevity of progressive rhetoric). Nor are encounters inevitably as undisciplined as Goodnight suggests. No doubt there are distinctly personal encounters dealing with matters idiomatic to private relationships, but why should we suppose that people never bring public disciplines—for instance, ethical constraints, habits of thought, and methods for evaluating evidence—to bear on private problems?

But the more important issue is the degree to which encounters are constrained and guided by, yet also constitutive of the structure of expert fields. Giddens (1979) calls this "structuration"—the idea being that organizational actors are both carriers and creators of structure (Riley 1983, 415). They simultaneously animate social structure, as for instance rules are brought to life in actual uses, yet are also guided by structure, and somehow, by this dual function, the possibilities for innovation arise. This is a striking theory: It suggests the possibility of explaining stability and change in the same language (Toulmin 1972), and a reply to the self-replicating discourses and institutions of Foucault and Douglas.

But before crowds gather to celebrate, it is important to notice that structuration has been more an organizational device for review essays (e.g., Poole and McPhee 1983) than an empirically confirmed—or especially clear—idea. Archer (1982, 479) calls the theory "incomplete because it provides an insufficient account of the *mechanisms* of stable replication versus the genesis of new social forms." And since Giddens suggested no method for unpacking the layers of practice and institutions, it is tempting to dismiss structuration as a Pascal's Wager for organizations—more a countergesture to Foucault and Douglas than an empirical refutation. But such a dismissal might be premature. Kanter (1977), for instance, concretely displays the tensions between pressures for stability and the tenuous possibilities for innovation, and in a similar vein, Poole (1985, 107) has proposed that "communication is the medium of all structurational processes," a proposal that presumably would bring encounters to center stage. And then, perhaps, the grand issue of human agency versus the iron cage will cease to be an essentially contested concept.

RELATIONSHIPS

Marriages, kinships, friendships, and professional bonds are founded on shared background knowledge that permits complex, elided, and implicit communication. Their epistemic and organizational importance lies in their meaning-constitutive function, the abbreviations and elisions they facilitate, the agreements and cooperative meanings they support. Intimate relationships are thus the clearest-cut argument fields imaginable.

The relationship idea also explains status effects. Professional socialization trades on mentoring and affects, for better and worse, the dissemination and acceptance of ideas. Status is a shield when individuals become establishments (Elias 1982). Corrupt lab chiefs make for corrupt labs (Price 1963, 1965). Where most science debunkers focus on government funding, citation traditions, and peer review, the relationship idea adds another dimension to the equation: it assumes that personal influence plays a role in advancing and protecting both structures (labs, programs, grants, etc.) and ideas.

GROUPS

A sizable literature has accumulated around the proposition that group decision-making is "how organizations think" (Abell 1975, Bass 1983). Groups, so to speak, are an organization's brains, its inner parliament that balances options and constraints. The more complex the organization, the greater its division of labor, and thus the greater its reliance on group rationality. This dependency is often for the best. Groups are, on the whole, better than individuals, though slower, at weighing options, identifying alternatives, managing information (both when there is too much and too little), and at balancing competing points of view. Asked to achieve a Foucauldian eventualization, then, group communication researchers would unanimously pick a team, not a lone historian. A team would hash things out, negotiate, and compromise. It might more accurately discern the effects of closed borders and pressures for agreement and recapture the group dynamics that create future inevitabilities.

The idea of dynamics has come rather far from Lewin's force fields. The literature is largely a variable-analytic tradition focusing, for instance, on the effects of democratic versus authoritarian leadership or on the effects of status on turns-at-talk or on the effects of emergent interpersonal perceptions on the tensions that wax and wane during group interaction. The goal is to determine how group dynamics go wrong. For in addition to their strengths, groups also "risky shift"—make riskier decisions than their members would alone. They "groupthink"—think single-mindedly because of their solidarity (Janis 1983). And they ratify self-fulfilling prophecies as the organizations in which they function set their agendas, circumscribe their power, and filter their information (Conrad 1983).

One interesting possibility is that the innovation side of structuration stems partly from accidents, a risky shift here makes for chaos there and thus weakens or subtly changes the larger structure. The study of group decision-making may thus reveal concrete instances of structuration in action. The thrust of the group communication literature is analogous to the critical thinking movement's goals for individuals, and if the principles of good decision-making demonstrably lead to good decisions, then structuration may become a clearer process, indeed one open to human control, and even fine-tuning.

One gathers from Kanter (1977), for instance, that the vigor and enthusiasm of participation in organizational groups is dependent on feelings of loyalty to the organization yet central to the success of group activities. High participation groups do best, and their members are likelier to participate when they feel upwardly mobile in the organization. Those feelings, I should think, are researchable mechanisms of structuration and perhaps clues to how groups depart (or fail to depart) from the deep ruts of Douglas's institutions.

I am content, incidentally, not to define the word *group* with any special precision. The idea implies some collective sense of "groupness," but as we've seen, shared identity covers a multitude of awarenesses, from the loosest and vaguest to the tightest and clearest. Groups are also defined by their histories of interaction. But there are de novo groups: For instance quality circles are problem-solving teams structured to discourage expressiveness, maximize brainstorming, and force decisions. And groups are sometimes defined by their size, though size, certainly, is in the eye of the beholder. One gathers from the literature that, since we have the word *dyad* for two people, "groupness" begins generally with three, and ends at some essentially contestable point where terms for larger aggregations seem more appropriate. So perhaps it is enough to say that a group is a band small enough to make its decision-making fit its desire for unanimity. Some synonyms for group suggest smallness: assembly, clique, circle, company, party, gathering. Hosts, hordes, and throngs are apparently bigger. And at the farthest reaches of throngness, I should think, the term *public* will do. A public, let's say, is anything bigger than a throng.

PUBLICS

Publics are not language systems. A public is a cluster of people with a field of attention; a language system is an idea in linguistic philosophy. The two have no known relations. And it is the language system, remember, where Foucault's trap springs shut.

The idea that discourse is balkanized into local languages, foci, subjects, and practices started, if not with the Sophists, with Wittgenstein (1953, 1969), who coined the expressions "forms of life" and "language games" to reject his own claim in the *Tractatus* that all propositions carry with them the whole of language. The *Tractatus*' picture theory of language says that elementary propositions are combinations of names; to know names one must know the objects in the world; to know any object is to know all objects; and "if elementary propositions are given, then at the same time all elementary propositions are given" (Wittgenstein 1922, 103, 5.524). The *Investigations* rejects this view: meanings arise in uses, not pictures. Language isn't isomorphic of objects but analogous to "an enormous toolbox, replete with the most diversified assortment of tools, practically none of which resembles those things in the world to which they may be applied" (Weitz 1966, 11). As there is no universal form of games (some are competitive, some are fun, some turn on zero sum conditions, some turn on cooperation, etc.), and only family resemblances among some, sentences do not carry with them the whole of language: they imply language games that in turn imply forms of life. Since "our empirical propositions do not form a homogeneous mass" (Wittgenstein 1969, 29e), the logical status of propositions is context-dependent—tied both to adaptations to situations and to the language games that guide them. So it is a mistake to want to "find an expression's meaning by contemplating the expression itself" (ibid., 601).

This was a radical claim for its time—as revolutionary as quantum dynamics. And it is still not universally accepted. Many argument scholars and informal logicians still look to the expression itself, deconstructionists are still unpacking the expression itself, and conversational analysts still focus on the moves and obligations wired into the act itself.

Still, the language game has been influential in the blurred genres, largely, I imagine, because those fields were already bent on defining knowledge by its functions and uses. Pragmatism, always an edge species in philosophy, had found its most receptive niches further afield. One notable migrating bird was Wittgenstein's student, Stephen Toulmin, who invented the argument field to reform logic, yet found his first audiences chiefly in rhetoric and policy studies. And the field that most energetically looked for uses of his *Uses of Argument* was argumentation, a little ecotone straddling the wetlands of rhetoric and the prairies of communication.

Language games were appealing because they seemed to rescue the idea of systems from the fate of "the cult of the system" (Toulmin 1972). It was a death and transfiguration, from prisonhouse of language to home incarceration. The closed system went local: The builder and his helper speak of blocks, pillars, slabs, and beams in a language game that is "complete in itself" (Wittgenstein 1953).

But language games are often incomplete in themselves. Getting a building up is a matter of coordinating the practices of carpenters, electricians, architects, cost-accountants, inspectors, and contractors. The organizations of modernity are complex versions of this coordination problem—pragmatic worlds in which "formal knowledge is transformed and modified by the activities of those participating in its use" (Freidson 1986, xi). NASA, for instance, manages projects of great complexity, often coordinating among hundreds of expert fields. But no one, so far as I know, has ever called NASA "a conversation" or likened a Challenger-scale blunder to a conversational glitch. The Challenger disaster is usually attributed to acquired organizational recklessness and policy momentum (Gouran 1985, 1987, Gouran, Hirokawa, and Martz 1986, Ice 1987, McConnell 1987, Miller 1989, Rowland 1986, Seeger 1986). But as we shall see, the movement of information and policy decisions through organizational time and space displays a quantum weirdness (Pagels 1983) analogous to chaos in computer networks.

If, then, many language games are not complete in themselves, it may be more informative to say that practices are given meaning by the publics in which they figure. Publics are organized around stances toward ideas. They are rhetorically constituted: They are audiences (McCloskey 1985); they have designated speakers; they use persuasion (Simons 1982); their discourses are bound to their styles of expression (Nelson, Megill, and McCloskey 1987); their members' faith is capital on which they draw (Bartley 1963); their knowledge claims are authorized by consensus (Finocciarò 1977); they capitalize upon illusions of rigor and precision (Geertz 1988) or of historical necessity, moral rightness, or divine purpose; and the more professionalized ones have authority structures for accrediting speakers and claims (Polanyi 1958).

The difference between publics organized around political goals and those centered on getting epistemically better is often thought to be clear-cut. Leff (1987) sees a difference as stark as Snow's "two cultures": Academic and public rhetorics differ in "complexity of reasoning, use of evidence, frequency and types of images, syntactic constructions, vocabulary, assumptions about the audience's knowledge, and almost every other category relevant to classification of types of rhetoric." If one doubts these contrasts, Leff says, one should compare texts of congressional debates with the prose in academic journals. The conditions "surrounding academic discourse require deviation from the practices of public deliberation. Rhetorical models for technical fields and for the public sphere do not correspond, and attempts to map one directly onto the other are bound to produce considerable distortion" (Leff 1987, 33–34).

Distortion may be too mild a word, but I prefer a continuum to a black-white contrast. One criticism of big science is that its subject matters are mapped all too well onto agency agendas and political fads. Environmentalism, though it is clearly a social movement, simply reeks of tweed and ivy: It is peopled largely by academics, deploys a decidedly technical patois, and numbers among its membership natural scientists whose professional work is allied with their movement activities. So a message complexity continuum might join Leff's list to other factors. For instance, professionalized schools of thought or issue fields may have more explicit epistemic norms and ideals than most social movements; they may be more reflective about their authority-dependence and more apt to see themselves as curators of a body of knowledge.

Perhaps it seems surprising that I even mention movements. The idea connotes strong agreement, indeed zealous quests for social or political change (Wilkinson 1971). One gathers from the literature that movements vary in their points and sources of unity (their members may coalesce around vague symbols or complex public positions), but their common rhetorical origins and continuing rhetorical conditions are founded on shared purpose (Bormann 1972, McGee 1983, Sillars 1980). The scholarly focus has been on their tactics and effects more than their internal constitution (Rosenau 1967). So movements are often described as if they function with the tactics of a single person.

So too are interest groups and lobbies. Both are seen as groups of variable power and cohesion organized around variously effective agents whose messages are directed at influencing governments. Interest groups range from diffuse ethnic lobbies to issue-specific action groups (Spanier and Uslaner 1978, Campbell 1971). Both genres propose that people organize around action goals—lobbies being formal organizations, movements being more informal and perhaps bigger. The right to life movement is at once a diffuse mass phenomenon, a demographically identifiable group arrayed against an equally identifiable opposing group, an orchestrated political movement, and a political lobby. One could say the same of Greenpeace, the Sierra Club, the Farm Labor Party, the IWW, and so on.

But agreement is scarcely the whole story. Populists and pluralists, remember, need one another. And the public behavior of some movements turns on internal divisions. With millennialist movements, for instance, splinter groups are the rule; and though the breakaways often latch onto charismatic leaders before taking to the woods, there is the continuing problem that with each passing day the world again doesn't end, thus ensuring internecine squabbles, hair-splitting, and the occasional try at helping Armageddon along. The more doctrinaire the movement, the more one can say of its internal divisions what Senator Moynihan says of ethnic conflict: Big differences aren't needed; "small will do."

Mass polling has to some extent diminished the power of movements and interest groups—or at least made it tricker to claim to speak for them: If one says one thing and the polls another, "almost invariably the polls are assumed to be correct" (Ginsberg 1986, 61). And it is harder than it used to be to define the contours of movements: There are too many media, messages, and leaders. One can perhaps spot the Aryan Nation by its campfires, the Skinheads by their tattoos; the Church of Scientology has membership roles. But labels such as "Feminism" cover so expansive a range of views that they are relatively uninformative. One needs a clear-cut dispute—say about censorship and the First Amendment—to glimpse the trajectories various groups are following.

This talk of movements isn't meant to imply that, for example, big bang physics is merely millennialism in the opposite direction or that the Critical Thinking movement has the group dynamics of the People's Temple. It is meant to suggest that the dynamics of opinion change and coalition formation take many forms, and if, as I believe, the expert fields are better able to correct for their social frailties, it is because they have disciplines unavailable to popular movements.

These disciplines ought to be most noticeable in schools of thought, the isms and ologies organized around ideas. This rubric includes social movements (astrology, scientology) as well as expert fields (chaos physics, cultural anthropology). Schools are definable largely by their beliefs (Freudians believe in the id, behaviorists don't), their agreed-upon problem foci (Toulmin 1972), their methods, and their judgmental and veridical standards. They are historically constituted social organizations. They have taken-for-granted background knowledge, a framework of assumptions about which there is enough consensus to keep an ism alive and to make normal science (or practice) possible. They function socially to maintain intellectual stability: They standardize authority and expertise and package knowledge for pedagogy. Their normal practices authorize canonical literatures.

We operationalize a school's local beliefs much as its members do—by their appearances in positions. Positions may be theories (as we might speak of the *Weltanschauungen* position) or political stances that presuppose many theories, or calls for action. They needn't be but often are associated with people (as we speak of the president's position on Nicaragua) or exemplary spokespersons (as the secretary of state exemplifies the State Department's position on *X*). They are often group productions. Characteristically, positions are designed to short-circuit hermeneutical speculations. Field actors often have specific intentions and zones of accountability in mind (ists are not free to say just anything or to appeal to just any order of evidence).

Disciplines and Institutions

The term *discipline* is often used as a loose synonym for "field." This way of speaking goes back to the medieval orders and reflects, for some, the intuition that all respectable fields (even ones riven by competing schools) aim to achieve a single definitive discipline. But I prefer a more Foucauldian convention: "Discipline" is an excellent label for particular packages of techniques and methods. A discipline, then, is a regimen, a compact body of constraints, methods, and assumptions, a set of procedures and strictures that might be called into play in any field. If one needs an analysis of variance, one plays by ANOVA rules; if one wants multidimensional computer modeling, one plays by other rules; and if one's arguments are supposed to contribute to the development of a theory, one plays by still other rules.

Not all disciplines are portable (electronmicroposy travels about as often as electron microscopes), but many—like statistics, contractarian ethics, cost-benefit analysis, and informal logic—are cosmopolitan. They can be described as self-standing discourse domains, complete with members, beliefs, literatures, practices, and as subdivisions in other fields—as imported methods and problem foci occupying niches in other ecologies. Similarly, chaos physics, a self-contained field, has found niches in mathematics, computer science, biology, astronomy, business, and others. So where Geertz says that philology has splintered into subspecialties, it seems better to say that the discipline has found niches in a variety of ecosystems, from ethnography to comparative and text linguistics, to psychology to rhetorical criticism.

This narrower usage brings discipline closer to institution—and perhaps recovers some of Douglas's intuitions. Both terms suggest cohesive complexes of values, beliefs, and practices that are analogous to a society's vital organs (Hertzler 1946). So just as slavery was called a peculiar institution—a package of laws, practices, mores, habits, and customs within southern culture—we can say that operationism is an institution within positivism, and confession, mass, and the roles of priests are institutions within Catholicism. Action within an institution is a matter of accommodating to expectations embedded in a public code. We thus expect to see institutions operating in encounters (e.g., in the politesse governing discourse among strangers), relationships (in their idiomatic histories as well as outside models called in for certain purposes), and issue fields. We expect them to have normative power and authority.

Institutions imply constraints: cost-benefit analysis is *meant* to be a suprapersonal closed system. And some societies *mean* to be carceral: Religions are *meant* to foster passivity, piety, and community. The Marine Corps *intends* to produce marines who think they are indestructible. Such cases confirm the determinists' intuitions, but I prefer the language of persuasion theory: of cognitive laziness, peripheral persuasion, disruptions of counterargument, and forced compliance (Petty and Cacioppo 1986). Within this vocabulary, individual differences in cognitive ability and communicative performance suggest proportionate differences in the ways actors use or succumb to institutions. We expect to find rebels, critics, and skeptics alongside fanatics—innocence side by side with bad faith, trust coexisting with Machiavellianism. And we will sometimes find conscientious attempts to promote critical thinking, critique, and rational intellectual progress. There are also psychological differences: People may create their own theories to order their cognitive affairs; their motives for seeking certainty in closed cognitive systems or reflective thinking in open-minded systems resemble the communal decisions that achieve the same results. So even in fields designed to promote reflective thinking, we are not surprised to find the occasional true believer.

If individual and field differences lead to variations in true-believership, reflectiveness,and adaptability, they also affect the facility with which people modify and use institutions—and for this, the language of rhetorical creativity is useful: Conventional and rhetorical communication may trade upon structure to accomplish ends. To move from one mode of thinking to another might seem disingenuous to O'Keefe's expressives, but we often applaud the intellectual flexibility that enables arguers to transcend intransigent disputes. So the rhetorical's solution—be someone else, find another language game—challenges the either-or choices some institutions pose.

PROFESSIONS

The term *profession* denotes a self-regulating, legally enfranchising field with a complex division of labor. Law and medicine come first to mind, but academic departments and organizations fit the definition. Their bureaucratic structures institutionalize expertise, credentialing, epistemic jurisdictions, and work jurisdictions (Abbott 1988); they publish journals and sponsor symposia; they administer (and package knowledge for) pedagogy; they enforce hiring patterns and codes of conduct (Berlant 1975, Bledstein 1976).

And as we've seen, in addition to these indispensable functions, professions also inspire considerable ambivalence. To put it all in one sentence, they are, or tend to be, predatory interest groups, oligarchical monopolies, with the social instincts of hyenas and the public spiritedness of arms merchants. This is perhaps too exuberant, and neither metaphor is entirely fair, but it does underscore two reasons for distinguishing professions from issue fields. First, it suggests that professionalism is a different order of awareness—overlaid, as it were, on issue fields. One does one's work; one belongs to one's professional organization; and if the twain do meet, the question is whether or to what degree the virtues and sins of the professions are visited on the specialties.

Second, though it isn't unheard of for a profession to be dominated by a single school of thought, professional labels are often epistemically uninformative. Medicine and economics are bureaucratically informative: They identify professional organizations and university departments. But they are not especially revealing about subject matter. Economists say all sorts of things, but a label such as cost-benefit analysis predicts the substance of what one will say, the drift of one's position. Ists make claims idiomatic to their isms: Behaviorists speak of paired-associate learning; cost-benefit analysts cast values into fiscal language; chaos physicists speak of extreme sensitivity to starting conditions; and pro-lifers speak of fetuses as human.

University departments and professional organizations may include any number of isms within their ambit. In 1933, for instance, Heidbreder (in Weimer 1979) divided psychology into seven schools—each envisioning itself as "the total field of psychology as a consistent and unified whole" (Heidbreder 1933, 18). Her reasoning was quite pre-Kuhnian. She saw the schools as alternative ways of looking at the same data. Psychology owns the data; the schools interpret it. Without the schools, "few facts would be forthcoming. For scientific knowledge does not merely accumulate; it is far more likely to grow about hypotheses that put definite questions and which act as centers of organization in the quest for knowledge. As a matter of historical fact, science has not grown by following the method Bacon described—that is, by the steady amassing of data and the emergence of generalizations" (ibid., 15). So there is nothing pathological about this pluralism. The practices of the schools are a strength. As in Quine's holism (scientific beliefs form a web meeting experience "as a corporate whole"), Heidbreder says that "A system may fulfill its function by proving itself either right or wrong, or [contra Quine, we might say] as is far more likely to be the case, by proving itself partly right or partly wrong. The very errors of systems, especially if they are clear-cut and decisive, may further the cause of science by revealing the mistakes that need not be repeated" (ibid., 15–16). Since 1933, of course, the schools have multiplied (artificial intelligence, S-O-R behaviorism, constructivism, third force psychology, cognitive psychology, social psychology, to name a few). So her point remains intact: Psychology is a profession, not an issue field.

The Functions of Fields

Normative Functions

The mingling of professions and issue fields is further illustrated by considering their functions as reference groups (Hyman and Singer 1968)—or in Hyman's (1960) words, "ego anchorages," groups to which individuals psychologically orient themselves to achieve a self-definition or to guide behavior. These orientations range, in all likelihood, from a Foucauldian governmentality—one's identity is lost in group values and norms—to a chameleon flexibility in which one dons one Goffmanesque mask after another. Somewhere in between, but closer to Goffman than Foucault, would be a conventional-but-flexible cosmopolitan—one of O'Keefe's rhetoricals—who would be polite everywhere in a pluralistic society, but who would also, perhaps only privately, hierarchically order the groups in which she moves—organizing her behavior vis-à-vis the prevailing values of the most important groups.

One can imagine shades and gradations along this continuum—which perhaps explains why the reference group was never an especially clear idea (Schmitt 1972). For some it covered a multitude of sins—"taking influence" being a kind of passive acquiescence, an abdication of reason. Others, however, saw a rational reflectiveness in reference groups: Shibutani (1955, 1961, 1962) likened them to Mead's "generalized other." They are implicit audiences of one's actions, whose expectations (and possible judgments) one deems relevant. One then weighs one's wants against situational constraints, adds the normative component into one's mix, and then makes choices.

At every point along the continuum, reference group effects resemble (and are sometimes indistinguishable from) ethos effects (Kelman 1961). We take influence, after all, from individuals as well as groups. So fields are seeable as sources of social comparison and confidence. To know them is to know their cardinal virtues and sins, their ideals and devils, their paradigm cases of excellence, and their lunatics and outcasts.

Discourse Functions

Small research traditions are animated by informal and deeply idiomatic communications. As they grow, they formalize paper exchanges and small journals. Bigger circles have bigger journals and conferences as well as textbooks. We might call these "relatively mass media." Though not everything said of mass communications applies to disciplined discourse (an expert field's public is comparatively more specialized than bigger publics, and even the biggest professions—the AMA, ABA, APA, or MLA—are small compared to the numbers represented by Nielsen points), some explanations of opinion change and influence do apply to big fields.

For instance, there is de facto selective exposure. To persuasion theorists, selective exposure is a weak general preference for information that supports one's views (O'Keefe 1990). But a more robust effect, I predict, will come from accidents of focus. One is attentive to information that drops into one's lap, as it were, that intrudes into one's habits. One is likeliest to notice information that is readily obtainable, apparently useful, or by some other measure relevant. The diffusion of medical information has thus been tied to selective exposure and literary density (Coleman, Katz, and Menzel 1966, Rogers 1962), and striking similarities have been reported between how farmers came to accept hybrid seed corn and how physicians decide to prescribe new drugs (Katz 1971).

De facto selectivity may mean de facto incommensurability. Big fields are divided into readerships—groups attentive to particular journals—so we are scarcely surprised if analytic philosophers avoid social epistemology or structuralists forego symbolic interaction. This is still another weakness of seeing fields as conversations. The bigger they are, the more they resemble the babble of multiple conversations at a cocktail party (Menzel 1962, Mullins 1968, Perrow 1984, Storer 1966, F. Williams 1987, Zaltman 1968).

Consider, too, the notorious two-step flow (Katz 1957), originally proposed as a repair of the bullet theory of mass communication. The idea was that mass influence filters down to individuals by the intervention of opinion leaders in smaller groups. But as researchers bit the bullet, unsurprisingly, there turned out to be many steps and many competing sources of influence. Influence turned out to be more lateral than horizontal: In political science, for instance, the two-step flow is called stratified pluralism and Neuman (1986, 37), for one, is dubious about it: "most political discussion takes place between people on equal levels of political interest." Still, though it is mostly an historical curiosity, and largley anecdotal, the two-step flow focused attention on the ethos of opinion leaders and its effects on group beliefs and attitudes. This credibility, I argue (1989a, 131–42) may be a rational attribution—just as we might think it rational for novices to be persuaded by their teachers or colleagues by esteemed colleagues. And if big fields are balkanized into smaller ones, then the two-step flow theory suggests not only an hermeticism in the smaller units but also a dilution effect as the ideas from one esoteric core filter outward to the relatively mass communications of the bigger field, and still more dilutions as these mass communications filter into other esoteric groups.

A similar filtering should occur as peripheral scholars interpret developments in other fields for their colleagues. Bruffee's (1986, 773) bibliographic essay explaining the importance of a new field for readers of

College English typifies the genre: "Although social construction has a venerable history . . . and although writers in a number of fields are engaged in an effort to develop the disciplinary implications of a nonfoundational social constructionist understanding of knowledge, that history remains largely unacknowledged and the effort fragmented. Terminology proliferates. The result is that in some cases positions not only similar but mutually supportive seem alien to one another. Writers find it difficult to draw upon each other's work."

So, grown from Pragmatism, seeded by Kuhn and Rorty, and articulated by Geertz, "social constructionist thought is a strikingly fruitful alternative to the way we normally think and talk about what we do" (Bruffee 1986, 776). The author's bibliography—a mere two pages—omits thousands of works from relevant research traditions. But this is typical: Most journals are intolerant of giant bibliographies, so the reader gets a tip-of-the-iceberg essay, and, as there are limits to footnote-chasing, the filtering process functions much like mass influence.

INTERFIELD DISCOURSE

The way analysts and field actors describe a field's internal organization and communication circumscribes what they are able and prone to say about discourse at its borders. Epistemic isolation makes for scant foreign affairs. Closed societies want hermetically sealed borders to protect a master narrative; relatively open societies tolerate multiple conversations, peripheral discourses, and permeable outer borders.

My defense of this thesis is organized around three claims: (1) that some but not all fields are marked by identifiable communication and cognitive styles; (2) that closure and openness are side effects of organizing metaphors; and (3) such stylistic choices may impede or promote peripheral discourse.

STYLE

The term *style* has many meanings. "Cognitive style" refers to one's dogmatism or openmindedness. Hofstadter (1967) speaks of the paranoid style of politics. Rhetorical theorists speak of the selection and management of language—word choices as well as grand, middle, or plain styles of delivery. In ordinary parlance, style means fashion, trend, or vogue. And as Charles Barkley has said, perspiration "shouldn't mess with one's style," by which he presumably meant élan, grace, and savoir faire.

All of these meanings figure in Fleck's (1979) proposal that thought collectives are marked by distinctive thought styles. Fleck opposed any dichotomy of substance and style. The foil is ancient rhetorical theory for its willingness to speak of the selection and management of language as if ("a rose by any other name . . . ") one has an obdurate reality that might be represented differently. Stylistic choices, on this view, depend not on the subject matter but on the rhetor's skill and adaptation to an audience. Fleck holds that form, manner, and technique are inseparable from substance; style affects substantive choices; it creates interpretive possibilities; it opens some interpretive doors while closing others. Thus, "the question of style arises not in trying to package a finished product of thought, but, rather, in actually producing the thought" (Fuller 1982, 3). The intertwining of style and substance is proved by contrasts between modern science and its ancient and medieval precursors. To ancient chemists, the metals were suns and moons, "kings and queens, red bridegrooms and lily brides. Gold was Apollo, sun of the lofty dome; . . . quicksilver was the wing-footed Mercury, Herald of the Gods, new lighted on a Heaven kissing hill" (Fleck 1979, 125), and so on.

Fleck is pressing an incommensurability thesis that turns on the differences between ancient and modern style—between seeing infections as demons, as portrayed in medieval paintings, versus seeing them as microbes or protozoa. The ancient and modern chemists aren't using different words to describe the same things. "These people thought and saw differently than we do" (1979, 125). If we could present our thinking about heredity, potentia, or physical constants to medieval thinkers, would the scales fall from their eyes? Would they applaud the correctness of our ideas and apologize for the literary excesses of their own age? Fleck thinks that they would find our ideas as fanciful and contrived as we find their seeing lead as "heavy-lidded Saturn, quiet as a stone, within the tangled forest of material forms" (1979, 125). They would see only the contrivances, not the reasons for them—the things hidden and the phenomena ruled out.

So a style is a perceptual readiness, a focusing of attention. It is an assimilative principle, a theory of admissible evidence. It is a mode of arguing that may be dogmatic and inflexible and a vocabulary that may be recondite and arcane. Fleck would say that style is where incommensurabilities grow; I see it as where closure begins: The cost-benefit style, remember, dictates the content of substantive claims. It favors some claims over others and prevents some claims from being made: that nature might be valued for itself (Tribe, Schelling, and Voss 1976) or that body counts are unreliable measures of success in war (Halberstam 1964,

1969). It changes the substantive outcome of disputes in jurisprudence and economics. And, some believe, it is substantively directing the increasingly corporatized sciences (Kornhauser 1962, Greenberg 1967, 1969, Gilpin 1962, Gilpin and Wright 1963, Haberer 1969).

Cost-benefit analysis isn't the only self-contained field. Analytic philosophy, phenomenology, behaviorism, Freudianism, and biotechnology seem to participate in external discourses largely by insisting on their own prerogatives. A field whose vernacular is completely arcane can't adjust its thinking to compromise with its neighbors. It can preach but not listen. Personality theorists often use the language of cognitive balance, symmetry, and cojudgment to describe a person's self image; and this applies to a field's self-image: If it sees its knowledge as a closed system it will restrict its communication within that closed system. Its borders will be impermeable, more like the Berlin Wall than the jagged, fractal nooks and crannies implied by the blurred genres thesis. At its core will be a nucleus, around which everything else orbits, harnessed in cooperative movement by covering laws. It will believe in knockdown arguments, for a properly put claim has the force of the whole system behind it.

Fuller (1982) holds that not all fields have completely unique styles. The grammar of economics, he says, is uniform enough that there exists an ideal prose style that allows competing schools to describe some phenomena in commensurable ways. The Marxist and neoclassical economist are thus linked in a discursive style that permits decisions about what counts as a better explanation. Fuller may be right to a degree, though it is an open question how much shallow quotation would be needed if the Marxist points to phenomena visible only to Marxist eyes or if the neoclassicist claims that, case by case, the two positions refer to different subject matters.

Argument requires a style common enough to recognize pertinent differences and rich enough to permit dispute. The Freudian and behaviorist may see phenomena (and research questions) invisible (or mystical) to each other, but they must lock horns (if they do) in a common style—even if the style isn't rich enough to settle their disputes. If the two fields share no ecotones, their common style will be too sparse. Their de facto differences may stem from as well as promote a lack of conflict. If two paradigms mirror realities so different that no common questions emerge, their proponents will ignore each other, publish in separate journals, attend separate conferences, and ignore each others' books. No disputes will arise between them, not because a common style is unachievable but because no one is interested in creating it.

Many interfield discourses require relatively mass media owing to the numbers of smaller media. Ideas may find advocates in new fields not by their esoteric expression in specialized media but in more popular guises in relatively mass media. In this way, as we saw, general relativity emanated out of physics into other expert fields and popular discourses. As the relatively mass media are more likely to present boundary-spanning material—the fringe stuff the esoteric circles would ignore—they are also the best platforms for making a case for a field's importation of a new idea.

There are, I think, general intellectual vernaculars—a bit richer than the writing in the *New York Times*, the *Chronicle of Higher Education*, or the mode of speech at collegewide faculty meetings. They are closer in complexity to the language of trade paperbacks and popular science. They are rich, powerful languages compared to the prose in *TV Guide* but diluted and weak compared to any esoteric journal and thus often too sparse to permit resolutions of interfield disputes. Book publishing often prefers such relatively mass idioms, for audience translates to sales. This works against distinct communication styles (and feeds Geertz's point about blurred genres). These general vernaculars, in other words, utilize relatively mass media—tiny compared to *USA Today*, enormous compared to the *Proceedings of the Aristotelian Society*.

If this picture is right, it is plausible to think that fields differ in cosmopolitanism because they differ in stylistic uniqueness. The more blurred genres are the ones accustomed to borrowing and lending ideas and so are more sensitive to the drawbacks of idiomatic expression or forced by their publishing organs to translate their specialized languages into a relatively mass public code or multiple mass vernaculars.

THE INSIDE VERSUS OUTSIDE DICHOTOMY REVISITED

The hermetically sealed field, then, is largely an artifact of a way of speaking. The inside versus outside dichotomy is posed as if a single individual confronts a single discursive formation. One might doubt this dichotomy for its individualism—arguing that intellectual life involves social comparison—and a certain gregariousness that makes the image of the solitary intellectual dubious. But the deeper defect is the field-as-single-cell-organism. For at the end of the day, the determinist is unable to explain how and why ideas cross field borders—hence my preference for the ecological way of putting things, which suggests borders teeming with ecotones, with edge species, fuzzy borders, and cosmopolitans.

But antideterminists risk an exaggeration of their own—describing cosmopolitans as if they are omniscient or completely free. Consider a recent proposal for the rhetoric of expertise which argues that the structural view of expertise—that experts who speak for special fields are protected by the closure of their discourses (Bazerman 1988, Mulkay 1979, Whitley 1984, 1986)—is only part of the story: "The structural view underestimates the capacity of certain influential experts to move freely about the intellectual landscape and enter new domains of discourse. This flexibility allows such persons to gain some control of the norms and standards by which their work will be judged. Rather than acting as a voice for stable professional standards, these experts can become like multinational corporations, able to appear in many locales and in many guises, without being under anyone's jurisdiction" (Lyne and Howe 1990, 134).

This proposal isn't unambiguous: It might be read as reviving Mannheim's free-floaters. The expression "move freely about" implies more flexibility and mobility than most fields permit. And the comparison with multinational corporations isn't entirely felicitous: Even the most gunboat-prone firms accommodate in nontrivial ways to local laws, customs, and folkways, and, once their local operations are up and running, with plants, equipment, and trained personnel in place, they are not completely free to leave. But Lyne and Howe seem to be thinking of a purely rhetorical possibility: "Instead of being hemmed in by disciplinary standards, the expert can blur the lines of demarcation between scientific paradigms and, thereby, elude accountability to any of them. Such experts are especially important to new fields and would-be fields of knowledge. They are often the celebrity scientists who bring their expertise to bear on broader public issues. . . . In such cases, the expert uses paradigms as strategies rather than as constraints, and becomes as much a rhetorician as a technician" (ibid.).

The good news is that Foucault's trap is broken. Cosmopolitans are moving from audience to audience. And so, presumably are audience members. Since audiences are not individuals, the onus for epistemic mastery is transferred from the individual to the group. But the bad news, as any persuasion researcher would say, is a diffusion of responsibility—which is why we hear of lynch mobs, not lynch persons. If the actors in peripheral fields are too accustomed to alien discourse and too open to using paradigms as rhetorical strategies, there may be a relaxation of accountability. For instance, E. O. Wilson "has been able to evade both scientific and social accountability because of the shifting discourse frames in which his work has been judged" (ibid., 135). Sociobiology has thus acquired a life of its own—with toe-holds in fields so disparate that even a robust Popperian falsification in one area might pass without notice in others.

The study of "shifting frames" may justify epistemics' existence, but the existence of shifting frames suggests a challenge to all peripheral fields. Their weaker conventions lead, no doubt, to more interesting conferences, but they also lend a hazy vagueness to the epistemic status of theories and claims. The belief that *any* field can problematize our knowledge possibly ensures that *no* field can convincingly do so. And this invulnerability should be not a permanent state-of-affairs. The problem is to know the point in time, during a peripheral field's maturation, when a positivist moment is needed. For just as O'Keefe's rhetoricals are sometimes entirely too creative, a field's rhetorical risks need occasionally to be put at risk. This, it seems to me, is an intellectual obligation—the price of cosmopolitanism—not to return necessarily to the old buffaloes, begging for affirmation, but to turn to someone else. For that, surely, is the whole idea of checks and balances.

ON LEARNING TO LIVE WITH INDETERMINACY

It is perhaps clear by now that the argument field is as much a way of thinking as it is a social knowledge scheme. It is a way of defining epistemics' subject matter by depicting the range of phenomena relevant to argument and knowledge. Of course, not everyone agrees about what is relevant. Some would dispense with the field of attention, for instance. Fearing subjectivism more than global warming, they would argue that the whole point of argument analysis is to get the *psycho* out of the *logic*. And as a purely empirical matter, others might say that since arguments can be analyzed as purely conventional affairs, personal perspectives are beside the point.

That would depend, I should think, on what the point is. If the point is to find the elements and interconnecting threads running through a propositional system, one can certainly focus on a Foucauldian corpus, a family of texts—as most field studies, in fact, do (Dunbar 1986, Jacobs 1983, Klumpp 1981, McKerrow 1980a, 1980b). I have certainly described liberalism in this way, and I will shortly do the same (though more briefly) for organizational studies.

But we sometimes want to know whether a person is speaking for a field, or the degree to which a person is influenced by a field; we sometimes need to know how a field socializes its young; and we often need to know the meanings of silences and ambiguities. It is thus a common practice among social knowledge schemes to match claims retrospectively to social domains. And the challenge in such cases is to balance the tension between descriptive determinacy and empirical fuzziness.

A common criticism of positivism is that matching claims to social domains reifies its objects. The social scientist wants precision and clarity, but lived experience is indeterminate and implicit. The scientist moves to disambiguate lived experience by tying it to a system—giving it "a determinate character . . . which it did not, in its original openness, actually possess." This is a fallacy "of the hermeneutical kind, to do with interpreting the meaning of statements or states of affairs, retrospectively from within such systems and ignoring the socio-historical processes of argument and contest" involved in their formulation (Shotter 1989, 149).

Perhaps the ambiguity and openness of lived experience can't be fully recaptured. And perhaps, too, one's assumptions about all-determining systems may be so abstract that everything confirms the diagnosis. The system will be phlogiston-like, pervading all the silences behind utterances. Still, when analysts find order in practices it is often because people have taken the trouble to put it there. Social life is more intersubjectively constrained than radically open. Pragmatic purposes often prefer clarity, so actors negotiate or impose precisely the reification Shotter sees as a scientific error. People with errands to run don't dawdle over hermeneutics. They order and punctuate events, they insist upon authorial privilege to limit interpretive openness, and they reify social entities in order to get their bearings. They share the problem Shotter imputes to the social scientist and solve it in the same way. They harness their actions to their aims and persuade others to follow suit. And field actors and analysts alike function within organizations that lend purpose, legal determinacy, authority, and structure to the discourses within and across their boundaries.

Still, Shotter's point is well taken. After all, the bent for clarity isn't unique to positivism; it is endemic to scientific curiosity. One acknowledges the fuzziness of social entities but still hopes to say clear and determinate things about them. One surrenders concreteness much as armies beat strategic retreats—fighting all the way, giving ground only when necessary. As Foucault might say, this attitude is indispensable but risky, for when researchers—and the actors they study—want more determinacy than is available, they may interpret safe options as inevitabilities and conjure retrospective rationality for whims and accidents. I assume that when I give ground to indeterminacy and fuzziness, I am surrendering to a frailty, like bad vision or a failed muse. The concrete boundaries are there, I just can't see or describe them. So I frustratedly speak of communities but mean towns. I operationalize the vagueness out of community by casting it in the language of concrete geographic-legal entities with precise boundaries, legally designated populations (whose memberships do not depend on the ebb and flow of belief but on the property tax and voting rolls).

The antidote is to assume that fuzziness is not a methodological flaw or a human handicap; it is an empirical fact (O'Keefe and Benoit 1982). Groups are not set in concrete, their natures fixed through time and boundaries sharply drawn. They exist in cognitive and social orientations—beliefs, attitudes, and practices. So analysts may be unable to make things clearer than field actors would or can. A field with ten members might have ten manifestations whose differences have costs ranging from zero to complete misunderstanding.

This respect for fuzziness as a fact is something of a cause célèbre in organizational studies, where the tolerance of ambiguity is seen more as a survival mechanism than a theoretical failure (Euske and Roberts 1987). One can appreciate why by considering the different interpretive challenges posed by (I may be lynched for putting it this way) dead and living things. It may seem unimaginative and historically naïve to say this, but there is a certain clarity to field borders in the past tense. One readily finds Enlightenment liberalism in the library, and only traces of its present-tense uncertainties. We can't know what it was like to argue with Locke, Mill, and Spinoza, to not know what they were going to say next. Our liberalism is rather fuzzier. There are too many voices to fit into an already bulging bibliography, and too many still talking. So I have at best caught liberalism at one moment in time—and certainly to some extent reified it. But if all has gone well, they might say that my version of liberalism *is* a coherent discourse made up of intelligible voices and that it catches some facets of the realities it is trying to map. Thus, one way to read Habermas is to ask how he lines up with Bernstein and Rorty against Bell and Nisbet. One way to read Foucault is to see how he lines up against the interactionists. And so on.

But argument fields are not best seen as equivalent to texts. Admittedly, we often encounter fields through their texts. We want to describe knowledge as concretely as we can, so we are drawn to the determinant corpus, the body of work. But texts must be understood in the context of the practices that produce and utilize them. For one thing, for theories that focus exclusively on texts, the fact that communication works—that interactants are able to disambiguate each others' messages, to select particular meanings—is either a miraculous puzzle or proof of a kind of stupidity in ordinary speakers. If the deconstructionist view of written discourse is applied to speech, we might see speakers spewing enigmas like buckshot, and listeners prosaically fixing on the one pellet luck permits them to catch. This isn't just a flawed view of communication: It isn't a view of communication at all.

And the determinacy of a text focus may be an artifact of selection. As we saw, literary density confers an indefiniteness—and thus a certain flexibility—on how terms like "modernity" and "postmodernity" are used. Depending on who one reads, one finds these terms used interchangeably or defined so expansively that they embrace the whole of the social sciences (see Aaron 1950 on class, Fisher 1987 on narrative, Barnett and Silverman 1979 on ideology, or Cole and Scribner 1974 on culture). One can cluster authors by usage similarities (*X*, *Y*, and *Z* use race in this way, not that way), but what does one then say of alternative views—especially if there has been no explicit debate? And what does one say about authors who use these terms as if they are unproblematic (e.g., Rorty's [1989] use of rhetoric and solidarity)? How does one know the difference between a text that presumes a clear consensus and one merely innocent of disputes and variations common elsewhere?

CODA: HARVESTING THE FIELD

The field idea can organize our thinking about epistemic problems and serve as an object of empirical analysis. In the former role, the field describes the frame of relevancy surrounding questions of knowledge. In the latter, it depicts the phenomena one deems germane to communicative acts. In both roles, the field emphasizes concrete cases as essential to understanding knowledge. But individual arguments are best studied in the context of speakers' intentions—which often requires placing speakers not only in concrete contexts but in larger contexts when their claims are indexical to fields.

Statements about what a field is may be complex, requiring the whole arsenal of terms—psychological, sociological, literary, and pragmatic. Constructivism is a literature, a set of beliefs and practices, a group of specific people, and a family of disciplines. A comprehensive field study, I think, capitalizes on all these perspectives plus some others. To describe a field is to see it in operation: socializing its novices, testing its hypotheses, codifying its knowledge, and changing its mind. And the academic field most experienced in such studies is the subject to which I now turn.

NINE

Fields as Organizations

The question now is how epistemics might read a closely related field—organizational studies. Ultimately, I think, the two fields will turn out to be interdependent—each complementing and problematizing the other's knowledge. But a literary merger must await events. Epistemics has scarcely begun its field work. It has no classics, no Evans-Pritchard or Malinowski. It could "adopt a classic," perhaps Latour (1987). But as things now stand, it is something of a cargo cult: The idea that the organization is a better epistemic model than the individual mind has more or less dropped out of the sky.

If the affinity between the two fields is as natural as it seems, we can begin—by definition at least—on solid ground. Fields plainly are organizations. They are "consciously coordinated activities" (Barnard 1983) that must be "continually reproduced or recreated through the actions of concrete individuals" (Perrow 1979, 246–47). They require a "flow of information and a mutual ordering of behavior. To paraphrase Freud, 'where interdependence is, there shall organization be'" (Greer 1964, 79).

The importance of interdependence and information flow to knowledge growth is scarcely a new idea. Crowther (1941, 448), catching the history of electricity in its factory period, so to speak, marveled at the "Laboratories" (Bell, Phillips, and others)—their myriad activities, organizational scale, and interconnections with the commercial world. The future of electricity, he thought, was in the hands of thousands of people working at countless tasks in organizations all over the world. The glowing modernity of 1941 was largely due to the profit motive—which since Edison had sparked permutations, derivations, and innovations, and would in the future, Crowther thought, be the mother of most inventions. And the past, in this case, had been very much prologue. The knowledge growth, Crowther argued, had always had a corporate character: Analyzing how Galvani got frog legs to kick, Volta electrified the Royal Society with the idea of current. Ampere then theorized; Faraday produced (thanks to Henry's electromagnet, itself made possible by methods owed to Watt) and Maxwell studied Faraday.

Nor in the same spirit would we speak of Newton's theory as if Newton had it all in his head and then transmitted it to others. The *Principia Mathematica* "took many years to write (and was unusable as a tool for predicting planetary motions until LaPlace cleaned up the proofs and added boundary conditions for the calculations). . . . Newton's book triggered a network of people [indeed the best work in eighteenth-century mathematics (Kuhn 1970a, 32–33)] who together (and only together) possess the theory of 'Newtonian mechanics'" (Steve Fuller, private correspondence 1991). And Newton's theory can be seen as part of a larger collective project—completing the Copernican revolution, a revolt barely visible in *De Revolutionibus* (Kuhn 1977a).

So it is plausible to think of epistemic mastery, knowledge growth, and the well-founded consensus as corporate achievements—as trading in some important ways on divisions of labor, equifinality, overlapping practices, local foci, and information channels. Most knowledge claims are made and tested in the context of organizations and transformed and revised in the activities of organizations. And most epistemic "tendencies," to oligarchy or diffusion, closure or openness, are organizational characteristics as much as individual frailties.

Of special interest, I think, is the fact that invisible hands have a way of showing themselves in organizational life. Not always, to be sure: Complex organizations have their mysteries, and the appeal to invisible hands is something of an art form in organizational studies. But organizations characteristically have a stake in not leaving matters to the tender mercies of markets or the gentle guidance of invisible forces. Organizations are reflectively contrived contexts: They exhibit the compromises people negotiate to maintain cooperation and order while remaining adaptive to environmental change. Their study thus provides an empirical basis for comparing rationalities, framing the issues of modernity, and clarifying the symbiosis of ideas and practices. If truth *happens* to ideas, as William James said, it arguably happens in organizational space and time.

THE FABIANS AND THE MUCKRAKERS

Unfortunately all sorts of things happen in organizational space and time, some unsavory. And even conceding that it might be valuable to understand the ill- founded consensus, some readers may fear that epistemics is going to hate itself in the morning. Organizational studies has that strumpet look—a history of satisfying businessmen for money. A theory that strays onto the commercial side of the tracks may confound curiosity with greed, knowledge with lucre. Others may doubt that there is much to be learned: Organizations *satisfice*, not *optimize* (March 1978, March and Olsen 1976, March and Simon 1958); they are deliberative *garbage cans* (Cohen, March, and Olsen 1972) cluttered with *groupthink* (Janis 1983). Their rationality is a *pose:* They act, rationalize, and then reap what they sow in bureaucratic momentum (Weber 1905). Intellectual fields are supposed to be above all this: Durkheim's *brain workers* seek truth, merit, and public welfare. They *optimize* and so escape or attenuate organizational flaws.

Others, however, will be puzzled that anyone could doubt the organizational bases of knowledge—and skeptical about claims to purity and intellectual supremacy (Elias 1982, Gaston 1969, Gieryn and Figert 1986, Greenberg 1967, 1969, Kenny 1986, Kitcher 1982, 1985, D. K. Price 1962, 1965). Some argue that big science has taken on the character of big business (D. Price 1961, 1963, 1970, Redner 1987a, Taub 1986). The structure, incentives, and language of large-scale research "have more in common with business than with the academy" (Nisbet 1969, 311). Science is structured like agencies and corporations because it is interdependent with them (Kohn 1986): Its research is channeled by funding priorities (Gilpin and Wright 1964); its images of objectivity are political face strategies to legitimize policies (Mukerji 1990).

The champions of science—call them Fabians—have not rushed to rebut the muckrakers, who they perhaps suspect of exaggerating aberrations exposed by science's self-policing. The muckrakers, however, argue that self-policing is inhibited by scale, literary density, personal relations, and ethos. Broad and Wade (1982) claim that replication is more private than public: Cheaters are likeliest to be exposed by colleagues; replicators often lack access to data; peer review is a poor check on honesty (Knoll 1990); universalism is observed mostly in the breach; and the pressures of funding and professional advancement encourage abuses.

Perhaps the Fabians feel that the muckraking is merely another version of arguing from hyperbolic standards. Broad and Wade are disappointed idealists, certainly. Nostalgic for a romanticized search for truth, they denounce a fall from grace: Science was once a church where Mertonian priests guarded a pristine order of immaculate conceptions. Now lab chiefs cum entrepreneurs resemble Trump more than Lavoisier.

Whatever the reason, it is perhaps fortunate that the Fabians and muckrakers have not locked horns. A debate that allowed no middle ground between the veneration or cynical dismissal of experts would present awkward choices—especially if it had funding repercussions in science policy debates. The Fabians, in such cases, might stand more firmly on middle ground. Claims to virginity are not unheard of inside the Beltway, but they are notoriously unwise. Chastity there is merely a challenge, and for muckrakers it is both fair game (the claim is assumed to be self-serving) and an inviting target (the claim is assumed to be false).

Intellectual supremacists are greeted more politely inside academe, partly I suppose because a contempt for the commercial is a fringe benefit. The plus side of one's poverty vows is that one gets to snub the less virtuous. In this spirit, it is both harmless and comforting to feel that the Philological Society is a nobler thing than ITT. But preferences of this sort are best expressed, if at all, sotto voce, for one can say of nobility what Nero Wolfe says of dignity—to assert it is to lose it.

Respecting more concrete claims—about how intellectual fields in fact stand vis-à-vis the societies with which they are intermeshed—the idea of purity should be belief, not an attitude. Beliefs can be tested, argued about, and linked to the evidence that justifies them. By focusing on the ways knowledge is corporatized, the organizational view permits the debate about the superiority of intellectual fields to turn on concrete cases (Knorr, Khron, and Whitley 1981, Knorr-Cetina 1981, 1982, Knorr-Cetina and Mulkay 1983, Kornhauser 1962). Such studies display more precisely how ideas are fitted to practices and how both are mingled with idealizations and professional canons, personal relations, and organizational structure (Latour and Woolgar 1979).

THE INVISIBLE HAND REVEALED?

The invisible hand (or mind) is never far from the surface in discussions of the well-founded consensus. It is hard to idealize deliberative processes—to imagine how decision-makers might best be rational—without also assuming (or hoping) that, if all goes well, the outcomes will be satisfactory. The Hobbesians among us thus believe that countless acts of greed sum up to utility. And Haskell (1984c, 211) reads much the same thing into Pierce: Fields thrive on competition, but gain consensus by a process "reminiscent of the price mechanism in economic markets. There in accordance with the natural laws of supply and demand, the jockeying of rival consumers and producers looking out for their own interests generates for each commodity a convergence toward its natural price. In the community of inquiry the clash of erring individuals produces eventually a convergence of opinion about reality."

This is Pierce, thank Heaven, not Dewey. One shudders to think of how ideas might find their *natural prices* in a public market, or what it would mean to find an idea like distributive justice in the sale bins. The dearest commodities are likely to be vaguely evocative ideas—*democracy, freedom, peace*. But beneath these abstractions we would find market mechanisms so bizarre as to call the whole metaphor into question. Scarcity, for instance, would not drive prices upward; it would be an epiphenomenon of demand. For if the critics of the melting pot culture teach us anything, it is that excess supply drives demand: the more the pricier.

Things might go more benevolently within a Piercean community of inquirers, but how ideas find their natural prices seems no clearer. Even if an idea's natural price lies in its ubiquity of uses, an elitist nose-count would not reveal how convergence works. Nor would it tell us whether we have a rational consensus of experts—as opposed, say, to opinion drift, accident, or a bandwagon.

Perhaps the more instructive economic parallel is a failure: Adam Smith's invisible hand presumed perfect competition—a condition hard to imagine in real markets, and still harder to defend as an ideal: Only a totalitarianism, Keynesians argued, could achieve it. Habermas's freedom requirement faces a parallel dilemma: If organizations value discipline and expertise, they *shouldn't* try to give everyone an equal voice. And it is hard to imagine how they could. Rawls (1971) avoids the latter problem by providing his *original position* with organizational details. The decision-makers' constraints, resources, and blindnesses are functionally integral to the ideas. They don't guarantee that people in the original position will be rational, but they lay the grounds for debating the requirements of being rational and whether decision-makers, *if* they are rational, will choose his principles of justice.

Perhaps organizational details can do the same for the well-founded consensus. Esoteric fields share with the most predatory corporations a need to transform equivocal, indefinite information into manageable communication to achieve a "workable level of certainty" (Weick 1979, 6). Every organization is a try at teleology, an attempt to make all its functions fit its purposes. It is someone's version of the link between theory and practice—a bundle of assumptions, rationales, and methods for adapting to multiple situations. Organizations, for all their satisficing, are operationalizations by which ideas are made flesh and structures are brought to life. They are cases in point of how ideas are accepted, used, and changed (Weick 1983)—concrete, observable tries at consummating the well-founded consensus. They are contexts, in other words, for explaining the force of better arguments.

How to Read the History of Organizational Studies

"When more and more people are thrown out of work, unemployment results."

—Calvin Coolidge

Many qualms about modernity concern its organizations—their scale, impersonality, and inauthenticity. Organizations, for some, are modernity's vile necessities: Peasant crafts can't build railroads; medieval guilds can't run airlines. Interdependency demands infrastructure (railroads, shipping, and communications), specialism (skills, professionalism, and licensing), and complexity (service industries, suppliers, and wholesalers).

Panglossian feelings are the flip side of the coin. A modern-day Ayn Rand may genuflect as she passes corporate headquarters. She will admire the postmodern architecture, not for its creativity but for its splendor. And she will advise one and all to know their stations and their duties and to otherwise be happy cogs in the capitalist machine.

This reverence may seem scarcely plausible. It is certainly unfashionable in academe, where even many pluralists agree with Woodrow Wilson: The system is basically heartless. Capitalism's apologists have grown squeamish: Even if they are as indifferent to the cruelty of disemployment as their critics say, they know lost purchasing power when they see it. Still, it is with corporate idolatry that we must begin, for the history of organizational studies is the Fall reenacted—complete with Eden and a serpent.

Genesis

In the beginning—between the day of the robber barons and the Great Depression—Henry Ford and others imbued business with the unction Hegel reserved for states. They saw corporations as wresting order from chaos and, by manifest destiny, turning philistines into productive workers. By organizing greed into a coherent capitalist spirit, the corporate superego was morally better than "each against all." So the late Victorian capitalists were both unrepentant and righteous: "God," Rockefeller said, "gave me my money," and William ("the public be damned") Vanderbilt wouldn't have said "greed is good," as in the film "Wall Street." He would have said "greed is Godly."

In fairness, what was good for General Motors in those days genuinely seemed good for the country. Capitalism had given the West unprecedented prosperity, so the conflation of public and corporate interests seemed plausible. Calvin Coolidge no doubt thought he was speaking plain truth when he coined 1925's most famous expression, "the business of America is business." Given that premise, government would be capitalism's guarantor. Its duty would be to *promote* business—and, from time to time, if needed, regulate. Universities, in this scheme, would seek knowledge to strengthen the institutions of the industrial revolution. Their faculties would be reserve labor pools. And science, a panacea for everything else, would go to bat for complex capitalism.

From this cozy womb, organizational studies was born. Rosemary's baby was called scientific management theory (Taylor 1913). And Taylorism, as it is now called, is what many people have in mind when they speak of modernity—an authoritarian pyramid, a hierarchical closed system, the ruling paradigm at the top governing all beneath it. Interestingly enough, this view is held today only outside organizational studies. The consensus within the field is that Taylorism survives today only as a local design; as a grand theory it would be a blueprint for organizational suicide. Adaptation is the first principle of management, so the focus is on ad hoc task forces, project teams, professionalization, and decentralization.

Perhaps Taylorism persists as the grand theory to be resisted because it evokes a powerful sympathy. It was a theory of shop design that reduced the humans therein to servo-mechanisms. To maximize efficiency, one used time-and-motion studies to reduce tasks to their simplest components and then eliminated worker discretion by standardizing each step in the process. Standardized selection tests and training programs would then assure a proper fit of worker to job. The cold-bloodedness of this vision has made Taylorism virtually synonymous with the words *dehumanizing* and *degrading*.

But Taylor was not the ogre he is made out to be. Textbooks often claim—quite mistakenly, by the way—that he coined the expression "time is money," but neglect to add that he advocated employee ownership—and a "mental revolution" for managers that would make the treatment of workers less capricious. He believed in a good day's work, certainly, but he also believed in a good day's pay. He is also blameless for the crime of which he most often accused—being one of the fathers of classical management. Classical management is a merger of Taylorism with Weber's (1947) views of bureaucracy that aimed to extend administrative control from the shop to whole organizations. The ideal structure is like a military chain of command. Power flows downward. Authority is delegated. Tasks are segmented and compartmentalized. Every move is monitored, calibrated, and regulated by a holistic intelligence. Classical management, in other words, is how authoritarian organizations *wish* they worked and how Foucault *fears* they work.

But the paternity suit against Taylor is dubious: The poor man died in

1915. Another oft-accused father, Henri Fayol, died in 1925. So by process of elimination, it might seem that the father of classical management must be Weber (who is also, in this literature, called the father of bureaucracy). This slander comes from reading Weber in a way that catches none of his pessimism and fear, that recommends that we strive to achieve the bureaucratic ideal type. And it illustrates, I think, another example of the limits of shallow quotation: One is doing so much violence to Weber that one really ought to read someone else.

Who, then, *is* the father of classical management? Is there a missing link—perhaps a long-buried or unpublished paper that brought Taylor and Fayol together with one book Weber happened to write? Or is this a case of Fullerian opinion drift? The ideas were simply in the air—at conferences, in conversations. Or, as I suspect, did classical management *just happen* as an artifact of textbook writing—an expositional convenience for lumping ideas together? There's a dissertation here, and perhaps a definitive answer. But for now, what the textbooks ought to say about the father of classical management is "whereabouts unknown."

EXODUS

The Hawthorne studies (circa 1927–32) convinced many that classical management needed humanizing (Mayo 1945). The human relations movement thus arose to find ways to align labor and management interests for the good of both (Argyris 1962, 1964, 1974). This was—and still is—a januslike project. Observed from the right, human relations is an internal reform, a critique of alienation in the workplace (Blackburn 1972, Blumberg 1976, Clawson 1980, Kaufman 1965, Seeman 1967), an attempt to humanize capitalism by finding a corporate *patriae,* a general will, that rids the system of irritants (Nisbet 1990, 133). Observed from the left, of course, human relations is a Judas goat. The corporate *patriae* is merely an ideology conducive to labor peace, a way to make current structures seem inevitable and management seem rational (Anthony 1977, Braverman 1974, Nord 1974, Storey 1983).

Both faces of human relations share with Taylorism the belief that human nature must be changed if people are to be happy in organizations. Standardized work is unfulfilling; line production makes one a servomechanism—"demanding little in the way of traditional craft skills" (Harvey 1989, 128). The separation of the worker from the material means of production is capitalism's highest crime. Line production is *inauthentic* compared to crafts—where the efficient, formal, and final causes rest with the craftsperson and there is personal satisfaction in a job well done. Work must be expressive to be rewarding. The servomechanism is a cog in a conventional structure. Any satisfaction it feels is false consciousness, for assembly line work expresses only the fraudulent spirit of capitalism.

LEVITICUS

But the degree to which Taylorism is (or was) a general western status quo is quite debatable. It met great resistance in America. Union negotiations as well as differences in tasks led to variations in assembly-line production—especially in worker input, rotation, and team structure. And such things as steel plants, once paradigm cases of labor-intensive Taylorism, now seek employees with "good communication skills; computer and robotics experience a plus." Beyond the shop, classical management is now said to be a long-lost fiction, eclipsed by decentralized, "loosely coupled," organizations (Browning and Hawes 1991).

And in at least one case where Taylorism survives, it is too blatant to be deceptive and too remunerative to be alienating. One example, certainly, does not a refutation make, but the United Parcel Service hub in Louisville is instructive nonetheless. For it is unquestionably a paradigm case of Taylorism, and so far as I can see it is critic-proof.

A package handling hub involves movement and sorting: Planes fly in, they disgorge package containers that are moved to a facility and unloaded. Each container holds packages that are sorted onto conveyor belts and then into other containers, which are then moved back out to the planes. The humans in this system are operators, stuffers, and sorters—in a word servomechanisms. Yet UPS enjoys by all accounts (and its record of labor peace) a happy labor force. This is perhaps owed to its stock purchase plan that has transformed it—as its founder intended—into an employee-owned company. UPS salaries are higher than unskilled labor can command elsewhere. And the corporate *patriae,* certainly, makes no pretenses that one will find the meaning of life sorting packages.

And no one, apparently, expects to. The hands and arms in this system belong mostly to part-time laborers, who must be able to lift 70 pounds to get the job. Many are students who work the graveyard shift then sleep through Western Civilization, broadly speaking, the next morning. And they have been saying, over the past ten years, roughly the same thing: The work is backbreaking. No one expects otherwise. Work conditions are as good as could be expected. The company is well-managed. The pilots have it easy. But chiefly the pay is excellent—and finances all sorts of self-expression after hours.

So what might the reformer-critic bring to UPS? Jameson and Harvey want something like self-actualization (Maslow 1954)—the idea being to realize one's potential, to grow as Bellah might say, or as the army says, "be all that you can be." In this spirit, a company might design tasks to maximize employee input, rotate workers among tasks to relieve boredom and to enlarge their understanding of the corporate whole, and it might expand its educational and social programs. UPS has done many of these things, but there are limits to task design and rotation: Ultimately packages must get sorted; there are only so many interchangeable tasks; and moving packages from one conveyor belt to another can scarcely be made to seem craftlike.

What sort of consciousness-raising is feasible here? The workers already know that their jobs are hard and tedious, but they might be persuaded that something they thought irrelevant to their jobs *is* relevant: Instead of expecting self-fulfillment in their private lives, they might come to expect it from their jobs—and thus be persuaded that their jobs are dehumanizing and degrading. Happy workers would become unhappy campers, and some would see this discontent as a success. Criticism is supposed to puncture bourgeois complacency and brandish truth in the face of power. This is a bit too holy a war for my taste—and too indifferent to consequences. But it is also the destruction of private property: One's illusions after all are arguably private property, and one might not agree that being happy in one's work is self-defeating. There are necessary fictions—face strategies not for others but for ourselves. They help us lead happier lives—to tolerate bad jobs or bad luck, to forgive ourselves for past mistakes and others for past wrongs. If I am a young person in a dull job, I rationalize it by thinking of the wages and that it is only temporary. If I am older, or stuck in the job, I tolerate it and seek fulfillment elsewhere. In either case, it does no good to tell me (assuming I don't know it) that my job is tedious. And it might do harm: If what I formerly thought tolerable now seems dehumanizing and degrading—and I can't change jobs—I will either seethe with rage, which is bad for my health, or become indifferent to my work, which is bad for my career.

I am not claiming that UPS vindicates human relations. Reconciliations of organizational and individual interests will always be open to dual interpretation, and Jameson and Harvey could certainly point to parallels between UPS' mollifying programs and the philosophy Harvey calls "Fordism." Ford favored good housing, good pay, company stores, and a short-lived experiment with moral oversight to protect workers from their base instincts (Harvey 1989). He was much like the character Undershaft in Shaw's *Major Barbara*. Both are committed capitalists. Both see line production as unsatisfying. Both try to humanize the workplace. And both can be praised or damned with equal logic.

One final point—and one of the most telling ironies of our century—is that Taylorism was a status quo chiefly in the Stalinist police states (Tompkins 1984, 667). Lenin, by all accounts, was obsessed with developing heavy industry, but championed Taylor in a totalitarian way. A proletarian rhetoric joined easily with Taylor's stress of employee-ownership. And a Marxist vision of central planning joined to Taylorism's mechanisms (an authoritarian pyramid, piecework reward structure, and devaluation of individual skills) yielded a society-scale blueprint. Thus arose the workers' paradises that should have been Foucault's focus. Had he kept his attention east, not west, he would have found his "carceral societies." And had he lived to see their dominolike disintegration, he might have revised his estimate of their cognitive determinism.

NUMBERS

Organizational studies is the *Pet Sematary* of the social sciences. Nothing dead stays buried there: The grand theories—Taylorism, human relations—have become local theories; theories that fail in one organization succeed in another; and all are set in literatures so big (or cast in terms so expansive) that falsification is only a local phenomenon. The only consensus is that the field is fragmented—or at least crowded with research programs that are proceeding simultaneously along multiple fronts and using as many methodologies as there are philosophies of science.

This proliferation of narrow-range theories reflects environmental adaptations (Hannan and Freeman 1981). Organizations vary in size, structure, interdependencies, aims, and practices because they are *splendid local adaptations* (Gould 1980). The organization rubric is thus like the phylum *mollusk*. Both are mixed bags of strange bedfellows: The Sunflower Society, Pentagon, and Ku Klux Klan are at least as different as the giant clam, octopus, and flatworm, and just as new discoveries swell the ranks of mollusks, the variety of organizations is growing.

Organizational theories have thus become increasingly local, for theory and practice in this field are closely intertwined. "The theories and the theorists are . . . part of the reality they describe" (Benson 1981, 220). Just as self-concept and the implicit theory view figure in personality theory, an organization's explanations of its own nature (its tables of authority, chain of command, internal and external public relations, accommodations to consultants, and its myths, ideals, and goals) affect its practices; its self-definition is part of its reality; its theories are its blueprints.

Perhaps this focus on environments, theories, and practices is another of Skinner's (1985) "grand theories explaining why there can be no grand theories." It does have a Derridian ring ("there is only difference"). If the diversity can't be blamed on the theorists' mistakes, then the only grand theory possible is a theory of differences. Anything else will either be so abstract as to be vacuous or radically false. As Wittgenstein says, forgetting the variety among language games leads to badly-put questions ("what is a question?").

But there is also Dewey's question about differences that make a difference. While there are differences galore—critical theory is as similar to aquatic biology as the Wheaties factory is to the John Deere factory—they may be uninteresting. A difference is interesting, I should think, when it helps or hinders something someone wants to do. The differences between Henry Ford's Dearborn and Toyota's high participation plants are pertinent to explanations of the effects of worker involvement. The differences between workers' attitudes—some are alienated, some love their jobs and define their self-worth by their careers (Argyris 1957, 1971, Bakke 1966)—are pertinent to sweeping claims about natural antagonisms between workers and management. And differences between workers' attitudes toward participatory control—some are indifferent to or afraid of it (Dunnett 1976)—are pertinent to the universality claims of participatory management advocates.

So the diversity in organizational studies suggests something more than sheer difference. If knowledge is embodied in organizations—brought to life in its uses—and if organizations evolve by virtue of functional fits with contexts and purposes, then the sweep of epistemic claims will always be problematic. Organizations and the theories that guide them will continue to evolve differently; organizational scholars will continue to have different motives, so they will continue to see organizations as embodying different abstractions. But the epistemic abstractions will be quite narrow. It would make no sense, for instance, to pose as general questions the problem of relativity or the hope for a final synthesis. Relativity and synthesis are local matters—turning on the concrete barriers people confront and concrete relationships they are able to achieve. Nor would it make sense to hope that the study of human knowledge might find completion as a single commensurating language. No one would claim that all tasks are alike, so there is no such thing as organization *in itself;* and it is puzzling that anyone would want it to be so.

Kings

The sources and functions of authority are "indistinguishable from organization" (Nisbet 1990, xxvi). Professions carve the world into jurisdictions and organize socialization, evaluation, and credentialling. This specialism creates a second economy—a *technostructure* (Galbraith 1971), an environment with its own momentum and market forces. Inside this economy, interests run with competencies: Workers may be as attached to a technology, method, or body of knowledge as to an employer (physicians and nurses, e.g., have more allegiance to their professions than to particular hospitals [Argyris 1964]).

The population ecology model explains the rise of professionalism as an effect, not of isomorphism between environments and organizations, but of the advantages of excess capacity: By employing professionals, organizations "increase their capacity to deal with a variable environment and the contingencies it produces" (Hannan and Freeman 1981, 190) The professionals' skills exceed immediate demands; their professional stature demands more autonomy, discretion, and pay than nonprofessionals; but the effect of excess capacity is enhanced flexibility. "Populations of organizational forms will be selected for or against depending on the amount of excess capacity they maintain and how they allocate it. . . . What would seem like waste to anyone assessing performance at one time may be the difference between survival and failure later" (190).

This picture of the sources and functions of authority suggests a way of balancing the tension between the two faces of human relations. Both faces put a premium on expertise. The modernist champions expertise as a natural result of the complexity of business and industry. The postmodernist sees specialism and expertise as ideological covers (Abravanel 1983). The increasing equivalence of organization with technocracy feeds their populist demonology—and some sweeping dichotomies (management versus labor and capital versus the working class) that basically come down to white versus blue collar.

But neither view can stand alone. To require expertise is in some respects to endorse it, and as expertise disenfranchises by exclusion, the modernists run the risk of becoming conservators of organizational purposes. If they are complacent, they will let entry requirements to the elite ranks perpetuate the class effects their critics denounce. On the other hand, the postmoderns need to revise their class antagonisms. Bureaucracy *is* a great equalizer; lateral complexity smothers vertical authority. The effects of hierarchy are mingled with and limited by pragmatic complexity. So the idea of an elite has become as much a matter of credentials and organizational function as of economics. Experts occupy an indefinitely large number of niches which vary in content, power, influence, rewards, and entry requirements.

The two faces of human relations can share an ambivalence about expertise and a belief in the malleability of organizations. Human contrivances are improvable; they can be better designed to reflectively appraise their pragmatic and moral options. But the path to this better design—inevitably, I think—is a still more powerful expertise.

THE NEW TESTAMENT

Had organizational theory stopped with Taylorism and human relations, the relation of fields to organizations might be a sort of mind-body problem—with materialists and vitalists imputing different relationships to organizations and their organizing intelligences or contents. Fortunately, Cartesian dualists dressed as sociologists now rarely appear in polite society. The current theoretical diversity canvasses the whole of the social sciences: contingency theory is a variable-analytic tradition like behaviorism; expectancy theory studies employee performance; motivational theory studies interactions of personality variables and performance. Group theory studies the strengths and weaknesses of group decision-making. Symbolic interactionism has spawned a family of theories—many describing structure in ways the *Wissensoziologists* might find unintelligible—as negotiated order (Day and Day 1977, Strauss 1978) or structuration (Giddens 1984). Despite differences, these approaches change the very language of structuralism. The common words now are *kinetic, adaptive,* and *dynamism;* and the common image is of organizations able to "connect the local and the global" (Giddens 1990, 20, Agor 1989, Sypher 1990).

Organizational studies hasn't dispensed with grand theory. The field remains as fascinated by utopian philosophies as any social science, and most of the themes associated with modernity and postmodernity have seeped inside. Indeed, one such theory is of special interest, for it displays the limits of rhetorical ingenuity.

METAPHORS: THE IMPORTANCE OF BEING EARNEST

The importance of metaphors is often underscored, but it is glaring in organizational studies. Few fields use metaphors so widely or vividly to organize explanations and methodological choices. Using a metaphor means calling up a system of ideas (Black 1962), a perspective, a package of ideas, methods, and values. Metaphors thus function like *Weltanschauungen,* and metaphorical analysis functions like perspective-taking: If I "use the Freudian metaphor," (playfully, hypothetically, analytically), I am, momentarily, claiming to "think like a Freudian."

Anthropologists and ethnographers know that "thinking like" someone else is a complicated maneuver. The alien must empathize with the native, capture the native's point of view, yet maintain distance. Too much enculturation, and the foreigner becomes a native—the report becomes a self-report. Too much distance, and the native's lived experience remains invisible. And if the alien cannot "translate" the native's rationalities, or can capture them only partially, or must imperialistically reform them in her own language (Fuller 1982, 1983, 1988), a powerful relativity arguably divides the insider and outsider.

Debates about these predicaments (Barnes and Bloor 1982, Bennett 1964, Wilson 1979, Winch 1958, 1964) often focus on striking anthropological differences—Western science versus Nuer religion, skyscrapers versus mud huts, but there are equivalent differences within cultures. If, say, behaviorism and Freudianism are as different as they seem, then the language in which we plot their differences might be less a translation then a shallow quotation—the best to be hoped for when fields are too exotic or closed. Not all fields are exotic and closed; many are bunched in families, stuck together by ecotones. But some fields are divided by fissures so sharp that cooperative projects are inconceivable.

I will defend this claim by considering a theory that seems to deny it—one that hopes to use contradictory metaphors as conceptual lenses. I will argue that this theory is too nimble. It understates the conventional constraints on public argument: A gestalt shift is not a license to suspend evidence that has been taken seriously. When the tensions among metaphors are set concretely in argumentative positions, they may be intransigencies best left to ideologues. "Thinking like" the denizens of a field is a perspective-taking problem best seen as a way of arguing (one test of the anthropologist's translation of the native's concepts is whether the anthropologist and native could then succeed at a cooperative project based on the reformatted concepts).

NIGHT OF THE LIVING METAPHORS

Popperians who want to see a field's history littered with the corpses of refuted theories will be disappointed with the organizational metaphor position. The dead have risen. What were once mirrors of nature have transmogrified into metaphors and now walk among us as interpretive tools. The transformation hasn't improved their appearance.

The organizational metaphor position holds that the use of alternative metaphors allows for flexibility and insight (Morgan 1986, Morgan, Frost, and Pondy 1983). Most metaphors (mechanistic, organismic, brain, populational, culture, political, psychic prison, flux, domination, and hermeneutic) are partial understandings—best seen as conceptual lenses to be imposed, one after another. The voice of each mingles with the others, revealing different aspects of organizations and enabling creative insights unavailable to one using a single metaphor. This counterpoint allows one "to go beyond the idea that symbols are variables influencing human behavior and the functioning of a wider social system, to explore the idea that such behavior and system characteristics represent no more than enacted symbolic forms" (Morgan, Frost, and Pondy 1983, 32). The goal is to "develop *a way of thinking* that can cope with ambiguity and paradox" (Morgan 1986, 342). Imagine pairing open systems theory (which stresses the integration of organism with environment) with closed systems theory (Morgan calls it *Autopoiesis,* the logic of self-producing, self-referential systems). The tensions between the two metaphors may be revealing. Organizational actors may better appreciate their balancing act between the need to be more open for some reasons yet more closed for others—adaptive and innovative for some reasons, oligarchical and self-preserving for others. There is, in other words, a continual and negotiable tension between an organization's tendencies for closure and self-reference, entropy and decay, and its need to interact, adapt, and innovate.

This is a plausible heuristic. It comports with our intuitions that different models are appropriate for different organizational features—for instance that theatrical metaphors illuminate organizational strategies and that Taylorism is humanized when its tensions with self-actualization are made explicit. But there is both less and more here than meets the eye. The organizational metaphor position capitalizes on a cavalier attitude toward the internal logics, concrete details, and empirical claims of metaphors. And it has a hidden agenda.

The cavalier attitude privileges the analyst: Metaphors are tools to be used for this and that chore. They are like lenses that an omniscient analyst inserts, one after another, discounting the distortions and capitalizing on the revelations of each. But the parallel with lenses suggests a predicament. Electronmicroscopy is a field devoted to determining the biases of lenses. This is a complex problem—not to be treated casually—because different lenses are *not* alternative views of the same thing. We might call this the "Heisenberg effect": The observer's stance doesn't merely affect the observation; the observation doesn't merely affect the phenomena. The observation is to some degree *sui generis*—not a reflection of reality but a reality in and of itself. There is also a "Hacking effect" (Hacking 1983): One can't just see through different lenses; one must be taught to see. And there is a "Hawthorne effect": Observation influences the observed; methods and techniques have social effects (the natural science parallel would presumably be quanta and microbes made angst-filled by a giant peering eye).

The organizational metaphor position presents itself as a rhetorical view. Its metaphors are Goffmanesque roles. Each voice must tell its tale. The various tales will then either coalesce to form a whole or their incommensurabilities will be *Rashoman*-like—integral to the reality being described. But the question, I think, is how rhetorically nimble the theorist should be, and the answer lies partly in how rhetorically flexible others are and should be. Communication capitalizes upon and creates social contracts; rhetorical creativity and flexibility may be checked by distance and formality. O'Keefe (1988) says that her rhetoricals tend to overestimate their ability to control events and thus find themselves in trouble with expressives and conventionals. Privately, I can use and discard metaphors like passing moods, and I may enjoy relationships with others that indulge whimsies. But what is frisky in private may be bad manners in public. If you and I are playing chess, you are not free to solve a board problem by changing the rules.

And if we are sharing *scientific* evidence, we are conventionally bound to prevalent rules of evidence—chief among them a sincerity condition: presentations of evidence invoke a social contract. In O'Keefe's vocabulary, expert communication is largely conventional. It is rule-governed, with sincerity conditions premised on the assumption of cooperative discourse. When one speaks, one means to be taken in a certain, conventionally understood way. This isn't the expressive's view of honesty-as-authenticity or a belief that facts are atheoretical; it is a claim about discourse norms. If I am taken seriously speaking within the institutions of one metaphor, the *Gestalt* shift to a second will feel the logical pull of the first: I am not free to disregard or suppress empirical states of affairs exposed by one metaphor as I shift to another. To be taken seriously is to be constrained.

If I assert that *X* must adapt to environmental effects *Y* and *N* to survive, I presumably take *Y* and *N* seriously: I prove my case by presenting evidence about *Y* and *N;* I ask others to take *Y* and *N* seriously. May I *then* assert that X must be closed to survive? If X is self-referential, what happens to the evidence about Y and N?

If I argue that *dominated* workers are *psychically imprisoned* in fraudulent language games, and present evidence of "social forces emanating either from the unconscious mind, or the power structure of the culture" (Morgan, Frost, and Pondy 1983, 32), what happens if I next enter the *theatrical* metaphor? Are the workers *feigning* submission? Are their ideological chains stage props? And what happens if I shift to the *protestant work ethic*? Are the workers occupying their proper places in life, *reflecting*, not enacting, the fruits of their efforts at self-improvement, and dominated because they ought to be?

This is not a deep theoretical problem, it is a mess—three moments on a mood ring. The organizational metaphor position works only if metaphors are loose labels whose details can be changed or suspended once we adopt a different metaphor. But unless this theory holds (which it doesn't) that all the competing details of all the metaphors are equally valid, it needs a mechanism for adjudicating among the competing claims. In other words, what assumptions guide the analyst in moving from one lens to another; what authorizes this flexibility?

The answer lies in the claim that discrepancies among metaphors reveal paradoxes *in* the organizations. We have been flipping lenses. Having seen the facts differently, we have exposed contradictions in the objects of study. But this claim, though it is the heart of the theory, is simply asserted. We aren't told why we shouldn't suspect that contradictions in our observations mean that our thinking is defective or incomplete or that different lenses are skewing our vision (since Morgan argues that reality is made, not given). The trouble lies with the mirror of nature at the core of the organizational metaphor position. Morgan isn't really impartial:

> I favor general use of the psychic prison metaphor . . . [broadened to include ideology] to free people from the traps of favored ways of thinking and to unleash their power and creativity. I favor the culture metaphor as a means of emphasizing the importance of enactment processes, and the political metaphor for decoding webs of interest and power relations. I favor the brain metaphor because of the fundamental challenge it presents to the bureaucratic mode of organization, and the flux and transformation metaphor for highlighting the tendencies and contradictions built into our general way of life. I believe that the domination metaphor helps us to confront the gross exploitation and inequality on which so many of

> our organizations build. I value aspects of the mechanistic and organismic metaphors for some of the practical insights they offer when used in a contingency mode, and am favorably disposed to the possibility of developing an ecologically based framework for interorganizational development. . . . we need to break the hold of bureaucratic thinking and to move toward newer, less exploitative, more equal modes of interaction in organizations (Morgan 1986, 382–83).

The only good metaphor is a dead metaphor. We have a reality—domination, the paradox of interests—and thus a standard against which other metaphors are measured. This family of "metaphors" no longer functions as but one set of possibilities (against which, presumably, a charitable reading of human relations would be equally valid). Instead we have a privileged vision for evaluating the motives behind the human relations model.

Still, who can oppose flexible thinking? Perhaps some of the organizational metaphor position's intuitions are salvageable. If the omniscient theorist is replaced by a focus on interfield tensions, then across field lines, some metaphors may compensate for the blindnesses of others, and others may turn out to have ideal niches.

The insistence on details and logics suggests the first step in reforming the organizational metaphor position—seeing each metaphor as an argumentative position. Positions are how argument fields come to life. The term *metaphor* is now functioning more like Kuhn's paradigms: the metaphors are labels or perhaps organizing images for argument fields—animated as arguers use them. And the tensions arising among metaphors are interfield tensions.

The epistemic view would first ask how the metaphors function in arguments. After all, the contradictions among them might reflect how they are put. The differences that divide people are sometimes side effects of ideological polemics, hysteria, and incommensurable values, and these particular metaphors may be contributors to liberalism's penchant for cranky polemics. The trio—"is" (psychic prison), "is not" (work ethic), and "can be both" (theatre)—looks like "thesis, antithesis, synthesis," but these metaphors yield expressive, conventional, and rhetorical positions; only the shallowest quotation, each of each, will permit the working consensus necessary to have a debate. If my truth is your false consciousness—and emphatically vice versa—you and I may not find points of compromise that would permit argument. Once we are talking about positions people will take publicly, the proponents of the psychic prison and of the protestant work ethic may not endure shallow quotation by their opponents, concede that a course of future cooperation lies between their positions, or concede the legitimacy of their opponent's position. The work ethic is the domination metaphor's paradigm case of false consciousness, and vice versa. To challenge either position is to be drawn into a logic that indicts the challenger in advance. The Goffmanite, on the other hand, might scold the prisoners and protestants for their zeal, but then issue a verdict even harder to swallow. We should sympathize with Willy Loman not because he has been deluded and exploited or had the bad luck to be a drone who can do nothing better, but because he has lost control of his metaphors; his facts are not indefinitely open to interpretation. When you fail as a simulacrum, suicide is the only good theatre you have left.

These arguments might go better in shallow quotation—argued best by those who argue like, but do not think like, the natives. Dispassionate partisans, by definition, are willing to abide by how the arguments turn out. Cooperation despite disagreement might thus be enabled. For instance, the tensions between the psychic prison, protestant work ethic, and theatrical metaphor might lead to a common resolve to tone the discourse down—or to blur the issues with enough ambiguity so that the tension between extreme positions can be profitable instead of irritating (Connolly 1987, 1988). Another project might be a search for the mechanism that enables discriminations among the details and evidence inside fields. Instead of claiming that the interplay among metaphors sorts itself, like an invisible hand, into a coherent picture, we might regard each metaphor as a point of leverage, an argumentative pivot on which one's attention shifts to different possibilities. On this view, metaphors neither sort themselves out nor reveal anomalies in the objects of study. Rather, the different argumentative moves one makes are tied together by an overarching view of communication. Krone, Jablin, and Putnam (1987, 37) thus join the mechanistic, psychological, interpretive symbolic, and systems-interactive metaphors on the premise that all are given meaning by a view of communication. They stress the prospect of incompatibilities between the details of the metaphors, and that the combined metaphor approach is advantageous "only if the constructs under study are conceptualized compatibly across the perspectives being merged." For instance, psychologies mustn't be described so deterministically that they preclude the interpretive and interactive models.

McCornack and Husband (1986) also capitalize on tensions between four models: constructivism, uncertainty reduction theory, attribution theory, and message design logic. These are selected from a larger list of metaphors, including psychodynamic theory, phase analysis, social exchange theory, game theory, and conflict style theory. The principle of selection is the degree to which a model exposes the communication practices underlying the conflict. So something like Morgan's program is feasible if grounded in particular data and in a general view of communication. Such particulars may be open to perpetual indefiniteness and alternative definition, but practices force decisions on actors and a respect for practices enforces practical limits on deconstructions.

So metaphors have internal logics and facts that invoke conventional restraints—chief among them, the need to translate one's insights into the conventions of public discourse: One takes a position and—expecting critique—takes care with details. Then we see how the arguments go. Two fields are not incommensurable, no matter how alien they seem, if one can figure out a common project for them. Conceiving common projects is a rhetorical maneuver of mingling conventional details—that either will or won't work depending on how the rhetorical negotiates her case.

ORGANIZATIONAL THEORIES AS POSITIONS

The term *position* means both coherences between intentions and performance and one's public stance (Willard 1989a). The latter is the focus here. Public stances include legal briefs, position papers, press releases, and speeches. They are conventional utterances; they come from individuals, groups, or spokespersons. They are not exclusively texts (they may capitalize on nonverbal ploys), but they are analyzable—and often subjected to intense scrutiny in the courts of law and public opinion.

As positions, organizational theories characteristically include (i) *a view of human nature;* (ii) *a theory of relevances,* of the phenomena constituting and affecting organizations; (iii) *an organizing metaphor,* living or dead; (iv) *an empirical picture,* assumptions or explicit claims about reality, infused with approval or opprobrium; (v) *a therapeutic program*—diagnostic methods, problem definitions, and treatment regimens; and (vi) *a picture of science*—a set of standards *imposed upon* or a legitimizing rationale *for* the theory.

There is no necessary order to these elements. Any of them might be regnant to the others depending on the theorist's interests. The organizing paradigm might, for instance, be a view of human nature: If workers are seen as irrational, unimaginative, and unreliable, they might also be seen as interchangeable spare parts best suited to narrowly defined, easily trainable tasks ruled by an authoritarian structure with a downward flow of information and decision-making. If workers are a "natural resource," they are objectified, measured, and used. Or the view of human nature might come last, to underwrite the status quo. One's empirical picture or financial interests might make one prefer a Hobbesian view of human nature because of its rationalizing power.

Thc *metaphor* has the same ambiguity. *Weltanschauungen* thinking makes us expect to find every element being molded by the organizing metaphor, but a look below at the biological and machine metaphors yields a different view. Both metaphors are selectively used—and set aside when they are argumentatively inconvenient. Both metaphors underwrite existing conditions, yield a theory of relevances, and suggest a therapeutic program.

Still differently, one might start with a picture of science and bring one's diagnostic and therapeutic programs into line with that model. Contingency theory, for example, is organizational studies' analogue to the factor-analytic tradition. As organizations and practices vary, one seeks systematic explanations of those variations in terms of each variation's function as an adaptation to some variable. Organizational design is thus seen as covarying with environmental, technological, motivational, and task factors. One might study covariations between any aspect of organizational life and organizational size, or employee motivation, education, and intelligence. Leadership style might be studied in association with factors such as group size, need for cooperation, aspects of the leader's job, task structure, the degree to which the leader clarifies path—goal relationships, and so forth.

And still differently, one might start from a therapeutic program—preferred for its ease, economy, or profitability. The other elements come into play as rationales for the therapy. The picture of human nature and theory of relevances buttress the program's methods and assumptions; the picture of science legitimizes the therapy; and the metaphor wraps the package, making it coherent, rhetorically attractive, or unthreatening. Put in another patois, if I defend a universal view of human nature and of organizations, it is likely because I am a consultant with a profitable therapeutic program. As con artists say, universalism is my *hook* or *story;* my role as a grand theorist is my *legend;* and my tenured position at a university, or best-seller, or reputation, is my *glow.* I peddle Maslow, or what-have-you, as a cure-all for getting the workers up to snuff.

Perhaps enough has been said about theories as positions to clarify the advantages of the position over the organizational metaphor position's view of metaphor—and to clarify a discussion below of the most influential single metaphor. The benefits of taking metaphors literally—of focusing on their concrete fit with the details of argumentative positions (in other words, killing them)—can be seen by examining some deployments of the biological metaphor.

THE BIOLOGICAL METAPHOR

My claims are that (1) once again, flexibility is a virtue only in moderation; (2) biological metaphors have kept open systems theory more closed than open; and (3) though it is the pick of the litter, the ecological metaphor needs to be argued as a local explanation, not a grand paradigm. An ecosystem implies both conflict and cooperation; the latter sometimes obscures the importance of the former.

Because the history of the biological metaphor is a familiar one, I will say only three things about it. First, though the biological metaphor was a successor to the Enlightenment's machine metaphor, it is only half right to say that the universe of gears and pulleys gave way to primal soup. Structural functionalism kept many features of the machine—preeminently, function—and its vision of organisms and systems had a machinelike simplicity. Second, in the nineteenth century the biological metaphor was largely gestural—a starting point for grandiose projects, a way to attract followers: "Organic analogies were in the air, and the development of psychology enabled these analogies to be used without any obligation on the part of theorists to tie themselves down to the precision of gross physical details" (Catlin 1938, xiii). The search was for universal principles of rationality. Since biology is nature's universal principle of organization, and since isomorphism and self-similarity undergird the Great Chain of Being, biological structure seemed to be a plausible model for understanding the structure, systematicity, and rationality underlying human practices. And third, structural functionalism's dominant metaphor is more Spencerian than Darwinian (Burrell and Morgan 1979, 56). Spencer, remember, made a move Darwin opposed: He made evolution whiggish (Gould 1980). Growth is a lawful progression toward differentiation and complexity, societal growth being the most complex kind of evolution. A society is an aggregation of parts locked in perennial struggle. The system selects for strength. Strife strengthens the competitors. In the society-as-mercantile casbah, countless acts of individual greed add up to social utility, so the effect of conflict is progress. Every day, in every way, the system gets better and better.

Spencer is often credited with seeing society as an organism, but this does not jibe with the rest of his views. An organism cannot tolerate internal dissent..Even in those pre-DNA days, Spencer saw that the organism metaphor did not easily fit social structure. So his biological metaphor stresses ecosystems. Evolutionary time was needed for Hobbes's jaundiced view of human nature to pass from favor and for functionalists to transform the metaphor from ecologies to organisms. Harmonious wholes supplanted Hobbesian jungles.

THE CLOSING OF THE AMERICAN SYSTEM

Now to systems theory (Homans 1950, Parsons 1951, Easton 1953). There is variation in this school in the meaning of *system,* but Von Bertalanffy's (1956) "complexes of elements standing in interaction" is often taken to typify the position. The vagueness of this view has been trenchantly criticized (Berlinski 1976). Its defects have perhaps been discussed enough that they needn't be rehashed. Suffice it to say that Von Bertalanffy wanted to unify the social sciences along a Vienna Circle model. He needed a formal construct of sufficient generality to cross disciplinary lines by demonstrating "an isomorphy of laws" across boundaries (Burrell and Morgan 1979, 58). That construct was the organismic metaphor, though by 1979 it was virtually unrecognizable:

> An open system can take a wide variety of forms. There are no general laws which dictate that it must achieve a steady state, be goal directed, evolve, regress or disintegrate. In theory anything can happen. One of the purposes of open system theory is to study the pattern of relationships which characterize a system and its relationship to its environment in order to understand the way in which it operates. The open systems approach does not carry with it the implication that any one particular kind of analogy is appropriate for studying all systems, since it is possible to discern different types of open system in practice (Burrell and Morgan 1979, 59).

Plainly, the word *open* has eclipsed the word *system.* "Anything can happen" is kissing kin to "anything goes," for the possible permutations of *system* are at least as abundant as possible variations in environments. So is the system so open that it is no longer a system?

Consider a famous example. Katz and Kahn (1978, 7) state that open systems theory "must avoid the fallacy of biological analogies," and then proceed to use biological analogies at every turn: Organizations are like "the human body and its various organs" (24). "The cell receives oxygen from the bloodstream; the body similarly takes in oxygen from the air and food from the external world" (23); "The body converts starch and sugar into heat and action" (24); "[E]ntropy is counteracted by the importation of energy and the living system is characterized by negative rather than positive entropy" (22–23). And "the catabolic and anabolic processes of tissue breakdown and restoration within the body preserve a steady state . . . [that] is seen in clear form in the homeostatic process for the regulation of body temperature" (27).

These are typical passages—and the only explanations of the difference between open and closed systems. Moreover they are pivotal to Katz and Kahn's explanation of change. Quantitative changes, we hear, proliferate specialized subsystems, like the progressive mechanization we would see in a small university that tripled in size. Open systems move toward differentiation and elaboration: "Diffuse global patterns are replaced by more specialized functions," much as cognitive development is *orthogenetic* (moving from simplicity to complexity): "The growth of personality proceeds from primitive, crude, organizations of mental functions to hierarchically structured and well-differentiated systems of beliefs and feelings" (29). "The steady state, which at the simple level is one of homeostasis over time, at more complex levels becomes one of preserving the system through growth and expansion. The most common growth pattern is a multiplication of the same type of cycles or subsystems—a change in quantity rather than quality. Animal and plant species grow by multiplication. An organization's subunits strive 'toward a closer approximation of their ideal form.' A social system adds more units of the same essential type as it already has" (Katz and Kahn 1978, 28). Foucault's trap once again springs shut: Systems, on the logic of this view, can only replicate themselves. So how, then, can qualitative change occur?

The solution? Suspend the organismic metaphor. Like a character who inexplicably wanders off stage, the metaphor does not happen to be there when Katz and Kahn discuss Coser's (1956) conflict dynamic:

> [O]rganizations are less integrated than biological systems; their patterns of cooperative interrelationships also represent constrained adjustments of conflict and struggle. The adjustment is not only the compromise of past antagonisms but also of immediate differences of feeling, belief, and interest. The contrived character of organizations means that by nature they contain built-in sources of conflict. Many facts of organizational life can be readily understood if the model of organizations is one which views social patterns not as fixed and rigid interrelations but as the outcome of a continuing tug of war.

> The implication of this model is that organizations are always in a process of change. (103–4).

So much for homeostasis. If the homeostatic principle ensures that systems replicate and maximize their basic character, it is not clear how and why newly differentiated subsystems would yield qualitative change. Malignancies aside, cells do not contradict the larger systemic imperatives in which they arise. Their DNA/RNA instructions are not only blueprints, they are miniteleologies linked coherently to the larger system. The thrust and parry of environment with the equilibrium-favoring system does not explain how the system internally reorders, and the explanation of how the system reorders to accommodate to internal conflict is no clearer, for organizational time is not evolutionary time. And the question of how accommodations are possible does not arise.

The orthogenetic system that is suddenly not orthogenetic is owed to Durkheim, who can be described as setting out to cross a river on one bridge, then midway insisting on finishing the crossing on another bridge because he has changed the name of the river. He uses the organismic analogy to say that differentiation emancipates resources, thus increasing functional capacity by enhancing a system's equifinality. But he wants to explain permanence, so he doesn't argue that equifinality explains qualitative change. Whenever the metaphor obstructs metaphysical claims, he scraps it in favor of a conservative system worship. Causality flows in *one* direction: from society to individual. The division of labor is an anomic force. And from his reading of the naturalist Espinas (Catlin 1938), he sees the value content of collective will as analogous to the instinctive cooperation one finds in anthills. The *collective unconsciousness* is an unfolding blueprint: The individuals in an ecosystem occupy their niches and play their roles for the collective good (Durkheim 1938, 105–6). The result is a naturalistic fallacy for moralists: *The ought* equals *the socially successful* (Catlin 1938, xxxi). So it is a civic duty to found sociology as a positive science—to undergird a stable political order by replacing speculative philosophy with unifying values.

In sum: If logical implication is seen as flowing downward, like determinism, from organizing principles to systematically organized particulars—in other words, if the stability of the thought system is explained *as if* it were like DNA/RNA—then one must *shift metaphors* to explain change. And if one has depicted an all-encompassing system, this shift is something of an out-of-theory experience.

The biological metaphor needs a Lamarckian mutation argument to explain qualitative change. Lamarckianism, of course, is a false theory of genetic inheritance, but still a popular vision of intellectual progress (Gould 1980, 84). Cultural history, Gould says, *is* Lamarckian—"in strong opposition to our biological history." So the claim would be that mutations arise randomly; some mutated species achieve local adaptations and thrive—passing on their enabling trait. Population ecologists find this explanation convincing (Aldrich 1979), but it is unattractive to systems theorists whose concern for rationality makes them want to keep randomness and accident out of their views of structure. But subdomains in organizations advocate their own perspectives, conflict with other subunits, intersect differently with the environment, and exert different influences on the larger organization (Bacharach and Lawler 1980, Biddle 1964, Blau and Schoenerr 1971, Brown 1973). Conflict among and within subunits is a social process (Burns 1961, 1966, 1967, Conrad 1985) whose outcomes are not uniformly predictable in terms of the organization's structure (McPhee 1985, Poole and McPhee 1983). As organizational change doesn't occur in evolutionary time, there is nothing in systems theory to explain how the proliferation of subdivisions would yield change rather than more of the same.

The idea of valuing dissensus, on the other hand, suggests that conflict plays a role analogous to the role of fever in the human body. Lowi's (1971) "iron law of decadence" holds that organizations conserve themselves at the expense of innovation. This is a political scientist's version of Foucault's trap, and it captures an important dimension of organizational life. It is harder to be competent than agreeable. Daily life favors agreement. Its architecture is functional. Its rhythms are set by tasks. Its normalcy has momentum. Everything about it works to minimize disruption and soothe disputes. Argument is how organizations think, and they do as little of it as possible.

Against this "iron law," there has arisen an organizational literature—especially the popular business literature—whose organizing value is the need to *balance* conservatism and adaptation. It attributes wise decisions and flashes of brilliance to openness: Adaptive organizations are able to get and interpret information because they nurture the tension between conserving the system and adapting to change. IBM, for instance, is *not* still doggedly manufacturing typewriters. It brought the advantages of size to bear on innovations in the computer field. It didn't sponsor innovations; it figured out which ones to buy—because it saw adaptation to a changing market as a core problematic. So the struggle of companies to resist their own conservatism and to make their corporate experience as

Lamarckian as possible is an oft-told story. Its chief lesson is the dangers of closure. And its success stories chiefly point to the saving grace—or organizational virtue—suggested by the expression "valuing dissensus." The companies who have opened the system are the ones who have institutionalized ways of managing dissent.

Systems without Systems Theory

Common parlance and *Webster's* condone seeing "systems" as plans, designs, strategies, routines, methods, contrivances, procedures, schemes, and the like. So organizations are seeable as systematically related communication practices—configurations of working agreements, conventions, and procedures arrayed around organizing aims and institutions. Social and conceptual systems are symbiotic and parallel—both based upon principled practices and both more or less open to refinement and adaptation.

This literal-mindedness has advantages. The organization idea structures one's thinking about the contexts and channels in which arguments occur. This focus yields a novel relationship between argument and decision-making—and forces the argument theorist to deal with commitment as an epistemic phenomenon. To see argument as a kind of interaction that occurs inside organizations of different complexity, is to change one's ways of conceptualizing dispute. It, inter alia, forces one to think concretely about contexts—and thus downplays processual models that depend on isolation of processes.

A case in point is the proposal that disputes reach *stases*. Deiter (1950) uses the *stasis* idea to explain the idea of a stopping point. In Greek physics, motion is seen as punctuated, not punctuated equilibria but starts and stops. The pendulum arcs to a critical point, stops for a moment, then begins its downward plunge. The momentary stop is the *stasis*. Translated into argumentation, *stasis* means stopping points—argumentative points we reach where the action cannot continue unless something happens, points of disagreement so fundamental that cooperative discourse cannot proceed until the *stasis* is breached. That arguments *do* come to full stops might seem to confirm Deiter's thesis, to describe a sort of incommensurability: One arrives at debilitating disagreements—points of dispute beyond which discourse cannot proceed unless some agreements are reached to permit transcending the obstacle.

But, though arguments stop, they are often replaced by other arguments, for organizational discourses can bypass intransigent disputes. Dispute localization and equifinality are essential to organizational survival. So arguments co-occur: They overlap and mingle with other discourses. And disputes admit of multiple solutions: One is not *either* stopped cold *or* forced to surmount a disagreement. Even deep differences can be submerged or bypassed if other motives take precedence. The preference for agreement *is* a regnant motive, but the press of events and the motives of other actors may take many forms. So the *stasis* metaphor is too stark and romantic. *Thesis-antithesis* has a cinematic air, like a showdown in a spaghetti western. But most arguments are punctuations of routine activities—of a piece with a tapestry of events whose organizational context gives them coherence.

The same can be said of Goffman's theatrical metaphor: An argument is not an isolated event on a stage. When arguments occur, other things are happening. Others are taking care of business, routines are being followed, other arguments are occurring. A better image is of a many-ringed circus: a jangle of performances, too many to keep track of in a big organization.

This is why the Challenger episode remains mysterious. By all accounts, many engineers opposed the launch; their opposition was not suppressed; yet NASA went ahead. It might seem that a clear narrative set on a clean stage, was mysteriously subverted. Seeing the decision-making process in the singular, I believe, is where the investigators went wrong. Putting the engineer's opposition in the larger organizational context makes it more believable that protests that seem powerful post facto may not have seemed so exigent at the time. The NASA decision-makers, trying to rationalize their decision, may be unable to satisfactorily describe the complexity of the goings on.

This may be a flaw in the narrative paradigm (Fisher 1987). Inside organizations, multiple stories, scattered voices, and tangled plots weave intricate webs. The stories used to explain and rationalize events may be fabulous, ways to dispel mystery or make the alien seem familiar. The genesis of decisions may lie along multiple tracks, jumping across one another, exchanging, and permutating. Organizations are not massively parallel processors (computerese for what computers have to be to simulate the human brain)—economic expediency disprefers redundancy—but every complex organization contains enough equifinality to complete projects. Given enough momentum, projects can plow past even entrenched opposition. The Challenger, for instance, was launched by multiple thrusters—including public relations (every delay prompted press scrutiny), institutional and bureaucratic momentum (the safety documents did get signed), and, very likely, the diffusion of responsibility that comes with organizational complexity. These elements do not touch on the same pressure points. It is not as if we have arrayed evidence and warrants building around a single practical syllogism (the conclusion being *launch*). The launch of Challenger did not issue from a single narrative thread extending unbroken from start to finish. That linear thinking is just why the ensuing disaster is mysterious. And, by parallel case, the reason why the *rational thread* of intellectual progress in the disciplines is hard to discern, or seems like a Foucauldian deception, lies largely in the organizational complexity of the disciplines. This explains why ideas sometimes seem to mysteriously appear and disappear and why the narrative thread of intellectual progress seems to be missing.

Identification and Commitment

Except for the human relations theorists who see humans and organizations as incompatible (and thus work to sugarcoat the inevitable), most organizational theorists recognize the importance of identification (Cheney 1983a, 1983b, Galbraith 1979, Katz 1964, Tompkins and Cheney 1985). In persuasion theory, identification designates feelings of affiliation—the followers identify with the leader. Organizational actors are likewise identifying when they fit their decisions to perceived consequences for the organization (Simon 1976), *internalize* organizational goals (Katz 1964), or see themselves as stakeholders (Mitroff 1983, Freeman 1984). Such fusions of person and organization are thought to be the glue that binds organizations together—an organizational resource on a par with liquid assets and plant capital.

But some readers may have qualms about commitment anywhere in the vicinity of the well-founded consensus. Knowledge, it may seem, can only be tainted by commitment. Commitment is what one has left when one runs out of justifications (Bartley 1963), a last epistemic refuge—like Hitler's Wolf's Lair—into which one is backed by skeptics.

Still, expert fields are not immune to *working faiths*. Experts may see themselves as curators of knowledge and disciples of disciplines. Curatorship is a kind of selflessness; discipline and professionalization are kinds of socialization. Thus Simon's (1976) exposition of organizational identification fits the expert fields—one's position in an organization focuses one's attention, and identification is a cognitive mechanism for coping with complexity (Tompkins and Cheney 1985, 191). Simon sees this as a mixed blessing, for focus implies exclusion. The things that make organizations useful also make them dangerous.

EPISTEMICS AND ITS METAPHORS

Having accused systems theory of indiscriminately shifting among metaphors, and setting them aside when their details are inconvenient, I admit that epistemics runs the same risk if it uses the language of ecology alongside the language of quantum dynamics (as I have been doing). Do the *quantum realities of organizations* make up its *matter* governed by a telos or élan vital? Does the ecological metaphor handle the vitalism while the quantum metaphor handles the materialism? Does the author see the connection (invisible to Democritus and left on a materialist horizon by Bohr and Heisenberg) between the nature of matter—the mathematical structures of atomic physics—and not only ecobiology but human social order?

Of course by its own logic, quantum dynamics *can't* contradict the ecological metaphor. The theory says that energy exists in different forms, so no particular arrangement of electrons, protons, and neutrons will deny that the "fundamental substance of which all reality consists" is *energy* (Heisenberg 1952, 103). The quantum metaphor undermines Newtonian scale descriptions. It clarifies organizational complexity. It exhibits chaos within order—that microcosmic unpredictability is often channelized by higher order structure. It tells us to look for strange attractors when behavior doesn't seem to fit circumstances. And it suggests that the relation of the observer and thing observed is fundamental; change the stance, position, and technology and the reality—the relationship—changes. As Heisenberg insisted, observation isn't an intervening variable between reality and theory; it is a reality in and of itself (which is why *function,* not truth, governs science). Every domain can be looked at from multiple perspectives, and, à la Heisenberg, its reality will change. This captures the intuitions of the organizational metaphor position while honoring "the importance of being earnest." One can speak of the quantum realities of organizations, local entropy, and chaos (in a materialistic way) and yet also speak of an organization's élan vital—perhaps its ideology or, more simply, *atmosphere.* Metaphors have vitalistic social effects, even if we don't believe in vitalism.

CODA: THE NEW LEVIATHAN

Fields are organizations. They have pragmatic conditions—structures, goals, practices, and actors—whose effects are pertinent to the genesis and use of ideas and the well-foundedness of consensuses. The organization rubric stresses interdependencies between ideas and structures: Every stance toward knowledge claims is a position someone takes inside a system of motives, practices, rules, roles, relations, myths, and ideals. This focus on interdependency recovers some of Foucault's intuitions: Organization favors conservation. Structures bear preferences and pronenesses; they suggest the functional value or irrelevance of ideas; they focus thinking and create implicit utilitarian jurisdictions. But organizations are also concrete tests of the determinist thesis, and the research does not bear out a general picture of actors trapped inside iron cages or caught up together as sheeplike bearers of corporate cultures. It has vindicated the symbolic interactionist's intuitions that structures are animated by practices and that action influences outcomes (Pettigrew 1973, 1975, 1979). Organizational unity serves its functions, certainly, but it is also imperfect, and thus open to interrogation and critique.

So why are some actors more trapped than others; why are some organizations less victimized by Lowi's iron law than others? The answer to these questions lies partly in the answer to another question: "Why are there so many kinds of organizations?" (Hannan and Freeman 1981). The answer is that organizations live and breath as their actors seek to balance organizational and adaptational interests. Adaptation suggests intercourse with surroundings—which is why modernity is made up of a near-infinity of organizational solutions. Organizations vary indefinitely because they fill an indefinite variety of niches and aims. If structures are the concrete manifestations of praxis, then "fit with local conditions" is a first principle of discourse. So every field, no matter how idiosyncratic it seems, reflects pragmatic coherences between intentions and institutions, ideas and activities. The *field* is thus not a universal template to be rigidly imposed on any community. Its only general claim is the tension between conservatism and adaptation. Beyond that, it assumes *differences*—in networks, structuration, information flow, human resources, psychology, power, politics, and conflict—and theoretical pluralism: Taylorism applies here but not there; human relations is ideological here but not there. The telling point is the loss of generality.

And the history of organizational studies has suggested a way of seeing shallow quotation as a communicative act: Mirrors of nature do not easily transform into metaphors. They are laden with facts. The substitution of multiple metaphors may allow us to triangulate (Denzin 1970b) toward refined views, but factual claims trade on a social contract. Thus metaphors cannot be deployed whimsically. The most promising method is to use a theory of communication as the basis for selecting metaphors and adjudicating among their contradictions. Communication, in other words, is a better dead metaphor than Marxism.

TEN

A Theory of Presumption

> In a culture that casts profound suspicion on all other forms of authority, judicial power assumes unique importance. It is the institutionalized expression of our dominant rhetorical ideal: the authority to determine who shall bear the burden of ignorance in a society where traditional and scientific forms of argument have long been stretched beyond capacity. . . . What we desperately want—but can never find—is a kind of authority from which there is no appeal, whose final determinations can lay claim to full legitimacy. (Gaskins 1992, xvi–xvii)

Untempered, adversarial democracy claims the legitimacy only of an ugly necessity. The killing fields in *Federalist* 10 are what they are, and Madison would likely be puzzled by Gaskins's hope to "moderate the adversarial strife that has become an inhibiting feature of public discourse" (xix). Without common interests, Madison might say, the only commonweal is the rule of law. Civilization can neither repeal natural law nor make silk purses of sows' ears. Factiousness simply is what it is, inevitably perpetual and ideally ineffectual.

A social contract with a dog fight is scarcely an inspiring ideal, and many people dismiss the late president's views as something of a family skeleton, an embarrassment best kept from the children. Except for pluralists, the majority view expects better things of adversaries and puts its trust in the legitimacy of procedures. This trust is not universal. Technocrats are often accused of being long on means when they are short on results. In the face of failure they valorize procedure and thus hold themselves accountable only for their disciplinary virtuosity. But even technocracy's severest critics concede that virtuosity has its virtues and not every turn to procedure is an empty retreat. And the majority instinct is to discipline public discourses, to constrain human frailties within principled procedures.

"Proceduralists," if I may call them that, are of two minds about the legitimation power of procedures. "High-voltage" proceduralists are concerned with the rationality of procedures and tenability of their defenses. Their arguments have a foundationalist feel. Procedures worth following rest on the bedrock not of precedent but of systematic justification, of warranted confidence. "Low-voltage" proceduralists, on the other hand, expect public actors to follow rules because they hope to be (or seem) rational or because the rules make public discourse tolerable. High-voltage legitimacy will never shine self-evidently from the balustrades of well-founded government, so procedures are best judged by their effects, intended and not, and a society could do worse—much worse—than the civilization of discourse.

Either outcome would be shocking, and, as might be expected given the case for blandness, I prefer low to high voltage. Public life is a mingling of things political, philosophy and flim-flam, and if one can't tell the difference, or suspects that there is more of the latter than the former behind a procedural principle, a case for weakening the principle suggests itself. The principle in question is the idea of presumption. The philosophy behind it is British idealism, a school of thought not unlike the human relations movement. Viewed one way, it is pluralism's exuberant ancestor. Viewed another way it is a shameless ideology underwriting ruling-class Victorian complacency.

The idea of presumption was born—with great expectations—in 1828, begotten respectably enough by the archbishop of Dublin, Richard Whately (1963), who used the term to mean a "preoccupation of the ground," a status quo best kept until a burden of proof is discharged. He took this notion from theology wherein an attitude in principle toward change was meant to prevent interminable debates. Doctrine was a default setting, so to speak, to which discourse would properly return if debates proved fruitless. Translated into British common law, the presumption of innocence puts the burden of proof on the prosecution. One is innocent till proven guilty, so in cases of doubt, one *remains* innocent.

Had the good bishop stopped with the restraint of police power, he would be remembered as the father of a well-grounded procedure. But being every inch an idealist, he extended the principle to the whole of society. The presumption, he wrote, favors "every existing institution" (Whately 1963, 114). In cases of uncertainty, which is to say in the absence of compelling proof, of overwhelming reasons for change, things as they are should remain as they are.

This entirely more dubious presumption, Gaskins argues, has degenerated into an argument from ignorance ("I am right because you cannot prove that I am wrong"). Given the uncertainties inherent in deliberative discourse, adversaries remain adversaries by assigning impossible burdens of proof to one another. But where Gaskins argues for shifting burdens of proof, and thus transforming uncertainty into a moderating influence, I think more radical surgery is needed. There are, I will contend, no generally tenable rules about what decision-makers should do in cases of doubt. Only the most vehement pluralists would say "do nothing." And the most generally defensible rule is "Obey epistemic authority," scarcely what one wants if one doubts authority, and not entirely satisfactory even to those who defend authority. So instead of a rote approval or censure of status quos, I will propose a stance toward argumentative prerogatives, an epistemic presumption meant to accentuate the tension between authority and public jurisdiction. This presumption—that every public jurisdiction is broader than any expert's span of authority—is arguably-indispensible. The corporatization of knowledge suggests corporate ownership, and alongside the authoritative voices of normal expertise, cosmopolitans may be marginalized by their pidgin dialectics, multilingual but ineffectual. So what is needed, I think, is a commonweal without common ground, a principle that defines a public interest while doing justice to the confusions of diversity.

The Conservative and Liberal Presumptions

It is pretentious and a thing of state

—With apologies to Sandburg

Presumption is the sort of idea one expects of bishops. It seems lofty, timeless, like the brittle hush of cathedrals. It forbids horseplay and inspires solemn prose. It is an idea *meant* to be an institution, and the result is not without irony: The serene grandeur of cathedrals is a well-understood technique—arguably a paradigm case of peripheral route persuasion. Cathedrals are meant to be felt, to bypass rationality, to inspire faith and soothe doubts. Presumption, however, is meant to be a principle of rational discourse.

Whately's presumption might be dismissed as Panglossian, whiggish, timid, or reactionary, but it was not exactly "the last refuge of all reactionaries" (Gaskins 1992, 272). It was more the first instinct of conservatives, so following Goodnight (1980), I will simply call it the "conservative presumption." The idea, then and now, is that change must be resisted *in principle*. Current institutions reflect an accumulation of advances, history's perfective outcomes, its accrued wisdom (Ross 1951). Bradley's ethics thus enjoins one to learn "my station and its duties," to appreciate the reasonableness of the established order, and from reasoning of this sort, Whately's presumption logically follows: Current institutions being justified in advance of any particular dispute, advocates of change bear the burden of proof, every time, everywhere.

The "liberal presumption" (Goodnight 1980) assumes the opposite: Every status quo is an aftermath. Current social structure is as likely the spawn of accident as of design. Historical forces don't aim toward anything, let alone perfection. Even the outcomes of design lack the grace of good motives. Prevailing institutions reflect episodic compromises, expediencies, the inertial weight of uninspired leadership, the sloppy traces of blunders, the residue of incompetence and mendacity, and the aftertaste of mean spiritedness. Since the human race botches most of its projects, the weight of history is dead weight. If defenders of the conservative presumption can be caricatured as Pollyannas, their dialectical counterpart is the Marcusian radical. At every degree of extremity, the liberal presumption mirrors its opposite. The more seriously we take it, the more open to change we become *in principle*.

Neither rationale is unambiguous. One might infer from the conservative presumption that one should be eager for change. If history moves toward perfection, and one stands not at the end of history but at a point along a road whose end one cannot see, then the soundest wager is that every status quo falls short of ideal completion. But the conservative presumption is never read this way, and the reason, perhaps, is all too human: Stuck with one's lifetime, one personally stands at the end of history and is thus more or less obliged to live happily ever after, like it or not. One clutches what one has, and then, Hamlet-like, sticks with the evils one knows. The clinical psycholgist George Kelly (1955) built a whole theory around this cognitive conservatism: One judges new ideas by their knowledge-enhancing effects. Preferring clarity to ambiguity, certainty to indecision, one construes people and events so as to make them explicable and tends to reject interpretations that jeopardize one's preferred way of thinking. Anxiety thus masquerades as a reflective grasp and control of events, and timidity passes as a theory of intellectual mastery (Ross 1951). This makes for whiggish politics: The litmus test of ideas is their consistency with the status quo. And as one's horizons determine not only the answers but also the questions one asks, the shape and structure of present society become blinders for the imagination. The result is a Uriah Heep semblance of open-mindedness: Mistaking one's prejudices for certainties, one expects the world to falsify them definitively. One is thus "open-minded" and ready to entertain "good and sufficient reasons for change." One just never happens to hear any.

The flip side of this ironic coin is the liberal presumption. One would think that if ineptness and avarice have ruled past episodes, they might affect current decisions. Power and corruption being matters of degree, and given that we do not entirely know how to thwart the Robespierres, Stalins, and Pol Pots of the world, one would think that liberals would be inordinately cautious and would choose incrementalism over upheaval every time. The liberal presumption is never read this way, of course, and the reason arguably has a psychological and a rhetorical side. The psychological side is that the courage of one's convictions is a necessary but potent brew. There would be no reform without convinced reformers, but embarked on crusades it is hard to keep one's "self" detached from one's righteousness. And it is especially hard when one is also caught up in the rhythms of an untamed trope. "Power" and "powerlessness" are human conditions, certainly, but they function in political discourse chiefly as face strategies. One characterizes, and thus *positions,* oneself and one's opponents. Positioning of this sort may be quite justified, and one can mount perfectly plausible arguments to the effect that some human foibles are entrenched in or magnified by positions of power. But if "power corrupts," as Lincoln said, it scarcely follows that *only* power corrupts or that powerlessness is an infallible sign of virginity. Yet notoriously in public life, these labels get out of hand. Lionizing leads to demonizing, dialectic masquerades as demonstration, and one concludes—all evidence to the contrary—that the Jacobins, Bolsheviks, and Khmer Rouge were corrupted only by power.

If impeccable logic isn't the strong suit of either presumption, neither are the substantive cases that might be marshalled in their favor. One can't always determine, for instance, which presumption is germane to issues such as environmental threats, apartheid, civil rights, and disarmament. And as we shall see, a debate about their comparative merits—a debate about progress—might extend indefinitely. Each presumption implies a critique of the other. Each can be buttressed by plausible arguments and harnessed to choice examples, yet also called into question by equally plausible arguments and examples. And though both are exaggerations, neither can be improved by moderation. They might seem more presentable as rules of thumb, stated guardedly, studded with caveats, but a modest presumption, a modest *general* attitude toward change, is a contradiction in terms: The vindication of the generality of one's attitude is the belief that one should win the preponderance of disputes, that one is generally likelier to be right than one's opponents.

Presumably one would hold such a belief because there is something behind one's presumption that distinguishes it from predispositions or default settings. But it isn't inconceivable that having a general attitude toward change is more a personality trait than a considered principle and that the principled appearances of the presumptions are merely prejudices putting on airs. Or at least it is hard to see the difference between the value constellations invoked by the presumptions and what happens in popular parlance when people call themselves "conservatives" or "liberals." These labels notoriously evoke a gestalt-like attitude that colors and informs a family of beliefs and public positions. The usual finding in cognitive balance research is that if one changes labels, one will reformat one's beliefs to stay consistent with the new gestalt. The two presumptions thus lend respectability to the hobgoblin of little minds. One is "principled," not "dogmatic." One has a "philosophy," not a "prejudice."

There is no good reason, in sum, to have a general attitude toward change. Unless the case-by-case disputes between the two presumptions can be settled, there are no viable general rules for knowing whether it is more prudent to do nothing or to change. And decision-making, of course, is rarely a choice between change and a steady state: Weber's whole point about bureaucracies is their cell-like differentiation and continual growth. Every status quo is Heraclitean: One can't step into the same bureaucracy twice.

The only remaining justification for a general attitude toward change is that it makes for better argument. If the ambiguity and irresolution of the two presumptions don't discourage this belief, perhaps a consideration of their ideological functions will. The choice between them, I submit, comes down to a comparison of gut intuitions about progress: Parsonian structuralism with unction versus poststructuralism as a state of grace. This is not a happy turn of events, for having a general posture toward progress is arguably a flimsier idea than having a general posture toward change.

Progress and Its Discontents

The idea of progress—to be brief—had a Reformation infancy, an Enlightenment adolescence, and a nineteenth-century prime. First, Bacon, Descartes, and Pascal attacked the veneration of the ancients. Age equals wisdom, so appeals to the authority of the ancients are analogous to seeking the counsel of children (Bury 1924). Each new age stands on the shoulders of its ancestors, and is thereby the epistemological superior of its predecessors (Frankel 1967, 483). Progress thus became the main point of enlightenment—a rejection of the scholastics' claim that history repeats itself and a proclamation that received authority should not set the boundaries of inquiry. Fallibilism and verificationism would supplant piety and faith, and knowledge would accumulate as these rational processes did their work. The encyclopedists, Diderot and d'Alembert, applied progressivism to social structure, psychology, politics, morals, and ethics, and thereby laid the groundwork for progress' nineteenth-century prime as social Darwinism and the Whig view of history (Butterfield 1951). Every day, in every way, it got better and better. Progress became a god term (Weaver 1953).

The god term fared less well in the more squeamish twentieth century. Lamentations of the price of progress started in the 1920s as cultural anthropologists saw themselves as *saving* cultures from passing into history, grew in the 1960s with the *Weltanschauungen* assault on positivism, and blossomed in the 1970s and 1980s as the environmental movement transformed progress claims into zero-sum calculations. In academic and popular parlance alike, progress ceased to be an automatic authority for anything done in its name. It had become, indeed, the paradigm case of a mixed blessing.

Nonetheless, four senses of progress seem to have survived: *communitarian progress*—the progressive expansion of familylike association onto a larger sociological scale; *conceptual progress,* the intellectual progress in expert fields; a *folk bromide,* the progress vaguely sensed in the world that leads us to expect that no one living today would trade places with any but the most privileged ancestors; and *institutional progress,* the idea of keeping institutions open to self-reform and of keeping inquiry free and open.

The communitarian sense of progress is found in Kant's claim that human conflicts aim toward a "universal civil society" and in the belief in moral progress debated by French philosophers in the 1800s. It is central to the unificationists's view of rhetoric, certainly, and to the valuing of the corporate *patriae* associated with Rousseau, Taylor, and the human relations movement. The idea, roughly, is to enlarge the scale of familial unity. The family being the ultimate idealization of affiliation, one thus wants small groups to be *like* families, communities to be such groups writ larger, states to be "communities of communities," and international community to be, allowing for a certain literary license, a human family.

Mutations of scale aside, it is worth remembering that if all men are brothers, so were Cain and Able. Most families, I imagine, fall somewhere between the Cleavers and the House of Atreus, or between Rousseau's cartoon bliss and O'Neill's emotional cannibals. But families are where most homicides happen. They may be dysfunctional, emotionally barren, and mutually destructive, and they may bind more tightly than people want, hence my earlier argument that Federated Europe's unfamilial feel is its strength. Indeed, the degree to which organizations mimic an idealized familial unity—the current argot is "strong culture"—is widely thought to be dysfunctional. When organizations measure their progress in terms of increasing unity, they become pathologically oblivious to their environments. Their tendencies to oligarchy and closure are intensified by a preference for agreement. And the more they insist on being like families, the more the inside-outside dichotomy becomes true: The choices are surrender or anomie.

Turning from communitarianism to the subject of conceptual progress used to be a turn from fish to fowl. Well before and well after Talcott Parsons, the whole point of the literature on conceptual progress was that social unity is incidental. Knowledge was impersonalized in systems whose stability came from logical structure and whose innovative capacities were thought to lie in their calculi (Suppe 1977, Lakatos and Musgrave 1970). Progress was thus a matter of subsuming new events under, say, covering laws or of new paradigms replacing old ones by solving their anomalies or of an idea's survival of repeated tries at falsification.

Something of the spirit of this thinking still survives, and rightly so. Knowing babies from bathwater, many who doubted the falsification idea never doubted the idea of communally validated tests. Thus, for instance: "A field of argument is an integrated complex of concepts, propositions, and arguments, persisting over time, directed to shared explanatory goals, embodying shared judgmental standards, held consensually by initiates of a discipline" (Wenzel 1982a, 211). An integrated complex persisting over time is not a "full Bertalanffy," so to speak. Instead of impersonality, Wenzel's writings emphasize public objectivity as an imperfectly realized ideal, one that social groups, frailties and all, try to achieve. Fields are thus seen as seeking to expand and elaborate conceptual systems. Cumulative intellectual progress is possible, for instance, in "research traditions" (Laudan 1977) or "conceptual ecologies" (Toulmin 1972), wherein variation and natural selection are used to explain a field's genealogy of problems, procedural traditions, conventions for expressing the meaning of concepts, and methods for legitimizing conceptual variations. Progress thus lies in problem solutions and in a domain's successive elaboration of methods of reasoning. As domains increase their sophistication, they produce increasingly subtle and adapted argumentative and expositive forms.

This reasoning is not unlike Whately's, but it differs sharply in spirit.

Rational enterprises are rational insofar as they reflectively monitor their practices. Some things inspire more confidence than others, but everything is open to argument, to what Habermas calls "relentless criticism." Defenders of a current consensus thus bear a remarkable burden of openmindedness: Not solely for compelling reasons, but merely on suspicion, they are obliged to adopt, in utter sincerity for the moment, the liberal presumption. This perhaps expects too much of flesh and blood, and fields might do better by nurturing their rebels and allowing role-players to play their roles. But in either case, warranted confidence is a matter of closely watched practices, of ideas severely looked after.

All of these more moderate progressivisms suppose some form of comparability. There are disputes about its nature, whether, for instance, successor ideas must solve old problems or merely offer more engaging puzzles. But rarely does one find a claim that a successor idea is better than what it replaces unbuttressed by some criterion for determining the successor's superiority or at least for justifying a preference for it. *Except,* that is, in public affairs, wherein for every successful faction, as Madison might say, there is an opponent crying *regress.* And among gatherings of factions, one finds compromise, arguably democracy's noblest but least Popperian invention. Public life presents a succession of disconnected decisions, fleeting coalitions, tradeoffs and truces, the frenzy of a stock exchange in the atmosphere of a Lutheran funeral. Competing parties sacrifice pieces of their positions, change their stances, and dilute other commitments. Within such working coalitions, an ad hoc rationality sets in: Decision-makers select the decision they have the votes for, and then, if needed, select the rationale that rationalizes their decision. This perhaps explains the adage that law, like sausage, is best appreciated when one doesn't watch it being made. But the more important implication is that public domains are not argument fields sui generis, having their own special concepts and epistemic claims and being capable of intellectual progress. Public ideas don't weather epistemic tests; they are not conceptual ecosystems with governing economies.

Still, some would argue that public life has progressed. Conceding that progress is in the eye of the beholder, there is something of a *consensus gentium* about at least some developments: the abolition of slavery, except for graduate students, of child labor, except in subsistence economies, and of the most egregious violations of human rights, again with exceptions. And even the exceptions show signs of improvement. The Burmas and Chinas of the world at least no longer torture and kill their dissidents unnoticed. International publics have coalesced around movements such as Amnesty International, and the human rights issue has found its way onto a number of hitherto detached agendas. International discourse has thus taken a turn for the better. Bismarck's world of cold horse-trading and Lewinian force fields has been replaced by a rhetoric of cooperation, equity, justice, and human rights. This progress is admittedly piecemeal, but even conceding exceptions, the late twentieth century is a better place to live than predecessor ages.

This argument, of course, is the folk bromide, the intuition that no one living today would change places with any but the most privileged people in former epochs. It is more a vague hunch than the precise, ecology-specific logics needed to determine conceptual progress. And it is harmless enough, perhaps, to marvel at the hardships of one's ancestors, to revel in the merits of indoor plumbing, and to wonder with a shudder what life must have been like without Pentium chips and tanning salons. Every generation, let's say, has a God-given right to frighten its young with tales of its own hardships. But the key to appreciating the folk bromide is to know when to take it seriously and how seriously to take it. It may be good for morale to appreciate what one has, but as with British idealism, morale can be too good, and as a serious argument the folk bromide has notorious flaws, for instance, the cost-benefit claims about the price of progress and environmental side effects. If events in achieving societies have consequences in nonachieving societies, the cost-benefit calculations justifying progress in one place at the expense of other places involve complex tradeoffs. If Americans eat beef at the expense of the world's grain supply, avoid domestic child labor by subsidizing foreign child labor, enjoy their freedom at the expense of the nuclear threat, and wallow in plenty, swilling gasoline, at the expense of developing countries, the arguments justifying such practices branch infinitely outward, taking in a sizable array of factors. Many people oppose such calculations: The grounds of argument that permit weighing our surpluses against their reverberations elsewhere smack of the vilest imaginable utilitarianism (so many ergs of happiness in one society balance so many ergs of misery in the places that must be plundered to fuel the happiness).

The bromide is also ethnocentric enough that it at least ought to be embarrassing (Bury 1924). Bangladeshis and Bosnians may not live all that much better or longer than their ancestors, and one would scarcely say that the march of progress has visited every Appalachian hamlet. Indeed one finds the march of progress, alongside a watered-down manifest destiny, chiefly in holiday rhetoric, the one medium that genuinely is the message. Picnic pluralism is a venerable art form and the expected entertainment at nationalist fiestas. The spectacle of private conceits bursting into public is the low-tech prelude to the fireworks display, and words and deeds in this case are birds of a feather. Both are meant to be experienced and remembered only as a warm glow.

Unfortunately, self-persuasion is among the most robust persuasion effects, and when pluralists believe their own rhetoric, and thus take the bromide seriously, their Realpolitik becomes increasingly self-congratulatory, which rarely makes for flexibility and an openness to the fourth sense of progress—self-reform. The gut feeling that one is caught up in an imperceptible process of gradual, perfective change is a psychological horizon on which it seems safest not to disturb the universe. One becomes a "low-risk reactionary," harmless enough in clubroom armchairs but stultifying in boardrooms and committee chambers.

This specter brings us to the last sense of progress, the idea of institutional progress as a feature of self-critical discourses:

> [T]he idea of progress in its most important aspect is a regulative moral idea, not simply a belief about history. It represents a directing principle of intellectual and social action, instructing men to regard all social arrangements with a critical eye and to reject any claim that any human problem has been finally solved or must be left finally unsolved. To the extent that this idea of progress is embodied in moral codes and social systems, these codes and systems will contain deliberate provision for self-reform. The idea of progress thus represents the social application of the principle that inquiry should be kept open and that no bounds can legitimately be set to the authority of such free inquiry. As such, it would appear to be an indispensable belief for a fully liberal civilization. (Frankel 1967, 487)

One can scarcely object to critique and reconstruction. Arguments are a field's open doors. One fully expects well-founded organizations to be adaptive to new conditions, which is to say open-minded, innovative. Trusting their procedures only provisionally, they show their rationality much as people do, by how they change their minds (Toulmin 1972).

But not, surely, by *constantly* changing their minds. It is often hard to know when people and organizations are open-minded enough, but when we find them frozen in place, or erratically vacillating, we might suspect that they have too much of a good thing. The word "progress," as a label for openness, suggests (to borrow from Douglas) "more of the same." Foreclosed options demand more openness, presumably to the point of complete openness, the sort of an ideal state of mind one associates with peyote-powered religions.

In using "progress" to label what most people would call "adaptation," Frankcl is perhaps trying to undo Spencer's damage, to wrest the word "progress" away from the Social Darwinists. Organizational progress; remember, is ideally Lamarckian. Enabling traits are passed on, *unless,* of course, we are too whiggish to appreciate them. Frankel thus turns Spencer's virtues into vices and allows the goal of free inquiry to capitalize on the ordinary language connotations of "progress." This is good public relations for a regulative moral principle, but it runs the risk of mirror-reversing social Darwinism. Frankel's progress principle mightily resembles the liberal presumption: Change is at minimum a wholesome symptom, and it will be tempting to judge an organization's open-mindedness by the degree to which it in fact changes. This is a gestalt, not logic, but it is the gestalt likeliest to be invoked when adaptation is called "progress." It is also, I think, the gestalt Frankel intends to invoke. Otherwise why make the point? Why insist upon provisions for self-reform? The answer is that organizations tend to be conservative, sluggish, maladaptive, and unimaginative—sometimes suicidally so. The conservative presumption being a powerful human frailty, Frankel's antidote is proportionately powerful, and precisely as justifiable as the liberal presumption.

Wither the Burden of Proof?

It might be objected that to abandon a general attitude toward change is to undercut the idea of burden of proof. The conservative presumption and the burden of proof have appeared in tandem for so long that they seem logically connected. But jurisprudence aside, the burden of proof is more a matter of audience predispositions, and it is sometimes impossible to decide who should benefit from a presumption. Environmental issues involve doubts and risks that are equally puzzling on both sides: With nuclear energy we risk low-level radiation and Chernobyl-like catastrophes; with fossil fuels we risk air pollution and the greenhouse effect. In Europe, the status quo is predominantly nuclear; in the U.S. it is predominantly fossil fuels. But since the pollution effects of either option are international, it is hard to say what the risks of *any* change might be. Neither the conservative nor liberal presumption tells us what playing it safe requires.

And what have we learned about disciplinary dogmatism? General attitudes toward change push some advocates toward a field's uncontroversial center. Once there, they display a resistance to change that might close a field entirely if unchecked by counterforces from the periphery. But one can defend the division of labor between conservators and innovators, and thus defend the protection of dissent, without mentioning the two presumptions. And there is another presumption, a change-of-subject to which I now turn, that though it might have been incomprehensible in the modernity of the 1790s, might prove to be more suitable to the modernity of the 1990s.

EPISTEMIC PRESUMPTION

The epistemic presumption is that breadth dilutes authority. Public issues cross field lines; their breadth exceeds any specialized authority. Nuclear safety, for instance, only partly belongs to nuclear engineering, for the nuclear engineer has no automatic bona fides for discussing distinctively public business—political expedience and compromise, efficiency engineering, administration, and economics. Safety is not simply a matter of nuclear engineering: it is also a matter of politicking, legislating, policy-making, and administration. So no one can claim complete epistemic hegemony over nuclear power policies. And if the creationism-versus-evolutionism dispute carries political, legal, constitutional, pedagogical, and moral implications, then the advocates of either side possess no special claims on the deliberative processes public decision-makers should employ in evaluating their dispute. The abortion question is not solely a medical or religious or sociological matter, so abortion expertise is always narrower than its political contexts.

These examples are unusually intransigent ones, but their breadth is typical. Public decision-makers are more often than not beset by competing field-dependent claims. There is as much breadth in issues of health care, highway construction, mass transportation, bank regulation, air safety, education, and foreign aid. These issues present decision-makers with complex options, esoteric knowledge, big literatures, and the claims of multiple fields. The existence of this competition suggests that none of the competitors can claim the right to adjudicate the dispute. By definition, they lack authoritative control over policy-making.

Epistemic jurisdiction is not a legal metaphor. Public interest arguments are always case-specific. And public jurisdiction is not a substantive question: It does not mean that certain topics straightforwardly belong to the public. Many of nuclear engineering's claims to hegemony are plausible: No one wants nuclear policy without nuclear expertise. But if public problems are usually broader than any expert's span of authority, this breadth can be the basis for public interest claims. The retreat to the field—which I earlier characterized as the proper behavior of actors defending true claims—is epistemologically but not epistemically correct. The retreat shuts off debate, or leaves it at a standstill, since it demands from the public a passive acquiescence to field authorities.

The breadth idea captures some of the intuitions behind the modernist fallacy, but it suggests that the fallacy lies not in making issues seem technical but in allowing single fields to dominate decision-making. Public issues will always have this breadth and complexity. Decision-making will always be a balancing process in which data and beliefs from competing fields are weighted and compared. And there is no reason to think that decision-making can get better by resembling science. To argue, as many do, that decision-making's fuzzy thinking and imprecision stem from its falling short of particular scientific models is to miss the point.

Experts *interpret* their facts. Testimony, as a rule, follows a set-piece format: Here are the facts; here in (my rendition of) your language is what these facts mean; and (often) here are the recommendations I infer from the facts. The first move is the most trustworthy, the last move the least, and the middle move is where the enforcement of jurisdiction is likeliest to blur or collapse. The decision-maker cannot evaluate the translation from esoteric to general parlance, so Brooks (1976) recommends the creation of an environmental "assessor of assessors" to evaluate technical testimony and clarify policy choices. This might create a new class of experts who intervene between expert testimony and public decision-makers—whose focus is partly on the translation of esoteric to general parlance and partly on shaping policy alternatives.

The jurisdictional principle dovetails with the "principle of attention" (Willard 1983), a public stance toward the obligations of advocates that enjoins us to listen to the fields for whom discourse is an open option and to listen skeptically, if at all, to fields that succeed by virtue of *closure* (preempting outside critique, closing off lines of argument, stipulating ground rules that ensure favorable outcomes). The cost-benefit analyst closes, remember, by insisting that her value judgments be refuted only by claims couched in the language of fiscal costs. Against the closed ranks of this expertise, decision-makers are presented with a brute take-it-or-leave-it choice.

This emphasis on closure obliges movements to be as expert as they can be and expert fields to remain as open to outside critique as possible. And there are success stories. Brashers and Jackson (1991) have studied one successful interaction between a public movement and experts—an experiment not in dominating expert domains but in influencing them. ACT UP (The AIDS Coalition to Unleash Power) was a populist movement—complete with demonstrations, "kiss-ins," and a demonizing of expertism—that gradually marshalled its own expert pool (including a Treatment and Data Committee) for dealing "behind the scenes" with federal agencies and the AIDS Clinical Trials Group. The aim was to challenge a bulwark of conventional wisdom—the traditional double-blind placebo study that randomly assigns subjects into experimental groups (who get the tested drug) and control groups (who get placebos). ACT UP denounced as morally objectionable the placebo controls, the time frame of phased research, and the insistence on homogeneous subject pools (white males). And ACT UP had a substitute for traditional science: Its document *National AIDS Treatment Research Agenda* included "detailed suggestions for alternative clinical trials designs, as well as many suggestions for more humane treatment of patients within the context of clinical research" (cited in Brashers and Jackson 1991, 13).

My earlier description of the authority dilemma would predict *either* that experts would dismiss public concerns *or* that populist values would contaminate the expert knowledge. "But what in fact happened was neither imposition of scientific values on the public nor sacrifice of scientific values to humanitarian values, but a genuine penetration of the public sphere" (ibid., 15–16). ACT UP didn't just object, it *critiqued*. "The medical community took these critiques seriously and invited participation in the creation of alternative designs" (ibid., 16). "The conflict between scientific interest and public interest was not resolved by exercise of power or by assertion of privilege on either side." ACT UP's critique of the assumptions behind AIDS research "penetrated the research community and stimulated a *general* reexamination of routine design and analysis decisions" (ibid., 18–19).

Brashers and Jackson argue that the key to reading the ACT UP story is not that humane values "defeated" the medical establishment or diluted its scientific rigor but that a public discourse evolved into a technical discourse (see Peters 1989) by engaging one set of experts with another and thus balancing technical and public concerns. The idea is *not* that the two sides of epistemic presumption should or can be in *balance.* There is no general equilibrium between expertise and jurisdiction. The public jurisdiction changes from subject to subject, context to context, where professional jurisdictions generally remain stable. And as expert prerogatives and organizational mandate differ in kind, *balances* between them are likely to be spurious. For instance, the Challenger disaster—in which experts were consulted, then forced into lockstep in the heat of organizational momentum—is a case in which NASA management believed it had balanced expert and organizational goals. The agreement between experts and activists to take a fresh look at clinical trials required less a balance than a measure of good will on both sides. ACT UP was willing to "try to understand the scientific principles behind the drug-testing policies" (Brashers and Jackson 1991, 20), and the experts were strikingly open to critique—open, that is, to tempering the conduct of AIDS research in light of the human consequences of AIDS.

CODA: THE NEW GLADIATORS?

The epistemic presumption doesn't solve the problem of incompetence, but it suggests a different way of seeing it. The presumption is that policy-making is more complex than any one span of expertise. Public issues cross specialties and thus require a division of labor in which, inter alia, experts interpret and challenge one another. The idea here is not of a new spectator sport, or still another version of science courts, but of taking more seriously the clash among experts as it already happens.

Defining the public jurisdiction is an ongoing feature of daily life. The resolution of interfield disputes requires an almost daily adjustment of one's working sense of the public jurisdiction. These jurisdictional decisions are apt to be case-specific and thus unlikely to yield an accumulation of case law upon which future decision-makers can base decisions. Conceptual progress is appropriate only to esoteric fields; the folk bromide functions in mass rhetorics but is ill-suited to policy-making, and provisions for self-reform can be maintained by speaking of adaptation, not progress. Adaptation, after all, can as easily as progress be seen as a regulative moral idea, thus preserving Frankel's intuitions about provisions for self-reform. The case for free and open inquiry, uncontaminated by power plays and authoritarianism, needn't be tied to progress.

ELEVEN

Desperately Seeking Dewey

Jeffersonians may feel that epistemics misses the whole point of a democracy. Quite apart from the plight of experts and organizations, the very idea of liberal democracy demands that some reasonably populist version of Dewey's public be redeemed, albeit one less naïve about expertise. Where Dewey championed the rule of experts and counted on liberal education to create an appreciative public, Jeffersonians, on the whole, prefer an activist public, which they see as the democratic alternative to a scientized politics on the one hand and a politicized science on the other.

Modernity *is* getting the worst of both. Parsons's fear that politics would contaminate science has been corroborated by the science debunkers who argue that technical fields are demand-sensitive to political whims and that universities have become shopping malls for evidence. At the same time, expertise has contaminated politics with more viruses than cost-benefit analysis. Experts may be as inept as senators at policy-making and as public spirited as lobbyists when funding is at stake. They may be true-believers who bring dogmatism and ideology into politics—witness Halberstam's (1969) and Janis's (1983) rosters of expert-driven fiascoes. Plainly, the Mertonian priesthood has sent more than a few Graham Greene priests to Washington, and if the intelligence of democracy is both scientized *and* obtuse, an enlightened public is an appealing alternative. Or that, at least, is an eminently debatable proposition.

Perhaps there are enough points of agreement between the epistemic and Jeffersonian positions to permit this debate. Epistemics has exhibited some democratic inclinations, certainly. It underscores the totalitarian drift of disciplines, the closure of isms, and the possibilities for reform. It wants to check organizational momentum with discussion and debate. It favors a separation of powers that pits experts against experts and exploits political and epistemic interdependencies. And Jeffersonians themselves may now be convinced that not every problem can be solved by more public participation. Even the fiercest populists surely don't literally want to be in the position of medieval peasants, going about their lives, hoping the outside world won't notice them. They see, perhaps, that local action may solve local problems, but not necessarily interdependence problems. Reduced scale makes community less menacing, but not authenticity. So an interesting debate may be possible. It may sharpen the tensions between the technocratic and Jeffersonian impulses and set the arguments onto more promising paths.

But it is one thing to speak vaguely of an enlightened public and quite another to define this enlightenment and to consider whether it is in any sense possible. The chief issue in this debate will be our comparative ignorance about how knowledge is translated from code to code. That admittedly is not the topic Jeffersonians want to debate, so the beginning move is to wheedle them into the debate, and then, in an admittedly sketchy way, to take stock of the ignorance within which the debate must proceed. No one, I submit, entirely knows how much is lost in translation.

THE PUBLIC AS GRAIL

What this book has chiefly done is ask liberalism to surrender a sweeping problematic: the problem of the public sphere. There is no problem, only a family of problems whose synergism yields a macro-incompetence for individuals and micro-incompetence for organizations. There is no public, only publics. Habermas's bourgeois public "was never *the* public." There were "competing counterpublics, including nationalist publics, popular peasant publics, elite women's publics, and working class publics" (Fraser 1991, 61). And finally there is no public sphere, only a pragmatically infinite number of channels, arenas, and theatres of operation.

If the vastness of this smorgasbord precludes a consensus about what and where the public sphere is, so do the expectations people bring to the subject. Consider, for instance, merely two differences in message-design logics. On the expressive side, Rousseau invidiously contrasts everything public with the privacy, warmth, and genuineness of hearth and home. Look for fraudulent emotion and counterfeit expression and you will find the public sphere. The solutions, on this view, are localism and authentic expression. Aristotle's view, on the other hand, is conventional—a matter of noticing why crowds gather. They gathered, one gathers, for legal, political, and ceremonial reasons, and, as one might conventionally expect, employed different discourse forms within the three spheres. Public life, on this view, is a matter of competent, rule-governed performance, and authentic expression therein would be at best a breach of etiquette and at worst a threat to the body politic. The only feature these two visions share is a fatal flaw: They get their unity from their smallness.

Our political modernity has its "Greek moments," certainly. Churchill's war speeches, Roosevelt's fireside chats, the JFK funeral, and the

Challenger disaster come to mind. But such galvanizing moments of mass attention are both evanescent and comparatively rare. Since the Vietnam era, presidential addresses, as a rule, and even military escapades have had mixed success in drawing audiences. Of course audience size is a comparative thing, and that, perhaps, is the point: If C-Span's small but steady following is dwarfed by any number of other audiences, then where *is* "the" public sphere?

But the best reason to doubt that there is any such thing as "the public" is that it can't be described as an argument field. It has too many subject matters. A regime is animated by a vast tapestry of activities—quantum contexts, multiple organizations, unmanageable information flows. Its operational range crosses *most* subject matters. So there is no public conceptual ecology with its own standards, subject focus, and veridical methods for measuring progress.

And where are its borders? Borders can be Berlin Walls or chicken wire, hermetic seals or Swiss cheese, but a good rule of thumb is that any border one can cross without noticing needs to be called something else. Rousseau noticed one border: Home and hearth are private; everything else is public. Dewey noticed a different border: Anything that affects one alone is private; anything that affects others is public. A debate about the comparative merits of these views will come down to whether it seems proper to call family life public. We might decide that family life is more public than, say, daydreams, more private than town meetings, and perhaps analogous to close-knit groups. But these distinctions are trivial beside the growing transnationalism of public life. If French sovereignty is dispersed to Brussels and Strasbourg and its economic and political horizons are European in scope, then its discourses of government, universities, mass media, and corporations will become more complex and interdependent. They will be more European and less French, and they will further blur the public-versus-private distinction with still more publics competing for attention.

And what are its beliefs and methods? Policy outcomes are rarely Popperian tests: The coalitions that enable decisions are often transient, so falsification is even more elusive in public life than in the sciences. The web of knowledge is too intricate; public practices do not sum up. And there is no theory-building: Public decision-makers can be content with local successes—one obeys the rules and abides by the outcomes of any number of decisions, but may use different scenarios for the next decision.

And what is its function? The function of an argument field is to illuminate the assumptions behind claims—to describe how and why people believe them. The field helps explain what political statements mean, what their truth conditions are, and why citizens vote as they do. The public, on the other hand, is often contrasted to fields by virtue of discourse distinctions: generalist versus specialist, ecumenical versus select, layman versus expert, broad versus narrow, consumer versus authority (Goodnight 1987b, Wenzel 1982a). In other words, the distinctive feature of *the* public is the sparseness of its discourse.

That sparseness explains why the discourse of presidents and senators *resembles* expert discourse. They talk about economics, military and foreign policy, and the like, and mimic to some degree the language of experts. But "the public" functions in arguments like "community": Broad appeals collapse to the local. The public can't be instantiated without changing meaning, without pointing for immediate purposes to a specific public. This is a modern variation on the Greco-Roman view of audiences. The difference between an audience and a public, arguably, is that an audience is paying attention to a common source; publics are busy with daily life and must be transformed (and thereby localized) into audiences.

This localization of the public occurs in tandem with its more concrete cousin, "the public interest." The idea of interest transforms an ineffable image into a concrete argumentative move. For instance, in the Radio Act of 1927 and Communications Act of 1934 the public interest is a move inside an argumentative position, a point of view defended as collectively valid. Public ownership of the airwaves is a legal principle, certainly, but it also directs future argumentation. Without knowing how the future will define broadcasting "in the public interest," the principle nonetheless ensures that some version of the public interest will be the starting point of future arguments. It is an abstract standard that will inevitably become concrete.

The most obvious stakes in distinctions between public and private are legal ones. Privacy checks police power. And the ownership of knowledge is becoming an increasingly litigious issue, one that pits governments and their espionage apparatuses against corporations. But aside from proprietary issues, the chief epistemic stakes lie with the public interest. Public interest arguments are by no means a panacea for pressing the case for distributive justice. Their legal efficacy in challenging bureaucracies and agencies has been mixed (Lazarus 1974). But they do suggest an alternative way of thinking, for like legal arguments they have less to do with defining the public sphere than with defining a public jurisdiction. Jurisdiction implies authority and span of control and thus turns our thinking in an epistemic direction.

KNOWLEDGE AS PUBLIC BUSINESS

Every society needs a sense of public knowledge to train future public actors and to assess their competence. Aristotle advised citizens to know the facts of war and peace, government and legislation, economics and commerce. By 1776, Jefferson added science and industry to the list. And by 1986, the classical intuitions were still operating—in the general education debate and the enfranchising pedagogies. Professionalism and specialism were still seen as problems to be conquered by an ecumenical public knowledge.

But professionalization was underway even in Jefferson's time, and it has dominated public life ever since. The legal profession, for instance, has served much of the training and evaluation function in American life, both because law is a body of public knowledge and because it is a traditional career path for politics. Schools of public administration and public policy produce professionalized corps of trained personnel equipped with bodies of knowledge thought to apply to the whole range of government. Political science departments have nurtured policy science and policy analysis. And journalism schools have joined a presumed general competence to the goal of maintaining opposition across the whole of government and society.

The Dalai Lama calls the twentieth century "the most complicated in human history," but this complexity is not evident in some of the curricula. In the 1960s, the public administration schools taught "applied political science, accounting, rudimentary public finance, and personnel administration." The public policy schools produce "Rand-style analysts" armed with cost-benefit analysis, statistical and methodological training, and macroeconomics (Fleishman 1991). The goal, it seems, is to produce Paladin decision-makers—have methods, will travel.

But there is a tension between these transportable methods and the project focus and division-of-labor governments in fact employ. Methods said to apply universally have limits that are well understood only by the specialists who focus on particular subjects and contexts. Cost-benefit analysis works the same way everywhere, but its policy implications may differ from case to case—just as writing, speaking, and informal logic pedagogies are universal in the abstract but variable in the concrete.

Handling this tension has not been the strong suit of the professional schools. As an accident of focus, and perhaps hubris, each profession has nurtured its own methods, leaving the tensions of local applications to others. Partial pictures, in other words, are projected as whole pictures, and authority-dependence is increased. The professionals are trained to respect but not evaluate authority, so they call in experts for this and that, and then either acquiesce to or disregard the advice.

This dependence is most pronounced in the professions that cover the most territory—journalism and law—which suggests a role for epistemics: playing the friendly skeptic to theories that ignore the problem of competence. For instance, Entman (1989) argues that the news system is caught in two vicious circles. In the first, the elites manage the news because journalists fumble complexity, but the journalists' ineptness stems from their hostility toward elites. In the second, journalists can't raise the quality of journalism without a more sophisticated audience, which they will never get without providing better journalism. There are no villains in this scenario: A low-common-denominator journalism makes it easier for elites to manipulate the media than to submit to public scrutiny; elite secretiveness and manipulation make for hostile and cynical journalism; and audience shortcomings require simplifications that ensure a low-common-denominator journalism. The result is power without control. Nobody—elites, journalists, or hidden cabals—controls the news system. The result is less a marketplace of ideas than a family of rituals that tell the same story again and again. This feeds a "spiral of demagoguery, diminished rationality in policy-making, [and a] heightened tendency toward symbolic reassurance and nostalgic evasion of concrete choices" (ibid., 128).

Entman is a mass enfranchiser. Like many journalists, he sees his profession much as humanists see liberal education. To raise the complexity of mass discourse and create new immunities to demagoguery, he proposes reworking the journalism curriculum, inviting the mass audience to demand better news, and creating a PBS-style print and broadcast news network. These moves might help Neuman's (1986) elite voters, and perhaps expand their ranks, but they scarcely ensure subject matter competence. Journalists freed from Entman's vicious circles will remain authority-dependent, conclusory, broadly incompetent, and no better prepared to translate esoteric claims into a language that the elites can comprehend.

And demagoguery does not thrive solely among the tensions between elites, journalists, and their audiences. It blossoms as well in the narrative structure of journalistic prose. Narrative, like community, spawns bizarre mutations with increasing scale. When matters of war, diplomacy, economics, and law become stories, much of importance about their dynamics is missed. And narrative structure can seep into these domains, just as Fleck says popular formulations seep back into the esoteric cores. So there is a third vicious circle in Entman's inferno: It will be hard to wean journalism away from narrative structure when the universities prize narratives for their authenticity and punish translations for their popularity.

EVALUATING EXPERTISE

I quoted Chomsky earlier to the effect that public knowledge isn't as intellectually demanding as academic specialities. The thrust of his argument was a populist one, and, though he didn't use the expression, one can easily imagine him saying of public knowledge: "It ain't rocket science." This expression is a familiar one on campus, often in the context of disparaging a subject matter or suggesting that it is manageable by less-than-first-rate intellects. But the meaning of this expression needs to be reversed. Public problems are much harder than rocket science. Were NASA merely rocket science, the Challenger might have flown, the Hubble Telescope might not have needed a billion dollar repair call. Bosnia, certainly, has been reduced to rocket science, or at least to the trigonometry needed for artillery. But most people, I imagine, would regard that reduction as a failure, just as no one wants the project of cajoling the North Koreans out of their nuclear weapons program to suddenly become as simple as rocket science.

If I am right about this, if public problems are more complex and thus more intellectually challenging than the problems of specialties, then where does the onus lie for preserving the public interest? The answer, I submit, is squarely on the best and the brightest—the academic specialities themselves.

The past several chapters have mustered a case for thinking that public knowledge—what decision-makers must know—is a package of discourse competencies for the appraisal of expert discourse. By appraisal I do not mean deciding whether experts are right or wrong—that is what experts are for—but deciding how expert testimony shall be taken. This includes knowledge about the dynamics of expertise. How do disciplines designate and monitor experts? How are intradisciplinary meanings, claims, and understandings translated into interdisciplinary or public claims? How do claims that are disputed within a field get translated into public claims? Does their controversial status get concealed as they are transformed into public ideas? Under what conditions do appearances of objectivity obstruct the decision-makers' evaluation of testimony?

This knowledge may be disciplinable. One can imagine progressive insight in the study of the organization of expert fields. The role of experts employed by government has been well studied (Apter 1971). And NASA's history of managing multiple disciplines and technologies is a realm of experience permitting comparative inferences about decision-making procedures. Where the expert fields coordinated by NASA judge the technical solutions, epistemics focuses on their uses and movement of information, their decision-making, their ways of arguing, and their methods of coordinating multiple discourses.

This organizational knowledge may neutralize professionalism's most oft-mentioned vice: its ethos strategy whereby experts claim privileged epistemic status (Wood 1964). The strategy exploits isolation and mystery, deliberately arcane testimony, so as to underscore the inferior status of public decision-makers (Abbott 1988, Bennett 1986). For instance, a prominent jurist calls psychiatry "the ultimate wizardry" (Bazelon 1974). It has, he says, a guild mentality that avoids public surveillance by guarding the mystery of its technologies. "One might hope that psychiatrists would open up their reservoirs of knowledge in the courtroom. Unfortunately, in my experience, they try to limit their testimony to conclusory statements couched in psychiatric terminology. Thereafter they take shelter in a defensive resistance to questions . . . [and] refuse to submit their opinions to the scrutiny that the adversary process demands" (ibid., 18). They also maintain a positivistic appearance: the effectiveness of psychiatric testimony depends on creating the "false impression" that the witness has discovered all that can be known about the issue at hand. The appearance of scientific certainty is the whole *point* of psychiatric testimony.

Bazelon says there is no substitute for the adversary process for monitoring the behavior of professions. This applies not only to psychiatry but "equally well to the public surveillance of other highly specialized professions on which the operation of our complex civilization depends" (ibid., 23). Whether the expert is a psychiatrist characterizing a defendant's mental state, a physicist predicting environmental impacts of nuclear reactors, or an engineer explaining why auto emission standards cannot be met, the adversary process involves "challenging the expert, digging into the facts behind his opinion."

But competing experts also rely on technical patois and argue at a conclusory level, leaving it to judges and juries to choose among them, often quixotically. We have already looked at some topics that one would think would be publicly accessible: creationism, scientific fraud. Yet the striking thing in the former case was the ineptness of experts in adapting to nonexpert audiences, and in the latter we concluded, unhappily, the less said the better.

Admittedly, experts are sometimes forced to take the low road. Scientific rationales lack the dazzle of new technologies, so the selling of supercolliders and space programs often resorts to what might be called "Teflon and Tang enticements," justifying research projects by their incidental payoffs. Applied benefits are the coin of the decision-makers' realm and sometimes, at least, the only viable public rationale. A case in point is a *60 Minutes* exposé (CBS, 26 February 1995) that broke the scandal that University of Arizona professors are doing research at public expense and publishing their work in what a Kentucky governor once called "itty-bitty journals." Philosopher Keith Lehrer, interviewed apparently for balance, pointed to the Gulf War, wherein all the successful technology came from basic research. We don't know, of course, what was snipped out of the interview, but it would have been interesting to hear Lehrer discuss his own work, and something of a spectacle, I imagine, if he had been able to draw Teflon and Tang arguments out of the epistemological work for which he is famous. By all appearances, Lehrer did what any candid humanist would have done, and I for one could have done no better: Lehrer was facing an interviewer, Leslie Stahl, whose nonverbals simply exuded shock and incredulity at the unfolding horror and whose questions betrayed the certainty that a defense of "doing philosophy" would have ended on the cutting room floor. Caught in a "full Winchell," the muckraker's version of a half-Nelson, one's choices are mystification, obfuscation, and when all else fails, Teflon and Tang arguments.

Context was part of the problem. Accustomed to meeting thieves and scoundrels on *60 Minutes,* the viewer could well imagine Milton scholars shielding their faces like Mafia dons as they scurry into their offices to *not* teach. But the tone of the segment heightened the effect. As the narrative gained momentum, university research became one more scandal, more or less indistinguishable from the S&L scandal. The "reporter" clearly had her "story," and her story, as stories tend to do, gathered the facts that fit it and rolled over ones that didn't. A number of the latter appeared in a rebuttal by the university's president, which suggested that rather more teaching was happening at Arizona than apparently met the CBS eye.

If one lesson of this episode is that expert fields should have modest expectations of journalists, then the important question is what expert fields should expect of themselves. The question is twofold. First, when research can't be publicly articulated or justified in a language of concrete payoffs, how much razzle-dazzle is tolerable? A good spiel is perhaps a vile necessity of funding, but in the process of hustling up the necessary mystery and reverence, fields might profitably consider whether they are also seducing themselves. No one, I imagine, ever intended the rhetoric of the liberal arts curriculum to be flim-flam. But if the idea of general knowledge is as empty as I claim, and if public issues are as technical as I claim, then functionally, at least, a public relations slogan has become a sacred cow. Jeffersonians needn't agree with this view, however, to consider the second aspect of the question, namely, what it would mean *if* the burden of redeeming the Jeffersonian promise lies with the expert fields. The underscored *if* is a bracketed disagreement, one we can put aside, for even the most fervent populists would assign *some* responsibilities to expert fields. Granting epistemics its donnée, pluralists and populists alike might agree that the price of public influence is the public interest, that experts who presume to direct government are obliged to enlighten it. The question, then, is how?

Translation across Discourse Levels

General discourses are generally meant to transcend local discourses, which is why the homogeneous "public" is often contrasted to the heterogeneity of technical fields. Unificationists thus insist that the traits that localize field discourses are not simply missing in public discourse, they are alien, even antagonistic to it. Specialists are a select elite trafficking in narrow expertise; the public is a lay audience dealing with broader issues. But differences between narrowness and breadth are scarcely the whole story. The degree to which any discourse can represent elements of another depends, inter alia, on its representational resources, which in turn depend on the competencies of the public to which the discourse must adapt. It seems perhaps obvious that discourses differ in complexity because their publics differ in cognitive complexity, but the extent and nature of these differences are perhaps less obvious.

The most robust finding in cognitive complexity research is that people differ in vocabulary size, the relationships they see among ideas, and the gradations of meaning or shades of gray they are able to see and express. One's "developmental complexity" thus consists of "differentiation," the number of constructs one uses, "integration," the connections one draws between constructs and construct systems, and "articulation," the differences in degree one is able to distinguish. Complexity, in this literature, is domain-specific: One may know much about Italian Renaissance art, nothing at all about auto mechanics, and only a little about politics. And cognitive simplicity makes for sparse communication, which is to say unnuanced, artless, and intolerant of ambiguity and cognitive dissonance. One uses fewer distinctions and is more prone to lump people, ideas, and events into "all liked" and "all disliked" categories.

Differences among individuals and discourses put a premium on translation. "Translation" is arguably the best word here. It evokes not a transparent mirroring or an unproblematic conversion of equivalencies, but a hazier process of imperfect matches, fuzzy commensurabilities, and missed connections. It suggests metamorphosis and transmutation, rendering and paraphrase. Indeed, its first synonym in *Roget*'s is "interpretation," a word that if it doesn't curdle the blood at least connotes a form of risk-taking.

The riskiest variety thereof is interpretation across dimly seen differences. In taking unassessed risks, one is left with only vague impressions of success or failure, and no dependable track record to guide future interpretations. That, I contend, is our situation, and to prove this claim I need to run the risk of seeming to belabor the obvious. But for Jeffersonians who believe that translation is merely a one-step process—one code to another—perhaps the following rough sketch will suggest something that is not at all obvious.

Imagine a continuum of what might be called "demographic sweep." At the left pole are messages meant to be understood by millions. At the right pole are the most esoteric, intricate, and recondite messages meant to be understood only by select groups. In between are any number of gradations that can be bunched into "latitudes of comprehension." The idea of latitudes comes from social judgment theory, but the latitudes below are meant to square with advertising and marketing research (see Cohen 1988).

Latitude 1: Mass Communication. Moving toward the left pole, messages are increasingly dependent on narrative and pictorial images. The sparser the code, the lower the common denominator, the clearer and better. Mass journalism is thus reduced to "this happened, and then that happened." Opinion and argument are matters of "*X* says *n; Y* says not-*n*." And expertise is institutionalized: "This happened, that happened, and here is an expert's opinion." And mass messages are about fewer topics, for a mass audience is a demographic potpourri. Aside from the usual suspects—war, crime, nationalism, and personalities—there are few topics of interest to audiences of millions. These topics give mass politics its tabloid traits and its need to mimic the marketing of mass commodities.

One wouldn't know it to read mass communication textbooks, but the idea of mass communication has remarkably limited utility (Elliott 1972).

Advertisers *wish* they could pitch everything to a mass audience, but for most marketing and advertising purposes, the mass is dispersed, heterogeneous, and disorganized (McQuail 1984). Unlike presidential candidates, luxury cars and champagne can't be peddled like toothpaste. So most audiences are demographically segmented—by income, race, lifestyle, education, locale, values, religion, beliefs, and interests. They are smaller than "mass," yet still bigger than most.

Latitude 2: Big Targets. "Positioning" in marketing and advertising aims at "penetrating" heterogeneous groups. "Message targeting" is a matter of accessibility: Messages are strategically fitted to an audience's abilities and predispositions. Self-help and popular business books thus differ in message complexity from science fiction and *The Wall Street Journal. Rolling Stone* is written more simply than *High Fidelity.* And if *Hard Copy* differs from *McNeil-Lehrer* both in kind and in code, the code to some extent determines the kind. For in entertainment, news, and marketing, "fog indexes" are used to keep content pegged to a common denominator that is determined by measuring the developmental complexity of a cross section of a potential public (Elliott 1972).

Latitude 3: Smaller Targets. The middle ranges of the continuum are best illustrated by magazines, for specialism is the driving force of the magazine world. Most students of the industry divide magazines by subject matter, circulation, regionalization, audience focus, price, and reader involvement. And it is conventional wisdom among advertisers that the trend away from mass media (*Life* and *Look* in their first incarnations) toward specialized publications directed at narrow audiences mirrors a growing heterogeneity in society's interests and competencies. To appreciate the extent of this heterogeneity, one needs only stand at some central point in the magazine section of a large general purpose bookstore. It needn't be one of those monstrous ones. A mere thousand or so magazines will illustrate that there are a thousand or so publics, many quite sophisticated. The rule of thumb is that the greater the specialization, the more arcane the content. One needs specialized knowledge to read, say, *Chess Life and Review, Flying, Yachting,* and *Antiques*—and professional-caliber expertise to read, say, *Flight International, Paris Review,* or any of the thousands of trade magazines one likely won't find in a bookstore.

This specialization exonerates television of what some see as its highest crime, the fact that it isn't more "magazine-like," meaning that it lacks the seriousness and depth of, say, *The New Republic* or *The Commonweal,* or even of such larger circulators as the *New York Times, Atlantic,* and *Omni.* Thus, the argument goes, by pandering to the lowest common denominator, television sharpens the schism between elites and masses (the former read magazines; the latter watch TV) and thus disenfranchises the public.

This criticism is not entirely mistaken. No one claims that broadcast news goes as deep as *The Public Interest.* And the readerships of esoteric magazines doubtless are participants in a higher level of discourse characterized by a greater reliance on written material. There is, for instance, a science-oriented public—its core perhaps embodied by the 700,000 subscriptions to the most arcane popular science magazine, *Scientific American* (Bennett 1986). But notice first that this criticism reduces television's content to level 1. It is directed at NBC not CNBC, at CBS not CNN. By ignoring so much of what is available (the History Channel, the Discovery Channel, Arts and Entertainment, Lifetime, a network for physicians, the Weather Channel, ESPN 1 and 2, and a rogue's gallery of adult channels, right-wing talk networks, and embryonic news networks), it ignores how magazinelike television has become: C-Span, for instance, gives Neuman's elites an unprecedented window on Washington, as close to Dewey's public sphere as one can imagine, and cable news networks have expanded the range and depth of available information.

If cable continues to mimic the specialization of magazines, the proliferation of channels will intensify. This might mean the extinction of the dinosaurs if broadcasting's audience dwindles to those who can't afford cable. But it is likelier that the broadcast networks have already found their niches on cable. Even in a world of 500 channels, there will always be an audience for mass entertainment. One can only speculate about whether that audience will continue to dwindle or become so dispersed over so many mass vehicles as to become only modestly profitable. But without the utopian future having arrived, Newton Minnow's "vast wasteland" is already, as fallacy theorists say, a straw man.

And television scarcely has a monopoly on plebeian content. For every vulgar talk show, there are a hundred coarse magazines that delve into their subject matters—from tattoos to tips for mercenaries—in more detail than even the worst of television's offenders. Moreover, the crisis of the public sphere was said to be full blown in the 1930s. Even if there was a magazine intelligentsia in Mencken's day, why should we expect television to achieve what the magazine world ultimately couldn't? If Neuman's (1986) political elites—the interested, engaged voters—don't read the *same* magazines, they might not agree on any particular ones as the house organs of the public sphere.

Latitude 4: Elite Targets. Toward the upper end of the magazine world, the prose is at a level of complexity that is in some respects indistinguishable from trade books. Trade books, of course, cross into latitudes 3 and 5, but latitude 4 is arguably the heart of the genre. The difference between the most arcane magazines and trade books may be largely quantitative: Book length treatments permit more abundant detail and intensity of focus than magazines and should thereby, on the whole, be more sophisticated. Trade books can target their audiences more narrowly and thus rely on the more highly specialized knowledge and abilities of their readers.

If journalism's prose stratosphere is captured, say, by Walter Lippmann's books, then latitude 4 is just beneath it. Its readership is educated enough to read, say, *Habits of the Heart, The Best and the Brightest,* or *Betrayers of the Truth,* and to read the sort of science-writing found in newspapers, magazines, and at least some trade books. This latitude includes books and essays about policy and politics, economics and legislation, and it perhaps represents the lingua if not the franca of Dewey's public sphere.

Latitude 5: Academe. Again with no clear demarcation from the previous level, there is, I think, a general discourse of academe—roughly the level at which academic committees function. It is a general discourse in the sense that any reasonably educated academic can read, say, *The Mismeasure of Man.* Some writers indeed (Jane Goodall, Richard Leakey, and Stephen Jay Gould) follow Darwin's lead and write for a general but high-level public. This realm doubtless has many levels differentiated by the degree to which readers can unpack and interpret the reasoning behind conclusions. Lewis Thomas's *The Lives of a Cell* is lucid but demanding, and recall that *Philosophy and the Mirror of Nature* advances widely accessible claims by virtue of technical assumptions and names-standing-for-positions that might be fuzzy to nonspecialists. In much the same way, it isn't inconceivable that *The Structure of Scientific Revolutions* is a creature of the next latitude but has gotten its myriad interpretations at least in part because of its wide dissemination.

Most translations of esoterica are into this general but high-level discourse. Lavoisier popularized the field he invented; Heisenberg translated quantum mechanics for philosophers; Gamow popularized the big bang. These translations are often successful (e.g., *The Cosmic Code*), but no one would mistake them for the esoteric knowledge. They are something else: more authority-dependent, metaphorical, and sparse; they are couched in a different language that conceals, more or less completely to the inexpert reader, what may have been lost and added in the translation.

Latitude 6: Professions. This level is not the sole locale of literary density, but it is dense enough to be analogous to a black hole. Ideas rarely escape its gravity and are able to do so only at the price of transformation into language appropriate to latitudes 4 or 5. The media of this latitude are apparent contradictions in terms—the "esoteric mass communications" of expert fields contained in "relatively mass media," by which I mean specialized books and journals. Their audiences are tiny compared to the audiences of magazines and network television, but enormous compared to interest groups and research programs. These media are characterized by indexicality to more clearly defined bodies of knowledge and their ability to enthymematically capitalize upon commonly known ideas. Toulmin (1964) thus feels free to define argument fields as "logical types" without defining the idea or footnoting it to send the reader to the right literature. Denizens of Oxbridge know what he means and know the relevant literature. Foreigners are on their own.

Latitude 7: The Quantum Domain—Esoteric Cores. These are discretely defined localities. They are smaller, more focused, and characterized by more frequent face-to-face interaction (Crane 1972, Taub 1986). Their members are more adept at catching errors in each other's work and more prone to appreciate each other's virtuosity. Their published work is more idiomatic, more elliptical than most professional writings, and more likely to rely on specialized media—newsletters, fax machines, and computer networks and bulletin boards. Their vernacular may need some translation even for fellow professionals.

In all likelihood, this sketch is too gross. One can imagine finer distinctions, certainly, but the intuitive idea is clear enough: Translation involves transformation; sparser codes lose the detail and precision of esoteric codes. There may be cases of complete incomprehension. Einstein, remember, thought that relativity described a reality incomprehensible to ordinary people, and Pagels sees "quantum weirdness" as so alien from ordinary experience that workable analogies are hard to find. More usually, though, different codes may be analogical in so intangible a way that it is pointless to debate whether the codes are commensurable but urgent to debate whether both sides of such analogies hold. Some transformations may be unproblematic, and others so difficult to evaluate that they are enigmas we must speak of much as the S-R behaviorists used to speak of mind: It is a black box we cannot open.

Some messages may risk incommensurability by spurious agreement, for when economists and senators make ostensibly similar claims about, say, the capital gains tax, can it be assumed that they are functioning at the same level? Can we tell from message characteristics alone whether they are saying the same things, or will more biographical and organizational information be needed? What would one have to know in order to answer these questions *and* avoid spurious agreements? The subject to which I now turn is one thing that one would always have to know.

TRANSLATION

From the perspective of esoteric fields, translations to broader discourses are dilutions, and perhaps distortions. The more general the discourse, the lower the complexity; so journalism is often blamed for distorting or twisting *the facts* or for being unable to convey complexity, technical information, nuance, and depth (Burger 1984). Economic journalism, for instance, has been said to be deficient in quality and quantity (Nelson 1992, Solow 1990). The reasons for these failings, however, lie not in a defective "mirror of science" but in the translation process itself. Translators are often field experts who may not know much about the discourse into which they translate. Their field expertise may not help as they search for simple ways to express complex ideas or images and metaphors that will get the idea across. Other times translators are science writers whose fluency with the general language exceeds their facility with the technical idiom. Science writers are often generalists, so they are translating the trade book, not the science. Whatever new creature the book writer has created, in other words, is transformed once again as it is cast into newspaper prose.

From the Jeffersonian perspective, however, the question is whether even diluted messages are beyond general publics. This raises the specter of scientific illiteracy—the fact that a large percent of American college graduates cannot answer even elementary questions about science. Hazen and Trefil (1991, 26) attribute this to a mismatch: Though scientists often agree on the proper content of a modern science curriculum, this curriculum doesn't jibe with professional/departmental structures:

> Think about what one needs to know to understand the scientific component of the greenhouse debate, for example: an understanding of the role of infrared radiation in the earth's heat balance (physics), the production of carbon dioxide by human activity (chemistry), the way climate can be affected from the greenhouse effect (earth science), the possible effects of climate changes on living things (ecology)—in other words, a little bit of physics, a little bit of chemistry, a little bit of biology, and a little bit of earth science, together with a general grounding in the way science works.

I earlier cited Trefil as a paragon science writer who ultimately succumbs to argument from authority. Here he is reprising Fleck's claim that popular images filter back into the esoteric core (Gleick's *Chaos,* for instance, has become the esoteric field's organizing document) and Klein's claim that fields grow by adapting to outside problems. So he would be open, I imagine, to the claim that science writing is a part of physics' problematic.

But one reason there are so few Trefils is that popularizing is academe's red light district—generally frowned upon, often visited with extradisciplinary motives, and snubbed by the genteel. The academic reward structure reflects this denigration: "Popularizer" is almost always an epithet, "popular" a red flag, and even "pedagogical" in many fields is a dismissal. Because popularization differs from esoteric subject matters, it is (like peripheral discourse) often seen as inferior work. Though the American Psychological Association at least gives an award for popular psychology, no expert field that I know of sees popularizing as a discipline, or as a problematic integral to its subject matter.

Perhaps they can be argued out of that prejudice—convinced, for starters, to dispense with the word *popularizing* in favor of the word *translation.* If the levels of discourse are as different as I claim, then the study of their interconnections will be a challenging discipline in its own right. Most expert fields have experience in translating their knowledge into at least one border language. Interfield coalitions are commonplace. So it is only a small next step for the expert fields that want to affect public policies to see translation as integral to their subject matters.

The actors in expert fields may also be Jeffersonians, or want to proselytize for their fields. One would think, for instance, that historians and physicists would be interested in popular histories and physics. If James Michener and Bruce Caton have taught history to more people than C. Van Woodward and Jacques Barzun, and Heinz Pagels has taught physics to more people than Richard Feyneman, then the question of whether they have their facts right and metaphors straight is scarcely a triviality.

And recall the big science critique. If the journalists are naïve, or fail to understand organized research, their work still attempts to translate technical issues into public vocabularies. The issues of fraud and self-deception in biotechnology are surely more accessible to popular translation than the technical details of biotechnology. If they can't be adequately debated by larger publics, then what can?

The Jeffersonians might point to the sizable number of journalists, science writers, public relations offices, and popularizing scientists whose ongoing activities would seem to deny my argument. They will find support for this view in *Scientists and Journalists* (Friedman, Dunwoody, and Rogers 1986)—a collection of essays from a workshop sponsored by the American Association for the Advancement of Science. The chief impression conveyed by this book is that translation is a process of simplification obstructed chiefly by the need to find ordinary analogues for esoteric concepts and hindered to lesser degrees by scientists' professional and public relations motives and journalists' lack of time and space. Since scientists sometimes praise journalists' reports of scientific work, objecting mostly to the lack of detail, and as most science writers and scientists believe that the essential problem is getting the facts right (Friedman 1986), the Jeffersonians may think that translation is a difficult but tractable problem.

But readers of *Scientists and Journalists* should bear two things in mind. First, throughout its pages, authority-dependence is not a problem; it is a taken-for-granted ideal. The onus for translation and burden of intelligibility rest exclusively with the experts (Miller 1986, 242): Journalists and science writers need merely "get it right." And second, the point is made repeatedly that journalists rely mainly on mainstream scientists and administrators and exclude dissident or fringe scientists (Dunwoody 1986, Goodell 1986, Pfund and Hofstadter 1981). This is a conservative reinforcement of authority-dependence that may work against attempts to open science up to public scrutiny (e.g., Fuller 1992).

Still, *Scientists and Journalists* is a good dialectical counterpart to my argument. It suggests that each translation level in our hierarchy of discourse complexity is not distinguished by a sharp cutoff point of complete incomprehension. Translation troubles will appear in shades and gradations; they will be dispersed among different publics, as individual variations in competency lead to pragmatically infinite differences in complexity.

CODA: MISS MANNERS GOES TO WASHINGTON

If "the public" is as poor a problematic as I claim, then the onus for preserving democratic values is on the expert fields. That's the carrot, at least for experts who are also Jeffersonians. The stick is the idea of public "jurisdiction": The public interest is to divide the loyalties of experts between their accountability to their special fields and their obligations to translate. The weighing of expert testimony is hard for the best and the brightest, and harder as the language gets sparser. Specialized expertise is needed to evaluate the expert's intervention between a field's facts and the interpretations needed to formulate policies. So translation is a public interest, a requirement not a courtesy. It should be seen as integral to any subject matter applicable to public policy.

The epistemic presumption narrows any expert's span of authority, so decision-makers need more effective ways to pit experts against experts. This public interest requires a certain sort of expert—one accountable not to interested parties but to the public interest and with the divided loyalties needed for translation. This squares with Cox's (1981) claim that visions of the public affect how the actors define their obligations and estimates of outcomes. His only mistake lies in seeing those visions of the public as the source of an empirical definition of the public sphere. A better assumption is that each expert's vision of the public interest will constrain (or not) her insistence on disciplinary hegemony.

The public jurisdiction requires accommodation to impersonal etiquettes, rules, and roles, and the policy-making etiquette proscribes closure (Willard 1983). Some of the discreditable behavior of experts stems from behaving as if the epistemic prerogatives of their fields are or should be widely shared. The epistemic presumption rules such closure out, for players on a broader court cannot stand only on their own principles.

The solution to authority-dependence is a blanket rejection of neither authority nor consensus: It is an appreciation of the side effects of consensus, its conservatism, organizing functions, instabilities, penchant for deceptive history. And it is a case for puncturing authority *at the right point,* not when experts are figuring out the facts but when their facts are used as the bases for policy inferences. Seeing expert fields as rhetorical structures takes the modernist fallacy seriously and confronts authority-dependence head on.

And the Jeffersonians need to stake out their turf and be a bit clearer about what they want. Preeminently they need to decide which latitude to defend. As the literature now stands, the crisis of liberal democracy seems to lie in latitudes 1 and 2. But it is doubtful that many serious issues, if any, can be translated into those codes. If, as I believe, the Jeffersonian's turf lies somewhere among latitudes 3 through 5, and the lion's share of it in latitude 4, then a careful consideration of what can be translated into those levels is the best point of embarkation for the Jeffersonian quest.

TWELVE

Epilogue: A Rhetoric for Modern Democracy

Now it may be useful to set liberalism and epistemics side by side, to capsulize their differences, see where the arguments stand, and clarify the stakes in the choice between them. Two distinct discourses are on the floor, and it is time to put the question: How do liberalism and epistemics stack up as rhetorics for modern democracy?

The answer lies in what the two have to say—and how they would say it—to three sorts of publics. Exaggerated aboriginal realities will play all too well to primitive publics, I will argue. Epistemics is the more informative discourse for the most interesting kind of modern public, people struggling to build democracies from scratch. And I will point to epistemics' aptness to postmodern publics, ones struggling with problems of transnationalism and interdependence.

HIGH ANXIETY

I ask you to indulge a personal reminiscence. I want to describe what it was like to be in Berlin on New Year's Eve, 1989. Though the moment is long past, and less consequential than the Soviet breakup, the last days of the Berlin Wall will be an indelible image of our century. It was a definitive, euphoric moment that seemed to punctuate the end of Mussolini's "fascist century" and symbolize an emphatic popular rejection of the totalitarian idea. It was also a deeply ambivalent moment. It sparked for some the most primitive sort of panic, for others the most postmodern anxieties, and for me a decidedly out-of-theory experience. Persuasion is an uneasy subject matter in Berlin, and those who believe that the world should work by persuasion are more or less doomed there to gain an empathy with liberalism's most aboriginal fears. Perhaps this empathy can overarch the emotional landscape we have been traversing and set epistemics' debate with the Jeffersonians on a more sympathetic and cooperative track.

At the time, no one knew how costly unification would be. Only a few foresaw the ethnic savagery that would sweep the East. Federated Europe seemed inevitable, not at all the long struggle with nationalist backlashes it has turned out to be. In retrospect, these blindnesses inspire a healthy respect for how long and winding the road to European union has been. As a likely critic of epistemics says: "If the partisans of the borderless world of commerce are as wrong in the future as they have been in the past, then the matter of Germany remains a very large question-mark" (Goldberg 1991, 56).

Like most partisans of a borderless world, I watched the first breaches of the Wall on television and like many, I imagine, felt a strong tug to go there. Perhaps some wanted a more authentic experience than the simulacrum on television. Others perhaps felt the pull of a McLuhanesque Lourdes: In the summer and fall of 1989, the gathering at the Wall seemed like the center of Europe, not one of Boorstin's pseudo-events but a bona fide miracle punctuating a series of miracles. It had a feel of historical importance, an event at the center of things, emblematic of the change sweeping the East.

My motives were more craven. To go there in late 1989 was to travel through the remnants of one of the world's vilest police states. The effect, for that brief time, was the faux menace of a Disney ride: Honnecker's Mountain, Fascists of the Crimean. One's train glided out of Hanover's sleek prosperity through horrifying concrete barriers into an Orwellian diorama, barbed wire, dim lights, and empty stations punctuated by grim border guards. Then, as all such rides end, one emerged, dazed, into a different order of reality.

One entered West Berlin back then by changing metaphors, at a train station whose name is as apt allegorically as literally: Berlin Zoo. Nothing about the station—its architecture or the wildlife therein—prepares one for the city outside. It is as if one has been teleported from a prison to a shopping mall, and the effect makes one appreciate Baudrillard's "hyperreality." The mall is entirely Western yet oddly unfamiliar, as if the trip east to west has revealed a reality without referent.

In the idiom of travel brochures, West Berlin was "the island city," a striking figure set against drab ground, Tokyo-scale neon surrounded by 40 watt dimness, a St. Denis trollop circled by church ladies. It is garish and engaging: Los Angeles shopping, Las Vegas food, and Los Alamos architecture. It is a place where modernity happened fast, a rabbit warren of tacky, 1950s tedium punctuated by ruins. The effect is postmodernity by accident: The relics are decorative but peppered among buildings a Kansas S&L might have commissioned in 1949. The result is fine for a commodity fetish, but weak in the history department. The most obvious history—and chief tourist attraction—was the Wall, and in December it was drawing the natives as well. It was the focal point, the Irish wake as public spectacle, and it wasn't going to last. So New Year's Eve 1989 found me walking with family and friends—and thousands of others—toward the point where the Wall used to cut between the Reichstag and the Brandenburg Gate.

Like many parties, this onc was audible before one got there. The dominant sound was a clattering that was puzzling until one got closer. The racket was a chorus of hammers and chisels chipping away, their produce being stuffed into knapsacks or being sold to tourists along with bratwurst, Vietnamese pot stickers, and beer, souvenirs of the end of an age, pieces of the True Wall.

The crowds to respect are the ones that ignore bad weather. This one was oblivious. Despite bitter cold, revelers by the thousands clustered on both sides and on top of the Wall. They were very happy, very young, and high not only on life. Some claimed to have been there since October, kept afloat no doubt by every mind-altering substance then available in Western Europe. Tourists were indistinguishable from participants, so the effect was Woodstock-by-the-Reichstag: A great and good thing was happening; the world was suspended; it was a time for being there, for mingling along the Wall, smiling, soaking up the crowd contagion.

It took effort to actually see the wall. People were perched on top, hanging on cracks, climbing up, jumping down, and walking along it. The thing itself, made uglier by layers of impotent graffiti, does soak in, and the effect has enlarged people's vocabularies. This, I remember thinking, is what the Bauhaus might have achieved with a little imagination. The Wall, remember, was first a necessity, not a symbol: The G.D.R. was a creature of concrete and concertina, untenable without borders. Form has followed function with a vengeance.

Night near the Ku'dam brought a different perspective. Standing in a twelfth-story window, one could watch the fireworks that continued till dawn. The launching points arced around the city following the Wall, and the effect was startling. The Wall seemed alive—a living, breathing organism venting enormous energy—and wonderful, like New Year's dragons in Chinatown. It had a new millennium feel: Freedom and dignity were back. The subjects were killing the experiment.

I remember thinking: Berlin is a good setting for modernity's next turn. Twentieth-century modernity was arguably born here, at the university on the Wilhelmstrasse where Einstein worked, where Heisenberg and Born nurtured the quantum revolution. Weil and Brecht invented modern theatre here; Hiller nurtured expressionism; Mannheim studied here; and Wagner put postmodernism on an operatic scale. Berlin has perfected the shallow quotation of history. The old buildings are replicas. The history is in museums where it belongs. The heart and soul of the city lie in the garish shopping districts and in the airport and train stations where a cosmopolitan populace moves to the rhythms of a global economy. If federated Europe works, it will be because shallow quotation works, because people prefer shopping sprees to pogroms.

You can see the future in Berlin, and it is frivolous: Serbs, Ruthenians, Slovenes, and Czechs jostle each other in department stores. Byelorussians, Ossetians, and Lithuanians fight for parking spaces at Ka De Ve. Ukrainians, Croats, Magyars, and Slovaks peddle their heritages to tourists. Tadzhiks, Moldavians, Georgians, Uzbeks, Tatars, and Kazakhs trade their ethnic identities for VCRs and see self-determination as a video store on every corner. This commodified utopia is flippant, superficial, and a vast improvement on the self-determination doctrine of the nineteenth and early twentieth centuries.

Imagine a dialectic, three of the worst ideas humans have ever had. *Thesis:* Hegel's state as an "end in itself" venerated as a "secular deity," or "march of God in the world." *Antithesis:* ethnic identity. Beneath the fraudulent state smolders an enduring reality, a people, Germans, Romanians, Armenians, Ladines, Azerbaijanis, Latvians, Poles. And *synthesis:* irredentism, Risorgimento, self-determination, each ethnic group becomes its own state (Johnson 1983). The result is a collective brain tumor.

The rhetoric works two ways. As an opposition strategy to states, it fanaticizes minorities, sharpens their differences, and intensifies their struggles. And as a state rationale, it sanctions persecution, purges, expatriation, and genocide. Both pathologies are operating now—from Iraq to Moldavia to Uzbekistan—and were operating in Europe more or less constantly from 1914 until the rise of the two concrete Golgothas, Lenin's in the East and Hitler's in the West (Johnson 1983).

FEAR AND LOATHING ON THE KURFURSTENDAMMSTRASSE

My thinking, you can see, was taking a nasty turn. A delightful moment prompted a little romanticism; the romanticism led to thoughts of continuity; and Berlin is a bad place to think of continuity. This city has seen delirious crowds before. The thought of them prompts a sudden feral dread, the kind that makes the hair on your arms stand up. D. H. Lawrence felt it in 1924, "a queer, *bristling* feeling of uncanny danger" (Johnson 1983, 136).

Hitler used to tell people that to understand national socialism, they had to understand Wagner, especially the decadence theme, the purity of the *Nibelungenlied* sullied by capitalist greed (Shirer 1960, 101). Transform this vision into a world historical conspiracy theory, add some show business, and Austrian corporals become Teutonic warlords, and in a bunker near the Potsdammerplatz decide to purify Germany with fire, a high tech *Götterdämmerung* fueled by allied napalm.

The stamp of that destruction is indelible: in preserved ruins, postwar architecture, and the fact that any cab driver can show you where Gestapo headquarters was. And there are the "lest we forget" signs that say (roughly) "from this station people went to their deaths at Auschwitz, Bergen-Belsen," and so on, all the death camps alphabetized. The length of the list is stunning: The scale and organizational infrastructure of the holocaust are the Weberian nightmare made flesh, and a potent image of modernity: Auschwitz and its factories, Faust on a grand, homicidal scale, I.G. Farben as modernity's maw. It eats people and passes petrochemicals.

This new turn of thought was more startling than the primal panic. It revived the imagery with which this book began: modernity as menace, democracy doomed. Forces roiling beneath fragile surfaces are about to erupt. Id is too strong for superego; Hyde will overpower Jekyll. Once you have "gone expressive," the *Gestalt* shift is easy: One minute Berlin is atavism's home town, the next minute it is "the tomb of Germanism" (Johnson 1983, 119). Marx, remember, took his view of alienation from the *Volk* movement (ibid., 118), its identification of people with land, its idealization of roots, and its demonizing of cities.

This primitive experience left me with an empathy for German intellectuals like Günter Grass, who have a feel both for "errors bred in the bone" (W. H. Auden's phrase) and for Cassandra journalism. Some of them shunned the carnival at the Wall and voiced a reluctance to belong, an impulse to flee. The specter of a unified German state was too menacing, indeed "doomed" by Auschwitz, Germany's "permanent wound" (Roberts 1991, 52). I don't know whether the *Volk* is expressive or rhetorical for Mr. Grass, but perhaps he sees an irony: Auschwitz is emblematic—perhaps the paradigm case—of modernity's menace; yet it was created by a pastoral movement. How, one wonders, did we get from hearty peasants resonating with nature in the Black Forest to the belching smoke stacks of Auschwitz?

You already know my answer: Modernity ruled by romanticism goes mad. Romanticism is quixotic, utopian, and whimsical; machines and organizations are designed to be steady, efficient, and practical. Machines driven by whimsies will try to get the job done. Organizations driven by an idealized purity will *purify.*

Romanticism, let's say, is an indulgence. It flourishes in quiet seclusion and blossoms with special brilliance in academe, which by design nurtures speculative thinking, utopian visions, and a concern for enduring values and historical truths. But in the German case, as we saw, atavism and anti-Semitism, and the idea of racial purification by expatriation or genocide, were brewed and simmered in the universities. The groundswell that lifted Hitler came partly from students, egged on by their professors: "The academic community as a whole was a forcing house for nationalist mythology. Instead of encouraging self-criticism and scepticism, the professors called for 'spiritual revivals' and peddled panaceas" (Johnson 1983, 125–26).

Schama (1989, 861) sees a similar drift in the French revolution. A revolutionary elite embraced a powerful romanticism "with its addiction to the Absolute and the Ideal; its fondness for the vertiginous and the macabre; its concept of political energy as, above all, electrical; its obsession with the heart; its preference for passion over reason, for virtue over peace." Danton, Robespierre, and Marat saw themselves as summoning a force. Volcanolike, the revolution would well out of the people. Citizens would weed out noncitizens. But the purification of society ultimately required a modernist turn. The mobs summoned by bells and whipped into killing frenzies gave way to the Committee of Public Safety. The demagogues became administrators, obsessed with finding new technologies to make the killing more efficient.

I mean no ad hominem here. My point isn't to malign the Eastern intellectuals who used ethnic identity as an opposition strategy, or the Germans who fear a revival of the *Volk,* or the American intellectuals calling for spiritual revivals, or for that matter anybody peddling a panacea. My point is about the track record of state-scale romanticism: To define a people is to define nonpeople; to fear the *Volk* powerfully is to confirm its existence; and to dabble with a politics of virtue is to risk Robespierre's "dictatorship of virtue."

CALAMITY-HOWLING IN A NEW KEY

Foucauldians defend a conventional version of these primitive qualms. It smacks less of the cave, and the parallel isn't perfect, but destiny is destiny, linguistic or racial. The two are functionally analogous, or at least the telos of the hermetically sealed discourse mightily resembles the dictatorship of the selfish gene. The Foucauldians fear that genre-blurring doesn't displace authority, it creates new ones. Border-crossings are mock escapes. Ecotones are prisons masquerading as sanctuaries.

But the Foucauldians are more wrong than right, about states or discourses. The fate of the Soviet Union proves that a 72-year Skinnerian nightmare failed to lobotomize its victims. The Stalinist police states were riddled with subterranean economies of people and ideas, "hidden publics," that grew in strength thanks to computers, Xerox machines, VCRs, and satellite dishes (Sukosd 1990, 49). The faux histories and cunning narratives were weaker than Foucault feared; the propaganda was less effective than Huxley and Orwell feared. If we date the experiment from 1917, when Lenin's firing squads began their work, or even from 1924 when Lenin died, the Stalinists had more than enough time to instantiate a totalitarian reality. Their narratives had all the seamlessness and linguistic closure feared by Foucault. Yet everywhere the histories, narratives, propaganda, and lockstep academies needed torture chambers and unmarked graves to stay in power. The master narratives—texts, outer seals, and all—were held together chiefly by the Soviet Army, and they disintegrated in the span of a summer.

Epistemic Albanias, held together only by their isolation, can perhaps persist longer. But in the blurred genres, at least, there are few single-cell organisms; their subdivisions are rarely self-contained. Porous borders weaken hegemonies, for new immigrants look with fresh eyes on the local folkways and new ideas are counterforces to old ones. Border discourses are thus on the whole less authoritative than mainstream discourses. They are more dissensual and diffuse, with more premises on the table and more competition.

Foucauldian trappers arguably run the risk of describing carceral discourses in so self-sealing a way as to underwrite a resigned unreflectiveness. The side effect is an ironic system worship: States and organizations can't be epistemically reconstructed; the only choices are substituting one system for another. This endorses field closure: It puts fields beyond critique. They stand alone, self-confirming: The cost-benefit analyst is responsible only for errors in arithmetic, the soldier is responsible only for miscalculation, the biotechnologist is responsible only to the profit margin. If alternative discourses are no less hegemonic than regime-sponsored systems, then hegemonic discourses can't be critiqued or rejected simply because they are hegemonic. And if field closure is thought to be politically immune to critique, then the trappers are as open to the charge of ineffectuality as Foucault's critics have claimed.

HABITATS OF THE LIBERAL HEART

Modernity's therapists share the qualms of the trappers. But theirs is the determinism of unexamined ideas. The rhetorical architectures of ethnicity, religion, culture, and state are coercive, but fueled by the inattention, nonchalance, and unreflective conformity of their victims. The premium, then, is on education. Since systematically distorted communication *can* be critiqued and reconstructed, the truth really ought to set us free.

The most compelling voice among the therapists is that of Habermas (1989b), who hopes that Germany's forty-five-year habituation to liberal institutions will prevent an atavistic revival. His call for "types of relations within which more subjectivity and more sentiment can find expression" may be vague, but, as Erik Doxtader has reminded me, the claim arose in the context of the German historical debates (surveyed in Roberts 1991), and it is of a piece with a broader call for a nonnationalist state, founded not on historical continuities but on civic responsibility and the rule of law. Historical continuities are out because there is no positive narrative beyond the catastrophic moment when German history begins: *Stunde Null,* zero hour, 1945 (Roberts 1991). Obstructing any continuity beyond that date is Auschwitz, the definitive answer to neoconservatives like Stürmer, who want to remedy the emptiness and fragmentation of modernity by finding a positive historical narrative. There can be no positive narrative, so the German public sphere must appeal to a higher court—by pinning its self-consciousness to the best enlightenment traditions.

But in arguing *with* Stürmer, must we argue *like* Stürmer? Must *History*—capitalized and uttered with reverence—be countered by some equally heavy-toned verity? Habermas perhaps comes by universal pragmatics because he is a philosopher by trade. But he seems to think that the claims of reason need a rhetorical boost, that they are less persuasive than the claims of technocracy, less glittery than the lifestyle enclaves of popular culture. Unificationists often make a similar point about the claims of distributive justice. Being rhetorical theorists by trade, they are inclined to distrust an emphasis on blandness, fearing that an empty sameness at the center of things may be alienating and that *Volk*-style realism strategies will ultimately outpull the weak ties of the melting pot. Lyne (1991, 54), for instance, argues that *rhetorical universals* are "vital." They are "appeals to realities that are either more basic or more ethereal, either more ancient or more utopian . . . than whatever it is they are being compared to." They are chiefly opposition strategies, places to stand against entrenched power. Because hegemonies characteristically wrap themselves in awe and mystery, dissenters need resistance rhetorics of equal power.

Estimable movements unquestionably appeal to noble sentiments. The abolition, suffrage, and civil rights movements appealed to universals of human nature, justice, and dignity. And crowds do sometimes gather around unassailable goals. From 1989 on, for instance, Nazi outrages in Germany have been denounced by large and small gatherings. And, Lyne might say, consider the scene in Berlin not in 1989 but on January 30, 1993, sixty years after the day Hitler took power. Again a crowd gathered—more than 100,000—but for a candlelight vigil gathered around an enormous sign that spelled out in candles, "Never again" (*New York Times,* 31 January 1993).

The Brandenburg Gate does look better by candlelight, and one can scarcely impugn the sentiment "Never again." But the issue isn't whether we should admire noble sentiments. Despicable movements also fly noble banners, and even the grace of impeccable intentions doesn't ensure consistency between pennants and the armies marching beneath them. Nor is it a question of what social movements will do. Searching for rhetorical resources, they will use, as Kenneth Burke says, all that is there to use. The question is whether intellectuals should endorse, or embody, or have nothing more to say about the most eminently twistable rhetoric.

The devil, in social movements, is sometimes in the rallying cries but always in the details. For proof, we have the testimony of the devil himself, or at least of a very shrewd student of revolution. The French and Russian revolutions, Hitler (1943, 475) argued, would never have sprung from lofty ideals without "an army of agitators led by demagogues in the grand style, who whipped up the passions of the people." Agitation, Hitler says, begins with grievances and proceeds by contagion. The idea of *contagion* suggests most obviously the great rallies with their orchestrated performances and torch-lit parades. But self-persuasion also happens in smaller groups and action cells. The first snare is small-group influence, and the second is to be caught up in the frenzy of activity. So *Mein Kampf* is also a textbook in organizational theory. Its author read the French and Bolshevik revolutions as case studies in grassroots organization. An organization "owes its existence to organic life, organic development" (ibid., 579), by which he meant, metaphorically, roots extending all the way up, and literally, totalitarian control extending all the way down. The lesson Hitler took from the Jacobins was the need of an organizational structure that could summon crowds when they were needed and just as quickly disperse them. And the lesson he took from the Bolsheviks was that ideas, on the whole, do not draw crowds. Agitators must find their audiences on street corners or at employment offices and taverns, places where small knots of people mutter their grievances.

As one would expect of a paranoid text, *Mein Kampf* is a dizzy mix of unbelievable candor and believable flim-flam. Its emphasis on grassroots organization is its least memorable content. Its most famous idea is the "big lie." Reduce ideas to slogans, then repeat them constantly. Its next most famous idea is a slogan Hitler repeats constantly, the power of the spoken word: All the great events of the world, he says, are not caused by ideas or doctrines but by "the firebrand of the word hurled among the masses." This image may seem quaint, but to connoisseurs of oratory it suggests that fire must be fought with fire. One combats evil by finding good firebrands to hurl.

But firebrand-hurling is merely pandering with delusions of grandeur. In films of Hitler's speeches, at least, one scarcely sees Wotan hurling thunderbolts. One sees a rather run-of-the-mill agitator rehearsing the crowd's grievances and demonizing the scapegoats in the usual way. Look at films of Huey Long and Father Coughlin and you have the species. Speeches in this genre are chiefly sincerity vehicles, ways of conveying emotion, fervor, and earnestness. One is meant to be more impressed by the man than by his words. And if the orator seems to glow with an unearthly light, this effect is not hindered by stage setting and lighting technicians. The great rallies were in some respects legitimation rituals to confirm persuasion that had already happened. Participation being the strongest opiate, the idea was, to use Douglas's expression, "more participation." They were meant to be felt, not heard. They were meant to be experienced in the most primitive way, and the result was to be something of a self-induced trance. The oratory at those occasions was variable, but on the whole tedious. Its emotional tenor, however, was an important part of the scenery, for many of the Nazi orators were early versions of what the business world now calls "motivational speakers." The idea was to raise morale by raising the blood pressure.

The lesson to be learned from *Mein Kampf* is that influence and organization are symbiotic. National socialism was a mixture of hot oratory and cold organization, but it was not a practical syllogism with a thousand legs (first a lofty ideal, then a hurled firebrand, then the ideal burns in every breast, and then action). Before every step, and intervening between every step, was organization. Hitler knew that organizations rarely run, or run for long, on firebrands. Indeed his chief management technique was to keep his associates at one another's throats. The Führer turned out to be a "detail man" and fortunately, from a military point of view, a dreadful micromanager.

One saving grace of relativity is that all sorts of things burn in human breasts, from dietary indiscretion to reflux narrativity. A narrative here, some coherence there may be scarcely noticeable alongside the myriad alternatives of a polyglot culture. The power of that culture mustn't be overstated, but neither should it be understated. One does gather from liberalism's rhetorics of loss that history dies easily in the West. When narratives lack state power, or when times are prosperous, historical identities weaken or become diluted and trivialized. The future, then, might not belong to whoever "fills memory," as Stürmer says, but to whoever fills bellies, wallets, and shopping malls.

It also bears saying that historical narratives legitimate states while Habermas's concerns are with the legitimacy of processes. So why not evaluate states for their nurturing of these processes, see them as dangerous tools to be evaluated by how well they maintain the rule of law, protect the rights of citizens, and achieve distributive justice? If postmodern states really are emerging, their dissenters may not need Lyne's universals. They may need only open borders and a reasonably level playing field. This will scarcely require communication rules written by God or Nature. It may be enough to say that Habermas's argumentation rules are good ideas. Deleting the "universal" from "universal pragmatics" and underscoring the "quasi" in "quasi-transcendental," Habermas's rules are much like the Amsterdam school's "pragma-dialectical" framework (van Eemeren and Grootendorst 1983). On this view, rational discussions are feasible if the discussants follow carefully contrived rules. The angels, so to speak, are in the details.

By shade and gradation, we are moving onto epistemics' ground. Epistemics shares the concern for the determinism of unexamined ideas, the preference for nonnationalist nations, the need to press the case for distributive justice, and the constitutional mission of finding as much openness as possible in organizations that prefer closure. And it shares at least one common plight with liberalism: Its origins are every bit as intuitive and emotional as liberalism's. Epistemics' founding emotion is no more useful than liberalism's and it is possibly as paralyzing. For where liberalism is prone to arm-waving, epistemics is agoraphobic.

Le Bon's Nightmare Revisited

Traveling to Berlin under the delusion that I had this book finished, my chief worry was rather like Lyne's: Epistemics is emotionally ugly. It seems anemic compared to liberalism: It taps no big questions; it prizes blandness; it impugns an issue agenda many people find engaging. It resembles (and in some respects is) a pallid replica of Lippmann's technocracy, a valorizing of "the bland Eurocrats in Brussels." There is something about corporate ethnography that seems dull if not tarnished, like putting the government department in the business school. Set the expression *public philosophy* beside *organizational studies* and you see the problem. Epistemics seems like an airline meal set beside the bounty of a great restaurant.

But when crowds gather in Berlin, one thinks of Le Bon. Epistemics' demon is a creature of the ironists, lurking in the shades and gradations between responsible speech and demagoguery and summoned by extravagant populism. If one simply must have demons, Le Bon's nightmare is at least as menacing as Capital. Think of the crowd of the French revolution raised to the *n*th power. That image has teeth in Paris, but fangs in Berlin. The crowds of modernity have deadlier things than pitchforks and guillotines, and the borders that kept the Terror on French soil are no longer there. Mobs in Baghdad mean bombs in Brussels. The primitive connects to the postmodern by changing planes in Athens.

If you summon this demon in Berlin, it will linger. You will sense with the same visceral shudder that it feels at home here. The thought of rhetoric will conjure not Pericles and Churchill but beer stube agitators, Speer's modernity in concrete, the Nuremberg rallies, and Goebbels's epistemology in jackboots:

> Like a rising star you appeared before our wondering eyes, you performed miracles to clear our minds and, in a world of skepticism and desperation, gave us faith. You towered above the masses, full of faith and certain of the future. . . . For the first time we saw with shining eyes a man who tore off the mask from the faces distorted by greed, the faces of mediocre parliamentary busybodies. . . . In the Munich Court you grew before us to the greatness of the Führer. What you said are the greatest words spoken in Germany since Bismarck. You expressed more than your own pain. . . . You named the need of a whole generation, searching in longing for men and task. What you said is the catechism of the new political belief, born out of the despair of a collapsing, godless world. (In Shirer 1960, 127)

This is a busy little passage: authenticity, community, and identity all nestled in primitive narrative. The call, in Ernst Huber's words, is to "awaken in a people its will to historical formation," to find "the natural community" where the *Reich* and *Volk* are "an inseparable unity" (Cohen 1972, 370).

The narrative is timeless, older than Barnum, older than the *commedia del arte*. Messiahs and Maudis are the oldest show business, and the arrival of the deliverer amid primitive struggle is the very linchpin of the Nazi imaginary. Swinging from that pin is the image management by which corporals become führers. The redeemer is not merely a handy guy to have around but the embodiment of a Rousseauian general will, the *Volkisch Reich* incarnate. This is stronger stuff than the "man of the people" technique. It is a claim to be extraordinary, not ordinary, so of necessity it is lent ethos. Others must say it, at least at first. "L'etat, c'est moi" didn't play all that well in Paris, but by the summer of 1934, when Hitler said essentially the same thing, he was by then only "modestly" repeating common knowledge.

And others must say it often. Credulity through repetition is something of a necessity when the goal is the aestheticization of a person. "Aestheticization" is often used to mean Speer's architecture and Goebbels's stage management, but the spectacle is also in the prose. For one becomes a "shining star," "towering above the masses," only when seen through "wondering eyes," "shining eyes." Goebbels is doing with words what Leni Riefenstahl did with her camera. Recall the lingering close-ups in *Triumph of the Will,* the faces beaming, shining, infatuated. Like Goebbels, they are "witnessing," a communication act that by all appearances has no illocutionary or perlocutionary meaning. It is persuasive because it doesn't seem meant to persuade. It just *is,* proving that the machinery of fame doesn't evoke the mysteries of adoration by rational argument but by the gentlest contagion: observed veneration, overheard worship.

You have to have a story to have a people, so notice the *from-to* images: confusion to clarity, chaos to order, aimlessness to purpose, decadence to reawakening. These images may seem like quack philosophy, but the better, purely technical classification is snake oil. Like all good scams, they trade on a frailty. Swindles capitalize on greed; *from-to* stories exploit fear. Both are fueled by the victim's flaw. And both often need to stoke the flaw. If "stoking the flaw" seems familiar, recall the criticism of advertising, that it create wants. One peddles the trinkets of consumerist culture by convincing people that they fill real needs. Much as therapists must convince their clients that they are ill (Hoffer's point), leaders create true believers by convincing them that something is wrong with them, something is missing in their lives. As Professor Harold Hill says, "You got trouble," confusion, chaos, aimlessness.

And primitive narrative is versatile. Look again at the Goebbels passage. It is all-purpose. One can whisper it to confidants, gently urge it to close gatherings, and shout it to assembled throngs. One can easily imagine Barnum's ringmaster announcing the first sentence, and any number of theologians intoning the last. It is a media chameleon: It could be the narration for a propaganda film, the voice-over for a political advertisement, the text of a pamphlet, or a personal letter. Its only changeless nature is its mythic, religious sound. It *sounds* timeless, eternal, just like Truth.

That sound is everything, the realism strategy in full flower. It is the engine of an identity politics that makes demographic categories "authentic mirrors of nature" while hiding its positivism in its level of prose, and it bears thereby the unmistakable mark of a rhetoric gone bad. Rhetoric is the only art that should not conceal itself, that ideally calls attention to its own instrumental intentions and thus puts persuadees on guard. The stammer of uncertainty is thus a virtue beside the fluency of certitude, and we have been considering, it seems to me, a family of overconfident discourses that are oblivious to, do not acknowledge, or would emphatically deny their rhetorical character. They assume a difference in kind between a sovereign reality and the constitution of discourses, a contrariety between surfaces and underlying realities. Much as Plato, Rousseau, and Marx claimed to see underlying realities, and much as expressives see the truth and must express it, liberalism's theories have been oracular stances, mirrors of nature, privileged positions, gifts of sight in kingdoms of the blind. Rhetoric is a fault to be found in others, and the truth shall set them free. The authoritarian drift of these theories has been noted (Popper 1950), but mine is an argument about foreseeable consequences. Realism and truth demand agreement. They criminalize pluralism, much as Rousseau's general will demanded that "there shall be no partial societies within the state" (1954, 29). The totalitarian reality, remember, "demands *one* point of view, *one* truth, *one* way of talking and writing, *one* type of behavior" (Popov 1990, 4).

Fortunately, partial societies are the rule. As Madison might put Scriven's point, relativity isn't a fault, it's a feature, and the social construction of reality is a very powerful feature, one that is hard to learn but worth the effort. Facing intransigent social difficulties, groups as well as individuals can mimic the solution of O'Keefe's rhetoricals, "be someone else." In this Goffmanesque spirit, epistemics is a new identity, aware of its own partiality and argumentative nature, and largely resigned to a democracy without collective omniscience. Managing discourse across differences is a big enough chore for the moment. For alongside the discourse differences we have traversed (primitive to modern to postmodern, or expression to convention to rhetorical), there are the pragmatic knowledge problems and their synergy. The medium, for once, really is the message, and it is to the gentleness of that message that I now turn.

WEIMAR REDUX?

The 1990s will be remembered whenever democracies struggle to rise from the ashes of police states. The death and transfiguration of Stalin's world will be a founding myth, or cautionary tale, for every fledgling democracy. Whether the glasnost democracies succeed or fail, they will be textbook cases of the politics and economics of sudden change, and perhaps to an unprecedented degree, paradigm cases of jerry-rigging under fire. Like most nascent democracies, they are hastily assembled experiments in economics and planning, statecraft, intellectual authority, and consensus-building, and like many, they are passing through an obligatory metamorphic moment during which they are queer composites of democratic institutions and autocratic remnants. What is extraordinary is that some of them are metamorphosing amid conditions that historically have been the fertilizer of tyrants. It is a modernist bromide that democracy is hard to value on an empty stomach, that democratic values are frightfully dependent on prosperity. But it is a postmodern truth that it is hard to have a commodity fetish with no commodities. Prosperity will come from integration with transnational markets, so infrastructure cannot be built in a vacuum, and political stability will come from interdependencies, which means, piquantly enough, that a new style nation-state must be fashioned without an entirely clear blueprint.

This prospect seemed unlikely in 1989. Liberation is a creature of volatile events. The energy that brings down tyrants is inimical to normalcy, yet everywhere crowds were in the streets. The classic moment of vacuum seemed to be at hand. Tocqueville warned that the most dangerous moment comes when people who have been unfree become free. They lack the habits of democracy and the stomach for raucousness. Accustomed to passivity, they may be fearful of freedom, and, inured to police states, they may recoil from the conflict on which democracies thrive. Having toppled one despot, they may enthrone another, or having forgotten how to think about the future, they may find their only touchstones in the past. The German social democrat Peter Glotz thus worried that populist uprisings might herald the "dawn of a new nationalism," a reintensified "balkanization," a strengthening of nation-states or a focus on building them at just the point in time that they are least useful (in Dahrendorf 1990, 132). Indeed many feared that "while Western Europe is leaving the twentieth century for the twenty-first, Eastern Europe is leaving the twentieth century for the nineteenth" (Dahrendorf 1990, 149).

The jury is still out on this prediction. There has been bad news, certainly. The Czechs and Slovaks parted company. The Balkans treated the world to the spectacle of rampant anti-Semitism in countries with no Semites to speak of. And "minority problems," to use the standard euphemism, flared up almost everywhere. The front page horror is Bosnia, which seems headed not for the nineteenth but the thirteenth century. These cases will be our cautionary tales about opposition strategies. Ethnic awarenesses and identity politics were one way to "read against the grain" of totalitarian narratives. But having served their purposes, these rhetorical tigers were difficult to dismount. The Foucauldians would say that the successor discourses became as domineering as their predecessors. Once a people is lionized and its minorities demonized, the architecture of ethnicity must play itself out. But the cynics among us would reply that race-baiting is a diversionary tactic governments use to deflect attention from their failures or, as in Bosnia, merely one tool in the devil's toolbox. And the more optimistic among us would add that the fires will burn themselves out without fuel and continued stoking.

Opposition strategies are notoriously bad governing strategies, but ethnic struggles are arguably the worst of the lot. They have always compromised human rights (Dahrendorf 1990), and they often spawn crusade-scale nest-fouling. The Serbs, the Hutu, and their ilk are thus mimicking an ageless tradition, hell-bent apparently on making their worlds as much like Beirut as possible. Once a vibrant, cosmopolitan city, "the Paris of the Middle East" now resembles Berlin in 1945. Efforts in the same direction have also marred the Paris of the West. Since Rousseau's day, and more emphatically since the 1960s, there has been something about Paris that makes fundamentalists want to bomb it. Perhaps it is the symbolism of the city: To lash out at cosmopolitanism, one goes, so to speak, to the capital. But Paris has its own ethnocentrics and cultural purists. So if epistemics' message about ethnicity is the sort of thing one expects to find pasted to a kiosk, it is also in Paris the sort of poster one expects to find half torn off. The message is this:

> Visit your ethnic heritage in museums. Wear it on tee-shirts. Hang it on your walls; sell it to tourists; eat it in restaurants; wear it on holidays. Give it the same depth as "Hoosier" or "Pepsi Generation."

Europeans can appreciate this flippancy-in-earnest if they "ask the German Question." The question is, how deeply should one feel one's ethnicity? And the answer is, how deeply does one want the Germans to feel the *Volk*? Europeans who want the Germans to think first of Europe, of interdependence and transnational integration, thus have a standard for weighing the risks of unity and the value of self-determination. An ethnic group that allows itself no more fervor than it would allow the Germans will not lay waste to its cities and mortgage its economic future in the name of ethnic cleansing.

Germany, I would venture to say, is answering the German Question, though whether for good or ill depends on who one reads. One gathers from "Germany Alert," a newsletter on the Worldwide Web, that the police crackdown on the Nazis was largely a sham and that the Kohl government is essentially rebuilding the Reich. This is leftist paranoia, perhaps, but it was provoked amply enough by events that bore a startling resemblance to the 1930s, real Julius Streicher stuff, beatings, murders, and firebombs, all within a year of Mr. Glotz's prediction. "Germany Alert" has thus followed the threat, much as a number of watchdogs in America track the aryan nationalists and militias.

No crackpot cult, I suppose, is too small to fear. As the various watchdogs are fond of saying, Hitler started small. But this scarcely means that smallness is an infallible sign of menace. So if one points out that only tiny numbers of people actually show up to shout *Sieg heil* and that rather more impressive majorities show up to say "Never again," one isn't automatically guilty of the blindness of the thirties. There are unquestionably people in the world who have not lost the taste for blood, so may the watchdogs ever walk the ramparts. But one gathers from the mainstream press a rather more complex story, and one that should remind us that there has also been some good news since 1989. Remembering Neville Chamberlin, we mustn't make too much of this, but there is reason to think that the nazi revival is an ugly little blip that will be slurped over by Euroculture. It festers almost exclusively in G.D.R. slums. Though the easterners have become to some extent a disemployed underclass ripe for agitation, the nazis are not only not growing as fast as Hitler did, there is no evidence that they are growing at all. And though it may be that forty-five years of Stalinism had left a young generation unprepared for freedom (*Newsweek,* 29 July 1991, 34), the best evidence for now is that the vast majority of that generation wants not *Lebensraum* but employment, better housing, and the accoutrements of civilization.

And though all is not quiet on the eastern front, there is some heartening news. During the years since Glotz's prediction, the eastern democracies turned to the West for advice. On every subject from economics and development to journalism, easterners searched for western models as they tried to integrate the apparatuses of states with a vision of civil society and human rights. They were more interested in first amendment and privacy law than in western leftist critique (Weinstein 1990). Apparently, having ample *Sturm und Drang* of their own, they saw no need to import someone else's. And they had not, as it turned out, put every egg in the ethnic basket; their opposition strategies had included a rhetoric of civil society, dignity, and solidarity (Kennedy 1991). Solidarity means cooperation, a rhetorical achievement bound by conventional constraints. So the democracies with the best prospects are the ones where the talk centers on law and citizenship and on economic integration and foreign investment. Hungary and Poland thus differed from Yugoslavia by turning to Western investment companies for advice on privatization and by building separation of powers into state institutions. Shallow centralization is feasible when localities keep enough sovereignty to check larger units. They thus didn't set out to mimic each developmental stage of the mature democracies, but sought instead a quantum leap forward, straight from the nineteenth to the twenty-first century.

Postmodern sovereignty is the breath-taking experiment. Unlike melting pots, interdependencies needn't "just happen," they can be engineered, and in matters of sovereignty, interdependence is the mother of shallow quotation. Nationalisms can evolve, so to speak, in a self-consciously Lamarckian way by adapting to new conditions. A nationalism of divided loyalties is no longer inconceivable in the east, not because states are withering, as Marx predicted, but because they are evolving in their relation to transnational organizations, in their attitudes toward their cultures, and in their need to pursue transnational projects. It may seem presumptious coming from an American, at a time when some Americans are dabbling in precisely the idols that most rile tribes, but it may not be too much to hope that if easterners can remember the historical grievances, they can also remember the carnage. They may thus find what some Americans seem intent on losing: Ethnicity will find its proper place in life, as one vulgarized, diluted item on a much larger smorgasbord.

One strength the new democracies may find in themselves is that they already know how badly things go when governments perform mass epistemology. Having been on the business end of what to Westerners is largely a metaphor, they know all too well that perestroika was a foregone conclusion masquerading as a decision. Having had to wait until totalitarianism reasoned its way to self-destruction, they may find democracy where Westerners see only power, blending socialist traditions with capitalist ambitions in ways that are invisible in the West. Their problem is to get commodities into the stores without gutting the humanity of their societies, so they will experiment with any number of commensurating discourses. But having seen firsthand where the impulse for universality leads, they will not rush headlong into borrowed totalities.

Nor, perhaps, will they be as immodest as Americans in their expectations of democracy. They already know that Americans seem to like the idea of democracy rather more than its practice. Disagreement may be the "lifeblood of democracy," but by all evidence, ordinary Americans loath disputation in their personal, public, and organizational lives. American organizations characteristically celebrate agreement and see disputation and disagreement as painful necessities to be gotten through as quickly as possible. And the Easterners have the evidence before them that the mature democracies have not found a way to balance the ideals of liberal democracy with their dependence on experts and specialists. The disciplines are indispensable, but not especially democratic, and democracies dependent on disciplines run a continual battle with the modernist fallacy. But the lesson to be learned from the West is that the problem is not simply one of a Jacobin devil whispering in one ear and a liberal seraph in the other. Populism and technocracy are not competing weights on the same scale. Experts are best constrained by experts and a public discourse, if it is any good, will be competent, and of necessity a babble of group projects moving across the space and time of multiple organizations.

If all goes well, they will achieve a "crisis of liberal democracy," at the latest, I should think, by the mid twenty-first century. Their intellectuals will feel marginalized, alienated, and not at all interested in walking the line between corporate idolatry and apologism on the one hand and the demonology of Capital on the other. Foucauldian fatalism may thus find a new life. Transnational corporations and consortia will be big and unwieldy and may thereby become mysteries, rather like ancient Greek gods or like Marxian forces. Their power fed by their apparent invulnerability, they will be gaped at in awe rather than regulated. And the history of the 1990s (circa 2050) will thus be a story of one totalitarianism replacing another. Just as Napoleon succeeded the Thermidore, the corporate Corsicans were patiently waiting for the crowds to go home. The choices were either-or, between government and corporate tyranny. And that, the eventualizing historian will conclude, is how a theory the communists couldn't make true by fiat and social engineering became true by accident.

But the 2060s needn't reprise the 1960s. Historians may repeat themselves, but perhaps we can convince them that things were much trickier in the 1990s than they seem from a distance. In this spirit, epistemics does have a message for Easterners. It is rather like a caution label on medicine bottles:

> The Western liberal tradition is a potent stimulant, not to be taken full strength; do not exceed recommended dosage; optimum therapeutic effect with moderate dosage; if paralysis, numbness, or acute depression occur, discontinue use.

I stress *moderate dosage:* I have not meant to denigrate every habit of the liberal heart. Some of liberalism's passions are as good as any. The shortcomings of one's times spark emotions; astute people see gaps between ideals and realities; the compassionate ones feel sad, threatened, and perhaps alienated; the passionate ones feel dwarfed, unable to summon enough outrage and sympathy to do justice to the wars, holocausts, and Gulags. The twentieth century unquestionably came at a high price, but the question is whether the twenty-first must begin in emotional paralysis.

Coda: Postmodernity's Delicate Condition

There comes a point when a line of thinking needs outside criticism before it can be carried further. Epistemics is sketched more sparsely than I would like. It would be better buttressed by studies of knowledge problems in concrete cases, especially ones in which experts are pitted against one another so as to optimize the critical effects of disagreements. We are only marginally better off than Dewey was in seeing rationality and competence as group achievements. Group flaws have been studied to a fare-thee-well, but group virtues are a bit vaguer, and epistemics is unquestionably dependent on group virtues. Still, dangling threads are like fishhooks: They snag disagreement and engagement, the things that keep ideas alive. Epistemics will thrive only if its claims spark dispute, revision, and use.

The cliff-hanger is Europe. Will its evolving corporate-governmental symbiosis simply replicate the corporate handmaiden on a larger scale? And is it done with primitive solidarities? Its allegorical "common currency" is fragile, certainly, and no more feasible in the foreseeable future in Bosnia than it is in Burundi and Rwanda. The future is hard to see through ancient lenses, but if the federation keeps its feeble hold on modernity's next stage while leading the developing democracies out of the nineteenth century, it will be remembered every time the primitive clashes with the modern. If it falters, it will be an object lesson about how best to talk about mass organization. For what we have learned, it seems to me, is that an effective modernity kills superstitions; a failed postmodernism revives them. But with some inventiveness, and a certain lightness of touch, postmodernity can be an effective dialectical partner to modern times.

Bibliography

For economy, the subtitles in books and articles are omitted except where necessary for identification and publication information is given in the shortest possible form.

AJS	*American Journal of Sociology*
AMR	*American Management Review*
AP	*American Psychologist*
APQ	*American Philosophical Quarterly*
APSR	*American Political Science Review*
ASQ	*Administrative Science Quarterly*
ASR	*American Sociological Review*
BJS	*British Journal of Sociology*
CM	*Communication Monographs*
CSMC	*Critical Studies in Mass Communication*
CSSJ	*Central States Speech Journal*
HBR	*Harvard Business Review*
HCR	*Human Communication Research*
JAMA	*The Journal of the American Medical Association*
JAFA	*Journal of the American Forensic Association*
JMS	*Journal of Management Studies*
PAS	*Proceedings of the Aristotelian Society*
POQ	*Public Opinion Quarterly*
PPA	*Philosophy and Public Affairs*
PPR	*Philosophy and Phenomenological Research*
PQ	*Philosophical Quarterly*
P&R	*Philosophy and Rhetoric*
QJS	*Quarterly Journal of Speech*
SCA	Speech Communication Association
SE	*Social Epistemology*
SM	*Speech Monographs*
SQ	*Sociological Quarterly*
SSS	*Social Studies of Science*
TCS	*Theory, Culture, and Society*

Aaron, R. 1950. "Social Structure and the Ruling Class." *BJS* 1:1–17; 126–44.
———. 1964. *German Sociology.* Free Press.
Abbott, A. 1988. *The System of Professions.* U. Chicago.
Abell, P., ed. 1975. *Organizations as Bargaining and Influence Systems.* Heinemann.

Abrams, E. 1983. "The New Effort to Control Information." *New York Times Magazine,* 25 September.
Abravanel, H. 1983. "Mediatory Myths in the Service of Organizational Ideology." In Pondy et al.
Adorno, T. W. 1973. *The Jargon of Authenticity.* Northwestern U.
Adorno, T., et al., 1950. *The Authoritarian Personality.* Norton.
Adorno, T. W., and M. Horkheimer. 1972. *Dialectic of Enlightenment.* Seabury.
Agor, W. H. 1989. *Intuition in Organizations.* Sage.
Albury, W. R. 1983. *The Politics of Objectivity.* Deak U.
Aldrich, H. 1979. *Organizations and Environments.* Prentice-Hall.
Alexander, J. C. 1991. "Bringing Democracy Back In." In Lemert.
Alford, R. R., and R. Friedland. 1985. *Powers of Theory.* Cambridge U.
Almond, G., and S. Verba. 1963. *The Civic Culture.* Princeton.
Allen, T., and S. Cohen. 1969. "Information Flow in Research and Development Laboratories." *ASQ* 14:12–20.
Allison, G. 1971. *Essence of Decision.* Little, Brown.
Altman, I., and D. A. Taylor. 1973. *Social Penetration.* Holt.
Alter, P. 1994. "Nationalism: An Overview." In P. C. Cozic, ed., *Nationalism and Ethnic Conflict.* Greenhaven.
Andrews, J. R. 1983. *The Practice of Rhetorical Criticism.* Macmillan.
Anderson, C. W. 1990. *Pragmatic Liberalism.* U. Chicago.
Anderson, J. E. 1979. *Public Policy-Making.* 2d ed. Holt.
Anderson, T. R., and S. Warkov. 1961. "Organizational Size and Functional Complexity." *ASR* 26:23–28.
Anthony, D. 1977. *The Ideology of Work.* Tavistock.
Anthony, L. J., et al. 1969. "The Growth of the Literature of Physics." *Reports on the Progress of Physics* 32:709–67.
Apel, K. P. 1980. *Towards a Transformation of Philosophy.* Routledge.
Apter, D. 1971. *Choice and the Politics of Allocation.* Yale U.
Archer, M. S. 1982. "Morphogenesis Versus Structuration." *BJS* 33:455–77.
Arendt, H. 1958. *The Human Condition.* U. Chicago.
Argyris, C. 1957. *Personality and Organization.* Harper & Row.
———. 1962. *Interpersonal Competence and Organizational Effectiveness.* Dorsey.
———. 1964. *Integrating the Individual and the Organization.* Wiley.
———. 1971. *Management and Organizational Development.* McGraw-Hill.
———. 1974. *The Applicability of Organizational Theory.* Cambridge U.
Ashford, N. 1976. *Crisis in the Workplace.* MIT.
Ashworth, P. D. 1979. *Social Interaction and Consciousness.* Wiley.
Astley, W. G. 1984. "Subjectivity, Sophistry and Symbolism in Management Science." *JMS* 21:259–72.
Babbili, A. S. 1986. "The New World Information Order." In W. M. Brasch and D. R. Ulloth, eds., *The Press and the State.* U. Press of America.
Bacharach, S. B., and E. J. Lawler. 1980. *Power and Politics in Organizations.* Jossey-Bass.
Bachrach, P. 1967. *The Theory of Democratic Elitism.* Little, Brown.

———. 1971. *Political Elites in a Democracy.* Atherton.
Back, K. H. 1962. "The Behavior of Scientists." *Sociological Inquiry* 32:82–87.
Bailey, F. G. 1987. *Humbuggery and Manipulation.* Cornell U.
Baillie, J. 1951. *The Belief in Progress.* Scribner's.
Baker, D. B. 1970. "Communication or Chaos?" *Science* 169:739–42.
Bakhtin, M. M., and P. M. Medvedev. 1985. *The Formal Method in Literary Scholarship.* Harvard U.
Bakke, E. W. 1966. *Bonds of Organization.* Archon.
Bagdikian, B. 1983. *The Media Monopoly.* Beacon.
Balthrop, V. W. 1989. "Wither the Public Sphere?" In Gronbeck.
Baltzell, E. D. 1958. *Philadelphia Gentlemen.* Free Press.
Banks, E. 1970. "Quick Publication Schemes." *Science* 169:739–42.
Bantz, C. R. 1983. "Naturalistic Research Traditions." In Putnam and Pacanowsky.
Barber, B. 1984. *Strong Democracy.* U. California.
———. 1988. *The Conquest of Politics.* Princeton U.
Barker, E. 1979. "Thus Spake the Scientist." *Annual Review of the Social Sciences of Religion* 3:79–103.
Barley, S. R. 1983. "Semiotics and the Study of Occupational and Organizational Cultures." *ASQ* 28:393–413.
Barnard, C. I. 1983. *The Functions of the Executive.* Harvard U. 1938; reissued 1968.
Barnes, B. 1974. *Scientific Knowledge and Sociological Theory.* Routledge.
———. 1977. *Interests and the Growth of Knowledge.* Routledge.
———. 1982. *T. S. Kuhn and Social Science.* Columbia U.
———. 1986. *About Science.* Blackwell.
Barnes, B., and D. Bloor. 1982. "Relativism, Rationalism, and the Sociology of Knowledge." In M. Hollis and S. Lukes, eds., *Rationality and Relativism.* MIT.
Barnett, S., and M. Silverman. 1979. *Ideology and Everyday Life.* U. Michigan.
Barry, B. 1964. "The Public Interest." *PAS* 1–18.
Bartley, W. W. 1963. *The Retreat to Commitment.* Knopf.
Bass, B. 1983. *Organizational Decision Making.* Irwin.
Baudrillard, J. 1983a. *Simulations.* Simiotext(e).
———. 1983b. *In the Shadow of the Silent Majorities.* Simiotext(e).
Bauman, Z. 1988. "Is There a Postmodern Sociology?" *TCS* 5:217–38.
Bavelas, A. 1950. "Communication Patterns in Task-oriented Groups." *Journal of the Statistical Society of America* 22:725–30.
Baynes, K., J. Bohman, and T. McCarthy. 1987. *After Philosophy.* MIT.
Bazelon, D. L. 1974. "Psychiatrists and the Adversary Process." *Scientific American* 230:16, 18–23.
Bazerman, C. 1981. "What Written Knowledge Does." *Philosophy of the Social Sciences* 11:361–87.
Beard, C. A., and W. Beard. 1930. *The American Leviathan.* Macmillan.
Becker, C. 1941. *Modern Democracy.* Yale U.
Becker, H. 1982. *Art Worlds.* U. California.

Begley, S. 1991. "Gridlock in the Labs." *Newsweek,* 14 January, p. 44.
Bell, D. 1960. *The End of Ideology.* Free Press.
———. 1964. "Authoritarian and Democratic Leadership." In Fein.
———. 1976a. *The Coming of Post-Industrial Society.* Basic Books.
———. 1976b. *The Cultural Contradictions of Capitalism.* Basic Books.
Bellah, R. N. 1964. "Religious Evolution." *ASR* 29:358–74.
Bellah, R. N., et al. 1985. *Habits of the Heart.* U. California.
———. 1991. *The Good Society.* Knopf.
Ben-David, J. 1960. "Roles and Innovation in Medicine." *AJS* 65:557–68.
———. 1964. "Scientific Growth." *Minerva* 2:455–76.
———. 1965. "The Scientific Role." *Minerva* 4:15–54.
Ben-David, J., and R. Collins. 1966. "Social Factors in the Origins of a New Science." *ASR* 31
Bendix, R. 1956. *Work and Authority in Industry.* Wiley.
Benn, S. I., and G. F. Gaus, eds. *Public and Private in Social Life.* Croom Helm.
Bennett, J. 1964. *Rationality.* Routledge.
Bennett, W. 1986. "The Medium Is Large, but How Good Is the Message?" In Friedman, Dunwoody, and Rogers.
Benson, J. K. 1981. "Organizations." In O. Grusky and G. A. Miller, eds., *The Sociology of Organizations.* 2d ed. Free Press.
Bentley, A. F. 1926. *Relativity in Man and Society.* Putnam.
Berelson, B. R., P. Lazarsfeld, and W. McPhee. 1954. *Voting.* U. Chicago.
Berger, P., and T. Luckmann. 1966. *The Social Construction of Reality.* Doubleday.
Berk, B. 1966. "Organizational Goals and Inmate Organization." *AJS* 71:522–34.
Berlant, J. L. 1975. *Profession and Monopoly.* U. California.
Berlinski, D. J. 1976. *On Systems Analysis.* MIT.
Berman, M. 1970. *The Politics of Authenticity.* Atheneum.
———. 1982. *All That Is Solid Melts into Air.* Simon & Schuster.
Bernstein, B. 1971. "On the Classification and Framing of Educational Knowledge." In Young.
Bernstein, R. J. 1968. *The Restructuring of Social and Political Theory.* U. California.
———. 1983. *Beyond Objectivism and Relativism.* U. Pennsylvania.
———. 1987. "One Step Forward, Two Steps Backward." *Political Theory.* 15:538–63.
Bernstein, R. 1992. *The New Constellation.* MIT.
Bershady, H. 1973. *Ideology and Social Knowledge.* Blackwell.
Biddle, B. J. 1964. "Roles, Goals and Value Structures in Organisations." In W. W. Cooper et al., eds., *New Perspectives Organization Research.* Wiley.
Biesecker, B. 1989. "Recalculating the Relation of the Public and Technical Spheres." In Gronbeck.
Billig, H. 1987. *Arguing and Thinking.* Cambridge U.
Birdsell, D. S. 1989. "Critics and Technocrats." In Gronbeck.
Birnbaum, N. 1960. "The Sociological Study of Ideology (1940–1960)." *Current Sociology* 9:91–117.

———. 1962. *The Sociological Study of Ideology.* Blackwell.
———. 1971. *Toward a Critical Sociology.* Oxford U.
———. 1988. *The Radical Renewal.* Pantheon.
Black, M. 1962. *Models and Metaphors.* Cornell U.
Blackburn, R., ed. 1972. *Ideology in Social Science.* Fontana.
Blair, J. A. 1987. "Everyday Argumentation from an Informal Logic Perspective." In Wenzel.
Blair, J. A., and R. H. Johnson, eds. 1980. *Informal Logic.* Edgepress.
Blau, J., and R. Alba. 1982. "Empowering Nets of Participation." *ASQ* 27:363–79.
Blau, P. M. 1955. *The Dynamics of Bureaucracy.* U. Chicago.
———. 1964. *Exchange and Power in Social Life.* Wiley.
———. 1970. "A Formal Theory of Differentiation in Organization." *ASR* 35:210–18.
Blau, P. M., and R. A. Schoenherr. 1971. *The Structure of Organization.* Basic Books.
Blau, P. M., and W. R. Scott. 1962. *Formal Organizations.* Routledge.
Bledstein, B. 1976. *The Culture of Professionalism.* Norton.
Bloor, D. 1976. *Knowledge and Social Imagery.* Routledge.
———. 1983. *Wittgenstein.* Columbia U.
———. 1984. "A Sociological Theory of Objectivity." In S. Brown, ed., *Objectivity and Cultural Divergence.* Cambridge U.
Bluhm, W. T. 1987. "Liberalism as the Aggregation of Individual Preferences." In Deutsch and Soffer.
Blum, A. F. 1971. "The Corpus of Knowledge as a Normative Order." In Young.
Blumberg, P. 1976. *Industrial Democracy.* Schocken Books.
Blumenberg, H. 1983. *The Legitimacy of the Modern Age.* MIT.
Blumer, H. 1964. *Symbolic Interactionism.* Prentice-Hall.
Blumstein, A. 1968. "The Choice of Analytic Techniques." In Goldman.
Bogart, L. 1982. "Newspapers in Transition." *The Wilson Quarterly* 6
Bohme, G. 1977. "Cognitive Norms, Knowledge Interests, and the Constitution of the Scientific Object." In E. Mendelsohn and P. Weingart, eds., *The Social Production of Scientific Knowledge.* Reidel.
Boon, James. 1982. *Other Tribes, Other Scribes.* Cambridge U.
Boorstin, D. J. 1961. *The Image.* Harper & Row.
Booth, W. C. 1974. *Modern Dogma and the Rhetoric of Assent.* U. Chicago.
Bormann, E. G. 1972 "Fantasy and Rhetorical Vision." *QJS* 58:396–407.
———. 1983. "Symbolic Convergence." In Putnam and Pacanowsky.
Bottomore, T. B. 1966. *Elites and Society.* Penguin.
Bourdieu, P. 1971. "Intellectual Field and Creative Project." In Young.
———. 1977. *Outline of a Theory of Practice.* Cambridge U.
———. 1984. *Distinction.* Routledge.
Bove, P. 1986. "The Ineluctability of Difference." In J. Arac, ed., *Postmodernism and Politics.* U. Minnesota.

Bové, P. A. 1988. "The Foucault Phenomenon." In Deleuze.
Braden, W. W. 1969. "The Available Means of Persuasion." In J. J. Auer, ed., *The Rhetoric of Our Time.* Appleton-Century-Crofts.
Brashers, D. E., and S. A. Jackson. 1991. "'Politically Savvy Sick People.'" In D. W. Parson, ed. *Argument in Controversy.* SCA.
Braverman, H. 1974. *Labor and Monopoly Capital.* Monthly Review Press.
Brigge, Morris L. 1971. *Positive Relativism.* Harper & Row.
Briskman, L. 1974. "Toulmin's Evolutionary Epistemology." *PQ.* 24:
Broad, W., and N. Wade. 1982. *Betrayers of the Truth.* Simon & Schuster.
Broadus, R. N. 1967. "A Citation Study for Sociology." *American Sociologist* 2:19–20.
Brooks, H. 1976. "Environmental Decision-Making." In Tribe, Schelling, and Voss.
Brown, R. H. 1973. "Bureaucracy as Praxis." *ASQ* 23:365–82.
———. 1976. "Social Theory as a Metaphor." *Theory and Society* 3:169–97.
———. 1977. *A Poetic for Sociology.* Cambridge U.
———. 1987. *Society as Text.* U. Chicago.
Browning, L. D. 1978. "Grounded Organizational Communication Theory Derived from Qualitative Data." *CM* 45:93–109.
Browning, L. D., and L. C. Hawes. 1991. "Style, Process, Surface, Context." *Journal of Applied Communication Research.* 19:32–54.
Bruce, C. 1976. *Social Cost Benefit Analysis.* World Bank Staff Working Paper No. 239.
Bruffee, K. A. 1986. "Social Construction, Language, and the Authority of Knowledge." *College English* 48:773–90.
Brummett, B. 1976. "Some Implications of 'Process' or 'Intersubjectivity' in Post-Modern Rhetoric." *Philosophy and Rhetoric* 9:21–51.
Buber, M. 1958. *Paths in Utopia.* Beacon.
Buchanan, S. 1958. *So Reason Can Rule.* Farrar, Straus, & Giroux.
Burch, P. H., Jr. 1980. *Elites in American History.* Holmes and Meier.
Burger, E. J., Jr. 1984. *Health Risks.* The Media Institute.
Burke, K. 1969. *A Grammar of Motives.* U. California.
Burke, T. E. 1979. "The Limits of Relativism." *PQ* 29:193–207.
Burns, T. 1961. "Micropolitics." *ASQ* 6:257–81.
———. 1966. "On the Plurality of Social Systems." In J. R. Lawrence, ed., *Operational Research and the Social Sciences.* Pergamon.
———. 1967. "The Comparative Study of Organizations." In V. Vroom, ed., *Methods of Organizational Research.* U. Pittsburgh.
Burns, T., and G. M. Stalker. 1961. *The Management of Innovation.* Tavistock.
Burrell, G., and Morgan, G. 1979. *Sociological Paradigms and Organizational Analysis.* Heinemann.
Bury, J. B. 1924. *The Idea of Progress.* Dover.
Butterfield, H. 1951. *The Whig Interpretation of History.* Norton.
Cahoone, L. E. 1988. *The Dilemma of Modernity.* State U. New York.
Cameron, W. B. 1966. *Modern Social Movements.* Random House.

Campbell, D. T. 1969. "Ethnocentrism of Disciplines and the Fish Scale Model of Omniscience." In M. Sherif and C. W. Sherif, eds., *Interdisciplinary Relationships in the Social Sciences*. Aldine.
———. 1982. "Experiments as Arguments." *Knowledge, Creation, Diffusion, Utilization* 3:327–37.
Campbell, J. A. 1983. "Creationism." In Zarefsky, Sillars, and Rhodes.
———. 1989. "Of Orchids, Insects, and Natural Theology." In Gronbeck.
Campbell, J. F. 1971. *The Foreign Affairs Fudge Factory*. Basic Books.
Campbell, K. K. 1972. *Critiques of Contemporary Rhetoric*. Wadsworth.
Cambrosio, A., and P. Keating. 1983. "The Disciplinary Stake." *SSS* 13:323–53.
Cantor, D., and J. Brown. 1981. "Explanatory Roles." In C. Antaki, ed., *The Psychology of Ordinary Explanations*. Academic.
Capron, W. M. 1968. "Cost Effectiveness Analysis for Government Domestic Programs." In T. A. Goldman.
Carey, J. W. 1982. "The Mass Media and Critical Theory." In M. Burgoon, ed., *Communication Yearbook 6*. Sage.
———. 1992. "The Press and the Public Discourse." *Kettering Review*, Winter, pp. 9–22.
Cantril, H. 1963. *The Psychology of Social Movements*. Wiley.
Carley, M. 1980. *Rational Techniques in Policy Analysis*. Heinemann.
Cartwright, D. 1959. "Lewinian Theory as a Contemporary Systematic Framework." In S. Koch, ed., *Psychology*. McGraw-Hill.
———. 1971. "Achieving Change in People." In D. E. Porter, P. B. Applewhite, and M. J. Misshauk, eds., *Studies in Organizational and Behavior Management*. 2d ed. InText.
Catlin, G. E. G. 1938. "Introduction to the Translation." E. Durkheim, *The Rules of Sociological Method*. Free Press.
Chafee, Z., Jr. 1947. *Government and Mass Communications*. U. Chicago.
Chalmers, T. C., C. S. Frank, and D. Reitman. 1990. "Minimizing the Three Stages of Publication Bias." *JAMA* 263:1392–95.
Chaney, D. 1986. "The Symbolic Form of Ritual in Mass Communication." In Golding, Murdock, and Schlesinger.
Chapman, J. W. 1956. *Rousseau—Totalitarian or Liberal?* Columbia U.
Charland, M. 1987. "Constitutive Rhetoric." *QJS* 73:133–50.
Cheney, G. 1983a. "On the Various and Changing Meanings of Organizational Membership." *CM* 50:343–63.
———. 1983b. "The Rhetoric of Identification and the Study of Organizational Communication." *QJS* 69:143–58.
Child, A. 1940–41a. "The Problem of Imputation in the Sociology of Knowledge." *Ethics* 51:200–219.
———. 1940–41b. "The Theoretical Possibility of the Sociology of Knowledge." *Ethics* 51:392–418.
———. 1941–42. "The Existential Determination of Thought." *Ethics* 52: 153–85.
———. 1943–44. "The Problem of Imputation Resolved." *Ethics* 54:96–109.

Chomsky, N. 1988. *Manufacturing Consent.* Pantheon.
———. 1989a. Interview in B. Moyers, ed., *A World of Ideas.* Doubleday.
———. 1989b. *Necessary Illusions.* CBC Enterprises.
Christenson, R. M., et al. 1975. *Ideologies and Modern Politics.* 2d ed. Dodd, Mead.
Chronicle of Higher Education Almanac, September 5, 1990.
Cicourel, A. V. 1964. *Method and Measurement in Sociology.* Free Press.
———. 1970. "Basic and Normative Rules in the Negotiation of Status and Role." In Dreitzel.
———. 1974. *Cognitive Sociology.* Free Press.
———. 1980. "Three Models of Discourse Analysis." *Discourse Process* 3:101–32.
———. 1982. "Interviews, Surveys, and Ecological Validity." *American Sociologist* 17:11–20.
———. 1983. "Language and the Structure of Belief in Medical Communication." *Proceedings of the Sixth World Congress of the International Association of Applied Linguistics.*
Clarke, B. L. 1964. "Multiple Authorship Trends in Scientific Papers." *Science* 143: 822–24.
Clawson, D. 1980. *Bureaucracy and the Labor Process.* Monthly Review Press.
Clegg, S. 1979. *Power, Rule, and Domination.* Routledge.
Clemmer, D. 1940. *The Prison Community.* Christopher Publishing House.
Clifford, J. 1986. "On Ethnographic Self-Fashioning." In T. C. Heller et al., eds., *Reconstructing Individualism.* Stanford U.
Cobb, A. T. 1980. "Informal Influence in the Formal Organization." *AMJ* 23, 1:155–67.
———. 1982. "A Social Psychological Approach to Coalition Membership." *GOS* 7:295–319.
———. 1984. "An Episodic Model of Power." *AMR* 9:482–93.
Cohen, C., ed. 1972. *Communism, Facism, and Democracy.* 2d ed. Random House.
Cohen, D. 1988. *Advertising.* Scott, Foresman.
Cohen, L. J. 1962. *The Diversity of Meaning.* Methuen.
Cohen, M. D., J. D. March, and J. P. Olsen. 1972. "A Garbage Can Model of Organizational Choice." *ASQ* 17:1–25.
Cohen, P. S. 1968. *Modern Social Theory.* Basic Books.
Cole, J. 1970. "Patterns of Intellectual Influence in Scientific Research." *Sociology of Education* 43:377–403.
Cole, S. 1970. "Professional Standing and the Reception of Scientific Discoveries." *AJS* 76:286–306.
Cole, M., and S. Scribner. 1974. *Culture and Thought.* Wiley.
Coleman, J. S., E. Katz, and H. Menzel. 1966. *Medical Innovation.* Bobbs-Merrill.
Collin, F. 1985. *Theory and Understanding.* Blackwell.
Collins, R. 1975. *Conflict Sociology.* Academic.
———. 1979. *The Credential Society.* Academic.
Commission on Freedom of the Press. 1947. *A Free and Responsible Press.* U. Chicago.

Conley, B. C. 1976. "The Value of Human Life in the Demand for Safety." *American Economics Review* 66:45–55.
Connerton, P. 1980. *The Tragedy of Enlightenment.* Cambridge U.
Connolly, W. E. 1969. *The Bias of Pluralism.* Atherton.
———. 1973. "Theoretical Self-Consciousness." *Polity* 5–35.
———. 1974. *The Terms of Political Discourse.* Heath.
———. 1977. *The State and the Public Interest.* American Political Science Association.
———. 1987. *Politics and Ambiguity.* U. Wisconsin.
———. 1988. *Political Theory and Modernity.* Blackwell.
Conner, S. 1989. *Postmodernist Culture.* Blackwell.
Conrad, C. 1983 "Organizational Power." In Putnam and Pacanowsky.
———. 1985. *Strategic Organizational Communication.* Holt.
Cook, P. J. 1978. "The Value of Human Life in the Demand for Safety." *American Economics Review* 68:710–11.
Cooke, P. 1988. "Modernity, Postmodernity, and the City." *TCS* 5:475–92.
Cordes, C. 1988. "Policymakers Ask: Who Should Set U.S. Research Agenda. Should Anyone?" *Chronicle of Higher Education,* June 15, 1988, pp. 1, A24.
Coser, L. A. 1956. *The Functions of Social Conflict.* Routledge.
———. 1974. *Greedy Institutions.* Free Press.
Coser, L., and B. Rosenberg. 1964. *Sociological Theory.* Macmillan.
Coulter, J. 1979. *The Social Construction of the Mind.* Rowman.
Cox, J. R. 1981. "Investigating Policy Argument as a Field." In Ziegelmueller and Rhodes.
Cox, J. R., and C. A. Willard, eds. 1982. *Advances in Argumentation Theory and Research.* Southern Illinois U.
Cox, J. R., M. O. Sillars, and G. B. Walker, eds. 1985. *Argument and Social Practice.* SCA.
Crane, D. 1972. *Invisible Colleges.* U. Chicago.
Crawford, John E. 1983. "Toward a Model of Effective Public Argumentation." In Zarefsky, Sillars, and Rhodes.
Crawshay-Williams, R. 1957. *Methods and Criteria of Reasoning.* Routledge & Kegan Paul.
Croley, H. D. 1909. *The Promise of American Life.* Macmillan.
Cronbach, L. J. 1982. "Prudent Aspirations for Social Inquiry." In W. H. Kruskal, ed., *The Social Sciences.* U. Chicago.
Crowther, J. G. 1941. *The Social Relations of Science.* Macmillan.
Crozier, M. 1964. *The Bureaucratic Phenomenon.* U. Chicago.
Cunningham, F. 1973. *Objectivity in Social Science.* U. Toronto.
Curtis, J. E., and J. W. Petras. 1967. "Social Conflict over Styles of Sociological Work." In J. E. Curtis and J. W. Petras, eds., *Social Theory and Social Structure.* Free Press.
———, eds. 1970. *The Sociology of Knowledge.* Praeger.

Cutlip, S. M. 1985. "The Impact of Public Relations in Public Communications." *Donald S. McNaughten Symposium Proceedings.* U. Syracuse.
Cyert, R. M., and J. G. March. 1963. *A Behavioural Theory of the Firm.* Wiley.
Dahl, R. A. 1956. *A Preface to Democratic Theory.* Little, Brown.
———. 1957. "The Concept of Power." *Behavioral Science* 2:201–15.
———. 1958. "A Critique of the Ruling Elite Model." *APSR* 52:463–69.
———. 1961. *Who Governs?* Yale U.
———. 1966. *Political Oppositions in Western Democracies.* Yale U.
———. 1967. *Pluralist Democracy in the United States.* Rand McNally.
———. 1970. *After the Revolution? Authority in a Good Society.* Yale U.
———. 1971. *Polyarchy.* Yale U.
———. 1972. *Democracy in the United States,* 2d ed. Rand McNally.
———. 1982. *Dilemmas of Pluralist Democracy.* Yale U.
Dahrendorf, R. 1968. *Essays on the Theory of Society.* Routledge.
———. 1990. *Reflections on the Revolution in Europe.* Times Books.
Damico. A. J. 1978. *Individuality and Community.* U. Florida.
Daniels, N., ed. 1975. *Reading Rawls.* Basic Books.
Darden, L., and N. Maull. 1977. "Interfield Theories." *Philosophy of Science* 44:43–64.
Davidson, D. 1967. "Truth and Meaning." *Synthese* 17:304–23.
———. 1968. "Actions, Reasons and Causes." In A. R. White, ed., *The Philosophy of Action.* Oxford U.
———. 1973–74. "On the Very Idea of a Conceptual Scheme." *Proceedings and Addresses of the American Philosophical Association* 47:5–20.
———. 1982. "On the Very Idea of a Conceptual Scheme." M. Krausz and J. W. Meiland, eds. *Relativism.* U. Notre Dame.
Davies, C. J. 1970. *The Politics of Pollution.* Pegasus.
Davies, P. C. W., and J. Brown. 1988. *Superstrings.* Cambridge U.
Davis, F. 1968. "Professional Socialization as Subjective Experience." In H. S. Becker, ed., *Institutions and the Person.* Aldine.
Day, R., and J. Day. 1977. "A Review of the Current State of Negotiated Order Theory." *SQ* 18:126–42.
Deal, T. E., and A. A. Kennedy. 1982. *Corporate Cultures.* Addison-Wesley.
DeGré, G. L. 1943. *Society and Ideology.* Columbia U.
———. 1970. "The Sociology of Knowledge and the Problem of Truth." In Curtis and Petras.
Deiter, O. A. L. 1950. "Stasis." *SM* 17:345–69.
Delia, J. G. 1983. "Social Psychology, Competency, and Individual Differences in Communication Action." *Journal of Language and Social Psychology* 2:207–18.
Delia, J. G., B. J. O'Keefe, and D. J. O'Keefe. "The Constructivist Approach to Communication." In F. E. X. Dance, ed., *Human Communication Theory.* Harper & Row.
Deleuze, G. 1988. *Foucault.* U. Minnesota.
Demac, D. 1984. *Keeping America Uninformed.* Pilgrim Press.

Denzin, N. K. 1970a. "Rules of Conduct and Study of Deviant Behavior." In G. J. McCall, ed., *Social Relationships*. Aldine.
———. 1970b. *The Research Act*. Aldine.
DeSario, J., and S. Langton. 1987. *Citizen Participation in Public Decision Making*. Greenwood Press.
De Soto, C. 1960. "Learning a Social Structure." In S. Lienhardt, ed., *Social Networks*. Academic.
Deutsch, K. L., and W. Soffer. 1987. *The Crisis of Liberal Democracy*. State U. New York.
Deutsch, M. 1954. "Field Theory in Social Psychology." In G. Lindzey, ed., *Handbook of Social Psychology*. Addison-Wesley.
Dewey, J. 1916. *Democracy and Education*. Macmillan.
———. 1920. *Reconstruction in Philosophy*. Holt.
———. 1929a. *Individualism Old and New*. Capricorn.
———. 1929b. *Experience and Nature*. Dover.
———. 1946. *Problems of Men*. Philosophical Library.
———. 1954. *The Public and Its Problems*. Swallow.
Dews, P., ed. 1986. *Habermas: Autonomy and Solidarity*. Verso.
Dickerson, K. 1990. "The Existence of Publication Bias and Risk Factors for Its Occurrence." *JAMA* 263:1385–89.
Dirac, P. A. M. 1982. "The Early Years of Relativity." G. Holton and Y. Elkana, eds. *Albert Einstein*. Princeton U.
Dixon, K. 1980. *The Sociology of Belief*. Routledge.
Dodd, S. C. 1955. "Diffusion Is Predictable." *ASR* 20:392–401.
Dolby, R. G. A. 1971. "Sociology of Knowledge in Natural Science." *Science Studies* 1:1–21.
Domhoff, W. 1967. *Who Rules America?* Prentice-Hall.
———. 1971. *The Higher Circles*. Vintage.
———. 1983. *Who Rules America Now?* Simon & Schuster.
———. 1990. *The Power Elite and the State*. De Gruyter.
Douglas, J. D. 1971."The Rhetoric of Science and the Origins of Social Thought." In E. Tiryakian, ed., *The Phenomenon of Sociology*. Appleton-Century-Crofts.
Douglas, M. 1975. *Implicit Meanings*. Routledge.
———. 1986. *How Institutions Think*. Syracuse U.
Douglas, M., and A. Wildavsky. 1982. *Risk and Culture*. U. California.
———. 1986. *Risk Acceptability According to the Social Sciences*. Basic Books.
Dreitzel, H. P., ed. *Recent Sociology, 2*. Macmillan.
Dretske, F. I. 1982. *Knowledge and the Flow of Information*. MIT.
Dreyfus, H. L., and P. Rabinow. 1982. *Michel Foucault: Beyond Structuralism and Hermeneutics*. 2d ed. U. Chicago.
Dumont, L. 1983. *Essais sur l'Individualisme*. Du Seuil.
Dunbar, N. R. 1986. "Laetrile." *JAFA* 22:196–211.
Dunn, W. N. 1981. *Public Policy Analysis*. Prentice-Hall.
———. 1983. *Values, Ethics, and the Practice of Public Policy*. Heath.

———, ed. 1986. *Policy Analysis*. JAI Press.
Dunnett, M. D., ed. 1976. *Handbook of Industrial and Organizational Psychology*. Rand McNally.
Dunwoody, S. 1986. "The Scientist as Source." In Friedman, Dunwoody, and Rogers.
Dunwoody, S., and R. Ryan. 1985. "Scientific Barriers to the Popularization of Science in the Mass Media." *Journal of Communication* 35:26–42.
Durkheim, E. 1938. *The Rules of Sociological Method*. Free Press.
———. 1961. *The Elementary Forms of the Religious Life*. Collier.
Dye, T. R. 1975. *Understanding Public Policy*. 2d ed. Prentice-Hall.
Dye, T. R., and H. Zeigler. 1981. *The Irony of Democracy*. 5th ed. Brooks/Cole.
Eagleton, T. 1985. "Capitalism, Modernism, and Postmodernism." *New Left Review* 152 (July–August).
———. 1987. "Awakening from Modernity." *Times Literary Supplement*, February, 1987.
Eagleton, T. 1991. *Ideology*. Verso.
Easton, D. 1953. *The Political System*. Knopf.
———. 1991a. "The Division, Integration, and Transfer of Knowledge." In Easton and Schelling.
———. 1991b. "Political Science in the United States." In Easton and Schelling.
Easton, D., and C. S. Schelling, eds. 1991. *Divided Knowledge*. Sage.
Edwards, G. C. 1978. *The Policy Predicament*. Freeman.
Eemeren, F. H. van. 1987. "Argumentation Studies' Five Estates." In Wenzel.
Eemeren, F. H. van, and R. Grootendorst. 1983. *Speech Acts in Argumentative Discussions*. Foris.
Eisenstadt, S. N. 1973. *Tradition, Change, and Modernity*. Wiley.
Elias, N. 1982. "Scientific Establishments." In Elias, Martins, and Whitley.
Elias, N., H. Martins, and R. Whitley, eds. 1982. *Scientific Establishments and Hierarchies*. Reidel.
Elliott, P. 1972. *The Making of a Television Series*. Constable.
———. 1974. "Uses and Gratifications Research." In J. Blumler and E. Katz, eds., *The Uses of Mass Communication*. Sage.
———. 1982. "Intellectuals, the 'Information Society,' and the Disappearance of the Public Sphere." *Media, Culture, and Society* 4:243–53.
Entman, R. M. 1989. *Democracy without Citizens*. Oxford U.
Etzioni, A. 1961a. *A Comparative Analysis of Complex Organizations*. Free Press.
———. 1993. *The Spirit of Community*. Crown.
———, ed. 1961b. *Complex Organizations*. Holt.
Euske, N. A., and K. H. Roberts. 1987. "Evolving Perspectives in Organizational Theory." In Jablin et al.
Evans-Pritchard, E. E. 1937. *Witchcraft*. Clarendon Press.
———. 1956. *Nuer Religion*. Oxford U.
———. 1965. *Theories of Primitive Religion*. Clarendon Press.
Ewen, S. 1976. *Captains of Consciousness*. McGraw-Hill.

Ezrahi, Y. 1982. "Einstein and the Light of Reason." G. Holton and Y. Elkana, eds. *Albert Einstein*. Princeton U.
Farrell, T. B. 1976. "Knowledge, Consensus, and Rhetorical Theory." *QJS* 62:1–14.
———. 1977. "Validity and Rationality." *JAFA* 13:142–49.
Farrell, T. B., and G. T. Goodnight. 1981. "Accidental Rhetoric." *CM* 48:271–300.
Faust, D. 1985. *The Limits of Scientific Reasoning*. U. Minnesota.
Featherstone, M. 1988. "In Pursuit of the Postmodern." *TCS* 5:195–216.
Fein, L. J., ed. 1964. *American Democracy*. Holt, Rinehart, & Winston.
Festinger, L. 1954. "A Theory of Social Comparison Processes." *Human Relations* 7:117–40.
———. 1957. *A Theory of Cognitive Dissonance*. Stanford U.
Feyerabend, P. 1965. "Problems of Empiricism." R. Colodny, ed. *Beyond the Edge of Certainty*. Prentice-Hall.
Finer, S. F. 1966. *Vilfredo Pareto*. Praeger.
Finocchiaro, M. 1977. "Logic and Rhetoric in Lavoisier's Sealed Note." *P&R* 10:111–22.
Firth, R. 1964. *Essays on Social Organisation and Values*. U. London.
Fischer, F. 1980. *Politics, Values, and Public Policy*. Westview.
———. 1990. *Technocracy and the Politics of Expertise*. Sage.
Fish, S. 1980. *Is There a Text in This Class?* Harvard U.
———. 1989. "Being Interdisciplinary Is So Very Hard To Do." *Profession* 89. Modern Language Association.
Fisher, W. R. 1987. *Human Communication as Narration*. U. South Carolina.
Flathman, R. 1966. *The Public Interest*. Wiley.
———. 1975. "Some Familiar but False Dichotomies Concerning Interests.'" *Political Theory* 3:277–88.
Fleck, L. 1935; reissued, 1979. *The Genesis and Development of a Scientific Fact*. U. Chicago.
Fleishman, J. L. 1991. "A New Framework for Integration." In Easton and Schelling.
Forgas, J. P. 1979. *Social Episodes*. Academic.
Fortes, M., ed. 1949. *Social Structure*. Oxford U.
Foucault, M. 1963; revised 1972. *Naissance de la Clinique*. Presses Universitaires de France.
———. 1966. *Le Mots et les Choses*. Editions Gallimard.
———. 1969. *L'Archaeologie du Savoir*. Editions Gallimard.
———. 1970. *The Order of Things*. Random House.
———. 1972a. *The Archaeology of Knowledge and the Discourse on Language*. Tavistock.
———. 1972b. *Histoire de la Folie à L'Age Classique*. Editions Gallimard.
———. 1976. *The History of Sexuality*. Pantheon.
———. 1977. *Discipline and Punish*. Random House.

———. 1980. *Power/Knowledge.* Ed. C. Gordon. Harvester.

———. 1984. "On the Genealogy of Ethics: An Overview of Work in Progress." In P. Rabinow, ed., *The Foucault Reader.* Pantheon.

———. 1988. *Politics, Philosophy, Culture.* Ed. L. D. Kritzman. Routledge.

———. 1991a. "Governmentality." In G. Burchell, C. Gordon, and P, Miller, eds., *The Foucault Effect.* U. Chicago.

———. 1991b. "Questions of Method." In G. Burchell, C. Gordon, and P. Miller, eds., *The Foucault Effect.* U. Chicago.

Frankel, C. 1962. *The Democratic Prospect.* Harper & Row.

———. 1967. "The Idea of Progress." In P. Edwards, ed., *The Encyclopedia of Philosophy.* Macmillan.

Fraser, N. 1991. "Rethinking the Public Sphere." In C. Calhoun, ed., *Habermas and the Public Sphere.* MIT.

Freeman, D. 1983. *The Making and Unmaking of an Anthropological Myth.* Harvard U.

Freeman, E. 1984. *Strategic Management.* Pittman.

Freidson, E. 1970. *Profession of Medicine.* U. Chicago.

———. 1986. *Professional Powers.* U. Chicago.

Freeman, M., R. Haveman, and A. Kneese. 1973. *The Economics of Environmental Policy.* John Wiley.

Friedman, P. J. 1990. "Correcting the Literature Following Fraudulent Publication." *JAMA* 263:1416–19.

Friedman, S. M. 1986. "The Journalist's World." In Friedman, Dunwoody, and Rogers.

Friedman, S. M., S. Dunwoody, and C. L. Rogers, eds. 1986. *Scientists and Journalists.* Free Press.

Friedrich, C. J., and Z. K. Brzezinski. 1965. *Totalitarian Dictatorship and Autocracy.* 2d ed. Praeger.

Frisby, D. 1985. *Fragments of Modernity.* Polity.

Frohock, F. 1974. *Normative Political Theory.* Prentice-Hall.

Fromm, E. 1955. *The Sane Society.* Rinehart.

Frost, M. J. 1971. *Values for Money.* Grower Press.

Frost, P. J., et al. 1985. *Organizational Culture.* Sage.

Frye, N. 1968. "On Value Judgments." In L. S. Dembo, ed., *Criticism.* U. Wisconsin.

Fuller, L. 1949. "The Case of the Speluncean Exploreres." *Harvard Law Review* 62:616–45.

Fuller, S. 1983. "Defense of Incommensurability." Seventh Regional Conference on the History and Philosophy of Science, U. Colorado.

———. 1986. "Consensus and Validation in Science." Philosophy of Science Association.

———. 1988. *Social Epistemology.* Indiana U.

———. 1989. *Philosophy of Science and Its Discontents.* Westview.

———. 1992. *Philosophy, Rhetoric, and the End of Knowledge.* U. Wisconsin.

Fuller, S., and C. A. Willard. 1987. "Defense of Relativism." In F. H. van Eemeren et al., eds., *Argumentation: Perspectives and Approaches*. Foris.
Galbraith, J. 1979. *Designing Complex Organizations*. Addison-Wesley.
Galbraith, J. K. 1971. *The New Industrial State*. 2d ed. Houghton Mifflin.
———. 1973. *Economics and the Public Purpose*. Houghton Mifflin.
Galgan, G. 1982. *The Logic of Modernity*. New York U.
Gallie, W. B. 1955–56. "Essentially Contested Concepts." *PAS* 56:167–98.
Gans, H. J. 1957. "The Creator-Audience Relationship in the Mass Media." In B. Rosenberg and D. M. White, eds., *Mass Culture*. Free Press.
———. 1980. *Deciding What's News*. Vintage.
Garfield, E., I. H. Sher, and R. J. Torpie. 1964. *The Use of Citation Data in Writing the History of Science*. Institute for Scientific Information.
Garfinkle, A. 1981. *Forms of Explanation*. Yale U.
Garnham, N. 1986. "The Media and the Public Sphere." In Golding, Murdock, and Schlesinger.
Garson, G. D. 1986. "From Policy Science to Policy Analysis." In Dunn.
Garvey, C. 1977. "Contingent Queries." In M. Lewis and L. Rosenblum, eds., *Interaction, Conversation, and the Development of Language*. Wiley.
Garvey, W. D., and B. C. Griffith. 1964. "Scientific Information Exchange Psychology." *Science* 146:1955–59.
———. 1966. "Studies of Social Innovations Scientific Communication Psychology." *AP* 21:1019–36.
Garvey, W. D., N. Lin, and C. E. Nelson. 1979. "Communication in the Social Sciences." In W. D. Garvey, ed., *Communication*. Pergamon Press.
Gaskins, R. H. 1992. *Burdens of Proof in Modern Discourse*. Yale U.
Gaston, J. 1969. "Big Science in Britain." Ph.D. diss. Yale U.
Geertz, C. 1964. "Ideology as a Cultural System." In D. Apter, ed., *Ideology and Discontent*. Free Press.
———. 1973. *Interpretation of Cultures*. Basic Books.
———. 1980. "Blurred Genres." *American Scholar* 49:165–79.
———. 1983. *Local Knowledge*. Basic Books.
———. 1984. "Anti-anti Relativism." *American Anthropologist* 86(2):263–77.
———. 1988. *Works and Lives*. Stanford U.
Geertz, C., H. Geertz, and L. Rosen. 1979. *Meaning and Order in Moroccan Society*. Cambridge U.
Gellner, E. 1973. *Cause and Meaning in the Social Sciences*. Routledge.
———. 1974. *Legitimation of Belief*. Cambridge U.
———. 1979. *Spectacles and Predicaments*. Cambridge U.
Gergen, K. J. 1982. *Toward Transformation in Social Knowledge*. Springer-Verlag.
———. 1985. "The Social Constructionist Movement in Modern Psychology." *AP* 40:266–75.
Gergen, K. J., and K. E. Davis, eds. *The Social Construction of the Person*. Springer-Verlag.
Gewirth, Alan. 1978. *Reason and Morality*. U. Chicago.

Gianos, P. 1974. "Scientists as Policy Advisors." *Western Political Quarterly* 27:429–56.
Gibb, J. P. 1961. "Defensive Communication." *Journal of Communication* 11:141–48.
Gibbs, J. 1966. "The Sociology of Law and Normative Phenomena." *ASR* 31:315–25.
Giddens, A. 1974. *Positivism and Sociology.* Heinemann.
———. 1976. *New Rules of Sociological Method.* Hutchinson.
———. 1979. *Central Problems in Social Theory.* U. California.
———. 1981. *A Contemporary Critique of Historical Materialism.* U. California.
———. 1984. *The Constitution of Society.* U. California.
———. 1990. *The Consequences of Modernity.* Stanford U.
Gieryn, T. F. 1983. "Boundary Work and the Demarcation of Science from Non-Science." *ASR* 48:781–95.
Gieryn, T. F., and A. E. Figert. 1986. "Scientists Protect Their Cognitive Authority." In G. Boehme and N. Sthr, eds., *The Knowledge Society.* Reidel.
Gilbert, G. N. 1976. "The Transformation of Research Findings into Scientific Knowledge." *SSS* 6:281–306.
Gilbert, G. N., and M. Mulkay. 1984. *Opening Pandora's Box.* Cambridge U.
Gilligan, C. 1982. *In a Different Voice.* Harvard U.
Gilpin, R. R. 1962. *American Scientists and Nuclear Weapons Policy.* Princeton U.
———. 1969. *France in the Age of the Scientific State.* Princeton U.
Gilpin, R., and C. Wright, eds. 1964. *Scientists and National Policy Making.* Columbia U.
Ginsberg, B. 1982. *The Consequences of Consent.* Random House.
———. 1986. *The Captive Public.* Basic Books.
Giroux, H. A. 1988. *Schooling and the Struggle for Public Life.* U. Minnesota.
Gleick, J. 1987. *Chaos.* Penguin.
Gluckman, M., ed. 1964. *Closed Systems and Open Minds.* Aldine.
Godfrey, L. R., ed. 1983. *Scientists Confront Creationism.* Norton.
Goffman, E. 1959. *The Presentation of Self in Everyday Life.* Anchor.
———. 1961a. *Encounters.* Bobbs-Merrill.
———. 1961b. *Asylums.* Doubleday.
———. 1963. *Behavior in Public Places.* Free Press.
———. 1964. *Stigma.* Prentice-Hall.
———. 1967. *Interaction Ritual.* Doubleday.
———. 1969. *Strategic Interaction.* U. Pennsylvania.
———. 1971. *Relations in Public.* Basic Books.
Goldberg, A. C. 1991. "Challenges to the Post–Cold War Balance of Power." *Washington Quarterly* 14:51–60.
Golding, P., G. Murdock, and P. Schlesinger, eds. 1986. *Communicating Politics.* Leicester U.
Goldman, P. 1978. "Sociologists and the Study of Bureaucracy." *Insurgent Sociologist* 3:21.
Goldman, T. A., ed. 1968. *Cost Effectiveness Analysis.* Praeger.

Goodell, R. 1986. "How to Kill a Controversy." In Friedman, Dunwoody, and Rogers.
Goodenough, W. 1964. "Cultural Anthropology and Linguistics." In D. Hymes, ed., *Language Culture and Society.* Harper & Row.
Goodman, N. 1972. *Problems and Projects.* Bobbs-Merrill.
———. 1978. *Ways of Worldmaking.* Hackett.
———. 1983. *Fact, Fiction, and Forecast.* 4th ed. Harvard U.
Goodman, P. 1962. *The Community of Scholars.* Random House.
Goodnight, G. T. 1980. "The Liberal and Conservative Presumptions." In Rhodes and Newell.
———. 1982. "The Personal, Technical, and Public Spheres of Argument." *JAFA* 18:214–27.
———. 1987a. "Argumentation, Criticism, and Rhetoric." In Wenzel
———. 1987b. "Generational Argument." In F. H. van Eemeren et al., eds., *Argumentation: Across the Lines of Discipline.* Foris.
———. 1987c. "Public Discourse." *CSMC* 4:428–32.
———. 1988. "Communities of Argument in Time." Wake Forest U. Conference on Argumentation and Community, Venice.
———. 1989. "Legitimation Issues." Temple U. Conference on Discourse Analysis, Philadelphia, Pennsylvania.
Gould, C. C. 1988. *Rethinking Democracy.* Cambridge U.
Gould, S. J. 1980. *The Panda's Thumb.* Norton.
———. 1981. *The Mismeasure of Man.* Norton.
Gouldner, A. 1954. *Patterns of Industrial Bureaucracy.* Free Press.
———. 1970. *The Coming Crisis of Western Sociology.* Basic Books.
———. 1976. *The Dialectic of Ideology and Technology.* Seabury.
Gouran, D. S. 1985. "A Critical Summary of Research on the Role of Argument Decision-Making Groups." In Cox, Sillars, and Walker.
———. 1987. "The Failure of Argument in Decisions Leading to the Challenger Disaster." In Wenzel.
Gouran, D. S., R. Y. Hirokawa, and A. E. Martz. 1986. "A Critical Analysis of Factors Related to the Decisional Process Involved in the Challenger Disaster." *CSSJ* 37:119–35.
Graebner, W. 1987. *The Engineering of Consent.* U. Wisconsin.
Graham, L. 1981. *Between Science and Values.* Columbia U.
———, ed. 1983. *The Functions and Uses of Disciplinary History.* Reidel.
Greenberg, D. S. 1967. *The Politics of Pure Science.* New American Library.
———. 1969. *The Politics of American Science.* Penguin.
Greer, S. 1964. "Community and Modern Urban Society." In Fein.
Grice, H. P. 1957. "Meaning." *Philosophical Review* 66:377–88.
———. 1975. "Logic and Conversation." In P. Cole and J. Morgan, eds., *Syntax and Semantics.* Academic.
Gronbeck, B. 1981. "Sociocultural Notions of Argument Fields." In Ziegelmueller and Rhodes.

Gronbeck, B. E., ed. 1989. *Spheres of Argument: Proceedings of the Sixth SCA/AFA Conference on Argumentation.* Annandale: SCA.
Grootendorst, R. 1989. "What a Pragma-Dialectical Approach to Fallacies Can and Cannot Do." Third International Symposium on Informal Logic, Windsor, Canada.
Gross, A. G. 1987. "A Tale Twice Told." In Wenzel
Grosse, R. N. 1971. "Cost Benefit Analysis Disease Control Programs." In M. G. Kendall, ed., *Cost-Benefit Analysis.* American Elsevier.
Guetzkow, H., and H. Simon. 1960. "The Impact of Certain Communication Nets upon Organization and Performance Task-Oriented Groups." In A. H. Rubensteand and C. J. Haverstroh, eds., *Some Theories of Organization.* Dorsey.
Gumperz, J. J., and Hymes, D., eds. *Directions in Sociolinguistics.* Holt.
Gurvitch, G. 1960. *Problemes de la Sociologie de la Connaissance.* Traité de Sociologie. Presses Universitaires de France.
———. 1971. *The Social Frameworks of Knowledge.* Blackwell.
Haan, N., E. Aerts, and B. Cooper. 1985. *On Moral Grounds.* New York U.
Haberer, J. 1969. *Politics and the Community of Science.* Van Nostrand.
Habermas, J. 1970a. "Toward a Theory of Communicative Competence." In Dreitzel.
———. 1970b. *Toward a Rational Society.* Beacon.
———. 1971. *Knowledge and Practice.* Beacon.
———. 1973. *Theory and Practice.* Beacon.
———. 1975. *Legitimation Crises.* Beacon.
———. 1979a. *Communication and the Evolution of Society.* Beacon.
———. 1979b. "The Public Sphere." In A. Matterlart and S. Siegelaub, eds., *Communication and Class Struggle,* Vol. 1. International General.
———. 1981. "Modernity versus Postmodernity." *New German Critique* Winter, pp. 3–4.
———. 1984. *The Theory of Communicative Action,* vol. 1. Beacon.
———. 1985a. "Modernity—an Incomplete Project." In H. Foster, ed., *Postmodern Culture.* Pluto Press.
———. 1985b. *Lectures on the Discourse of Modernity.* Harvard U.
———. 1986. "Taking Aim at the Heart of the Present." In D. C. Hoy, ed., *Foucault.* Blackwell.
———. 1987. *The Philosophical Discourse of Modernity.* Polity Press.
———. 1989a. *The Structural Transformation of the Public Sphere.* MIT.
———. 1989b. *The New Conservatism.* MIT.
Hacking, Ian. 1982. "Language, Truth, and Reason." In M. Hollis and S. Lukes, eds., *Rationality and Relativism.* MIT.
———. 1983. *Representing and Intervening.* Cambridge U.
———. 1985. "Making Up People." *Reconstructing Individualism.* Stanford U.
———. 1992. "Statistical Language, Statistical Truth, and Statistical Reason." E. McMullin, ed. *The Social Dimensions of Science.* U. Notre Dame.

Hackman, J. D. 1985. "Power and Centrality in the Allocation of Resources in Colleges and Universities." *ASQ* 30:61–77.
Hagstrom, W. 1965. *The Scientific Community.* Basic Books.
Halberstam, D. 1964. *The Making of a Quagmire.* Random House.
———. 1969. *The Best and the Brightest.* Random House.
Hall, E. T. 1977. *Beyond Culture.* Anchor.
Hall, S. 1980. "Cultural Studies." *Media, Culture, and Society* 2:57–72.
Hamilton, R. 1975. *Restraining Myths.* Sage.
Hancher, M. 1979. "The Classification of Cooperative Illocutionary Acts." *Language and Society* 8:1–14.
Hannan, M. T., and J. Freeman. 1981. "The Population Ecology of Organizations." In O. Grusky and G. A. Miller, eds., *The Sociology of Organizations.* 2d ed. Free Press.
Hanson, N. R. 1958. *Patterns of Discovery.* Cambridge U.
Hanson, R. L. 1985. *The Democratic Imagination in America.* Princeton U.
Hardin, R. 1982. *Collective Action.* Johns Hopkins U.
Hardt, H. 1993. "Authenticity, Communication, and Critical Theory." *Critical Studies in Mass Communication* 10:49–69.
Hardwig, J. 1973. "The Achievement of Moral Rationality." *P&R* 6:171–85.
Hargens, L. L. 1990. "Variation in Journal Peer Review Systems." *JAMA* 263:1348–52.
Harre, R. 1980. *Social Being.* Littlefield, Adams.
———. 1981. "Rituals, Rhetoric, and Social Cognitions." In J. P. Forgas, ed., *Social Cognition.* Academic.
———. 1984. *Personal Being.* Harvard U.
Harre, R., and P. F. Secord. 1972. *The Explanation of Social Behavior.* Blackwell.
Hart, R. P., and D. M. Burkes. 1972. "Rhetorical Sensitivity and Social Interaction." *SM* 39:75–91.
Hartman, G. H. 1980. *Criticism in the Wilderness.* Yale U.
Hartung, F. E. 1970. "Problems of the Sociology of Knowledge." In Curtis and Petras.
Harvey, D. 1989. *The Condition of Postmodernity.* Blackwell.
Haskell, T. L., ed. 1977. *The Emergence of Professional Social Science.* U. Illinois.
———. 1984a. *The Authority of Experts.* Indiana U.
———. 1984b. "Introduction." In Haskell.
———. 1984c. "Professionalism versus Capitalism." In Haskell.
Hauerwas, S. 1981. *A Community of Character.* U. Notre Dame.
Hawkesworth. M. E. 1988. *Theoretical Issues in Policy Analysis.* State U. New York.
Hawley, A. H. 1944. "Ecology and Human Ecology." *Social Forces* 22:398–405.
———. 1950. *Human Ecology.* Ronald.
Hayes, J. T. "'Creation Science' Is Not 'Science.'" In Zarefsky, Sillars, and Rhodes.
Hazen, R. M., and J. Trefil. 1991. "Quick! What's a Quark?" *New York Times Magazine,* 13 January, pp. 24–26.
Hegel, G. W. F. 1967. *The Philosophy of Right.* Ed. T. M. Knox. Oxford U.
Heidbreder, E. 1933. *Seven Psychologies.* Appleton-Century-Crofts.

Heisenberg, W. 1952. *Philosophic Problems of Nuclear Science.* Pantheon.
———. 1958. *Physics and Philosophy.* Harper & Row.
Hennessy, B. C. 1970. *Public Opinion.* Wadsworth.
Hertzler, J. O. 1946. *Social Institutions.* U. Nebraska.
Hesse, M. 1980. *Revolutions and Reconstructions in the Philosophy of Science.* Harvester.
Hikins, J. W., and K. S. Zagacki. 1988. "Rhetoric, Philosophy, and Objectivism." *QJS* 74:201–28.
Hitler, A. 1943. *Mein Kampf.* Houghton Mifflin.
Hobbes, T. 1968. *The Leviathan.* Penguin.
Hocking, W. E. 1947. *Freedom of the Press.* U. Chicago.
Hoffer, E. 1951. *The True Believer.* Harper & Row.
Hofstadter, R. 1944. *Social Darwinism in American Thought.* Beacon.
———. 1948. *The American Political Tradition.* Knopf.
———. 1960. *The Age of Reform.* Random House.
———. 1963. *Anti-Intellectualism in American Life.* Random House.
———. 1967. *The Paranoid Style of American Politics.* Knopf.
Hofstadter, R., W. Miller, and D. Aaron. 1964. *The United States.* Prentice-Hall.
Hogwood, B. W., and B. G. Peters. 1985. *The Pathology of Public Policy.* Oxford U.
Hohenberg, J. 1971. *Free Press, Free People.* Macmillan.
Hollis, M. 1977. *Models of Man.* Cambridge U.
Holton, G. 1982. "Introduction." In G. Holton and Y. Elkana, eds., *Albert Einstein.* Princeton U.
Homans, G. C. 1950. *The Human Group.* Harcourt Brace.
Horowitz, I. L. 1961. *Philosophy, Science, and the Sociology of Knowledge.* Thomas.
Hoy, D. C. 1986. *Foucault.* Blackwell.
Hunter, F. 1953. *Community Power Structure.* U. North Carolina.
———. 1959. *Top Leadership.* U. North Carolina.
Huntington, S. P. 1974. "Postindustrial Politics." *Comparative Politics* 6:163–91.
Huxley, A. 1932. *Brave New World.* Doubleday, Doran.
———. 1958. *Brave New World Revisited.* Harper & Row.
Hyman, H. H. 1960. "Reflections on Reference Groups." *POQ* 269:1–94.
Hyman, H. H., and E. Singer. 1968. *Readings in Reference Group Theory and Research.* Free Press.
Hynes, T. J. 1987. "Risk, Vulnerability, and Policy Analysis." In Wenzel.
———. 1989. "Can You Buy Cold Fusion by the Six Pack? Or Bubba and Billy-Bob Discover Pons and Fleischmann." In Gronbeck.
Ice, R. 1987. "Presumption as Problematic in Group Decision-Making." In Wenzel.
International Commission for the Study of Communal Problems, UNESCO. 1980. *Final Report.* UNESCO.
Irvin, G. 1978. *Modern Cost Benefit Methods.* Macmillan.
Jablin, F. M., et al., eds. 1987. *Handbook of Organizational Communication.* Sage.
Jackson, S. A. 1985. "What Can Speech Acts Do for Argumentation?" In Cox, Sillars, and Walker.

———. 1987. "Engineering Argument." Northwestern U. Conference on Language, Argument and the Public Sphere, Evanston.

———. In Press. "What Can Argumentative Practice Tell Us about Argumentative Norms?" In R. Maier, ed., *Norms in Argumentation.* Foris.

Jackson, S. A., and S. Jacobs. 1980. "Structure of Conversational Argument." *QJS* 66:251–65.

———. 1981. "The Collaborative Production of Proposals in Conversational Argument and Persuasion." *JAFA* 18:77–90.

Jacobs, J. 1976. "Stratification and Conflict among Prison Inmates." *Journal of Criminal Law and Criminology* 66:476–82.

Jacobs, S. 1983. "When Worlds Collide." In Zarefsky, Sillars, and Rhodes.

———. 1987. "Finding 'Common Ground' and 'Zones of Agreement.'" Northwestern U. Conference on Language, Argument and the Public Sphere, Evanston.

Jacobs, S., and S. A. Jackson. 1982. "Conversational Argument." In Cox and Willard.

———. 1983. "Strategy and Structure in Conversational Influence Attempts." *CM* 50:285–304.

Jacobs, S., and C. Laufersweiler. 1981. "The Social Enactment of Dramatic Forms." SCA Convention, Anaheim, California.

Jacoby, R. 1975. *Social Amnesia.* Beacon.

Jameson, F. 1988. "Postmodernism and Consumer Society." In E. A. Kaplan, ed. *Postmodernism and Its Discontents.* Verso.

———. 1991. *Postmodernism.* Duke U.

Janis, I. 1983. *Groupthink.* 2d ed. Houghton Mifflin.

Jarvie, I. C. 1964. *Revolution in Anthropology.* Humanities.

———. 1972. *Concepts and Society.* Routledge.

Jay, M. 1984. *Adorno.* Harvard U.

Jensen, J. 1990. *Redeeming Modernity.* Sage.

Johannesen, R. L. 1971. "The Emerging Concept of Communication as Dialogue." *QJS* 57:373–83.

Johnson, D. W. 1972. *Reaching Out.* Prentice-Hall.

Johnson, P. 1983. *Modern Times.* Harper & Row.

Johnson, R. H., and J. A. Blair. 1985. *Logical Self-Defense.* McGraw-Hill Ryerson.

Jones, L. 1994. "Nationalism Can Be Beneficial." In P. C. Cozic, ed., *Nationalism and Ethnic Conflict.* Greenhaven.

Jourard, S. 1974. *The Transparent Self.* Rev. ed. Van Nostrand Reinhold.

Kadushin, C. 1966. "The Friends and Supporters of Psychotherapy." *ASR* 31:786–802.

———. 1968. "Power, Influence, and Social Circles." *ASR* 33:685–99.

Kahn, R. L., and E. Goulding, eds. 1964. *Power and Conflict in Organisations.* Tavistock.

Kanter, R. M. 1968. "Committment and Social Organization." *ASR* 33:499–517.

———. 1972. *Committment and Community.* Harvard U.

———. 1977. *Men and Women of the Corporation.* Basic Books.

———. 1983. *The Change Masters*. Simon & Schuster.
Kaplan, A. 1961. *The New World of Philosophy*. Random House.
Kaufman, A. S. 1965. "On Alienation." *Inquiry* 8:141–65.
Kariel, H. 1961. *The Decline of American Pluralism*. Stanford U.
———. 1977. *Beyond Liberalism*. Harper & Row.
Karp, I., and M. B. Kendall. 1982. "Reflexivity in Field Work." In P. F. Secord, ed., *Explaining Human Behavior*. Sage.
Katz, E. 1957. "The Two-Step Flow of Communication." *POQ* 21:61–78.
Katz, E., and P. F. Lazarsfeld. 1968. "On Reopening the Question of Selectivity in Exposure to Mass Communications." In Abelson et al., eds., *Theories of Cognitive Consistency*. Rand McNally.
Katz, D. 1964. "The Motivational Basis of Organizational Behavior." *Behavioral Science* 9:131–46.
———. 1971. "Psychological Barriers to Communication." In H. Bosmajian, ed., *Readings in Speech*. 2d ed. Harper & Row.
Katz, D., and R. Kahn. 1966. *The Social Psychology of Organizations*. Wiley. 2d ed. 1978.
Kellner, D. 1988. "Postmodernism as Social Theory." *TCS* 5:239–70.
Kelly, G. A. 1955. *A Theory of Personality*. Norton.
Kelly, M. 1993. "The Politics of Meaning." Louisville *Courier-Journal*, May 23, D1.
Kelman, H. 1961. "Processes of Opinion Change." *POQ* 25:58–78.
Kennedy, M. D. 1991. "Eastern Europe's Lessons for Critical Intellectuals." In Lemert.
Kenny, M. 1986. *Biotechnology*. Yale U.
Key, V. O., Jr. 1961. *Public Opinion and American Democracy*. Knopf.
Killian, L. M. 1964. "Social Movements." In R. E. L. Faris, ed., *Handbook of Modern Sociology*. Rand McNally.
Kimball, P. 1972. *The Disconnected*. Columbia U.
Kirkpatrick, F. G. 1986. *Community*. Georgetown U.
Kitcher, P. 1982. *Abusing Science*. MIT.
———. 1985. *Vaulting Ambition*. MIT.
Klein, J. T. 1990a. *Interdisciplinarity*. Wayne State U.
———. 1990b. "Across the Boundaries." *SE* 4:267–80.
Klumpp, J. F. 1981."A Dramatistic Approach to Argument Fields." Ziegelmueller and Rhodes.
Knoll, E. 1990. "The Communities of Scientists and Journal Peer Review." *JAMA* 263:133–1332.
Knorr, K. D., R. Khron, and R. Whitley, eds. 1981. *The Social Process of Scientific Investigation*. Reidel.
Knorr-Cetina, K. D. 1981. *The Manufacture of Knowledge*. Pergamon.
———. 1982. "Scientific Communities or Transepistemic Arenas of Research?" *SSS* 12:101–30.
———. 1988. "The Internal Environment of Knowledge Claims." *Argumentation* 2:369–89.
Knorr-Cetina, K. D., and M. Mulkay. 1983. *Science Observed*. Sage.

Kohn, A. 1986. *False Prophets.* Blackwell.
Kolko, G. 1962. *Wealth and Power in America.* Praeger.
Kornhauser, W. 1959. *The Politics of Mass Society.* Free Press.
———. 1962. *Scientists in Industry.* U. California.
Kramer, F. 1975. "Policy Analysis and Ideology." *Public Administration Review* 35:509–17.
Kristol, I. 1983. *Reflections of a Neoconservative.* Basic Books.
Kroker, A., and D. Cook. 1987. *The Post-Modern Scene.* St. Martin's.
Krone, K. J., F. M. Jablin, and L. L. Putnam. 1987. "Communication Theory and Organizational Communication." In Jablin et al.
Kuhn, T. S. 1970a. *The Structure of Scientific Revolutions.* U. Chicago.
———. 1970b. "Reflections on My Critics." In I. Lakatos and A. Musgrave, eds., *Criticism and the Growth of Knowledge.* Cambridge U.
———. 1977a. *The Essential Tension.* U. Chicago.
———. 1977b. "Theory Change as Structure Change." In R. Butts and J. Hintikka, eds., *Historical and Philosophical Dimensions of Logic, Methodology, and Philosophy of Science.* Reidel.
———. 1979. Foreword to Ludwik Fleck, *The Genesis and Development of a Scientific Fact.* U. Chicago.
Lakatos, I., and A. Musgrave, eds. 1970. *Criticism and the Growth of Knowledge.* Cambridge U.
Lambert, R. D. 1991. "Blurring the Disciplinary Boundaries." In Easton and Schelling.
Lane, R. E., and D. O. Sears. 1964. *Public Opinion.* Prentice-Hall.
Lang, K., and G. E. Lang. 1966. *Collective Dynamics.* Random House.
Larson, M. S. 1984. "The Production of Expertise and the Constitution of Expert Power." In Haskell.
Lasch, C. 1979. *The Culture of Narcissism.* Warner.
———. 1984. *The Minimal Self.* Norton.
Lasswell, H. D., and D. Lerner, eds. 1965. *World Revolutionary Elites.* MIT.
Lasswell, H. D., D. Lerner, and C. E. Rothwell. 1952. *The Comparative Study of Elites.* Stanford U.
Latour, B. 1987. *Science in Action.* Harvard U.
Latour, B., and S. Woolgar. 1979. *Laboratory Life.* Sage.
Laudan, L. 1977. *Progress and Its Problems.* U. California.
———. 1984. *Science and Values.* U. California.
Layard, R., ed. 1972. *Cost Benefit Analysis.* Penguin.
Lazarsfeld, P. F., B. Berelson, and H. Gaudet. 1968 [1944]. *The People's Choice.* Columbia U.
Lazarus, S. 1974. *The Genteel Populists.* Holt, Rinehart, & Winston.
Le Bon, G. 1879. *The Crowd.* Unwin.
Lee, A. M. 1966. *Multivalent Man.* Braziller.
Leff, M. C. 1987. "Modern Sophistic and the Unity of Rhetoric." In Nelson, Megill, and McCloskey.
Leiserson, A. 1965. "Scientists and the Policy Process." *APSR* 59:408–16.

Lemert, C. C., ed. 1991. *Intellectuals and Politics*. Sage.
Leps, M.-C. 1990. "Crossdisciplinary Inquiry in the Information Age." *SE* 4:281–91.
Levin, M. 1960. *The Alienated Voter*. Holt, Rinehart, & Winston.
Lewin, K. 1935. *A Dynamic Theory of Personality*. McGraw-Hill.
———. 1947. "Group Decisions and Social Change." In T. Newcomb and E. Hartley, eds., *Readings in Social Psychology*. Holt.
———. 1948. *Resolving Social Conflicts*. Harper & Row.
———. 1951. *Field Theory in Social Science*. Harper & Row.
Lindberg, L. N., ed. 1975. *Stress and Contradiction in Modern Capitalism*. Lexington Books.
Lindblom, C. E. 1965. *The Intelligence of Democracy*. Macmillan.
———. 1977. *Politics and Markets*. Basic Books.
Lippmann, W. 1925. *The Phantom Public*. Macmillan.
———. 1963. "The Dilemma of Liberal Democracy." In C. Rossiter and J. Lare, eds., *The Essential Lippmann*. Vintage.
———. 1965. *Public Opinion*. Free Press.
Litt, E. 1973. *Democracy's Ordeal in America*. Dryden.
Longino, H. 1990. *Science as Social Knowledge*. Princeton U.
Lourenco, S., and J. C. Gildwell. 1975. "A Dialectical Analysis of Organizational Conflict." *Administrative Science Quarterly* 20:489–508.
Lowery, S. A., and M. L. DeFluer. 1988. *Milestones in Mass Communication Research*. 2d ed. Longman.
Lowi, T. 1969. *The End of Liberalism*. Norton.
———. 1971. *The Politics of Disorder*. Basic Books.
Luhmann, N. 1990. *Essays on Self-Reference*. Columbia U.
Lukes, S. 1973. *Individualism*. Harper Torchbooks.
———. 1977. *Essays in Social Theory*. Macmillan
Lundberg, G. A. 1939. *Foundations of Sociology*. Macmillan.
Luszki, M. B. 1958. *Interdisciplinary Team Research Methods and Problems*. National Training Laboratories. Cited in Klein 1990a.
Lyne, J. R. 1983. "Ways of Going Public." In Zarefsky, Sillars, and Rhodes.
———. 1989. "Arguing Science." In Gronbeck.
———. 1990a. "The Culture of Inquiry." *QJS* 76:192–224.
———. 1990b. "Bio-Rhetorics." In H. W. Simons, ed., *The Rhetorical Turn*. U. Chicago.
———. 1991. "Claiming the High Ground." In D. W. Parsons, ed., *Argument in Controversy*. SCA.
Lyne, J. R., and H. F. Howe. 1986. "Punctuated Equilibria." *QJS* 72:132–47.
———. 1990. "The Rhetoric of Expertise." *QJS* 76:134–51.
Lyotard, J.-F. 1984. *The Postmodern Condition*. U. Minnesota.
———. 1988. Interview (by W. van Reijen and D. Veerman). *TCS* 5:277–310.
Mabbott, T. D. 1948. *The State and the Citizen*. Hutchison Library.
Maciariello, J. A. 1975. *Dynamic Benefit-Cost Analysis*. Heath.

MacIntyre, A. 1971. "Rationality and the Explanation of Action." *Against the Self Images of the Age*. Schocken.
———. 1979 "The Idea of a Social Science." In B. R. Wilson, ed. *Rationality*. Blackwell.
———. 1981. *After Virtue*. U. Notre Dame.
Mackenzie, D. 1980. *Statistics in Britain, 1865–1930*. Edinburgh U.
Macnamara, J. 1986. *A Border Dispute*. MIT.
Macnamara, R. 1987. *Blundering into disaster*. Pantheon.
MacPherson, C. B. 1977. *The Life and Times of Liberal Democracy*. Oxford U.
Madison, J. 1954. "Federalist No. 10. " In R. H. Gabriel, ed., *On the Constitution*. Bobbs-Merrill.
Maier, J., and R. W. Weatherhead, eds. 1964. *Politics of Change in Latin America*. Praeger.
Malinowski, B. 1923. "The Context of Situation." In C. K. Ogden and I. A. Richards, *The Meaning of Meaning*. Harcourt.
Mandel, E. 1975. *Late Capitalism*. Humanities Press.
Mandelbaum, M. 1982. "Subjective, Objective, and Conceptual Relativisms." In M. Krausz and J. W. Meiland, eds. *Relativism*. U. Notre Dame.
Mannheim, K. 1936. *Ideology and Utopia*. Harcourt.
———. 1952. *Essays on the Sociology of Knowledge*. Ed. P. Keckemeti. Routledge.
Mansbridge, J. J. 1976. "Town Meeting Democracy." In P. Collier, ed., *Dilemmas of Democracy*. Harcourt Brace Jovanovich.
Maquet, J. J. 1949. *Sociologie de la Connaissance*. Nauwelaerts.
March, J. G. 1962. "The Business Firm as a Political Coalition." *Journal of Politics* 24:662–78.
———. 1978. "Bounded Rationality, Ambiguity, and the Engineering of Choice." *Bell Journal of Economics*. 587–608.
———, ed. 1965. *The Handbook of Organizations*. Rand McNally.
March, J. G., and J. P. Olsen. 1976. *Ambiguity and Choice in Organizations*. Universitetsforlaget.
March, J. G., and H. A. Simon. 1958. *Organizations*. Wiley.
Marcus, G. E., and M. J. Fischer. 1986. *Anthropology as Cultural Critique*. U. Chicago.
Marger, M. N. 1987. *Elites and Masses*. 2d ed. Wadsworth.
Marshall, J. 1977. "Minds, Machines and Metaphors." *SSS* 7:475–88.
Martin, E. D. 1920. *The Behavior of Crowds*. Harper & Row.
Maslow, A. H. 1954. *Motivation and Personality*. Harper & Row.
May, A., and K. Rowan, eds. 1982. *Inside Information*. Constable.
Mayo, E. 1945. *The Social Problems of an Industrial Civilization*. Harvard U.
McCarthy, T. 1982. *The Critical Theory of Jurgen Habermas*. MIT.
McCloskey, D. N. 1983. "Notes on the Character of Argument in Modern Economics." In Zarefsky, Sillars, and Rhodes.
———. 1985. *The Rhetoric of Economics*. U. Wisconsin.
———. 1987. "Rhetoric within the Citadel." In Wenzel.

McConnell, G. 1966. *Private Power and American Democracy.* Knopf.
McConnell, M. 1987. *Challenger.* Doubleday.
McCornack, S., and R. L. Husband, 1986. "Long-Term Organizational Conflict." Conference on Organizational Policy and Development, University of Louisville.
McCrae, D., Jr. 1973. "Science and the Formation of Policy in a Democracy." *Minerva* 11:228–42.
McGee, M. C. 1983. "Social Movement as Meaning." *CSSJ* 34:74–77.
McGregor, D. 1960. *The Human Side of Enterprise.* McGraw-Hill.
———. 1966. *Leadership and Motivation.* MIT.
———. 1967. *The Professional Manager.* McGraw-Hill.
McGuire, J. W. 1982. "Management Theory." *Business Horizons* 25:31–37.
McKerrow, R. E. 1980a. "Argument Communities." In Rhodes and Newell.
———. 1980b. "On Fields and Rational Enterprises." In Rhodes and Newell.
McKiernan, D. 1989. "Television and the Dialectic of Community." *Media Development* 1:33–36.
McPhee, R. D. 1985. "Formal Structure and Organizational Communication." In McPhee and Tompkins.
McPhee, R. D., and P. K. Tompkins, eds. 1985. *Organizational Communication.* Sage.
McQuail, D. 1984. *Mass Communication Theory.* Sage.
———. 1986. "Diversity in Political Communication." In Golding, Murdock, and Schlesinger.
Mead, G. H. 1932. *Philosophy of the Present.* Open Court.
———. 1954. *Mind, Self, and Society.* U. Chicago.
Meadows, A. J. 1967. "The Citation Characteristics of Astronomical Research Literature." *Journal of Documentation* 23:28–33.
Megill, A. 1983. "Some Tentative Reflections on Ethos, Argument, and Methodology in the History of Ideas." In Zarefsky, Sillars, and Rhodes.
Meier, R., ed. 1989. *Norms in Argumentation.* Foris.
Meiklejohn, A. 1948. *Free Speech and Its Relation to Self-Government.* Harper & Row.
Mendelsohn, E. 1977. "The Social Construction of Scientific Knowledge." In E. Mendelsohn, P. Weingert, and P. Whitley, eds., *The Social Production of Scientific Knowledge.* Reidel.
Mencken, H. L. 1955. "On Being an American." In J. T. Farrell, ed., *Prejudices.* Vintage.
Menzel, H. 1962. "Planned and Unplanned Scientific Communication." In B. Barber and W. Hirsch, eds., *The Sociology of Science.* Free Press.
Merriam, C. E., and H. F. Gosnell. 1924. *Non-Voting.* U. Chicago.
Merton, R. K. 1949. *Social Theory and Social Structure.* Free Press.
———. 1957a. The Role-Set." *BJS* 8:106–20.
———. 1957b. *Social Theory and Social Structure.* Free Press.
———. 1961. *The Bureaucratic Personality.*

———. 1970. "Paradigm for the Sociology of Knowledge." In Curtis and Petras.
Meyer, J. W., and B. Rowan. 1977. "Institutionalized Organizations." *AJS* 83:340–63.
Meyer, M. W. 1972. *Bureaucratic Structure and Authority.* Harper & Row.
Meyrowitz, J. 1985. *No Sense of Place.* Oxford U.
Michels, R. 1962. *Political Parties.* Collier.
Mickunas, A. 1987. "Perelman on Justice and Political Institutions." In J. C. Golden and J. J. Pilotta, eds. *Practical Reasoning in Human Affairs.* Reidel.
Mill, J. S. 1956. *On Liberty.* Bobbs-Merrill.
Miller, C. R. 1983. "Fields of Argument and Special *Topoi.*" In Zarefsky, Sillars, and Rhodes.
Miller, C. M. 1989. "Assuming Burdens of Advocacy in a Technical Controversy." In Gronbeck.
Miller, G. R., and H. W. Simons, eds. 1974. *Perspectives on Communication in Social Conflict.* Prentice-Hall.
Mill, J. S. 1956. *On Liberty.* Bobbs-Merrill.
Milliken, J. 1990. "Traveling across Borders." *SE* 4:317–21.
Mills, C. W. 1956. *The Power Elite.* Oxford U.
———. 1959. *The Sociological Imagination.* Oxford U.
———. 1963. *Power, Politics, and People.* Ed. I. Horowitz. Oxford U.
———. 1970. "Social Psychology." In Stone and Farberman.
Mitroff, I. I. 1974. *The Subjective Side of Science.* Elsevier.
———. 1983. *Stakeholders of the Organizational Mind.* Jossey-Bass.
Mitroff, I. I., and W. Bennis. 1993. *The Unreality Industry.* Oxford U.
Montag, W. 1988. "What Is at Stake in the Debate on Postmodernism?" In E. A. Kaplan, ed., *Postmodernism and its Discontents.* Verso.
Morone, J. A. 1990. *The Democratic Wish.* Basic Books.
Moore, W., ed. 1972. *Technology and Social Change.* Quadrangle.
Morgan, G. 1986. *Images of Organization.* Sage.
Morgan, G., P. J. Frost, and L. R. Pondy, "Organizational Symbolism." In Pondy et al.
Morgan, G., and L. Smircich. 1980. "The Case for Qualitative Research." *AMR* 5:491–500.
Morone, J. A. 1992. *The Democratic Wish.* Basic Books.
Mosca, G. 1939. *The Ruling Class.* McGraw-Hill.
Mouzelis, N. P. 1967. *Organisation and Bureaucracy.* Routledge.
Mowlana, H., and L. Wilson. 1990. *The Passing of Modernity.* Longman.
Moyers, B. 1989. *A World of Ideas.* Doubleday.
Moynihan, D. P. 1993. *Pandaemonium.* Oxford U.
Mulkay, M. 1979. *Science and the Sociology of Knowledge.* Allen & Unwin.
Mullins, N. C. 1968. "The Distribution of Social and Cultural Properties in Informal Communication Networks among Biological Scientists." *ASR* 33:786–97.
Mukerji, C. 1990. *A Fragile Power.* Princeton U.
Nadel, S. F. 1963. *The Theory of Social Structure.* Cohen and West.

Naess, A. 1966. *Communication and Argument.* Allen & Unwin.
Nagel, E. 1961. *The Structure of Science.* Harcourt, Brace & World.
Negt, O., and A. Kluge. 1979. "The Proletarian Public Sphere." In A. Matterlart and S. Seigelaub, eds., *Communication and Class Struggle,* vol. 1. International General.
Neitzsche, F. 1968. *The Will to Power.* Vintage.
Nelkin, D. 1981. "Science and Technology Policy and the Democratic Process." In A. Teich, ed., *Technology and Man's Future.* 3d ed. St. Martin's.
———. 1987. *Selling Science.* Freeman.
Nelson, B. 1981. *On the Roads to Modernity.* Rowman & Littlefield.
Nelson, J. S. 1983. "Models, Statistics, and Other Tropes of Politics." In Zarefsky, Sillars, and Rhodes.
———. 1988. "Approaches, Opportunities, and Priorities in the Rhetorical of Political Inquiry." *SE* 2:21–42.
Nelson, J. S., and A. Megill. 1986. "Rhetoric of Inquiry." *QJS* 72:20–37.
Nelson, J. S., A. Megill, and D. N. McCloskey, eds. 1987. *The Rhetoric of the Human Sciences.* U. Wisconsin.
Nelson, D. E. 1992. *Business and Economic Reporting.* Ohio Journalism Monograph Series, 2. Scripps School of Journalism, Ohio U.
Neuman, W. R. 1986. *The Paradox of Mass Politics.* Harvard U.
Newcomb, T. M., R. H. Turner, and P. E. Converse. 1965. *Social Psychology.* Holt.
Newell, N. D. 1982. *Creation and Evolution.* Columbia U.
Nisbet, R. 1953; reissued 1990. *The Quest for Community.* ICS Press.
Nisbet, R. 1969. "Project Camelot." In P. Rieff, ed., *On Intellectuals.* Doubleday.
Nisbett, R. E., and L. Ross. 1980. *Human Inference.* Prentice-Hall.
Nisbett, R. E., and T. D. Wilson. 1977a. "The Halo Effect." *JASP* 35:250–56.
———. 1977b. "Telling More Than We Can Know." *Psychological Review* 84:231–59.
Nodia, G. 1994. "Nationalism Is Vital to Democracy." In P. C. Cozic, ed. *Nationalism and Ethnic Conflict.* Greenhaven.
Nord, W. R. 1974. "The Failure of Current Applied Behavioral Science—A Marxian Perspective." *Journal of Applied Behavioral Science* 10:557–73.
Oberschall, A. 1973. *Social Conflict and Social Movements.* Prentice-Hall.
O'Connor, J. 1974. *The Corporations and the State.* Harper & Row.
Offe, C., and V. Ronge. 1975. "Theses on the Theory of the State." *New German Critique* 2:137–47.
O'Keefe, B. J. 1988. "The Logic of Message Design." *CM* 55:80–103.
———. 1989a. "Theory and Practice in the Constitution of Communication Processes." Tenth Annual Conference on Discourse Processes, Temple U., Philadelphia, Pennsylvania.
———. 1989b. "Recent Developments in the Study of Message Design Logic." Southern Communication Association, Louisville, Kentucky.
———. 1990. "The Logic of Regulative Communication: Understanding the Ra-

tionality of Message Designs." In J. Dillard, ed., *Seeking Compliance*. Gorsuch-Scarisbrick.
———. 1992. "Developing and Testing Rational Models of Message Design." *HCR* 18:637–49.
O'Keefe, B. J., and P. J. Benoit. 1982. "Childrens' Arguments." In Cox and Willard.
O'Keefe, B. J., and S. A. McCornack. 1987. "Message Design Logic and Message Goal Structure." *HCR* 1987:68–92.
O'Keefe, D. J. 1987. "Describing Messages." Speech Communication Association, Boston, Massachusetts.
Olson, M. 1965. *The Logic of Collective Action*. Harvard U.
———. 1970. *Power in Societies*. Macmillan.
Oppenheim, Felix. 1975. "Self-Interest and Public Interest." *Political Theory* 3:259–77.
Ortega y Gassett, J. 1950. *The Revolt of the Masses*. New American Library.
Orwell, G. 1949. *Nineteen Eighty-Four, a Novel*. Harcourt, Brace.
Osborn, Michael. 1983. "Rhetoric in the Human Sciences." In Zarefsky, Sillars, and Rhodes.
Ozick, C. 1987. "Science and Letters." *New York Times Book Review*, 27 September, p. 3.
Pagels, H. 1983. *The Cosmic Code*. Bantam.
Pangle, T. L. 1992. *The Enobling of Democracy*. Johns Hopkins U.
Parenti, M. 1983. *Democracy for the Few*. 4th ed. Heath.
Pareto, V. 1966. *Sociological Writings*. Praeger.
Park, R. E. 1936. "Human Ecology." *AJS* 17:1–15.
Parry, G. 1969. *Political Elites*. Praeger.
Parsons, T. 1949. *The Structure of Social Action*. Free Press.
———. 1951a. *The Social System*. Free Press.
———. 1951b. "An Approach to the Sociology of Knowledge." In Curtis and Petras.
———. 1961a. *Suggestions for a Sociological Approach to the Theory of Organizations*. Free Press.
———. 1961b."Culture and the Social System." In T. Parsons et al., eds. *Theories of Society*, vol. 2. Free Press.
Pateman, C. 1970. *Participation and Democratic Theory*. Cambridge U.
Perrow, C. 1961. "The Analysis of Goals in Complex Organizations." *ASR* 26:854–66.
———. 1979. *Complex Organizations*. 2d ed. Scott, Foresman.
———. 1984. *Normal Accidents*. Basic.
Peters, J. D. 1989. "Democracy and American Mass Communication Theory." *Communication* 11:199–220.
Peters, T. N. 1989. "On the Natural Development of Public Activity." In Gronbeck.
Pettigrew, A. M. 1973. *The Politics of Organizational Decision Making*. Tavistock.

———. 1975. "Towards a Political Theory of Organizational Intervention." *Human Relations* 28:191–208.
———. 1979. "On Studying Organizational Cultures." *ASQ* 24:570–81.
Petty, R. E., and J. T. Cacioppo. 1986. "The Elaboration Likelihood Model of Persuasion." In L. Berkowitz, ed., *Advances in Experimental Social Psychology,* vol. 19. Academic.
Pfeifer, M. P., and G. L. Snodgrass. 1990. "The Continued Use of Retracted, Invalid Scientific Literature." *JAMA* 263:1420–23.
Pfeil, F. 1988. "Postmodernism as a 'Structure of Feeling.'" In C. Nelson and L. Grossberg, eds., *Marxism and the Interpretation of Culture.* U. Illinois.
Pfund, N., and L. Hofstadter. 1981. "Biomedical Innovation and the Press." *Journal of Communication* 31:138–54.
Pierce, C. S. 1934. *Collected Papers of Charles S. Pierce,* vol. 5. Ed. C. Hartshorne and P. Weiss. Harvard U.
Polanyi, M. 1958. *Personal Knowledge.* Harper & Row.
———. 1962. "The Republic of Science." *Minerva* 1:54–73.
———. 1967. "The Growth of Science in Society." *Minerva* 5:533–45.
Polsby, N. 1980. *Community Power and Political Theory.* 2d ed. Yale U.
Pondy, L., et al., eds. *Organizational Symbolism.* JAI.
Poole, M. S. 1985. "Communication and Organizational Climates." In McPhee and Tompkins.
Poole, M. S., and R. D. McPhee. 1983. "A Structurational Theory of Organizational Climate." In Putnam and Pacanowsky.
Popov, Z. 1990. "Totalitarianism and Education." *Inquiry* 6:3–4.
Popper, K. R. 1950. *The Open Society and Its Enemies.* Rev. ed. Princeton U.
———. 1959. *The Logic of Scientific Discovery.* Harper & Row.
———. 1963. *Conjectures and Refutations.* Routledge.
———. 1970. "Normal Science and its Dangers." In I. Lakatos and A. Musgrave, eds., *Criticism and the Growth of Knowledge.* Cambridge U.
———. 1972. *Objective Knowledge.* Oxford U.
Postman, N. 1985. *Amusing Ourselves to Death.* Viking.
Pranger, R. J. 1968. *The Eclipse of Citizenship.* Holt.
President's Commission for a National Agenda for the Eighties. 1980. *Science and Technology Promises and Dangers in the Eighties.* U.S. Government Printing Office.
Price, D. K. 1962. *Government and Science.* Oxford U.
———. 1965. *The Scientific Estate.* Harvard U.
Price, D. de S. 1961. *Science Since Babylon.* Yale U.
———. 1963. *Little Science, Big Science.* Columbia U.
———. 1965. "Networks of Scientific Papers." *Science* 149:510–15.
———. 1970. "Citation Measures of Hard Science, Soft Science, Technology and Nonscience." *Communication Among Scientists and Engineers.* Heath.
Price, D. de S., and D. Beaver. 1966. "Collaboration in an Invisible College." *AP* 21: 1011–18.

Procter, D. E. 1990. "The Dynamic Spectacle." *QJS* 76:117–33.
Pugh, D. S., et al. 1973. "The Context of Organization Structures." In Scott and Cummings.
Putnam, L. L. 1983. "The Interpretive Perspective." In Putnam and Pacanowsky.
Putnam, L. L., and M. E. Pacanowsky, eds. 1983. *Communication and Organizations.* Sage.
Putnam, R. D. 1976. *The Comparative Study of Political Elites.* Prentice-Hall.
Quine, W. V. O. 1960. *Word and Object.* Wiley.
———. 1969. *Ontological Relativity and Other Essays.* Columbia U.
Rapaczynski, A. 1987. *Nature and Politics.* Cornell U.
Rawls, J. 1971. *A Theory of Justice.* Harvard U.
Reagan, M. D. 1969. *Science and the Federal Patron.* Oxford U.
Redner, H. 1987a. "Pathologies of Science." *SE* 1:215–47.
———. 1987b. "The Institutionalization of Science." *SE* 1:37–59.
Reich, R. B., ed. 1988. *The Power of Public Ideas.* Ballinger.
Reijen, W. van, and D. Veerman. 1988. "An Interview with Jean-François Lyotard." *TCS* 5:277–310.
Reisman, D. 1950. *The Lonely Crowd.* Yale U.
Reiter, H. L. 1987. *Parties and Elections in Corporate America.* St. Martin's.
Rescher, N. 1973. *The Primacy of Practice.* Oxford U.
———. 1977a. *Methodological Pragmatism.* Oxford U.
———. 1977b. *Dialectics.* SUNY.
Rhodes, J., and S. Newell. 1980. *Proceedings of the [first] Summer Conference on Argumentation.* SCA.
Ricci, D. M. 1971. *Community Power and Democratic Theory.* Random House.
Ricoeur, P. 1965. *History and Truth.* Northwestern U.
———. 1972."The Political Paradox." In H. Y. Jung, ed., *Existential Phenomenology and Political Theory.* Henry Regnery.
Richards, I. A. 1965. *The Philosophy of Rhetoric.* Oxford.
Rieke, R. 1981. "Investigating Legal Argument as a Field." In Ziegelmueller and Rhodes.
Riesman, D., N. Glazer, and R. Denny. 1950. *The Lonely Crowd.* Yale U.
Riley, P. "A Structurationist Account of Political Culture." *ASQ* 28:414–37.
Roberts, D. 1991. "The *Historikerstreit.*" *Thesis Eleven.* 30:33–55.
Rogers, C. 1970. *On Becoming a Person.* Houghton Mifflin.
Rogers, E. M. 1962. *Diffusion of Innovations.* Free Press.
Rogers, L. 1958. "Political Philosophy in the Twentieth Century." In R. Young, ed. *Approaches to the Study of Politics.* Northwestern U.
Roloff, M. E., and C. R. Berger, eds. 1982. *Social Cognition and Communication.* Sage.
Rorty, R. 1979. *Philosophy and the Mirror of Nature.* Princeton U.
———. 1982. *Consequences of Pragmatism.* U. Minnesota.
———. 1983. "Postmodernist Bourgeois Liberalism." *Journal of Philosophy* 80:583–89.
———. 1987a. "Science as Solidarity." In Nelson, Megill, and McCloskey.

———. 1987b. "Thugs and Theorists." *Political Theory* 15:564–80.
———. 1989. *Contingency, Irony, and Solidarity.* Cambridge U.
Rosaldo, M. Z. 1980. *Knowledge and Passion.* Cambridge U.
Rose, D. 1982. "Occasions and Forms of Anthropological Experience." In J. Ruby, ed. *A Crack in the Mirror.* U. Pennsylvania.
Rosen, J. 1991. "The Erosion of Public Time." *Quill* 79:22–23.
Rosen, L. 1984. *Bargaining for Reality.* U. Chicago.
Rosenau, J. N. 1967. "Foreign Policy as an Issue Area." In J. N. Rosenau, ed., *Domestic Sources of Foreign Policy.* Free Press.
Rosenbaum, W. A. 1973. *The Politics of Environmental Concern.* Praeger.
———. 1975. *Political Culture.* Praeger.
Rosenberg, A. 1983a. "Human Science and Biological Science." In N. Rescher, ed., *Scientific Explanation and Understanding.* U. Press of America.
Ross, R. G. 1951. Editor's Introduction. In R. G. Ross, ed. *Bradley—Ethical Studies.* Bobbs-Merrill.
Rourke, F. E. 1973. *Bureaucracy and Foreign Policy.* Johns Hopkins U.
Rouse, J. 1987. *Knowledge and Power.* Cornell U.
Rousseau, J. J. 1954. *The Social Contract.* Henry Regnery.
Rowland, R. 1986. "The Relationship between the Public and Technical Spheres of Argument." *Science* 236:267–70.
Ryan, M. 1988. "Postmodern Politics." *TCS* 5:559–76.
Sahlins, M. 1976. *Culture and Practical Reason.* U. Chicago.
Said, E. 1986. "Foucault and the Imagination of Power." In D. C. Hoy, ed. *Foucault.* Blackwell.
Salkever, S. G. 1987. "The Crisis of Liberal Democracy." In Deutsch and Soffer.
Saunders, J. J. 1949. *The Age of Revolution.* Roy Publishers.
Schama, S. 1989. *Citizens.* Knopf.
Schambra, W. A. 1990. "Foreword" to R. Nisbet, *The Quest for Community.* ICS Press.
Schattschneider, E. E. 1960. *The Semisovereign People.* Holt.
Schein, E. H. 1965. *Organizational Psychology.* Prentice-Hall.
Scheler, M. 1924 "Probleme einer Soziologie des Wissens." *Versuche zu einer Soziologie des Wissens,* vol. 2. Dunker and Humbolt.
———. 1926. *Die Wissenformen und die Gesellschaft.* Verlag.
———. 1973. *Formalism in Ethics and Nonformal Ethics of Values.* Northwestern U.
Schelling, T. 1948. *Toward a Theory of Strategy for International Conflict.* Rand.
———. 1960. *The Strategy of Conflict.* Oxford U.
———. 1978. *Micromotives and Macrobehavior.* Norton.
Schiappa, E. 1983. "Theorists Understanding 'The Public': An Informal Study in Technical Argument." In Zarefsky, Sillars, and Rhodes.
———. 1989. "'Spheres of Argument' as *Topoi* for the Critical Study of Power/Knowledge." In Gronbeck.
Schiller, D. 1986. "Transformation of News in the U.S. Information Market." In Golding, Murdock, and Schlesinger.

Schiller, H. I. 1969. *Mass Communications and American Empire.* Kelley.
———. 1981. *Who Knows: Information in the Age of the Fortune 500.* Ablex.
———. 1986. *Information and the Crisis Economy.* Oxford U.
Schlesinger, A. M. Jr. 1992. *The Disuniting of America.* Norton.
Schmitt, R. L. 1972. *The Reference Other Orientation.* Southern Illinois U.
Schoek, H., and J. Wiggins. 1960. *Scientism and Values.* Van Nostrand.
Schrag, C. O. 1985. *Communication Praxis and the Space of Subjectivity.* U. Indiana.
Schumpeter, J. A. 1942. *Capitalism, Socialism, and Democracy.* 3d ed. Harper & Row.
Schusterman, R. 1988. "Postmodernist Aestheticism." *TCS* 5:337–56.
Schutz, A. 1962. *Collected Papers,* vol. 1. Ed. M. Natanson. Nijhoff.
Schweder, R. A. 1986. "Storytelling among the Anthropologists." *New York Times Book Review.* 21 September, 1 and 3–6.
Scott, M. B. 1970. "Functional Analysis." In Stone and Farberman.
Scott, W. H., et al. 1956. *Technical Change and Industrial Relations.* Liverpool U.
Scott, W. E., and L. L. Cummings. 1973. *Readings in Organizational Behavior and Human Performance.* Irwin.
Scriven, M. 1980. "The Philosophical and Pragmatic Significance of Informal Logic." In Blair and Johnson.
———. 1989. Plenary Address. Second Conference on Informal Logic, U. of Windsor.
Seeman, M. 1967. "On the Personal Consequences of Alienation in Work." In L. W. Porter et al., eds., *Studies in Organizational Behavior and Management.* 2d ed. InText.
Seeger, M. W. 1986. "The Challenger Tragedy and Search for Legitimacy." *CSSJ* 37:147–57.
Seibert, F. S., T. Peterson, and W. Schramm. 1956. *Four Theories of the Press.* U. Illinois.
Sen, A. 1977. "Rational Fools." *PPA* 6:317–44.
Sennett, R. 1974. *The Fall of Public Man.* Vintage.
———. 1980. *Authority.* Vintage.
Shaw, M. E., and P. R. Costanzo. 1970. *Theories of Social Psychology.* McGraw-Hill.
Sheppard, S. A., and R. D. Rieke. 1983. "Categories of Reasoning Legal Argument." In Zarefsky, Sillars, and Rhodes.
Sherif, M., and C. Hovland. 1961. *Social Judgement.* Yale U.
Sherif, M., and C. W. Sherif. 1966. *Groups in Harmony and Tension.* Octagon.
———. 1969. "Interdisciplinary Coordination as a Validity Check." In M. Sherif and C. W. Sherif, eds., *Interdisciplinary Relationships in the Social Sciences.* Aldine.
Shibutani, T. 1955. "Reference Groups as Perspectives." *AJS* 60:562–69.
———. 1961. *Society and Personality.* Prentice-Hall.
———. 1962. "Reference Groups and Social Control." In A. Rose, ed., *Human Behavior and Social Processes.* Houghton Mifflin.

Shils, E. A. 1962. "The Theory of Mass Society." *Diogenes* 39:45–66.
———. 1967. "Primordial, Personal, Sacred, and Civil Ties." In P. O. Rose, ed., *The Study of Society*. Michigan State U.
Shirer, W. L. 1960. *The Rise and Fall of the Third Reich*. Simon & Schuster.
Shotter, J. 1984. *Social Accountability and Selfhood*. Blackwell.
———. 1989. "What Is Special about Normal Circumstances." In Meier.
Shweder, R. A., and R. A. LeVine. 1984. *Culture Theory*. Cambridge U.
Sillars, M. O. 1980. "Defining Movements Rhetorically." *Southern Speech Communication Journal* 46:17–32.
Simmel, G. 1955. *Conflict and the Web of Group-Affiliations*. Free Press.
Simon, H. A. 1945. *Administrative Behavior*. Macmillan.
———. 1957. *Models of Man*. Wiley.
———. 1964. "On the Concept of Organizational Goals." *ASQ* 9:1–22.
———. 1977. *The New Science of Management Decision*. Rev. ed. Prentice-Hall.
———. 1976. *Administrative Behavior*. 3d ed. Macmillan.
———. 1986. "Alternative Visions of Rationality." In H. Arkes and K. Hammond, eds., *Judgment and Decision-Making*. Cambridge U.
Simons, H. W. 1982. "Genres, Rules, and Collective Rhetorics." *QJS* 30:181–88.
———, ed. 1989. *Rhetoric in the Human Sciences*. Sage.
Simons, H. W., and E. W. Mechling. 1981."The Rhetoric of Political Movements." In D. Nimmo and K. Sanders, ed., *Handbook of Political Communication*. Sage.
Skinner, Q., ed. 1985. *The Return of Grand Theory in the Human Sciences*. Cambridge U.
Skolnick, J. H. 1969. *The Politics of Protest*. Ballantine.
Slavin, R. E. 1983. *Cooperative Learning*. Longman.
Small, H. G. 1978. "Cited Documents as Concept Symbols." *SSS* 8:327–40.
Smircich, L. 1983. "Concepts of Culture and Organizational Analysis." *ASQ* 28:339–58.
Smircich, L., and M. B. Calas. 1987. "Organizational Culture." In Jablin, Putnam, Roberts, and Porter.
Smith, A. 1981. *The Geopolitics of Information*. Oxford U.
Smith, Douglas Bradley. 1983. "Technical Writing as Argumentation." In Zarefsky, Sillars, and Rhodes.
Snyder, L. L. 1976. *Varieties of Nationalism*. Dryden.
Socolow, R. H. 1976. "Failures of Discourse." In Tribe, Schelling, and Voss.
Solow, R. M. 1990. "Can Economics Be Made Easy?" *New York Times Book Review*. March 4:9.
Spanier, J., and E. M. Uslaner. 1978. *How American Foreign Policy Is Made*. 2d ed. Holt.
Speier, H. 1970. "The Social Determination of Ideas." In Curtis and Petras.
Stam, R. 1988. "Mikhail Bakhtin and Left Cultural Critique." In E. A. Kaplan, ed. *Postmodernism and Its Discontents*. Verso.
Stark, W. 1958. *The Sociology of Knowledge*. Free Press.

———. 1967. "Sociology of Knowledge." In P. Edwards, ed., *Encyclopedia of Philosophy.* Collier/Macmillan.
Stewart, C., C. Smith, and R. E. Denton, Jr. 1984. *Persuasion and Social Movements.* Waveland.
Stich, S., and R. Nisbett. 1984. "Expertise, Justification, and the Psychology of Inductive Reasoning." In Haskell.
Stone, G. P., and H. A. Farberman. 1970. *Social Psychology through Symbolic Interaction.* Ginn.
Storer. N. 1966. *The Social System of Science.* Holt.
Storey, J. 1983. *Managerial Prerogative and the Question of Control.* Routledge & Kegan Paul.
Strauss, A. 1978. *Negotiations.* Jossey-Bass.
Sukosd, M. 1990. "From Propaganda to 'Offentlichkeit' in Eastern Europe." *Praxis International.* 10:39–63.
Sullivan, W. M. 1982. *Reconstructing Public Philosophy.* U. California.
Suppe, F., ed. 1977. *The Structure of Scientific Theories.* U. Illinois.
Sypher, B. D. 1990. *Case Studies in Organizational Communication.* Guilford.
Tannenbaum, A. S. 1966. *Social Psychology of the Work Organization.* Tavistock.
Tarski, A. 1956. *Logic, Semantics, Metamathematics.* Clarendon.
Taub, G. 1986. *Nobel Dreams.* Random House.
Taylor, C. A., and C. M. Condit. 1988. "Objectivity and Elites." *CSMC* 5:293–312.
Taylor, C. 1967. "Neutrality in Political Science." In P. Laslett and W. G. Runciman, eds., *Philosophy, Politics and Society.* 3d ser. Barnes & Noble.
———. 1971. "Interpretation and the Sciences of Man." *Review of Metaphysics.* 25:3–51.
———. 1986. "Foucault on Freedom and Truth." In D. C. Hoy, ed., *Foucault.* Blackwell.
Taylor, F. W. 1913. *The Principles of Scientific Management.* Harper.
Taylor, M., and C. Lomas. 1976. *The Rhetoric of the British Peace Movement.* Random House.
Taylor, Michael. 1982. *Community, Anarchy, and Liberty.* Cambridge U.
Thompson, E. T., and E. C. Hughes, eds. 1958. *Race.* Free Press.
Thompson, J. D. 1967. *Organizations in Action.* McGraw-Hill.
Tinder, Glen. 1976. "Community." *Yale Review* 550–64.
Tocqueville, A. de. 1945. *Democracy in America.* 2 vols. Vintage.
Tolbert, P. S. 1985. "Institutional Environments and Resource Dependence." *ASQ* 30:1–13.
Tompkins, P. K. 1981. "On Seeing the Rhetorical Situation with an Omniscient Eye." *QJS* 67:93–95.
———. 1984. "The Functions of Human Communication in Organization." In C. C. Arnold and J. W. Bowers, eds., *Handbook of Rhetorical and Communication Theory.* Allyn & Bacon.
———. 1987. "Translating Organizational Theory." In Jablin et al.

Tompkins, P. K., and G. Cheney. 1983. "Account Analysis of Organizations." In Putnam and Pacanowsky.

———. 1985. "Communication and Unobtrusive Control in Contemporary Organizations." In McPhee and Tompkins.

Tönnies, F. 1957. *Community and Society.* Michigan State U.

Toulmin, S. E. 1964. *The Uses of Argument.* Cambridge U.

———. 1972. *Human Understanding.* Princeton U.

———. 1976. *Knowing and Acting.* Macmillan.

———. 1990. *Cosmopolis.* Free Press.

Traber, M., ed. 1986. *The Myth of the Information Revolution.* Sage.

Trefil, J. 1989. "Beyond the Quark." *New York Times Magazine.* April 30:24–46.

Trenn, T. J. 1979. Preface to Ludwick Fleck, *Genesis and Development of a Scientific Fact.* U. Chicago.

Tribe, L. H., C. S. Schelling, and J. Voss, eds. 1976. *When Values Conflict.* Ballinger.

Tribe, L. H. 1972. "Policy Science." *PPA* 2:66–110.

Trigg, R. 1973. *Reason and Commitment.* Cambridge U.

Truman, D. 1951. *The Governmental Process.* Knopf.

———. 1959. "The American System in Crisis." *Political Science Quarterly.*

Turner, R., and L. M. Killian. 1957. *Collective Behavior.* Prentice-Hall.

Turner, S. 1980. *Sociological Explanation as Translation.* Cambridge U.

Ulam, S. M. 1976. *Adventures of a Mathematician.* Scribner's.

Unger, R. 1975. *Knowledge and Politics.* Free Press.

Veerman, D. 1988. "Introduction to Lyotard." *TCS* 5:271–76.

Verba, S., and N. Nie. 1972. *Participation in America.* Harper & Row.

Verba, S., N. Nie, and J. Kim. 1978. *Participation and Political Equality.* Harper & Row.

Von Bertalanffy, L. 1956. "General Systems Theory." *General Systems* 1:1–10.

Vroom, V. H. 1964. *Methods of Organizational Research.* U. Pittsburgh.

Wade, N. 1981. *The Nobel Dual.* Doubleday.

Walker, J. L. 1966. "A Critique of the Elitist Theory of Democracy." *APSR* 60:285–95.

Wall, Grenville. 1975. "The Concept of Interest Politics." *Politics and Society.* 487–510.

Wallinger, H. 1985. "Argumentation in Utility Hearings." In Cox, Sillars, and Walker.

Walter, B. 1967. "The Sociology of Knowledge and the Problem of Objectivity." In L. Gross, ed., *Sociological Theory.* Harper & Row.

Walton, D. N. 1989. "Reasoned Use of Expertise in Argumentation." *Argumentation* 3: 59–74.

Walton, R. E., and R. B. McKersie. 1965. *A Behavioral Theory of Labor Negotiations.* McGraw-Hill.

Walzer, Michael. 1983. *Spheres of Justice.* Basic Books.

Ward, L. 1883. *Dynamic Sociology.* 2 vols. Appleton.

Weaver, R. 1953. *The Ethics of Rhetoric.* Regnery.

Weber, M. 1905. *The Protestant Ethic and the Spirit of Capitalism.* Scribners.

———. 1946. *Essays in Sociology.* Oxford U.
———. 1947. *The Theory of Social and Economic Organization.* Glencoe.
Weick, K. E. 1976. "Educational Organizations as Loosely Coupled Systems." *ASQ* 21:1–19.
———. 1979. *The Social Psychology of Organizing.* 2d ed. Addison-Wesley.
———. 1983. "Organizational Communication." In Putnam and Pacanowsky.
———. 1987. "Theorizing about Organizational Communication." In Jablin et al.
Weimer, W. B. 1979. *Notes on the Methodology of Scientific Research.* Erlbaum.
———. 1984. "Why All Knowing Is Rhetorical." *JAFA* 20:63–71.
Weinstein, M. 1990. "Reflections on Democracy and Education." *Inquiry* 6:1 and 19.
Weisskopf, T. E. 1978. "The Irrationality of Capitalist Economic Growth." In R. C. Edwards, M. Reich, and T. E. Weisskopf, ed., *The Capitalist System.* 2d ed. Prentice-Hall.
Weitz, M., ed. 1966. *20th Century Philosophy.* Free Press.
Wenger, D. M., and T. Giuliano. 1982. "The Forms of Social Awareness." In W. J. Ickes and E. S. Knowles, eds., *Personality, Roles, and Social Behavior.* Springer-Verlag.
Wenzel, J. W. 1982a. "On Fields of Argument as Propositional Systems." *JAFA* 18:204–13.
———. 1982b. "Some Uses of Rhetoric in a Technological Age." SCA Convention paper.
———, ed. 1987. *Argument and Critical Practices.* SCA.
Westerlund, G., and S. Sjostrand. 1979. *Organizational Myths.* Harper & Row.
Westin, A. F., ed. 1971. *Information Technology in a Democracy.* Harvard U.
Whately, R. 1963. *Elements of Rhetoric.* Southern Illinois U.
Wheeless, L. R., and J. Grotz. 1976. "Communication and Measurement of Reported Self-Disclosure." *HCR* 3:338–46.
Whitley, R. 1984. "The Scientific Status of Management Research as a Practically Oriented Social Science." *JMS* 21:369–90.
———. 1986. *The Intellectual and Social Organization of the Sciences.* Oxford U.
Whittenberger-Keith, K. 1986. "Behaving Oneself: The Place of Manners in Contemporary American Culture." *Communication Yearbook 10.* M. L. McLaughlin, ed. Sage.
Whorf, B. L. 1956. *Language, Thought, and Reality.* MIT.
Whyte, W. H. 1956. *The Organization Man.* Simon & Schuster.
Wilkinson, P. 1971. *Social Movements.* Praeger.
Willard, C. A. 1981. "Argument Fields and Theories of Logical Types." *JAFA* 17:129–45.
———. 1982. "Argument Fields." In Cox and Willard.
———. 1983. *Argumentation and the Social Grounds of Knowledge.* U. Alabama.
———. 1987a. "Valuing Dissensus." In F. H. van Eemeren et al., eds., *Argumentation: Across the Lines of Discipline.* Foris.
———. 1987b. "L'argumentation et les Fondements Sociaux de la Connaisance." In A. Lempereur, ed. *L'argumentation.* Mardaga.

———. 1989a. *A Theory of Argumentation.* U. Alabama.
———. 1989b. "Argument as a Social Process." In Meier.
———. 1989c. "The Problem of the Public Sphere." In M. D. Hazen and D. C. Williams, eds., *Argumentation Theory and the Rhetoric of Assent.* U. Alabama.
Willard, C. A., and T. J. Hynes. 1991. "Valuing dissensus." Department of Communication, U. Louisville.
Williams, A. 1973. "Cost Benefit Analysis." In Wolfe.
Williams, D. C. 1987. "The Assent of Rhetoric." In Wenzel
Williams, F. 1987. *Technology and Communication Behavior.* Wadsworth.
Williams, M. 1970. "Reference Groups." *SQ* 11:545–54.
Williams, R. 1961. *Culture and Society.* Penguin.
———. 1979. *Politics and Letters.* Verso.
———. 1981. *Culture.* Fontana Books.
Wilson, B. R. 1979. *Rationality.* Blackwell.
Wilson, J. 1973. *Introduction to Social Movements.* Basic Books.
Wilson, T. P. 1970. "Normative and Interpretive Paradigms in Sociology." In J. D. Douglas, ed., *Understanding Everyday Life.* Aldine.
Winch, P. 1958. *The Idea of a Social Science and Its Relation to Philosophy.* Routledge.
———. 1964. "Understanding a Primitive Society." *APQ* 1:307–24.
Wiseman, H. 1967. *Political Systems.* Routledge.
Wittgenstein, L. 1922. *Tractatus Logico-Philosophicus.* Routledge.
———. 1953. *Philosophical Investigations.* Oxford U.
———. 1969. *On Certainty.* Harper & Row.
Wolfe, A. 1977. *The Limits of Legitimacy.* Free Press.
Wolfe, J. N., ed. 1973. *Cost Benefit and Cost Effectiveness.* Allen & Unwin.
Wolff, K. H. 1959. "The Sociology of Knowledge and Sociological Theory." In L. Gross, ed., *Symposium on Sociological Theory.* Harper & Row.
———. 1965. "Ernst Grunwald and the Sociology of Knowledge." *Journal of the History of the Behavioral Sciences* 1:152–64.
Wolff, R. P. 1968. *The Poverty of Liberalism.* Beacon.
———. 1970. *In Defense of Anarchism.* Harper & Row.
Wolin, S. 1960. *Politics and Vision.* Little, Brown.
Wood, J. L., and M. Jackson. 1982. *Social Movements.* Wadsworth.
Wood, R. C. 1964. "Scientists and Politics." In Gilpin and Wright.
Woodward, J. 1965. *Industrial Organization.* Oxford U.
Wright, J. D. 1976. *The Dissent of the Governed.* Academic.
Wrong, D. H. 1980. *Power.* Harper & Row.
Wyle, W. E. 1912. *The New Democracy.* Harper.
Young, F. D., ed. 1971. *Knowledge and Control.* Macmillan.
Zaleznik, A., and D. Moment. 1964. *The Dynamics of Interpersonal Behavior.* Wiley.
Zaltman, G. 1968. *Scientific Recognition and Communication Behavior in High Energy Physics.* American Institute of Physics.
Zaltman, G., and J. Blau. 1969. "A Note on an International Invisible College in Theoretical High Energy Physics." Quoted in Crane 1972.

Zarefsky, D. 1981. "'Reasonableness' in Public Policy." In Ziegelmueller and Rhodes.

———. 1982. "Persistent Questions in the Theory of Argument Fields." *JAFA* 18:191–203.

———. 1987. "Argumentation and the Politics of Criticism." In Wenzel.

Zarefsky, D., M. O. Sillars, and J. Rhodes, eds. *Argument in Transition*. SCA.

Zaretsky, I. I., and M. P. Leone, eds. 1974. *Religious Movements in Contemporary America*. Princeton U.

Zeckhauser, R. 1986. "The Muddled Responsibilities of Public and Private America." In W. Knowlton and R. Zeckhauser, eds., *American Society*. Ballinger.

Ziegelmueller, G., and J. Rhodes, eds. 1981. *Dimensions of Argument*. SCA.

Ziman, J. 1968. *Public Knowledge*. Cambridge U.

Znaniecki, F. W. 1934. *The Method of Sociology*. Rinehart.

———. 1940. *The Social Role of the Man of Knowledge*. Columbia U.

———. 1952. *Cultural Sciences*. U. Illinois.

———. 1955. *Social Relations and Social Roles*. Chandler.

Zucker, L. G. 1983. "Organizations as Institutions." In S. B. Bacharach, ed., *Research in the Sociology of Organizations*, vol. 2. JAI.

Index

Aaron, D., 121
Aaron, R., 22, 154, 244
Abbott, A., 154, 232, 300
Abell, P., 224
Abrams, E., 37, 155
Abravanel, H., 257
ACT UP (AIDS Coalition), 291–292. *See also* public, influence on science
Adams, J., 8, 119–121, 124, 148, 210
Adams, J. Q., 121
Adorno, T. W., 13, 76–77, 111, 115
adversarial relationship, 217
advertising, 45, 152, 162, 172, 304
Agor, W. H., 258
Albury, W. R., 134
Aldrich, H., 271
Alexander, P., 160
Almond, G., 76
Alter, P., 52
American studies, 191, 214
amusement parks, 62, 175
analytic philosophy, 238
Andrews, J. R., 75
Anthony, D., 252
Apel, K. P., 69
Apter, D., 300
Arafat, Y., 37–38
Archer, M. S., 224
Arendt, H., 76, 158
argument, 128, 185, 218, 223, 238, 249, 272–273
argumentation, 73, 101, 124, 145, 213
argument fields, 73, 83, 92, 104, 110, 126–129, 184–185, 217–244, 276, 295, 307
Argyris, C., 252, 256–257
Aristotle, 55, 71, 145, 151, 162, 197, 215, 294, 297
Arnold, M., 221
Aronson, E., 2
Aryan Nation, 66, 202, 229
Astley, W. G., 182
astrology, 122, 230
Auden, W. H., 12, 48
Auschwitz, 77, 316, 319
authenticity, 4, 6,16, 25–39, 252, 294
authority-dependence, 72, 74–75, 108, 128–129, 134–141, 172, 211, 228, 298, 310

Bachelard, G., 94
Bachrach, S. B., 36, 155, 271
Bacon, F., 14, 282
Bagdikian, B., 37, 155
Bailey, F. G., 16
Bakhtin, M. M., 202
Bakke, E. W., 256
Balthrop, V. W., 155
Balzac, H., 33
Barber, B., 155
Barker, E., 103
Barnard, C., 245
Barnes, B., 259
Barnett, S., 244
Bartley, W. W., 228, 274
Baudrillard, J., 16, 28–29, 176, 313
Baynes, K., 69, 72
Bazelon, D. L., 300
Bazerman, C., 240
Beard, C. A., 76, 134, 157
Beard, W., 76, 134, 157
Becker, H., 217
Behan, D., 48
behavioral medicine, 191
behaviorism, 92, 230, 233, 238, 259
Beisecker, B., 171
Bell, D., 151, 158, 243
Bellah, R. N., 12, 40, 42, 45, 52, 125
Bennett, J., 259, 300
Bennis, W., 29, 174–175
Benoit, P. J., 199, 243
Benson, J. K., 255
Berelson, B., 151, 153
Berger, P., 217

Berlant, J. L., 232
Berlinski, D. J., 268
Berman, M. 20, 24, 29, 71, 91, 117
Bernstein, R. J., 13, 22, 89, 91, 111, 115–116, 243
Beruit, 48, 113
Biddle, B. J., 271
biochemistry, 191, 214
bioecology, 194
biological/organismic metaphors, 267–270
biology, 73, 193, 214, 231
biophysics, 191
biopsychology, 191
biotechnology, 238, 309
Birnbaum, N., 11, 154, 168
Black, M., 258
Blackburn, R., 154, 252
Blair, J. A., 158
Blau, P. M., 271
Bledstein, B., 232
Bloor, D., 259
Blumberg, P., 252
Blumenberg, H., 12, 76
Blumer, H., 93
Blumstein, A., 144
Bogart, L., 37
Bohman, J., 69, 72
Bohr, N., 70, 92, 111
Bolsheviks, 281, 320–321
Boorstin, D., 11, 30
Booth, W., 71
borders, boundaries, border discourse, interfield or peripheral discourse, 94, 98, 114, 133, 166, 183–184, 191–192, 196, 207, 209, 212, 235–236, 239–240, 295, 318
Bormann, E. G., 229
Bosnia, 3, 44, 65, 299, 327, 331
Bourdieu, P., 201
Bové, P., 19, 91
Braden, W. W., 56
Bradley, F. H., 23, 279
Brashers, D. E., 290–292
Braverman, H., 252
Bryan, W. J., 121–122
Broad, W., 131, 247
Brooks, C., 114
Brooks, H., 290
Brown, J., 142
Brown, R. H., 190, 273
Browning, L. D., 253
Bruce, C., 144
Bruffee, K. A., 235–236
Brzezinski, Z. K., 85
Buber, M., 28, 41
Buchanan, S., 71, 81
Burch, P. H., Jr., 157
bureaucracy, 257–258
Burger, E. J., Jr., 308
Burgess, A., 92
Burke, K., 56, 189, 320
Burkes, D. M., 28
Burleson, B., 218
Burns, T., 271
Burrell, G., 267–268
Burundi, 3, 54, 331
Bury, J. B., 282, 286
Bush, G., 22, 121

Cacioppo, J. T., 80, 231
Cahoone, L. E., 76
Cambrosio, A., 193
Campbell, D. T., 182
Campbell, J. A., 93
Campbell, J. F., 229
Campbell, K. K., 56
Capra, F., 2, 33, 161
Capron, W. M., 144
Carey, J. W., 11, 158
Carnap, R., 98, 110
Cassirer, E., 72
Catlin, G. E. G., 267, 270
CBS, 301–302, 305
Chafee, Z., Jr., 158
Challenger disaster, 104, 273–274, 292, 295, 299
chaos physics, chaos metaphor, 92, 95, 193, 227, 230, 233, 275
Cheney, G., 274
Child, A., 101
Chomsky, N., 92, 154–156, 160, 299
Christenson, R. M., 85
Cicourel, A. V., 27, 98, 216
classical management theory, 251
class warfare, language of, 166–169
Clawson, D., 252
Clegg, S., 36
Clemmer, D., 92
Clinton, H. R., 12, 40–41, 46–47
Closure, 127–129, 237, 240, 290, 311, 318
CNN, 305

cognitive: complexity, 195, 207, 302–303; dissonance, 1, 195, 198
Cohen, C., 50, 324
Cohen, L. J., 217
Cole, M., 244
Coleman, J. S., 235
Collins, R., 193
commensurating discourse, 211–216. *See also* epistemology; incommensurability
Commission on Freedom of the Press, 158
common ground, 55–60
community, 40–67, 185, 294, 296, 298, 324; communitarians, 2, 17
Competition, conflict, opposition, 94–95, 130, 181, 198–200, 330. *See also* valuing dissensus
Comte, A., 57, 110
Conan Doyle, A., 33
Condit, C. M., 122–123
Conley, B. C., 144
Conner, S., 15, 29, 76
Connerton, P., 12
Connolly, W. E., 143, 154–155, 201, 264
Conrad, C., 271
consensus, 73, 133, 171, 206, 210, 228, 249
conventional message design logic, 27, 220, 261
conversation, 199, 205, 218–219, 222–223
Cook, D., 20
Cook, P. J., 144
Coolidge, C., 121, 250
Cordes, C., 136
Coser, L. A., 267–270
cost-benefit analysis, 9, 77, 101, 126–128, 143–145, 165, 170, 173, 209–211, 231, 237, 238, 297, 318
Cox, J. R., 311
Crawshay-Williams, R., 37
creationism, 128, 300–301
criminology, 192
critical theory, 172–174. *See also* Habermas
criticism, critics, and critique, 14, 68–86, 108–109, 140, 155
Croatia and Croats, 2–3, 59
Croly, H., 40, 46
Crowther, J. G., 245
C-SPAN, 295, 305
cultural: anthropology, 214, 230, 259; ecology, 191; history, 271
culture, 116–117, 146, 215, 218
Curtis, J. E., 100
Cutlip, S. M., 158
Cytology, 191

Dahl, R. A., 152, 158, 198
Dahrendorf, R., 326–327
Daniels, N., 77
Danton, G. J., 4, 119, 317
Darden, L., 193
Darwin, C., 61, 90, 138, 195, 197, 306
Darwinism, social, 120, 181, 197, 283, 288
Davidson, D., 98, 212
Davies, C. J., 144
Davies, P. C. W., 142
Davis, F., 222
Day, J., 258
Day, R., 258
decision-making, 145, 211, 225, 285
deconstruction, 227, 243–244
DeFluer, M. L., 161
Deiter, O. A. L., 272
Deleuze, G., 91, 97, 99
Delia, J. G., 205, 208, 218
Demac, D., 37, 155
demagoguery, 121–123, 152, 157, 162, 186, 298
demographics, 112–113, 117, 214
Denzin, N. K., 200, 276
Derrida, J., 63, 72, 115, 256
DeSario, J., 134
Descartes, R., 14–15, 22, 89, 282
determinism and freedom, 77, 89, 92, 97, 108, 110–116, 140, 276, 322. *See also* existential determination of thought
Deutsch, M., 11
Dewey, J., 1, 11, 13, 58, 69, 89, 98, 101, 119–121, 124–126, 149, 163, 166, 171, 178, 181–182, 197, 199, 207, 211, 248–249, 255, 293, 295, 306
Dews, P., 51
diffusion of medical information, 235
Dirac, P. A. M., 111
discipline and disciplines, 22, 88, 153–154, 171, 206, 219, 230–232, 293
Disney, 175, 313
distributive justice, 77, 101, 142, 171–172
Dixon, K., 222
Domhoff, W., 167
Douglas, M., 108–110, 223–225, 231, 287–288, 321
Doxtader, E., 319

Dretske, F. I., 28
Dreyfus, H. L., 96–97
Dunbar, N. R., 241
Dunn, W. N., 209, 211
Dunnett, M. D., 256
Dunwoody, S., 310
Durkheim, E., 57, 72, 100, 105, 108, 247, 270
Dye, T. R., 161, 169, 209

Eagleton, T., 142
Easton, D., 268
ecology: metaphor, 138, 190–200, 204, 217, 219, 257, 275; ecosystems, 137–138; ecotones, 191–192, 215, 238, 318; population, 271. *See also* argument fields; borders
economics, 233
Eddington, A., 111
education or pedagogy, 120, 124–126, 130, 159, 168, 206, 215, 297, 302
Eemeren, F. H. van, 322
Einstein, A., 68, 111, 307, 314
Eisenstadt, S. N., 15
electronmicroscopy, 260–261
Elias, N., 224, 247
elites: scientific, 106; political, 153, 157, 169, 298, 305; elite oligarchy, 123, 148, versus masses, 164, 167. *See also* pluralism
Elliott, P., 11, 37, 155
engineering, environmental, 191
Enlightenment, 12, 160, 267
enthymeme, 55, 98
Entman, R. M., 155, 298–299
environmentalism, 23, 64, 143, 154, 171, 173–174, 213–214, 228
epistemics, 3–5, 7, 10, 110, 163, 184–185, 189–216, 245, 275, 293
epistemology, 68–86, 100, 105, 126, 206, 209, 211–214, 323
equilibrium or homeostasis, 112–114, 195, 270. *See also* systems
Esperanto, 61–65
ethnography, 218, 231
ethos, 103, 134, 192, 198, 220, 235, 324–325
etiquette, 145–146, 218
Etzioni, A., 11
Euroculture, 60–67. *See also* Federated Europe
Euske, N. A., 243
Ewen, S., 11, 30
existential determination of thought, 100–104, 201
expertise, expert knowledge, and expert fields, 36, 73–75, 78, 82–83, 98, 104, 123, 124, 126, 130, 134, 138–141, 146–147, 153–154, 164, 169, 186, 223, 232, 257, 299, 310. *See also* argument fields; disciplines; professions
expressive: message design logic, 16, 26–29, 33–34, 163, 205, 232; politics, 38, 163
Ezrahi, Y., 111

Fallacies and fallacy theory, 74, 83, 137, 140, 170
false consciousness, ideology, 100, 102, 161, 163, 222, 263. *See also* systematically distorted communication
falsification, 136, 184, 240, 259, 284, 295
Farrell, T. B., 217
Faust, D., 129
Fayol, H., 252
Featherstone, M., 15
Federalist, 1, 66, 120–121, 149, 181, 277
Federated Europe, 60–67, 78, 163, 187, 284, 312–332
feminism, 229
Feyerabend, P., 212
Figert, A. E., 247
Fillmore, M., 61
Finocchiaro, M., 228
Fischer, F., 187
Fish, S., 19, 97
Fishbein, M., 162
Fisher, W. R., 244, 273
Fleck, L., 88, 105–110, 133, 193, 222–223, 236–237, 299
Fleishman, J. L., 297
Ford, H., 123, 250, 254–256
forensic psychiatry, 147, 170, 192, 300
Foucault, M., 6, 13–14, 17, 22, 80–81, 87–118, 140, 148, 155, 166, 176, 183, 191, 201, 207, 220, 223–226, 234, 240–241, 251, 255, 274, 317–318
Frankel, C., 4, 41, 153, 282, 287–288, 292
Frankfurt school, 13. *See also* Habermas

Fraser, N., 294
free-floating intellectuals, 14, 102–104, 125, 240. *See also Wissensoziologie*
Freeman, J., 255, 257, 274, 276
Frege, W. G., 69
Freidson, E., 153
French Revolution, 162–163, 203, 320
Freud, S., 92, 245; Freudian school, 230, 238, 259
Friedman, S. M., 310
Friedrich, C. J., 85
Fromm, E., 28
Frost, M. J., 144
Frost, P. J., 260, 262
Fuller, S., 4, 133, 142–143, 170, 182, 206, 209, 212, 238, 246, 252, 259, 310

Galbraith, J. K., 123, 257, 274
Galgan, G., 12, 76
Garnham, N., 168, 172–174
Garson, G. D., 210
Gaskins, R. H., 277–279
Gaston, J., 247
Gaudet, H., 152
Geertz, C., 1, 61, 66, 92, 97, 129, 189–190, 208, 213, 220, 228, 231, 236
Gemeinschaft und Gesellschaft, 28, 43. *See also* community
general: discourse, *see* public sphere; education, *see* education; will, *see* Rousseau
Germany, 44, 50, 328; GDR, 314, 328
gestalt, 25, 91, 109
gestalts, 87, 105, 112, 114, 151, 163, 259, 282, 288
Giddens, A., 92, 194, 223–224, 258
Gieryn, T. F., 247
Gilbert, G. N., 133
Gilpin, R. R., 238, 247
Ginsberg, B., 29, 42, 161, 167–168, 171
Giroux, H. A., 76
Gleick, J., 92, 309
Glotz, P., 326, 328
Gödel, K., 69
Goebbles, J., 8, 10, 50, 163, 323–326
Goffman, E., 27, 92, 189, 220, 234, 273
Goldberg, A. C., 313
Goldman, T. A., 144
Goodell, R., 310
Goodman, N., 212, 217
Goodnight, G. T., 11, 127–128, 134, 159, 170, 209, 223, 279–280, 296
Gosnell, H. F., 161
Gould, S. J., 53, 75, 147, 151, 218, 255, 267, 271, 306
Gouran, D. S., 227
Graebner, W., 118
Greenberg, D. S., 247
Greer, S., 245
Grootendorst, R., 81, 322
Gross, A. G., 133, 212
Grotz, J., 28
groups and group decision-making, 224–226; interest groups, 229; reference groups, 233–234

Haberer, J., 238
Habermas, J., 11, 13–15, 17, 22, 50–51, 69, 77, 82, 88–89, 94, 96, 108, 113, 124, 134, 140, 159–160, 170, 173–174, 209, 243, 249, 285, 294, 319, 322
Hacking, I., 89, 95, 261
Halberstam, D., 148, 154, 200, 237, 293
Hall, E. T., 116–117
Hall, S., 97
Hamilton, A., 8, 119–121, 197
Hamilton, R., 154
Hannan, M. T., 255, 257, 276
Hanson, N. R., 115
Harre, R., 69
Hart, R. P., 28
Hartman, G., 72–73
Hartung, F. E., 101–102
Harvey, D., 15, 28, 33, 203, 252, 254
Haskell, T. L., 138–139, 248
Hauerwas, S., 57
Hawes, L., 253
Hawkesworth, M. E., 209–211
Hawley, A., 194–196
Hayes, J. T., 128
Hazen, R. M., 122, 308
Hegel, G. W. F., 14–15, 49, 78, 85, 89, 115, 141, 215–216, 250
Heidbreder, E., 233
Heidegger, M., 28, 34, 49, 69, 72, 115
Heisenberg, W., 70 , 92, 111, 212, 261, 275, 306, 314
Hennessy, B. C., 158
Herder, J., 49, 60
Hesse, M., 69

Hikins, J. W., 56
Hilbert, D., 69
history, 201. *See also* Stürmer
Hitler, A., 8, 29, 46, 274, 315–316, 320–325
Hobbes, T., 12, 14, 140, 172–173, 190
Hocking, W. E., 155, 158
Hoffer, E., 35, 46, 324
Hofstadter, L., 310
Hofstadter, R., 23, 121, 152, 236
Hohenberg, J., 158
holism, 78, 129–130, 193–194
Holton, G., 68
Homans, G. C., 268
Horkheimer, M., 13, 76–77
Howe, H. F., 170, 240
Hoy, D. C., 95, 97
humanities, 217
human relations, 252–255, 258, 276, 283
Hume, D., 15
Hungary, 44, 329
Hunter, F., 154
Huntington, S. P., 153
Husband, R. L., 26, 264–265
Hutu, 2, 54, 327
Huxley, A., 46, 84
Huxley, T. H., 318
Hyman, H. H., 233
Hynes, T. J., 23, 171, 200

identification and commitment, 274
immunopharmacology, 192
incommensurability, 21, 23, 72, 105, 114, 126, 129, 142–143, 205, 307–308
indexicality, 126, 128–129, 222–223
individualism, 35, 95, 105
informal logic, 72–73, 124, 213, 227, 297
information, 37, 225, 227; kept from public, 155, 178; society, 37
inside versus outside dichotomy, 98, 111, 166–167, 239–241
institutions, 108–110, 231
intentionality, 218–219
interdisciplinarity, 207–208, 214–216
interfield communication, 207. *See also* borders; interdisciplinarity
irony of democracy, 21, 152. *See also* elites, elite oligarchy
Irvin, G., 144
Israelis, 39, 212

Jablin, F. M., 264
Jackson, A., 121
Jackson, S. A., 199, 205, 218–219, 290–292
Jacobins, 120, 281
Jacobs, J., 92
Jacobs, S., 128, 205, 218–219, 241
Jacoby, R., 28
James, W., 98, 207, 246
Jameson, F., 14, 33, 38, 78, 254
Janis, I., 89, 200, 247, 293
Japan, 50, 62
Jaspers, K., 28
Jay, M., 115
Jefferson, T., 1–2, 11, 46, 119–121, 124, 148, 168, 197, 210, 297; Jeffersonians, 293–311
Jensen, J., 30
Johannesen, R. L., 28
Johnson, B., 48
Johnson, L. B., 40
Johnson, P., 49–50, 315–317
Johnson, R. H., 158
Jones, L., 41
Jourard, S., 28
journalism and journalists, 7, 37–38, 42, 121–123, 146, 158–159, 187, 297–299, 301–311, 316; economic journalism, 156, 308
Jukun, 54

Kahn, R., 268–270
Kant, I., 14, 49, 72, 162, 215, 283
Kanter, R. M., 224–225
Kaplan, A., 62, 67
Kasai, 54
Katangans, 54
Katz, D., 56, 235, 268–270, 274
Kaufman, A. S., 252
Keating, P., 193
Kelly, G. A., 89, 201, 280
Kelly, M., 40–41
Kelman, H., 47, 234
Kennedy, M. D., 329
Kenny, M., 247
Key, V. O., Jr., 152
Khmer Rouge, 281
Khron, R., 248
Kimbell, P., 161
Kirkpatrick, F. G., 41
Kitcher, P., 128, 247

Klein, J. T.,143, 192, 203, 214–216, 309
Kline, S. L., 218
Kluge, A., 155, 168
Klumpp, J. F., 241
Knoll, E., 247
Knorr-Cetina, K. D., 93, 248
knowledge, general, 19, 124, 132–133, 138, 302
know-nothings, 65, 121
Kohn, A., 247
Kolko, G., 155
Kornhauser, W., 248
Kramer, F., 210
Kroker, A., 20
Krone, K. J., 264
Kristol, I., 119
Kuhn, T. S., 69, 94, 104–105, 114–115, 193, 212, 236, 246, 263

Lakatos, I., 284
Lamarckian mutation argument, 270–272
Lane, R. E., 152
Langton, S., 134
language: games, 70, 226–227; system, 226
latitudes of demographic sweep, 303–308
Latour, B., 183, 185, 245, 248
Laudan, L., 284
Laufersweiler, C., 128
law, 36, 138, 146, 232, 238, 297
Lawler, E. J., 36, 271
Layard, R., 144
Lazarsfeld, P. F., 151–153
Lazarus, S., 296
Le Bon, G., 122, 162, 323
Lee, A. M., 101, 204
Leff, M. C., 84, 228
Lehrer, K., 301–302
Leiserson, A., 134
Lenin, V. I., 84, 255, 315, 318
Lerner, M., 41
leveling, 122–123
Levin, M., 161
Lewin, K., 111–114, 225, 286
liberalism, 6–7, 11–24, 241, 243, 263, 312, 322, 325, 331
liberal theory of the press, 173, 178–179. *See also* journalism
libertarian argument, 4, 46–48, 51, 167–168
library science, 132
Lindberg, L. N., 155
Lippmann, W., 9, 123, 157, 168, 171, 197, 199, 306, 323
literary: density, 131–134, 193, 235
Litt, E., 43
Locke, J., 13, 168, 198, 243
Long, H., 65, 321
Longino, H., 217
Lowery, S. A., 161
Lowi, T., 23, 90, 271, 276
Luckmann, T., 217
Luhmann, N., 111, 113
Luszki, M. B., 143
Lyne, J. R., 170, 190, 240, 319, 322
Lyotard, J.-F., 12–13, 76, 115

MacIntyre, A., 23, 41, 88, 158, 201
Madison, J., 1, 120, 149, 153, 181, 198, 277, 285
magazines, 80, 178, 304–305
Maier, J., 52
Mandelbaum, M., 212
Mannheim, K., 12–14, 72, 100–102, 125, 240, 314
Mansbridge, J. J., 177
Marat, J.-P., 317
March, J. G., 247
Marger, M. N., 155
marginal man, 97, 106–108, 112–114, 118, 207
marketplace of ideas, 6, 11, 83, 153, 249, 298
Martin, E. D., 122
Martz, A., 227
Marx, K., 8, 13, 85, 100, 118, 179, 190, 316, 325
Marxists, 6–7, 14, 16, 68, 96, 165, 168, 179, 185, 201–203, 238, 255, 276
Maslow, A. H., 254, 266
mass: communication, 161, 210, 303; media, 79, 83–84, 153–154, 159, 161; programming, 177; relatively mass media, 234, 239, 307. *See also* movements
Maull, N., 193
May, A., 37
Mayo, E., 252
McCarthy, T., 69, 72
McCarthy, J., 8

McCloskey, D. N., 69, 83–84, 99, 133, 170, 190, 212, 228
McConnell, M., 227
McCornack, S. A., 26, 264–265
McDonald, D., 30
McGee, M. C., 229
McGuire, J. W., 182
McKerrow, R. E., 217, 241
McKiernan, D., 47
McLean v. Arkansas, 122–123
McLuhan, M., 79
McPhee, R. D., 223, 271
McPhee, W., 153
McQuail, D., 37, 304
Mead, G. H., 101, 207, 234
medicine, 232–233
Megill, A., 69, 83–84, 99, 170, 228
Meiklejohn, A., 158
melting pot, 40, 46, 58, 60–61, 185–186, 249, 322
Mencken, H. L., 21, 119, 121–123, 152, 158, 186
Menzel, H., 235
Merriam, C. E., 161
Merton, R. K., 103, 109
message design logic, 26–27, 220. *See also* conventional; expressive; rhetorical
Meyrowitz, J., 26, 80–81
Michels, R., 152
Mickunas, A., 125
Mill, J. S., 13, 151, 197–199, 243
Miller, C. M., 227
Miller, W., 121
Mills, C. W., 21, 71, 76, 123, 157
Mitroff, I. I., 29, 103, 174–175, 274
modernism, modernists, modernity's therapists, 6, 13, 16, 17, 87, 115, 141, 146, 201, 257, 316–317
modernist fallacy, 134, 170–171, 209
modernity, 14–15, 68, 78, 115, 150, 164, 250, 258
Montag, W., 78
Moore, M. H., 132
Morgan, G., 260, 262–263, 265, 267–268
Mosca, G., 152
Moses, R., 20
movements, 192, 228–229; critical thinking, 230
Mowlana, H., 15
Moynihan, D. P., 3, 58–59, 185–186, 216, 229
Mukerji, C., 247
Mulkay, M., 73, 93, 103, 170, 240, 248
multinational organizations, 240, 330–331
Musgrave, A., 284
Mussolini, A., 65
Mussolini, B., 85, 312
Myanmar, 3

Naess, A., 37, 213
Nagorno-Karabakh, 3
narrative and narrative paradigm, 107, 273, 298–299, 301, 322, 325
NASA, 104, 227, 273, 299–300
nationalism, 17, 44, 48–55, 77, 169, 187, 312–313, 329
Nazis, 51–52, 162, 320–321, 324, 328
Negt, O., 155, 168
Nelkin, D., 134
Nelson, J. S., 69, 83–84, 99, 170, 207, 228, 308
Neuman, W. R., 42, 123–124, 235, 298, 305
Newman, Cardinal, 81, 130
Newton, I., 245–246
Newtonian metaphor, 111
Nie, N., 155
Nietzsche, F., 13, 72, 164
Nigeria, 54
Nisbet, R., 43, 46, 243, 247, 257
Nisbett, R. E., 140
Nixon, R. M., 33
Nodia, G., 52
Nord, W. R., 252
nuclear power and engineering, 128

objectifying, 219–220
objectivity, as rhetorical claim, 136, 247, 300. *See also* realism
O'Keefe, B. J., 26–27, 205, 232, 234, 241, 243, 261, 325
O'Keefe, D. J., 218
Olsen, J. P., 247
organization and organizations, 77, 90–91, 95, 129–130, 140–141, 154–155, 165, 185, 200, 222, 224, 227, 245–276, 284, 320–321
organizational: complexity and scale, 141–142; metaphors, 258–274; studies, 72, 111, 116, 173, 183, 246–276
Ortega y Gassett, 152

Orwell, G., 46–47, 85, 318
Ozick, C., 131

Pagels, H., 227, 307, 309
Palestinians, 38, 212
Pangle, T. L., 43
Papua New Guinea, 3
Parenti, M., 11, 148
Pareto, V., 152
Paris, 25–26, 30–31, 62, 327
Parsons, T.,103, 154, 268, 282, 284, 293
Pateman, C., 158
Paul, R., 82
Pauli, W., 92
Perelman, Ch., 82
Perot, R., 7–8
Perrow, C., 245
persuasion and influence: versus coercion, 210; as cooperative activity, 117–118; oratory, 321–322; by participation, 108, 225, 287, 321; peripheral route, 231; as process, 192; as subject matter, 162, 312
Peters, J. D., 153
Peterson, T., 158
Petras, J. W., 100
Pettigrew, A. M., 276
Petty, R. E., 80, 231
Pfeifer, M. P., 140
Pfeil, F., 29
Pfund, N., 310
physical chemistry, 192
physics, 73, 135–137, 138, 205, 215, 223, 229, 239, 309
physiology, 73
Pierce, C. S., 207, 248–249
Plato, 8–9, 81, 85, 120, 142, 153, 198, 209, 325
PLO, 37–38
pluralism and pluralists, 6, 18, 21, 123–124, 148, 279, 287; pluralists at their worst (connoisseurs),151–154, 158, 160, 162–165, 169
Poland, 44, 329
Polanyi, M., 219, 228
policy: analysis, 209–211; freezes, 143–144; science, 9–10, 165, 170, 209–211
political: geography, 192; science, 124, 297; sociology, 192; theory, 72
polls and polling, 42, 122, 128, 157, 161, 171, 229
Pol Pot, 47
Pondy, L. R., 260, 262
Poole, M. S., 223, 271
Pope, A., 48
Popov, Z., 85, 325
Popper, K. R., 85, 325; Popperian school, 70. *See also* falsification
populism, 65, 119–126, 148–149, 152, 155, 163, 210, 293
position, argumentative, 230, 265–267; positioning in advertising, 304
positivism, 9, 70, 100, 165, 173, 209
Postman, N., 11, 30, 177
postmodernism and postmodernists, 6, 13, 17, 38, 201, 257, 329
postmodernity, 14–16, 78, 115, 258
practical wisdom, 210–211. *See also* knowledge
pragmatism and pragmatists, 98–99, 101, 227
Pranger, R. J., 158
Pratkanis, A., 2
presumption: conservative, 186–187, 278–280, 288; epistemic, 187, 289–292; liberal, 186–187, 280–282, 288
Price, D. K., 247
Price, D. de S., 224, 247
prisons and inmate cultures, 92
private or personal sphere, 223
proceduralism, 277–279
professionalization and professionalism, 145–146, 297, 300
professions, 87, 232–233, 306–307; professional authority, 137–138, 228, 257
progress, 73, 91, 136, 232, 282–288
progressives, 40–41, 199, 223
prose levels, 157. *See also* latitudes of demographic sweep
psychology, 111, 138, 215, 233
public: apathy, 152–153; decision-making, 126–129, 133–134, 160, 228, 295; discourse, 75, 79, 159; godterm of journalism, 158; influence on science, 107–108, 291–292; interest, 296; knowledge, 126, 148, 206, 297–311; opinion, 123, 138; participation, 154–156, 293–294; pluralists view of,

public (*continued*)
151–165; versus private distinction, 25, 31, 296; relations, 136, 152, 172–173, 205; sphere, 79–81, 83, 166–168, 174, 178, 294–297; as symbol, 150. *See also* Mencken; polls
publics, as audiences, 205, 226–230, 296
Putnam, L. L., 264

quantum physics and metaphor, 70–71, 91, 109, 111, 205, 275, 307, 314
Quine, W. V. O., 98, 129–130, 193, 212, 233

Rabinow, P., 96–97
race, 112, 169, 201
Rapaczynski, A., 30
rationality, 102, 104, 127–128, 134, 140, 145, 207, 220–221, 224, 249, 259, 274, 322
Ratzinger, Cardinal, 195
Rawls, J., 77, 101, 127, 142, 159–160, 249
Reagan, R., 33, 124
realism, 9–10, 30–31, 165, 319–322, 325
Reason, 82, 221
Redner, H., 93, 154, 247
reflective thinking, 101, 109–110, 141, 232
Reich, R. B., 173
Reisman, D., 35
Reiter, H. L., 11, 148
relativism, 103, 129, 211
relativity, 17, 75, 83, 89, 100, 111, 126–129, 239; de facto, 130–131, 211, 259, 322
republican instinct, 119–123. *See also* pluralism
Rescher, N., 16 , 74, 220
rhetoric, 7–9, 72–73, 83–84, 86, 164–166, 170, 213, 223, 325; of inquiry, 192–193, 211
rhetorical: message design logic, 26–28, 220, 232, 234, 261; universals, 319–322
Richards, I. A., 37, 213
Riefenstahl, L., 50, 324
Riley, P., 223
Roberts, D., 44, 316, 319
Roberts, K. H., 243
Robespierre, M. de, 119, 317
Rockefeller, J. D., 250
Rogers, C., 28
Rogers, C. L., 310
Rogers, E. M., 235
Rogers, L., 132
Romanticism, 17, 29, 81, 160–162, 316–317
Rorty, R., 1, 10, 22, 63, 69, 94, 98–99, 115, 140, 236, 243–244
Rose, A., 244
Rosen, J., 11
Rosenau, J. N., 229
Rosenbaum, W. A., 64, 116
Rosenberg, A., 50
Ross, R. G., 279–280
Rousseau, J. J., 9, 13, 16, 25–39, 43, 54, 76, 81, 83, 160, 174, 198, 283, 294–295, 325
Rowland, R., 227
Russell, B., 37, 145, 213
Rwanda, 54, 331
Ryan, M., 19

Said, E., 91
Salkever, S. G., 11, 16
Sammuelson, P., 156
Sammuelson, R., 156
Sapir-Whorf, 90
Schama, S., 317
Schambra, W. A., 40, 46
Schattschneider, E. E., 148
Scheler, M.,100–101
Schelling, C. S., 127, 173, 237
Schiller, D., 37, 155
Schiller, H. I., 37
Schlesinger, A. N., 40, 44, 58–59, 186
Schmitt, R. L., 234
Schoek, H., 210
Schoenerr, R. A., 271
Schramm, W., 158
Schumpeter, J. A., 123, 152
Schutz, A., 219
Schweder, R. A., 74
Schweitzer, A., 41
science, 78, 192, 247, 259, 265
science writing, 137, 148, 156, 308–310. *See also* journalism; public
scientific: versus astrology, 122; commu-

nities, 106–108; versus creationism, 122–123; fraud, 300–301, 309; versus humanism, 130–131; identity, 205; illiteracy, 122, 308–309; journals, 132; revolutions, 107, 114; versus social, 103–104; stature or ethos, 73, 103, 110, 220
scientism, 111, 211
Scientology, 229
Scribner, S., 244
Scriven, M., 152
Sears, D. O., 152
Seeger, M. W., 227
Seeman, M., 252
Seibert, F. S., 158
selective exposure, 234–235
Sellars, W., 98–99
Sennett, R., 25–39, 94
Serbs, 2, 44, 59, 315, 327
shallow quotation, 94, 200–204, 252, 264, 276
Sherif, C. W., 73
Sherif, M., 73
Shibutani, T., 234
Shirer, W. L., 316
Shotter, J., 142, 190, 242
Sillars, M. O., 229
Simmel, G., 198
Simon, H. A., 247, 274
Simons, H. W., 84
Singer, E., 233
skepticism, 211–212, 220
Skinner, B. F., 110
Skinner, Q., 76, 256
Small, H. G., 133
Smith, A., 9, 37, 95, 120, 153
Snodgrass, G. L., 140
Snow, E., 131, 228
Snyder, L. L., 48
social: Darwinism, 23; epistemology, 192, 211, 235; psychology, 192; sciences, 189–190, 206, 217
socialization, into expert fields, 223
sociobiology, 192, 240
sociology, 73, 104
sociology of knowledge, 73, 100. *See also* *Wissensoziologie*
Socolow, R. H., 143–145
Soffer, W., 11
Solow, R. M., 156, 308
sovereignty, 3, 295, 329
specialism, 172. *See also* expertise; technical, versus public discourse
Speer, A., 33, 163, 323–324
Speier, H.,103
Spencer, H., 196, 267
Spinoza, B., 13
Sri Lanka, 54
Stahl, L., 301–302
Stalin, J., 46, 84–85, 326
Stam, R., 201, 212–213
statistics, 138, 214, 231
Stich, S., 140
Storey, J., 252
Strauss, A. L., 258
structuralism, 105, 155
structuration, 223–225, 258
Stürmer, M., 44, 319
style: 78, 105, 236–239. *See also* institutions
subjectivity and intersubjectivity, 219, 241–242
Sukosd, M., 318
Sullivan, W. M., 41
Sumner, W. G., 151, 197
supercollider, 80, 135–136, 148
Suppe, F., 284
symbolic interactionism, 93, 97, 195, 258
systematically distorted communication, 155, 222, 319. *See also* false consciousness
systems: closed, 110–111, 113, 236, 238; open, 194, 268–270; theory, 113, 138, 142, 194, 268, 272–274

Tamils, 54
Tarski, A., 212
Tatars, 2, 38
Tajiks, 2, 212
Taub, G., 247
Taylor, C., 93
Taylor, C. A., 122–123
Taylor, F. W., and Taylorism, 84–85, 251–255, 258, 260, 276, 283
technical: versus public discourse, 164, 170, 172–174; sphere, 223. *See also* expertise; public
technocracy, 84, 123, 187, 209–211
television, 11, 79, 169, 176–179, 304–305; cable, 305
texts, focus on, 93–96, 222, 243–244, 265
Thatcher, M., 64

theologians, 41, 57, 71
thought collectives, 105–110. *See also* argument fields
thought style. *See* style
Tocqueville, A. de, 3, 11–12, 44–46, 120, 130, 166, 177, 326
Tolstoy, L., 48
Tompkins, P. K., 255, 274
Tonnies, F., 28
total institutions. *See* Foucault
Toulmin, S. E., 68–69, 88, 191, 196, 204, 206, 223, 227, 230, 284, 287, 307
trade books, 306–308
translation: from esoteric to broader publics, 107, 156, 302–311
Trefil, J., 122, 135, 137, 308–309
Tribe, L. H., 127, 144, 173, 237
Truman, H., 7
Trumbo, D., 48
Turner, V., 189
Tutsi, 54
Twain, M., 48, 195–196

Ulam, S. M., 133
Unger, R., 158
unificationism, 79–84, 283
United Parcel Service, 253–255
unity, 79, 116, 171, 214, 276, 294
universality, 206, 211, 247
urban studies, 192
Uzbeks, 212

valuing dissensus, 94, 181, 199, 217, 271
Verba, S., 76, 155
Vienna Circle, 70, 73
Volk, 34, 49–50, 52, 58, 316–317, 319
Von Bertalanffy, L., 268
Voss, J., 127, 173, 237

Wade, N., 131, 247
Walton, D., 139
Ward, L., 158
Weatherhead, R. W., 52
Weaver, R., 162, 283
Weber, M., 12, 22, 23, 33, 36, 50, 165, 199, 209, 251–252, 282
Weick, K. E., 182–183, 216, 249
Weimer, W. B., 170
Weinstein, M., 329
Weisskopf, T. E., 155
Weitz, M., 226
Weltanschauungen, 210, 230, 259, 266
Wenzel, J. W., 83, 284, 296
Whately, R., 23, 278, 279, 284
Wheeless, L. R., 28
whiggishness, 73, 91, 267, 283
Whitley, R., 170, 182, 240, 248
Whittenberger-Keith, K., 145
Whyte, W. H., 35
Wiggins, J., 210
Wilkinson, P., 228
Willard, C. A., 23, 94, 185, 200, 207, 212, 265
Williams, A., 144
Wilson, B. R., 259
Wilson, E. O., 240
Wilson, L., 15
Wilson, W., 40, 197, 250
Winch, P., 259
Wissensoziologie (Franco-German sociology of knowledge), 72, 87, 100–104, 223, 258
Wittgenstein, L., 25, 69, 70, 76, 98, 189, 226–227, 256
Wolfe, A., 155
Wolin, S., 158
women's studies, 192
Wood, J. L., 300
Woods, J., 139
Woolgar, S., 185, 248
Wright, C., 247
Wyle, W., 13, 40–41, 46

Yeats, W. B., 12

Zagacki, K. S., 56
Zaltman, G., 170
Zeigler, H., 161, 169
Znaniecki, F. W., 72